Python GUI with PyQt

Learn to build modern and stunning GUIs in Python with PyQt5 and Qt Designer

Saurabh Chandrakar

Dr. Nilesh Bhaskarrao Bahadure

www.bpbonline.com

FIRST EDITION 2024
REPRINT 2025

ISBN: 978-93-5551-557-5

Distributors:

BPB PUBLICATIONS
20, Ansari Road, Darya Ganj
New Delhi-110002
Ph: 23254990/23254991

DECCAN AGENCIES
4-3-329, Bank Street,
Hyderabad-500195
Ph: 24756967/24756400

MICRO MEDIA
Shop No. 5, Mahendra Chambers,
150 DN Rd. Next to Capital Cinema,
V.T. (C.S.T.) Station, MUMBAI-400 001
Ph: 22078296/22078297

To View Complete BPB Publications Catalogue Scan the QR Code:

Published by Manish Jain for BPB Publications, 20 Ansari Road, Darya Ganj, New Delhi-110002 and Printed by him at Manipal Technologies, Manipal

www.bpbonline.com

Dedicated to

My Parents
***Dr. Surendra Kumar Chandrakar** and*
Smt. Bhuneshwari Chandrakar
brother
Shri Pranav Chandrakar,
Sister in law
Smt. Silky Chandrakar
to my wife
Smt. Priyanka Chandrakar
and to my lovely son
Master Yathartha Chandrakar

- Saurabh Chandrakar

My Parents
Smt. Kamal B. Bahadure** and **Late Bhaskarrao M. Bahadure
to my in-laws
Smt. Saroj R. Lokhande** and **Shri Ravikant A. Lokhande
and to my wife
Shilpa N. Bahadure
and to beautiful daughters
Nishita** and **Mrunmayee
and to all my beloved students

- Dr. Nilesh Bhaskarrao Bahadure

About the Authors

- **Saurabh Chandrakar** is a Research & Development Engineer (Dy. Manager) at **Bharat Heavy Electricals Limited** (BHEL) Hyderabad. He is the winner of the best executive award on Operations Division by BHEL Hyderabad. Recently, he has been awarded the prestigious BHEL Excellence Award under Anusandhan category for Redundant Composite Monitoring System of Power Transformers project. He has 23 copyrights and 3 patent granted. Additionally, he has 4 patents filed. Moreover, he has published 5 books in reputed publications such as BPB New Delhi (*Programming Techniques using Python, Python for everyone. Building Modern GUIs with tkinter and python*), Scitech Publications Chennai (*Programming Techniques using matlab*) and IK International publishers (*Microcontrollers and Embedded System Design*). Additionally, he has also launched one video course on BPB titled *"First Time Play with Basic, Advanced Python concepts and complete guide for different python certification exams all in one umbrella."*

- **Dr. Nilesh Bhaskarrao Bahadure** received the Bachelor of Engineering degree in Electronics Engineering in 2000, the Master of Engineering degree in Digital Electronics in 2005, and the Ph.D. degree in Electronics in 2017 from KIIT Deemed to be University, Bhubaneswar, India. He is currently an Associate Professor in the Department of Computer Science and Engineering at Symbiosis Institute of Technology (SIT), Nagpur, Symbiosis International (Deemed University) (SIU), Pune, Maharashtra, India. He has more than 20 years of experience. Dr. Bahadure is a life member of IE(I), IETE, ISTE, ISCA, SESI, ISRS, and IAENG professional organizations. He has published more than 40 articles in reputed international journals and conferences, and has five books to his credit. He is the reviewer of many indexed journals such as IEEE Access, IET, Springer, Elsevier, Wiley and so on. His research interests are in the areas of Sensor Technology, the Internet of Things, and Biomedical Image Processing.

About the Reviewer

Prasenjeet Damodar Patil is currently working as an Associate Professor at the School of Computing, M.I.T A.D.T University, Pune. He has completed his B.E. in E&TC Engg. and M. Tech. in Electronics from Walchand College of Engineering Sangli, India. He did his Ph.D. in E&TC Engineering in 2018. Prasanjeet has 14+ years of teaching experience and has published more than 16 papers in reputed Journals. His research interest includes Computational Electromagnetics applications in Integrated Optics, IoT, and digital Image Processing.

Acknowledgements

- First and foremost, I would like to thank you all for selecting this book. It has been written with the beginner reader in mind. First of all, I take this opportunity to greet and thank my mentor "Prof. Nilesh Bahadure Sir" for motivating me and always communicating his expertise fully on topics related to Python. I am very thankful for being his protégé. I appreciate his belief in me for always standing behind me and pushing me to achieve more. The phrase "Journey of a Thousand Miles Begins with a Single Step" is something he always reminds me of.

  My parents, Dr. Surendra Kumar Chandrakar and Smt. Bhuneshwari Chandrakar, my brother, Shri Pranav Chandrakar, my sister-in-law Silky Chandrakar, my beloved wife, Mrs. Priyanka Chandrakar, my adorable son Yathartha Chandrakar, and all of my friends have inspired me and given me confidence over the years. Last but not the least, I would like to express my sincere gratitude to the staff at BPB Publications for their contributions and insights that made parts of this book possible.

  — Saurabh Chandrakar

- It was my privilege to thank Dr. S. B. Mujumdar, Chancellor of the Symbiosis International University, Pune, and Shri. Vijay Kumar Gupta, Chairman of Beekay Industries Bhilai and BIT Trust, for his encouragement and support. I thank my mentors, Dr. Arun Kumar Ray, Dean, School of Electronics Engineering, KIIT Deemed to be University, Bhubaneswar, and Dr. Anupam Shukla, Director, SVNIT Surat. I would like to thank Dr. Vidya Yeravdekar, Principal Director of Symbiosis Society and the Pro Chancellor of Symbiosis International University, Pune, Dr. Ramakrishnan Raman, Vice Chancellor of the Symbiosis International University, Pune, and Dr.Ketan Kotecha, Dean, Faculty of Engineering, Symbiosis International University, Pune, and Dr. Nitin Rakesh, Director, SIT Nagpur, for their advice, and encouragement throughout the preparation of the book.

  I would also like to thank Dr. Sanjeev Khandal, HOD, Department of Aeronautical Engineering, SGU Kolhapur, my well-wisher Dr. Prasenjeet D. Patil, Associate Professor, MIT ADT University, Pune, and my colleagues in Symbiosis Institute of Technology Nagpur for providing valuable suggestions and lots of encouragement throughout the project.

I am thankful to Prof. Dr. N. Raju, Sr. Assistant Professor, SASTRA University, Thanjavur, Tamil Nadu, for his support, assistance during writing, and for his valuable suggestions.

I would also like to thank Dr. Ravi M. Potdar, Sr. Associate Professor, BIT Durg, and Dr. Md. Khwaja Mohiddin, Associate Professor, BIT Raipur, for providing valuable suggestions and encouragement throughout the project. Writing a beautiful, well-balanced, and acquainted book is not a work of one or two days or a month; it takes a lot of time and patience, as well as hours of hard work. Many thanks to my family members, my parents, wife, children, and well-wishers for their kind support. Without them and their faith and support, writing this classic book would have remained just a dream. I also like to thank my students, who have always been with me, for relating problems and finding solutions too. The perfection in any work does not come in a day. It needs a lot of effort, time, hard work, and sometimes, proper guidance.

It is my privilege to thank Prof. (Dr.) Ram Dhekekar, Professor, Department of Electronics & Telecommunication Engineering, SSGMCE Shegaon, and Dr. C. G. Dethe, Director UGC Staff College Nagpur. Last but not the least, I would like to offer an extra special thanks to the staff at "BPB Publications Private Limited" for their insight and contribution in polishing this book.

Most significantly, I want to thank Lord Ganesha for all of the work I was able to put into the book's preparation. I would not be as zealous as I am now if it weren't for God's amazing creation of the universe.

For since the creation of the world God's invisible qualities - his eternal power and divine nature - have been clearly seen, being understood from what has been made, so that men are without excuse."

— Dr. Nilesh Bhaskarrao Bahadure

Preface

The purpose of this book is to introduce readers with little to no programming experience in Python Graphical User Interface (GUI) to use Python binding for the GUI toolkit called PyQt5. A GUI application can be created in any programming language, whether VB.Net, C#.Net etc. In this book, we will see how to create a GUI application using PyQt5. The readers will get the foundational knowledge and skills necessary to start writing code for creating a GUI app in Python language. We will use a Graphical tool for creating user interfaces in Qt called Qt Designer. By mastering PyQt5, readers can apply this knowledge to solve real-world problems and create various useful applications according to their needs.

The first part of the book covers PyQt5 library and the overall layout of Qt Designer tool. Then we will see some insights into layout management and the concept of event-driven programming and its implementation in the context of Python programming with the usage of the concept of signals and slots. Finally, in the later part of the book, we shall see an insight into various widgets related to buttons, container item views, container, input, and display widgets.

This book covers a wide range of topics, from the basic definitions of different widgets to various solved examples with well-explanatory code. Overall, the book provides a solid foundation for beginners to start their journey for getting trained in Python GUI using the PyQt5 library along with the Qt Designer layout tool.

This book is divided into **9 chapters**. Each chapter description is listed as follows.

Chapter 1: Introduction to PyQt5 and Qt Designer Tool – This chapter will start by comparing powerful and cross-platform toolkit graphical PyQt5 with the tkinter library. You will learn how to install PyQt5 framework installation along with the creation of a basic GUI form using PyQt5 without and with using the class. We shall explore the components inside Qt Designer along with different pre-defined templates. In the latter half of the chapter, we will create a user credential app initially focusing on view in Qt Designer (.ui file, which is an XML file), then converting it into a python code (.py) using pyuic5 command and finally creating a new python file which will be importing the python code for user interface design and adding some useful logic to create a basic Login application for the user.

Chapter 2: Getting Insights of Layout Management – will cover the concept on widgets placement using absolute positioning approach. We shall see widgets placement using layout classes where initially we will see how to organize widgets either horizontally or vertically using QBoxLayout class. We will explore how to arrange the widgets in a row side by side using QHBoxLayout with the usage of methods viz addStretch, addWidget, addLayout. Alternatively, we will look into arranging the widgets vertically with addStretch method using QVBoxLayout. Then we shall find out arranging widgets in a grid of rows and columns using QGridLayout. Also, we will look into creating an application using QFormLayout. In the end, we will be confident to create " User Credential App " application using absolute positioning , QBoxLayout, QGridLayout and QFormLayout class.

Chapter 3: Getting Insights of Events, Signals and Slots – will explore the concept of event-driven programming and how it is implemented in the context of Python programming using signals and slots. The above chapter will guide us through utilizing signals and slots to create and manage events. We will discover how to define signals and connect them to slots so that our program can respond to events in a useful way. We will also investigate various events and signals and how to use them to create interactive user interfaces or handle external inputs.

Chapter 4: Getting Insights of Button Widgets in Qt Designer – will cover the concept of button widgets which are commonly used for creating interactive user interfaces and make them understand their properties, functionality, and customization options. By exploring the features and settings related to button widgets, user can effectively design and implement user-friendly interfaces in our Qt applications. Qt Designer offers a number of different button widgets, including CheckBox, Push Button, Tool Button, Radio Button, Command Link Button etc and shall explore description, properties, important methods , important signals and an application example with output display of each button widget in detail. The important properties of QObject, QWidget and QAbstractButton will be covered with images at the end as an addon information.

Chapter 5: Getting Insights of Item Views in Qt Designer – will cover the concept of Item Views in Qt Designer which are commonly used for creating user interactive interfaces. We will look into their properties, functionality, and customization options. We will explore Qt Designer's item view widgets, like QTableView, QTreeView, and QListView, which are effective tools for presenting data in an organised and ordered way. User can use these widgets to display data in simple list formats (QListView), hierarchical tree structures (QTreeView), or rows and columns (QTableView).

Chapter 6: Getting Insights of Item Widgets (Item-Based) in Qt Designer – will cover the concept of Item Widgets in Qt Designer which are commonly used for creating interactive user interfaces. We shall look to understand their properties, functionality, customization options and also will gain a thorough grasp of how to create and operate item-based widgets within the Qt Designer environment. User will be able to create dynamic, interactive user interfaces using the power of item-based widgets and will also discover different features and characteristics to personalize the look and behavior of widgets viz list widget, tree widget and table widget. In order to facilitate user interaction and implement functionality, user will learn to manage the events and signals connected to item-based widgets.

Chapter 7: Getting Insights of Containers in Qt Designer – will cover the concept of container widgets offered by Qt Designer, their features, and how to customize them to design aesthetically pleasing and user-friendly interfaces. User will investigate various container widget types and will obtain knowledge of the precise features and capabilities provided by each widget. They will get to know what container widgets are and how they work, its different types, its usage to create layouts and shall also explore customizing appearance of container widgets.

Chapter 8: Getting Insights of Input Widgets in Qt Designer – will deal with concept of many input widgets available and how to utilize them effectively to create interactive user interfaces. Users will have a solid understanding of input widgets including QLineEdit, QSpinBox, QComboBox, QTextEdit etc. as well as their corresponding characteristics, functionality, and customization choices. They all shall experience the knowledge needed to incorporate these input widgets into their designs so that they may enter data, select options, and interact with the program. The use of input validation methods, processing user input events, and linking signals and slots to accomplish required functionality are also covered for the benefit of the readers. In the end, they will be able to develop simple, user-friendly interfaces which will effectively collect user input and deliver a smooth user experience by mastering input widgets in Qt Designer.

Chapter 9: Getting Insights of Display Widgets in Qt Designer – will explain the concept of display widgets in Qt Designer. Initially we will learn how to display static text or images using labels and how to change their font, color, alignment, and size. And then understand how labels can improve the GUI's visual presentation of information. We will examine the TextBrowser widget's features to learn how to display and control rich text content. Also, we will learn how to add hyperlinks, graphics, and formatting choices to text displays to make them dynamic and interactive. Next, we will explore how to add a calendar widget to our GUI application. We shall discover how to customize the calendar widget's look, structure, and behavior to meet specific application requirements. We will explore how to display numerical values, such as counters using the LCDNumber widget and also how to modify the LCDNumber widget's digit count, decimal accuracy, look, and style. Finally, we will look into exploring ProgressBar widget to show how a task or operation is progressing. We will learn how to dynamically update the progress bar based on our application.

Code Bundle and Coloured Images

Please follow the link to download the
Code Bundle and the *Coloured Images* of the book:

https://rebrand.ly/s2nzbop

The code bundle for the book is also hosted on GitHub at:
https://github.com/bpbpublications/Python-GUI-with-PyQt.
In case there's an update to the code, it will be updated on the existing GitHub repository.

We have code bundles from our rich catalogue of books and videos available at **https://github.com/bpbpublications**. Check them out!

Errata

We take immense pride in our work at BPB Publications and follow best practices to ensure the accuracy of our content to provide with an indulging reading experience to our subscribers. Our readers are our mirrors, and we use their inputs to reflect and improve upon human errors, if any, that may have occurred during the publishing processes involved. To let us maintain the quality and help us reach out to any readers who might be having difficulties due to any unforeseen errors, please write to us at :

errata@bpbonline.com

Your support, suggestions and feedbacks are highly appreciated by the BPB Publications' Family.

Piracy

If you come across any illegal copies of our works in any form on the internet, we would be grateful if you would provide us with the location address or website name. Please contact us at **business@bpbonline.com** with a link to the material.

If you are interested in becoming an author

If there is a topic that you have expertise in, and you are interested in either writing or contributing to a book, please visit **www.bpbonline.com**. We have worked with thousands of developers and tech professionals, just like you, to help them share their insights with the global tech community. You can make a general application, apply for a specific hot topic that we are recruiting an author for, or submit your own idea.

Reviews

Please leave a review. Once you have read and used this book, why not leave a review on the site that you purchased it from? Potential readers can then see and use your unbiased opinion to make purchase decisions. We at BPB can understand what you think about our products, and our authors can see your feedback on their book. Thank you!

For more information about BPB, please visit **www.bpbonline.com**.

Join our book's Discord space

Join the book's Discord Workspace for Latest updates, Offers, Tech happenings around the world, New Release and Sessions with the Authors:

https://discord.bpbonline.com

Table of Contents

CHAPTER 1

Introduction to PyQt5 and Qt Designer Tool

Introduction

In our previously launched book *Building Modern GUIs with tkinter and Python*, we learned how to create GUI forms using the Tk interface library. Now, we will be looking at another approach to create the same GUI forms using one of the most popular cross-platform libraries, known as PyQt5 library, which was developed by Riverbank Computing. A robust and cross-platform graphical toolkit called Qt has a Python binding called PyQt5. Python is a well-known and simple-to-learn programming language, and with PyQt5 developers, we can simply construct GUI applications using Python. With PyQt5, a visual layout tool called Qt Designer is included. Without having to write any code explicitly, it enables developers to construct GUI layouts quickly and easily by dragging and dropping widgets onto a canvas. Additionally, Qt Designer offers a selection of editable widgets that may be used to design distinctive user interfaces with eye-catching visuals.

Structure

In this chapter, we will discuss the following topics:

- Comparison of PyQt5 with tkinter library
- PyQt5 framework installation

- First GUI form creation using PyQt5 without using class
- GUI form creation using PyQt5 by using class
- Installation of Qt Designer tool with pre-defined templates
- Components of Qt Designer
- User Credential App Demo

Objectives

By the end of this chapter, the reader will be able to compare the powerful and cross-platform toolkit graphical PyQt5, with the tkinter library. We shall see how to install the PyQt5 framework installation, along with the creation of a basic GUI form using PyQt5, first without, and then using the class. Moreover, we will be looking into the components inside Qt Designer along with different pre-defined templates. Finally, we will be creating a user credential app, initially focusing on the view in Qt Designer (`.ui` file which is a XML file), then converting it into a Python code (`.py`) using `pyuic5` command, and finally creating a new Python file, which will be importing the Python code for user interface design and adding some useful logic to create a basic login application for the user.

Comparison of PyQt5 with tkinter library

There are numerous Qt classes in a set of Python modules, which are compatible with many operating systems such as iOS, Windows, Linux, Unix, Android, and so on, which is a part of the top-level Python package, that is, PyQt5 library. Qt5 in PyQt5 stands for **Qt version 5.** This library provides us the advantage of Python binding with the Qt C++ toolkit. An important point to note is that under the **GNU General Public License** (**GNU GPL** or **GPL**) v3 license, the PyQt5 license is being released. One may wonder that if we have already learned about tkinter, then why we should learn about PyQt5 as well? To better understand this, let us check the advantages of PyQt5 over other library packages such as tkinter:

- **Flexibility in coding**: In order to establish simple communication between objects, there is a concept of signals and slots, which gives us flexibility for GUI programming using PyQt5, when dealing with events.
- **More than GUI toolkit:** Using PyQt5, we can build entire applications using its graphics, printer support, networking, database access, and so on. It is like an application framework.
- **Numerous UI components:** PyQt5 offers numerous widgets such as `QLabel`, `QButton`, `QCombobox`, and so on, such that each widget has some basic image well suited in all the platforms. Numerous advanced widgets are also available on the topic in this library.

- **Numerous study resources:** If there is no documentation, then you might wonder what the point of learning is. PyQt5 comes with a rich array of documentation since it is one of the most commonly used Python packages for GUI creation.
- **Easy to understand:** We can easily use previous knowledge of either Python, Qt or C++, thus making PyQt5 easy to understand.
- **Preferred choice of GUI developers**: Due to simplicity and ease of use, many GUI developers opt for functionalities that come with PyQt5 to develop their own applications.
- **GUI widget appearance:** The appearance of PyQt5 is nice and pleasing to the eyes.

Now, we may wonder which library to choose to create GUI forms using PyQt5 or tkinter. This generally depends on user application and the willingness to learn and explore. *Table 1.1* further shows the differences between the libraries:

Fundamental points	PyQt5	tkinter
Licensing	Commercial license is applicable if not complying to provide an application to the end user under GPL license.	It is free if needed to supply commercially.
Library	Vast	Small compared to PyQt5.
Understanding time	More	Less
Widgets appearance	Nice and modern look	Orthodox and quite old-fashioned
Provision of advanced widgets	Yes	No
Interfacing with other designer tool	Yes, Qt Designer	Qt Designer is not there for tkinter
Default supply of inbuilt libraries	No, we need to install it separately	Yes, as it comes along with default standard Python library
Concept of signals and slots for communication	Yes	No

***Table 1.1:** Differences between libraries PyQt5 and tkinter*

You can decide which library to choose to create GUI forms, depending on your application. We will later discuss how to create a **UI form** using Qt Designer in detail, as well as the widgets associated with it and the Python code with logic written by importing the auto-code generated by creating the UI form in detail.

PyQt5 framework installation

The Python version we will be using for discussing PyQt5 will be 3.7.3. (You can try working with new version as on today, that is, 3.11.5 dated Aug 24, 2023) From the location where we have installed our Python, first type the command **`python --version`** to check the version installed and then type the following command to install pyqt5:

```
pip install pyqt5
```

Refer to *Figure 1.1*:

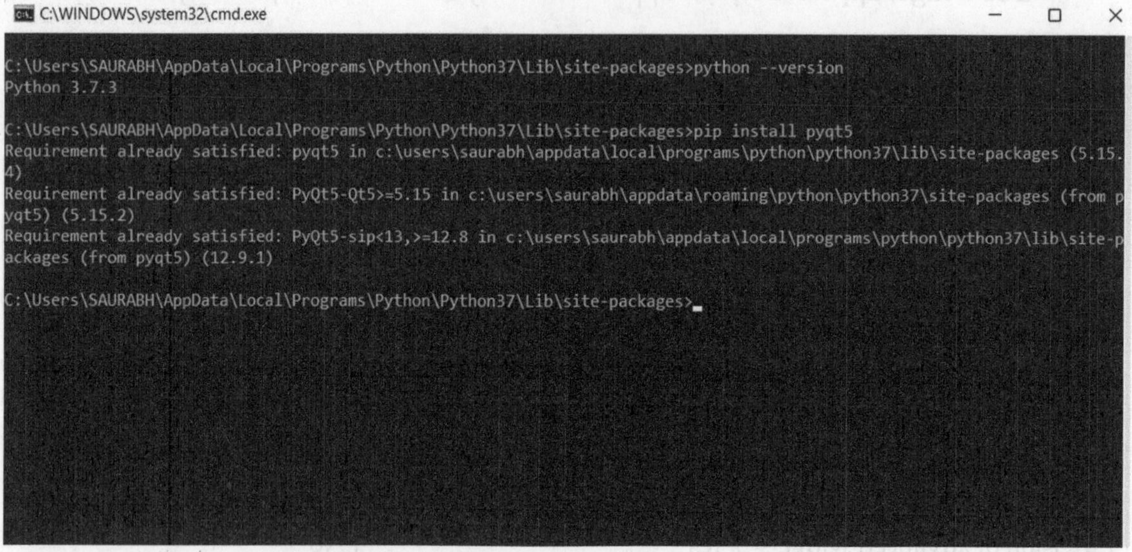

***Figure 1.1:** PyQt5 installation*

Once installed, we can verify the installation of PyQt5 under Python site-packages folder, as shown in *Figure 1.2*:

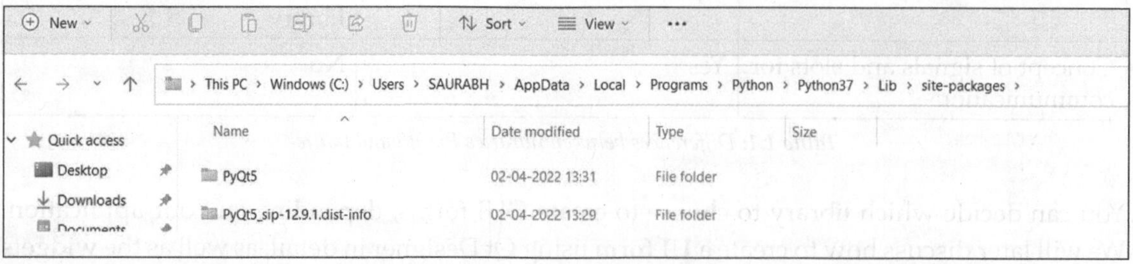

***Figure 1.2:** PyQt5 folder*

We can check some of the modules present in PyQt5. If we do not get any error, then we can again cross verify that PyQt5 is successfully installed, as shown in *Figure 1.3:*

```
C:\Users\SAURABH>python
Python 3.7.3 (v3.7.3:ef4ec6ed12, Mar 25 2019, 22:22:05) [MSC v.1916 64 bit (AMD64)] on win32
Type "help", "copyright", "credits" or "license" for more information.
>>> from PyQt5 import QtGui
>>>
```

***Figure 1.3:** PyQt5 package verification*

First GUI form creation using PyQt5 without using class

Now, we shall see a basic UI form creation using PyQt5 without using class. This is quite important. As you might have realized, most of the UI forms which we will be creating will be using the concept of class and object. It is highly recommended that you go through the concept of class before moving further in this chapter. It is well explained in our previous books, *Programming Techniques using Python* and *Python for Everyone*. Here, we will only focus on our basic UI form creation. So, without any further delay, let us start. Refer to the following code which can be checked in some IEDs like VSCode, Spyder, Anaconda and so on:

```
import sys # L1
from PyQt5.QtWidgets import QWidget, QApplication # L2

myapp = QApplication(sys.argv) # L3
mywindow = QWidget() # L4
mywindow.show() # L5
sys.exit(myapp.exec_()) # L6
```

Output:

The output can be seen in the following *Figure 1.4:*

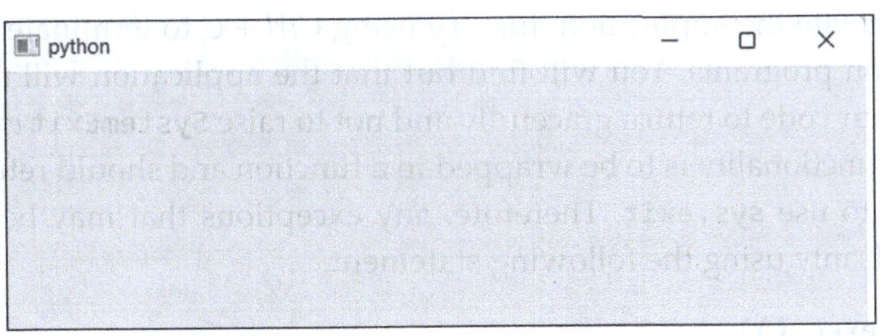

***Figure 1.4:** Output of Chap1_Example1.py*

Note: The preceding code is covered in Program Name: Chap1_Example1.py

You will be surprised that by writing few lines of code, we can create our GUI form, and that too, as fully functional. Now let us see the explanation of this code, line by line.

In **L1**, we are first importing the **sys** module for accessing the command line arguments.

In **L2**, we are importing from class, which creates desktop style UIs of PyQt5 package, that is, Qt Widgets. **QWidget** is used for creating an empty GUI and **QApplication** is nothing but an application handler. We can see that from the above statement, we are importing the modules for creating the GUI form.

In **L3**, we are creating an instance, that is, object of **QApplication** class using the variable name **myapp** and passing command-line parameters list **sys.argv** to the application. When we are sure that we will be passing command line parameters to control Qt form through shell launching or during the course of interface automating, we can pass this as an argument to **QApplication** class, or else we can pass as an empty list as:

```
myapp = QApplication([])
```

In **L4**, we are creating an object of **QWidget** class using the variable name **mywindow**. This **QWidget** class is the parent class of all the User Interface objects in Qt. The top-level window is created by not passing any parameter to the **QWidget** class.

In **L5**, in order to make the widgets visible after creating the object of **QWidget** class, we must call **show()** method with the object. Now, you may wonder what will happen if we do not call this show method. Since after running the application, there is no way to close or quit it, show() will be called to simply display widgets.

In **L6**, for implementing parallel execution, PyQt5 uses an event-loop mechanism as it is largely written in C++, So, to start up the event-loop mechanism, we are calling **myapp.exec_()** method, which will be held by the application object. Some will even think that at some places, we have seen **myapp.exec**. This exec was a reserved word in Python 2. So, to avoid the naming conflict with this reserved word, we are using **exec_()** in PyQt5. Therefore, when there will be a requirement by the user to close the GUI, this **myapp.exec_()** will allow the control to pass over to Qt to terminate the application. Just try using *Ctrl* + C to terminate the application as done in our Python programs. You will find out that the application will not be terminated. Now, if we want our code to return gracefully and not to raise **SystemExit** *exception*, this event loop mechanism functionality is to be wrapped in a function and should return from the place where we intend to use **sys.exit**. Therefore, any exceptions that may be thrown or might occur, must exit cleanly using the following statement:

```
sys.exit(myapp.exec_())
```

You will be wondering that in the above code, many classes start with a capital letter **Q** so that it can be distinguished from other namespaces.

We can resize the window, drag it around to any conformable place, maximize it or close it. Just make sure that do not use the following, as it is best to avoid wild imports:

```
fromPyQt5.Qtwidgets import *
```

One important point to observe is that the GUI form comes up with the default title **Python** and with default size.

Now, let us put some of our own title text in Python GUI form:

```
import sys
from PyQt5.QtWidgets import QWidget, QApplication

myapp = QApplication(sys.argv)
mywindow = QWidget()
mywindow.setWindowTitle('Basic GUI Form') # BG1
mywindow.show()
sys.exit(myapp.exec_())
```

Output:

The output can be seen in the following *Figure 1.5:*

Figure 1.5: *Output of Chap1_Example2.py*

Note: The preceding code is covered in Program Name: Chap1_Example2.py

In **BG1**, we are calling **setWindowTitle()** method from **QWidget** object and passing parameter as **Basic GUI Form**. Therefore, we can see that our GUI form has a title that we wanted to display at the top-left. The rest of the code is the same as previous program.

Now, we can also specify the size of our GUI form, that is, by specifying width and height by calling the resize method as shown:

```
import sys
from PyQt5.QtWidgets import QWidget, QApplication

myapp = QApplication(sys.argv)
mywindow = QWidget()
mywindow.setWindowTitle('Basic GUI Form')
mywindow.resize(400,350) # RS1
mywindow.show()
sys.exit(myapp.exec_())
```

Output:

The output can be seen in the following *Figure 1.6:*

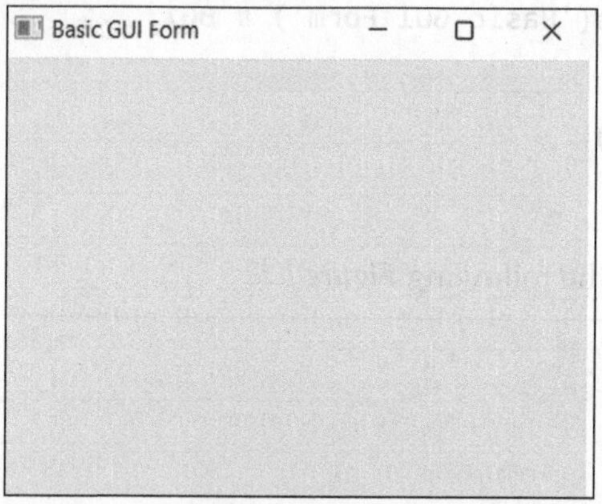

Figure 1.6: Output of Chap1_Example3.py

Note: The preceding code is covered in Program Name: Chap1_Example3.py

In **`RS1`**, we are calling the **`resize()`** method using the **`QWidget`** object and passing parameters as 400 and 300. So, here we are setting width as 400 and height as 300, which sets our GUI form.

Therefore, we have learned the basic structure of creating a GUI form using PyQt5 without the usage of class.

Now, we will learn the similar examples , with usage of classes and objects concept.

GUI form creation using PyQt5 by using class

It is very important that you understand the concept of objects and classes. Before we proceed further, one program can be written in **n** number of ways. The best approach is to program systematically, in a structured way with as few lines as possible. Let us learn the same examples by creating class approach:

```
import sys # CL1
from PyQt5.QtWidgets import QWidget, QApplication # CL2

class GUIWindow(QWidget):
    def __init__(self):
        super(GUIWindow, self).__init__() # CL6
        self.initializationUI() # CL7

    def initializationUI(self):
        self.show() # CL8


if __name__ == '__main__':
    myapp = QApplication(sys.argv) # CL3
    mywindow = GUIWindow() #CL4
    sys.exit(myapp.exec_()) # CL5
```

Output:

The output can be seen in the following *Figure 1.7:*

Figure 1.7: *Output of Chap1_Example4.py*

Note: The preceding code is covered in Program Name: Chap1_Example4.py

Explanation of **CL1**, **CL2**, **CL3** and **CL5** is similar to that of **L1**, **L2**, **L3** and **L6** of code **Chap1_Example1.py**

In **CL4**, we are creating an object of user-defined class **GUIWindow** class. We can see that **GUIWindow** class is being derived from the parent class **QWidget,** from which spaces and windows are inherited either directly or indirectly. Moreover, all UI objects will be derived from this **QWidget** class.

In **CL6**, we are calling the **__init__** method of our parent class **QWidget**. In other words, we can say that the default constructor of **QWidget** class is created.

In **CL7**, we have created the **initializationUI** method in our **GUIWindow** class.

In **CL8**, inside the **initializationUI** method, we are calling the show method on our GUI Window object for displaying:

```
import sys # CL1

from PyQt5.QtWidgets import QWidget, QApplication # CL2


class GUIWindow(QWidget):

    def __init__(self):

        super(GUIWindow, self).__init__() # CL6

        self.initializationUI() # CL7


    def initializationUI(self):

        self.setWindowTitle("Basic GUI Form") #CL9

        self.show() # CL8


if __name__ == '__main__':

    myapp = QApplication(sys.argv) # CL3

    mywindow = GUIWindow() #CL4

    sys.exit(myapp.exec_()) # CL5
```

Output:

The output can be seen in the following *Figure 1.8:*

Figure 1.8: Output of Chap1_Example5.py

Note: The preceding code is covered in Program Name: Chap1_Example5.py

In the above code, everything is similar to that of code **`Chap1_Example4.py`** except that in **`CL9`**, we are calling **`setWindowTitle()`** method on our GUI Window object and passing the parameter as **Basic GUI Form**. This will set the title to the text at the top-left side of the GUI form, as shown:

```
import sys # CL1
from PyQt5.QtWidgets import QWidget, QApplication # CL2


class GUIWindow(QWidget):
    def __init__(self):
        super(GUIWindow, self).__init__() # CL6
        self.initializationUI() # CL7


    def initializationUI(self):
        self.setGeometry(300,300,400,300) # CL10
        self.setWindowTitle("Basic GUI Form") # CL9
        self.show() # CL8


if __name__ == '__main__':
    myapp = QApplication(sys.argv) # CL3
    mywindow = GUIWindow() #CL4
    sys.exit(myapp.exec_()) # CL5
```

Output:

The output can be seen in the following *Figure 1.9:*

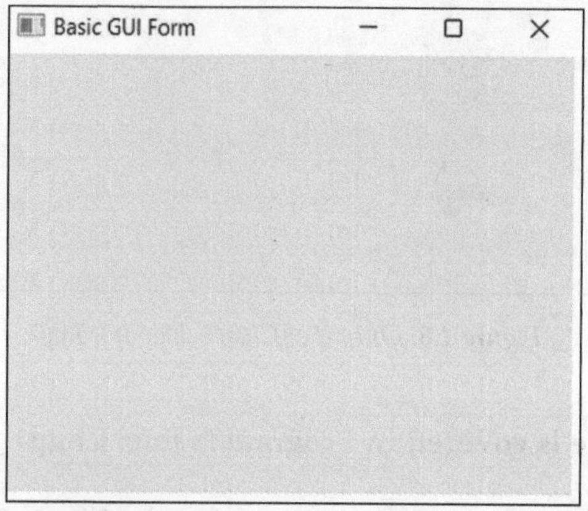

Figure 1.9: *Output of Chap1_Example6.py*

Note: The preceding code is covered in Program Name: Chap1_Example6.py

In the above code, everything is similar to that of code **`Chap1_Example5.py`** except that in **`CL10`**, we are trying to define the geometry of PyQt5 GUI form by setting the four arguments :

`self.setGeometry(300,300,400,300) (# self.setGeometry(x-axis, y-axis, width, height))`

The first argument is X-coordinate, which is set as **`300`**.

The second argument is Y-coordinate, which is set as **`300`**.

The third argument is window width, which is set as **`400`**.

The fourth argument is window height, which is set as **`300`**.

So, we can see that with the help of the usage of classes as well, we can create a GUI form, set the title, define the geometry, and neatly exit the form.

Now, we have written some lines of code to get our desired result. What if we can just create our own GUI form by using some user interface design tool. We are lucky that we can create the same GUI forms that we have seen till now using interface tools such as Qt Designer. Now, we will learn all the GUI forms using Qt Designer tool from here.

Qt Designer is one of the handiest tools for designing your imagination into a working product by building GUI forms with existing Qt Widgets. In this book, we will cover the creation and usage of Qt Designer widgets and its interfaces to create newly designed UI forms. We will study about the concept of signals and slots, drag and drop interfaces, customization of signals, dialogs, windows, and so on. For more documentation on Qt Designer and some other insights, you may visit the official website through the link: **https://doc.qt.io/qt-6/qt-intro.html**

Installation of Qt Designer with pre-defined templates

Till now, we have seen that for any package we want to install, we will be using the `pip` command. But Qt Designer cannot be installed in your system using `pip` command like this `pip install pyQt Designer`. So, you can either download it from sourceforge or install it using `pip install pyqt5-tools`.

After this, run the designer from the following path:

```
C:\Users\%USERNAME%\AppData\Local\Programs\Python\Python37\Lib\site-packages\
pyqt5-tools\designer\designer.exe.
```

Launch the Qt Designer application, and on executing, the following GUI window, as shown in *Figure 1.10*, will be displayed to the user. Here, we can create our own GUI forms as per our need:

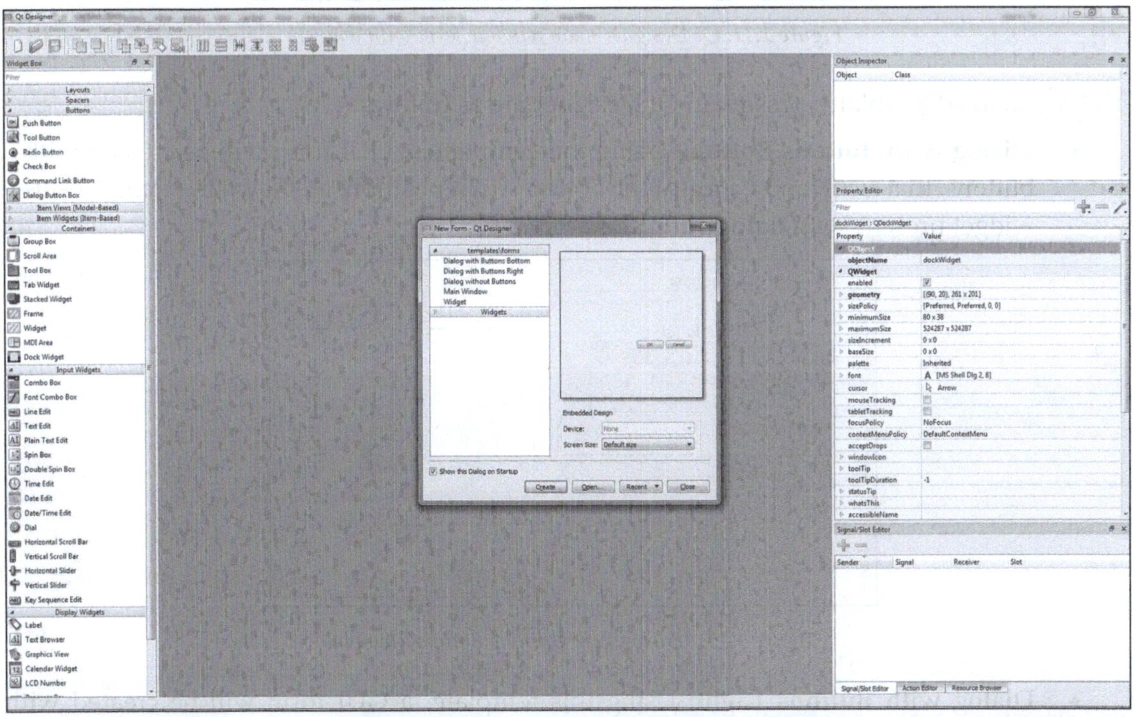

***Figure 1.10:** Qt Designer main window form*

Let us see some insights of Qt Designer. From *Figure 1.10*, we can see that there is an open dialog box with title as **New Form**, prompting the user to select any of the templates/forms or widgets on launching the designer. The widgets selection is shown in *Figure 1.11*:

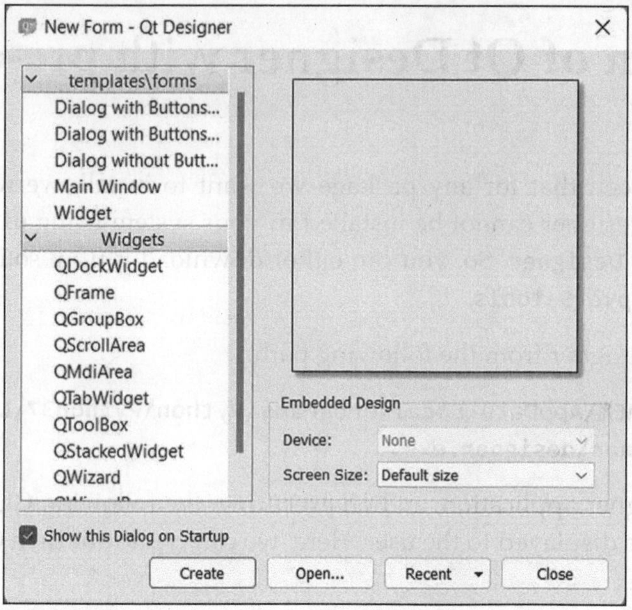

Figure 1.11: *Qt Designer main window form with widgets*

The pre-defined templates present in Qt Designer are as follows:

- **Dialog with Buttons Bottom:** Using this template, a GUI form will be created with 2 buttons, that is, **OK** and **Cancel** at the bottom-right position, as shown in *Figure 1.12*. The widget present is **QDialogButtonBox**.

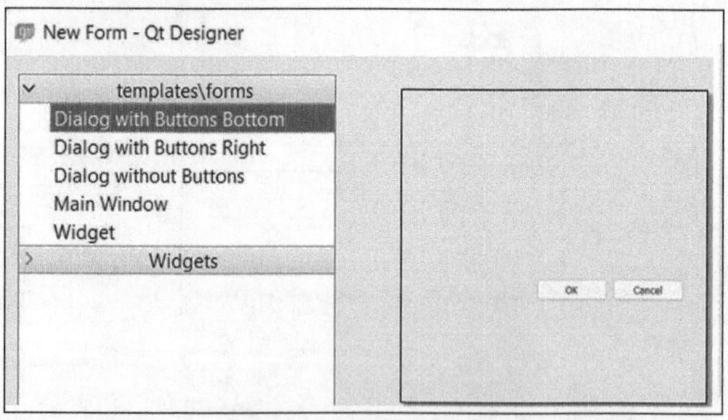

Figure 1.12: *"Dialog with Buttons Bottom" template*

- **Dialog with Buttons Right:** Using this template, a GUI form will be created with presence of two buttons, that is, **OK** and **Cancel**, at top-right position, as shown in the following *Figure 1.13*. The widget present is **QDialogButtonBox**:

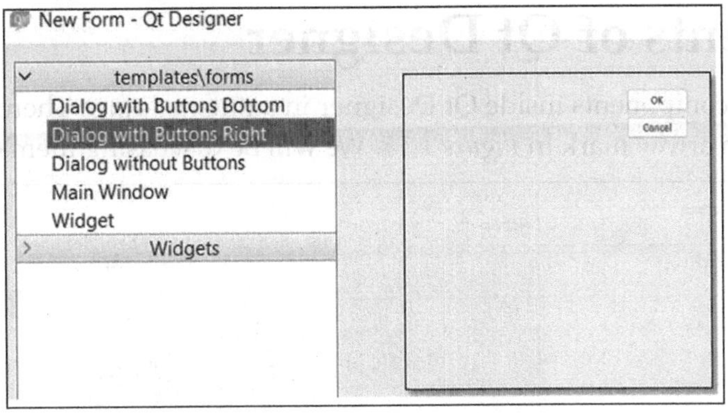

Figure 1.13: "Dialog with Buttons Right" template

- **Dialog without Buttons:** Using this template, an empty GUI form will be created with superclass as **`QDialog`**, where the user can place widgets and create applications as per their own requirement.
- **Main Window:** Using this template, the main application GUI form will be created with superclass as **`QMainWindow`**, along with the presence of *menubar* and *toolbar* for the user. The user may use it or may delete it as per the need.
- **Widget:** Using this template, an empty GUI form will be created with superclass as **`QWidget`**.

These **`QDialog`** , **`QMainWindow`** and **`QWidget`** classes have their own importance.

Suppose there is a requirement to create a GUI form by choosing **dialog** template. In that case, all the widgets used will be inherited from the superclass **`QDialog`**.

Suppose there is a requirement to create a GUI form by choosing **main window** template. Then, all the widgets used will be inherited from the superclass **`QMainWindow`**.

Suppose there is a requirement to create a GUI form by choosing **widget** template. Here, all the widgets used will be inherited from the superclass **`QWidget`**.

Moreover, the screen size is selected as **Default size**, as shown in *Figure 1.14*. We can select the screen size from the list of items mentioned in the combobox:

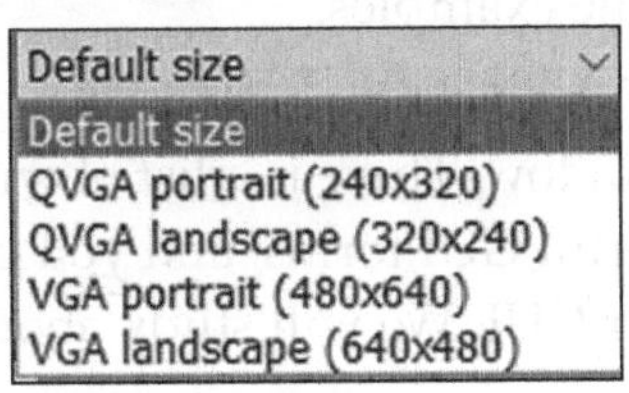

Figure 1.14: Screen size selection

Components of Qt Designer

We will see all the components inside Qt Designer in a nutshell now. There are some numbers present across each arrow mark in *Figure 1.15*. We will be discussing them one by one:

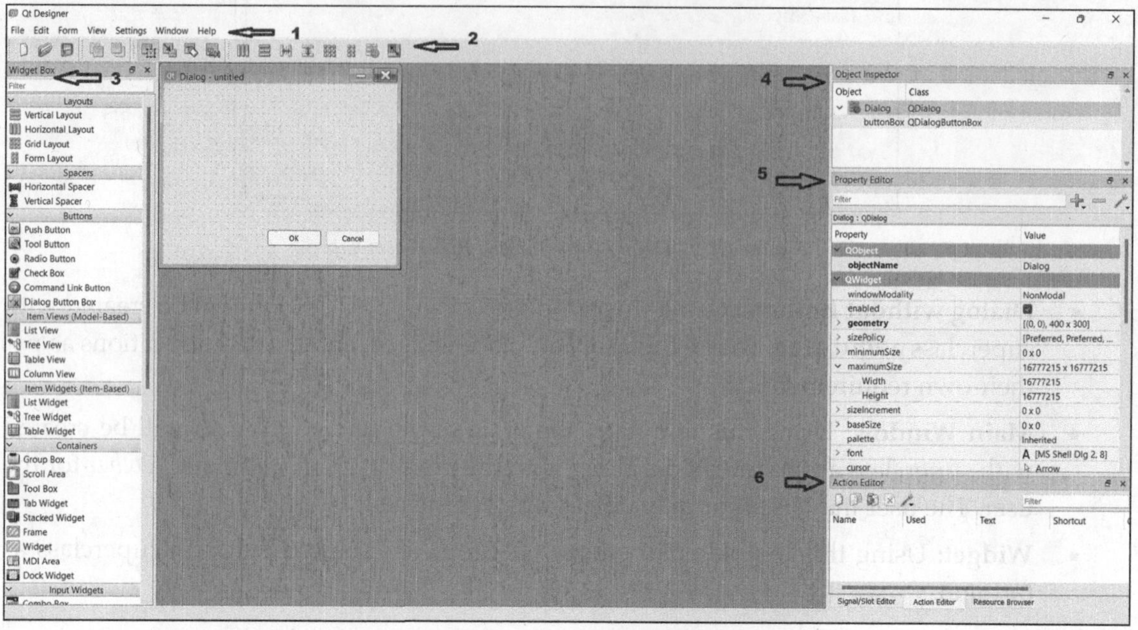

Figure 1.15: Qt Designer tool

Here are the different numerically marked components:

1. **Menubar:** The first thing which we noticed at the top will be nothing but the menubar of Qt Designer for GUI managing. It has **File, Edit, Form View, Settings, Window**, and the **Help** options, for interacting with the user.

2. **Toolbar:** What we can manage using Menubar can also be replicated using Toolbar. The icons are placed instead of text for user interaction. It provides shortcut icons for most useful functions. There are options like **Edit Widgets, Edit Signals/Slots, Edit Buddies** and **Edit Tab order**, in this toolbar of Qt Designer. We will be using all these features with demonstration of some examples.

3. **Widget Box:** This is one of the most important areas of Qt Designer. It is located on the left side of Qt Designer window. There is a list of widgets and layouts which provides flexibility to create wonderful GUI forms, and you can access it by using the drag and drop to any location of our GUI. We will study about all these widgets and layouts in detail.

4. **Object Inspector (OI):** OI is located on the right side of Qt Designer window, which displays the list of objects used in the form along with their layout display in hierarchical manner.
5. **Property Editor:** Under OI, there is a Property Editor dock widget. In this dock widget, we can change the property of a widget, layout or of a window as per our requirement.
6. **Action Editor:** Under Property Editor, there is Signals / Slot Editor , Action editor and Resource browser:
   a. In **Signals/Slot Editor**, signals and slots between the objects can be created, deleted or edited as per our requirement. It may be noted that while using the widget, complete configuration will not be possible as it requires possible amount of coding by the user to get the end result.
   b. In **Action editor**, we can create new actions, and delete actions. Moreover, there is a checkable option for **`Used`** column, we can write text under **"`Text column`"**, provide a shortcut key under **"`Shortcut column`"**, make checkable under **"`Checkable column`"** as well as a tooltip that has been provided under **"`Tooltip column`"**. This Action editor will allow us to work with Actions.
   c. Whenever there will be a requirement to manage resources like images, icons, translation files and any binary files in our application, then we will be using **Resource Browser**. We will be learning this with examples.

User credential app demo

Finally, let us see the first example of Qt Designer. We will be creating a user credentials application where the username and password will be prompted from the user. If they both match, then we will display some message. This example is quite important to understand because first, we will simply display them by just dragging and dropping **without using the concept of layout and spacers**. Then we will learn the concept of layouts and spacers. Refer to the following *Figure 1.16:*

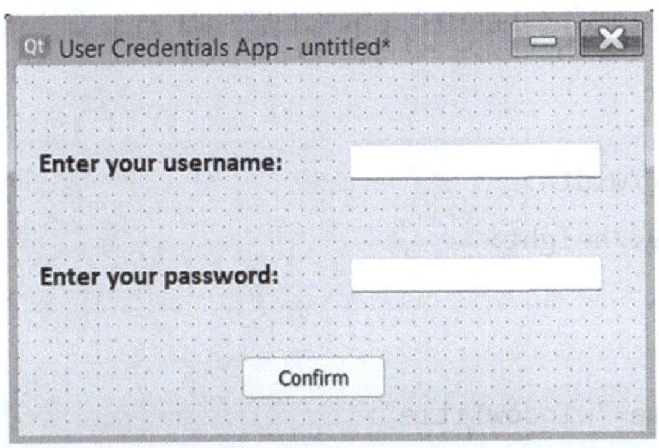

Figure 1.16: *User credentials app without usage of layout and spacers*

The steps to create user credentials app are as follows:

1. We have selected the new template as **Widget** for creating the user credentials app GUI form.
2. First drag 2 **Label** widgets under display widgets dock and drop it on the GUI form. We are changing a few properties of these **Label** widgets. First is the **text** property, of which we have changed the text to **Enter your username**: and **Enter your password:** respectively. Next, we have changed the **font** property. Moreover, we have also changed their object names as **mylbl_username** and **mylbl_password** using the **objectName** property.
3. Then drag 2 **Line Edit** widgets from the widget box and drop it on the GUI form. Using **objectName** property, their names have been changed to **lineEdit_username** and **lineEdit_password** .
4. Finally drag a **Push Button** widget into the GUI form and change its text to **Confirm** using its **text** property. Then, using **objectName** property, its name has been changed to **mybtn_confirm**.
5. Now, we are saving this GUI form with name as "**user_credential_app.ui**". This **.ui** file is nothing but an XML file which depicts form information, that is, widgets, layouts and so on. In simple ways, we can understand that Qt Designer is independent of any programming language and does not generate code in any of the programming languages but generates a XML based .ui file as it is easy to understand.

   The data contents inside **user_credential_app.ui** file is as follows:

```
<?xml version="1.0" encoding="UTF-8"?>
<ui version="4.0">
 <class>Form</class>
 <widget class="QWidget" name="Form">
  <property name="geometry">
   <rect>
    <x>0</x>
    <y>0</y>
    <width>398</width>
    <height>229</height>
   </rect>
  </property>
  <property name="windowTitle">
   <string>User Credentials App</string>
```

```
</property>
<widget class="QLabel" name="mylbl_username">
 <property name="geometry">
  <rect>
   <x>14</x>
   <y>50</y>
   <width>161</width>
   <height>20</height>
  </rect>
 </property>
 <property name="font">
  <font>
   <family>Calibri</family>
   <pointsize>10</pointsize>
   <weight>75</weight>
   <bold>true</bold>
  </font>
 </property>
 <property name="text">
  <string>Enter your username:</string>
 </property>
</widget>
<widget class="QLabel" name="mylbl_password">
 <property name="geometry">
  <rect>
   <x>14</x>
   <y>120</y>
   <width>161</width>
   <height>20</height>
  </rect>
 </property>
 <property name="font">
```

```
      <font>
       <family>Calibri</family>
       <pointsize>10</pointsize>
       <weight>75</weight>
       <bold>true</bold>
      </font>
     </property>
     <property name="text">
      <string>Enter your password:</string>
     </property>
    </widget>
    <widget class="QPushButton" name="mybtn_confirm">
     <property name="geometry">
      <rect>
       <x>140</x>
       <y>180</y>
       <width>93</width>
       <height>28</height>
      </rect>
     </property>
     <property name="text">
      <string>Confirm</string>
     </property>
    </widget>
    <widget class="QLineEdit" name="lineEdit_username">
     <property name="geometry">
      <rect>
       <x>210</x>
       <y>50</y>
       <width>161</width>
       <height>22</height>
      </rect>
```

```
    </property>
   </widget>
   <widget class="QLineEdit" name="lineEdit_password">
    <property name="geometry">
     <rect>
      <x>210</x>
      <y>120</y>
      <width>161</width>
      <height>22</height>
     </rect>
    </property>
   </widget>
  </widget>
  <resources/>
  <connections/>
 </ui>
```

Note: The preceding code is covered in Program Name: User Credential App/user_credential_app.ui

Some important observations from **user_credential_app.ui** file are:

- We can see that whatever property we have changed, such as **text**, **font**, and **objectName**, all have been reflected in their respective widgets.
- Moreover, default geometry property with x, y, width, and height is mentioned with values for each widget.
- Just observe the Qt Designer property for each widget. The property whose color is black (object with bold text property) will be displayed in the **.ui** file.

Let us now move on to the next step in creating the User Credentials App.

6. Our next task is to convert this XML based **.ui** file to Python scripting with the help of command utility **pyuic5**. It is a dev tool to make the conversion of Qt Designer **.ui** file to Python **.py** file. A good thing is that it is tied together with PyQt5. Therefore, we go to the folder where we have saved this "**user_credential_app.ui**" file which is saved in the folder "**E:\my_pythonbook\PyQt5\Chapter_1\User Credential app**" as shown in the following *Figure 1.17*, by opening the command prompt window:

Figure 1.17: Saving of file user_credential_app.ui

Therefore, after opening of command window and navigating to the folder, we are writing following command:

```
pyuic5 user_credential_app.ui -o user_credential_app.py
```

This is illustrated in the following *Figure 1.18:*

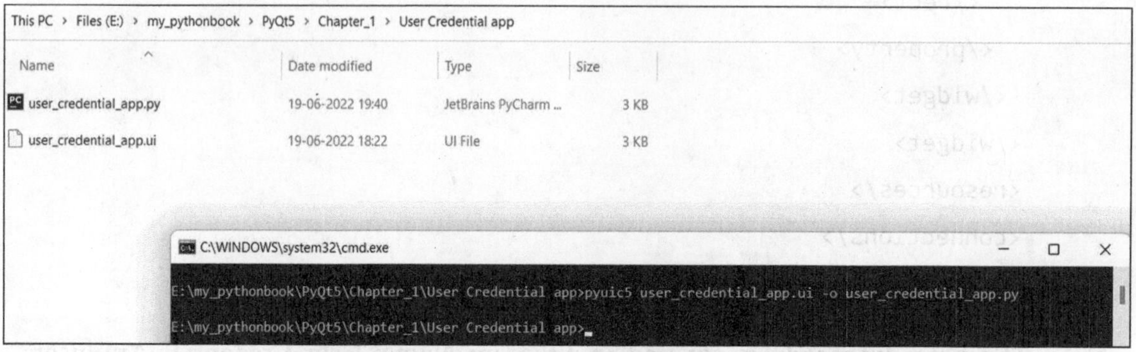

Figure 1.18: Creation of file "user_credential_app.py"

After execution of the above command, we can see from *Figure 1.18* that **user_credential_app.py** file has been created and the python code inside this file is as follows:

```
# -*- coding: utf-8 -*-


# Form implementation generated from reading ui file 'user_credential_app.
ui'
#
# Created by: PyQt5 UI code generator 5.15.4
#
# WARNING: Any manual changes made to this file will be lost when pyuic5
is
# run again.  Do not edit this file unless you know what you are doing.


from PyQt5 import QtCore, QtGui, QtWidgets
```

```
class Ui_Form(object):
    def setupUi(self, Form):
        Form.setObjectName("Form")
        Form.resize(398, 229)
        self.mylbl_username = QtWidgets.QLabel(Form)
        self.mylbl_username.setGeometry(QtCore.QRect(14, 50, 161, 20))
        font = QtGui.QFont()
        font.setFamily("Calibri")
        font.setPointSize(10)
        font.setBold(True)
        font.setWeight(75)
        self.mylbl_username.setFont(font)
        self.mylbl_username.setObjectName("mylbl_username")
        self.mylbl_password = QtWidgets.QLabel(Form)
        self.mylbl_password.setGeometry(QtCore.QRect(14, 120, 161, 20))
        font = QtGui.QFont()
        font.setFamily("Calibri")
        font.setPointSize(10)
        font.setBold(True)
        font.setWeight(75)
        self.mylbl_password.setFont(font)
        self.mylbl_password.setObjectName("mylbl_password")
        self.mybtn_confirm = QtWidgets.QPushButton(Form)
        self.mybtn_confirm.setGeometry(QtCore.QRect(140, 180, 93, 28))
        self.mybtn_confirm.setObjectName("mybtn_confirm")
        self.lineEdit_username = QtWidgets.QLineEdit(Form)
        self.lineEdit_username.setGeometry(QtCore.QRect(210, 50, 161, 22))
        self.lineEdit_username.setObjectName("lineEdit_username")
        self.lineEdit_password = QtWidgets.QLineEdit(Form)
        self.lineEdit_password.setGeometry(QtCore.QRect(210, 120, 161,
        22))
```

```
        self.lineEdit_password.setObjectName("lineEdit_password")

        self.retranslateUi(Form)
        QtCore.QMetaObject.connectSlotsByName(Form)

    def retranslateUi(self, Form):
        _translate = QtCore.QCoreApplication.translate
        Form.setWindowTitle(_translate("Form", "User Credentials App"))
        self.mylbl_username.setText(_translate("Form", "Enter your
        username:"))
        self.mylbl_password.setText(_translate("Form", "Enter your
        password:"))
        self.mybtn_confirm.setText(_translate("Form", "Confirm"))
```

Note: The preceding code is covered in Program Name: User Credential App/user_credential_app.py

So, here we can convert a **.ui** file into **.py** file.

This '**-o**' in **pyuic5** command which we had run here, stands for - **-output**, that is, writing the generated Python code to **user_credential_app.py** file.

Note: Since this is our first time looking into .ui and Python script code .py file, we have learned whole process. From the next time, whenever we will be creating any application form, then you will find the .ui and .py file in the source code bundle. We will only be displaying the actual usage code by creating a new Python file, which we will learn shortly by using the above automated generated code .py file.

One of the most important points to note after converting **.ui** file to **.py** file, is that **the modification of the Python code generated must not be done manually**. This is since any modification done will be overwritten the next time we will be creating **.py** file from **.ui** file, when running using **pyuic5** command.

7. It is now time to create a new Python file called **run_user_credential_app.py.** Here, we will be importing **user_credential_app.py** file and write some code into it such that when username and password is matched/unmatched, some message will be displayed to the user. Refer to the following code:

```
import sys
from PyQt5.QtWidgets import QWidget, QApplication, QMessageBox # RUCA1
from user_credential_app import * # RUCA2
```

```
class MyWidget(QWidget):
    def __init__(self):
        super(MyWidget, self).__init__()
        self.myui = Ui_Form() # RUCA3
        self.myui.setupUi(self) # RUCA4
        self.myui.mybtn_confirm.clicked.connect(self.myuser_credentials_
check) # RUCA5
        self.show() # RUCA6

    def myuser_credentials_check(self):
        if(self.myui.lineEdit_username.text() == ""): # RUCA7
            QMessageBox.information(self, "Enter Username", "Username
cannot be  empty!", QMessageBox.Ok, QMessageBox.Ok)
            return

        if(self.myui.lineEdit_username.text() != ""and self.myui.lineEdit_
password.text() == ""): # RUCA8
            QMessageBox.information(self, "Enter Password", "Password
cannot be empty!", QMessageBox.Ok, QMessageBox.Ok)
            return

        if(self.myui.lineEdit_username.text() == self.myui.lineEdit_
password.text() ): # RUCA9
            QMessageBox.information(self, "Credentials check", "Welcome",
QMessageBox.Ok, QMessageBox.Ok)
        else:
            QMessageBox.information(self, "Credentials check", "Credentials
does not match", QMessageBox.Ok, QMessageBox.Ok)

if __name__ == '__main__':
    myapp = QApplication(sys.argv) # RUCA10
    mywindow = MyWidget() # RUCA11
    sys.exit(myapp.exec_()) # RUCA12
```

Note: The preceding code is covered in Program Name: User Credential App/run_user_credential_app.py

Let us now understand the explanation of the source code.

In **RUCA1**, after importing the sys module for accessing the command line arguments, we are importing from class, which creates desktop style UIs of PyQt5 package, that is, **QtWidgets**. **QWidget** is used for creating an empty GUI and an application handler, that is, **QApplication**. In addition to it, we are also importing a widget for creating dialogs, which is, **QMessageBox**. We will be learning about this later. For your information right now, we are displaying a pop up window with some informative text to the user.

We have created a new Python file **run_user_credential_app.py** to utilize **Ui_Form** class, which was created using **pyuic5** command from Qt Designer **.ui** file . Here, **MyWidget** class will inherit from **Ui_Form** class. So in **RUCA2**, from **user_credential_app** Python file, we are importing all the members of a module.

In **RUCA3**, we are creating an instance of **Ui_Form** class.

For representing organization of widgets in a UI, a widget tree is built on the parent widget Form by the method **setupUi** of the class **Ui_Form**. This generated class contains a method called **setupUi** that configures the widgets and layout in accordance with the data in the **.ui** file. When the Python code is run, the instance of the top-level widget class receives a call to the **setupUi** method, which initialises all the widgets and configures the layout in accordance with the data in the **.ui** file. The graphical user interface of the application is essentially created using this method. There is also a **retranslateUi** method for translating the interface, that is, for multi-language support logic handling, regarding how the text is to be displayed in the GUI. In **RUCA4**, we are passing a single positional argument **self**.

In **RUCA5**, we are using the concept of signals and slots. Here, when the **whenmybtn_confirmbutton** is clicked (click **event | signal**), **myuser_credentials_check** method (slot) will be invoked. We will study about signals and slots in detail later in this book. Just understand the flow of concepts right now.

In **RUCA6**, we are displaying widgets by calling the **show()** method with the object.

Now, we shall see what exactly we are doing inside **myuser_credentials_check** method which is event handling for the **mybtn_confirmbutton**.

In **RUCA7**, we are first checking whether text inside **lineEdit_username** is empty or not. If it is empty, then a message is being displayed **Username cannot be empty** as informative text, in new window, when you click on the **Confirm** button, as shown in the following *Figure 1.19:*

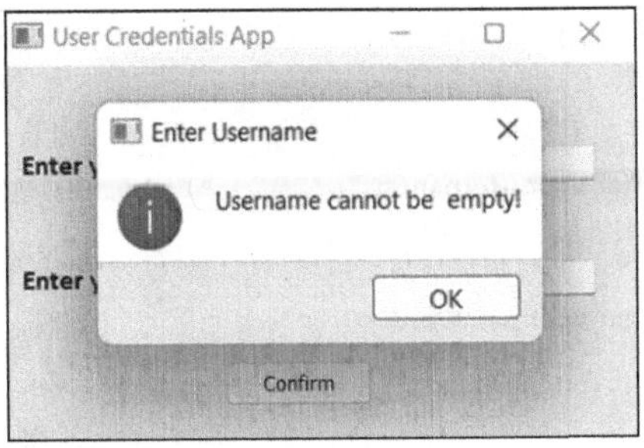

Figure 1.19: *When username is empty*

The control will be then returned after clicking the **Ok** button. This message on the new window is possible due to **`QMessageBox`** widget.

In **RUCA8**, we are then checking whether text inside **`lineEdit_password`** is empty or not. This indicates that **`lineEdit_username`** is not empty. If **`lineEdit_password`** is empty, then the message **Password cannot be empty!** is displayed as informative text in a new window, on clicking the **Confirm** button, as shown in *Figure 1.20:*

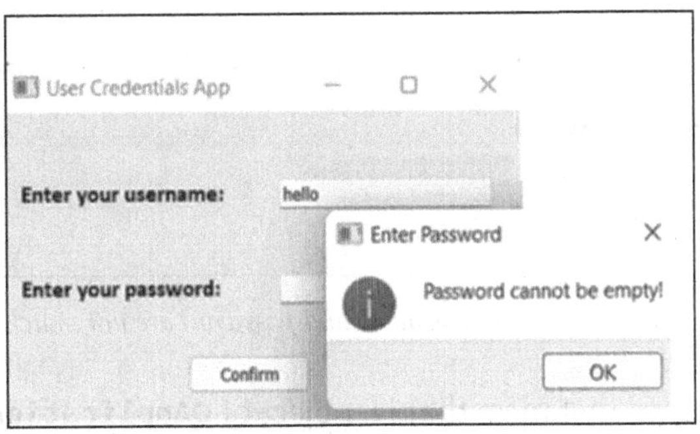

Figure 1.20: *When password is empty*

We can see that the text **`hello`** is written in **`lineEdit_username`** widget. The control will be then returned after clicking the **Ok** button.

In **RUCA9**, we are checking whether text of **`lineEdit_username`** and **`lineEdit_password`** matches or not. If it matches, then the text with **`Welcome`** message will pop up in new window, as shown in *Figure 1.21*:

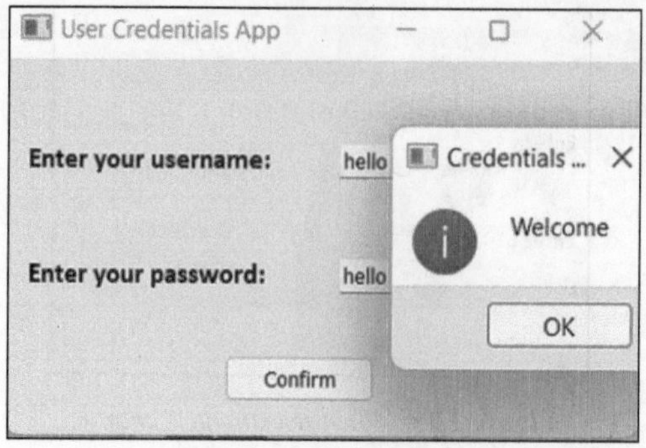

Figure 1.21: When username and password matches

If the text is not matched, then **Credentials does not match** message will pop up in a new window, as shown in *Figure 1.22*:

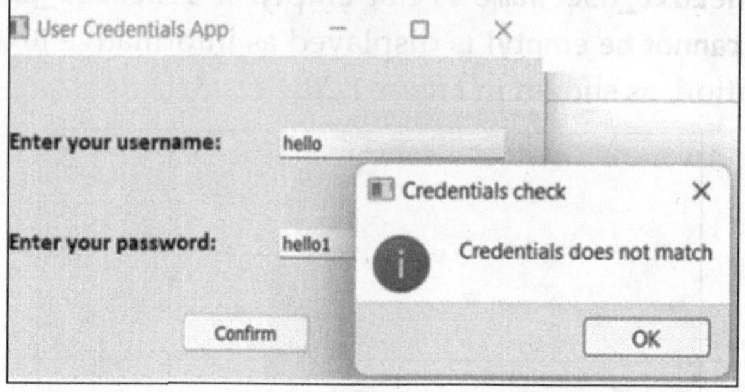

Figure 1.22: When username and password are not matched

In **RUCA10**, we are creating an instance, that is, object of **QApplication** class using the variable name **myapp** and passing command-line parameters list **sys.argv** to the application.

In **RUCA11**, we are creating an object of **MyWidget** class using the variable name **mywindow**.

In **RUCA12**, for starting up the event loop mechanism, we are calling **myapp.exec_()** method, which will hold by the application object. If we want our code to return gracefully and not to raise **SystemExit** exception, this event loop mechanism functionality is to be wrapped in a function and should return from the place where we intend to use **sys.exit**. So, any exceptions thrown or might occur must exit cleanly using the statement

```
sys.exit(myapp.exec_())
```

Note: Please note that from RUCA10 to RUCA12, the explanation will be the same for almost all the examples we will be further discussing. The only change you can find is that the mywindow object name will be the same for creating an object of different classes, which we will be creating in all these examples.

We can see that we have created an application user credentials app without the usage of any layout management, that is, without any arranging of widgets in our UI form. Now, in the next chapter, we will study how to create the same application by using layout management.

Conclusion

In this chapter, we learned about the difference between PyQt5 and tkinter library. We learned about the installation of PyQt5 framework, along with the creation of a basic GUI form using PyQt5, first without using the class, and then with the class. We saw various components inside Qt Designer, along with different pre-defined templates. We created a user credential app by initially focusing on view in Qt Designer (**.ui** file), which was then converted into a Python code (**.py**) using **pyuic5** command. Finally, a new Python file was written by first importing the Python code for user interface design where some useful logic was built, so that a basic Login application can be designed at run-time for the user.

In the next chapter, we will learn about layout management, which is the process of organizing the widgets on a GUI. We will learn how child widgets will be arranged within any parent or container widget. We will look into some commonly used layout managers, which will include **QVBoxLayout**, **QHBoxLayout**, **QGridLayout,** and **QFormLayout**.

Points to remember

- Qt5 in PyQt5 stands for Qt version 5, which provides us the advantage of Python binding with Qt C++ toolkit.
- Simple command to install pyqt5: **pip install pyqt5**
- When there is a requirement by the user to close the GUI, **myapp.exec_()** will allow the control to pass over to Qt to terminate the application.
- If we want our code to return without errors and not to raise **SystemExit** exception, the event loop mechanism functionality is to be wrapped in a function and should return from the place where we intend to use **sys.exit**.
- Use some pre-defined templates in Qt Designer and save them with **.ui** file.
- Command to convert a **.ui** file (XML file) to **.py** file is: **pyuic5 user_credential_app.ui -o user_credential_app.py**
- Create some logic as per need in a newly generated Python file (**.py**) by importing the **.py** file for user interface design, which was converted from **.ui** file.

Questions

1. Explain the difference between PyQt5 GUI toolkit and tkinter library. Which library should you choose while creating GUI app?
2. Write the command to install PyQt5 in your system.
3. Explain basic GUI form creation, both with and without using class concept.
4. What are different pre-defined templates present in the Qt Designer?
5. Explain the components of Qt Designer.
6. What is the command to convert a Qt Designer `.ui` file to Python `.py` file?
7. Design a user credential app in Qt Designer, convert it into a Python code and then write a functional Python code by checking its credentials.

CHAPTER 2

Getting Insights of Layout Management

Introduction

Any application can be created by just dragging and dropping the widgets in our GUI form from the widget box of Qt Designer. It may look good when we are using multiple widgets on the same GUI form and creating an application. We can place the widgets in any location on the GUI form, without giving a notion of their appearance. However, it may look shabby if we do not place it in a proper location on the GUI form, with any arrangement of widgets. Such an arrangement leads to the concept of layout management; an approach to place the widgets on our GUI form. All professional GUI application forms creation uses the concept of layout managers as it is important for the user to create an application with a nice look. If we want to organize our widgets, the preferred approach is to manage the layout with layout managers. Therefore, whenever there is a requirement to arrange widgets on a GUI form, we will use the methods present inside the class of layout manager. The space between parent and child widgets can be properly utilized in a GUI form and is useful for communicating between them.

Let us start learning the different ways for layout management in PyQt5. We will be creating the same application user credentials app (*appearance only*) but now, with the usage of the concept of layouts.

Structure

In this chapter, we will learn the following topics:

- Widgets placement using absolute positioning
- Widgets placement using layout classes
  - QBoxLayout
    - QHBoxLayout
    - QVBoxLayout
  - QGridLayout
    - Basic QGridLayout
    - QGridLayout Span
    - QGridLayout Stretch
  - QFormLayout

Objectives

After studying this chapter, the reader will learn about widgets placement using absolute positioning approach. Then, we shall see widgets placement using layout classes, beginning with learning how to organize widgets either horizontally or vertically using **`QBoxLayout`** class. We will also explore how to arrange the widgets in a row, side-by-side using **`QHBoxLayout`** with the usage of methods viz **`addStretch`**, **`addWidget`**, **`addLayout`**. Alternatively, we will also look into arranging the widgets vertically with **`addStretch`** method using **`QVBoxLayout`**. Then, we shall look into arranging widgets in a grid of rows and columns using **`QGridLayout`**. Finally, we will look into creating an application using QFormLayout. In the end, we can confidently create "User Credential App" application using absolute positioning , **`QBoxLayout`**, **`QGridLayout`** and **`QFormLayout`** class.

Widgets placement using absolute positioning

Without using a layout manager, the first approach of creating layouts in a GUI form that we will learn is, using the absolute positioning. We can place the widgets in any position in a GUI form by specifying explicitly the size or position values for each widget in pixels. It is mainly used in the applications where there is a requirement to size values and set positions of the widgets which have to be accommodated within other widgets. Widgets can be positioned in a GUI form using the absolute positioning approach, with the help of **`move(x,y)`** method.

Here, x and y will be the coordinates of the respective widget which starts from the upper top left corner (0,0), as shown in the following *Figure 2.1*:

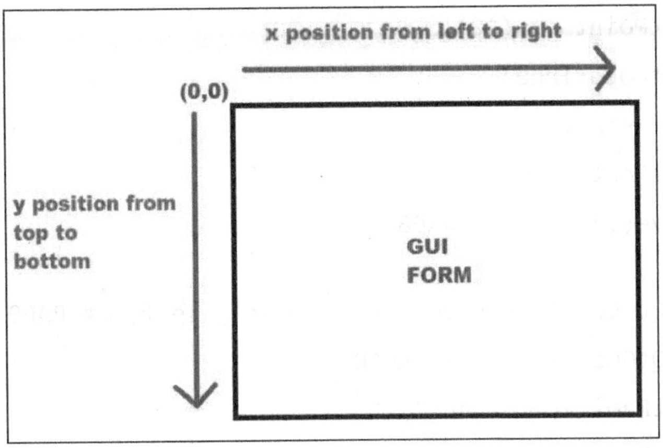

Figure 2.1: *Coordinate system of GUI form*

From *Figure 2.1*, we can see that the x position will increase from left to right and the y position from top to bottom.

Now, we shall create the same GUI form, similar to **run_user_credential_app.py** using absolute positioning.

Observe the following code:

```
import sys
from PyQt5.QtWidgets import QWidget, QApplication, QLabel, QLineEdit, QPushButton
# RAP1
from PyQt5 import QtGui


class Absolute_Position(QWidget): # RAP2
    def __init__(self):
        super().__init__()
        self.display_widgets() # RAP3
        self.setGeometry(0, 0, 398, 229)  # RAP4
        self.setWindowTitle('User Credentials App') # RAP5
        self.show()

    def display_widgets(self):
        mylbl1 = QLabel('Enter your username:', self)  # RAP6
```

```
        myfont = QtGui.QFont() # RAP7
        myfont.setFamily("Calibri")
        myfont.setPointSize(10)
        myfont.setBold(True)
        myfont.setWeight(75)
        mylbl1.setFont(myfont)
        mylbl1.move(14, 50)  # RAP8

        mylbl2 = QLabel('Enter your password:', self)  # RAP9
        myfont = QtGui.QFont() # RAP10
        myfont.setFamily("Calibri")
        myfont.setPointSize(10)
        myfont.setBold(True)
        myfont.setWeight(75)
        mylbl2.setFont(myfont)
        mylbl2.move(14, 120) # RAP11

        mylineedit1 = QLineEdit(self) # RAP12
        mylineedit1.move(210, 50) # RAP13

        mylineedit2 = QLineEdit(self) # RAP14
        mylineedit2.move(210, 120) # RAP15

        mybtn = QPushButton(self) # RAP16
        mybtn.setText('Confirm') # RAP17
        mybtn.move(140, 180) # RAP18

if __name__ == '__main__':
    myapp = QApplication(sys.argv)
    mywindow = Absolute_Position()
    sys.exit(myapp.exec_())
```

Output:

The output can be seen in the following *Figure 2.2:*

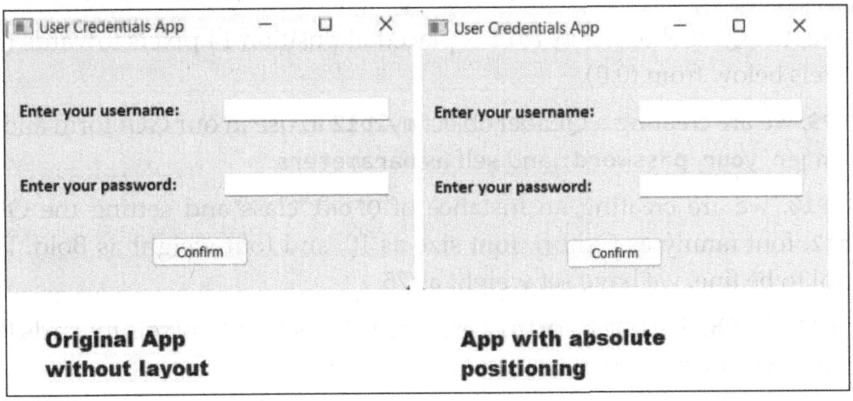

***Figure 2.2:** Output of Chap2_Example1.py*

Note: The preceding code is covered in Program Name: Chap2_Example1.py

On comparing with the original user credentials app, (refer to *Figure 2.2*), we can see that there is hardly any difference between the original code and the one we wrote using absolute positioning. Now, let us understand the code.

- In **RAP1**, first import the sys module for accessing the command line arguments. Then we will be importing from the class which creates desktop-style UIs of PyQt5 package .i.e. QtWidgets , for creating an empty GUI and an application handler, that is, QApplication . In addition to it, we are also importing other widgets like **QLabel**, **QLineEdit**, and **QPushButton**.
- In **RAP2**, we are creating a class named **Absolute_Position** inheriting from the base class QWidget.
- In **RAP3**, we are calling the **display_widgets** method present inside the class QWidget.
- In **RAP4**, we are displaying the GUI form of 398 (width) by 229 (height) pixels at position (0,0) on the screen. It can be displayed anywhere on the screen by changing the xpos and ypos which is at present set at (0,0).
- In **RAP5**, we are setting the title of our GUI form, that is, window as *User Credentials App*.
- In **RAP6**, we are creating a QLabel object **mylbl1** for using in our GUI form and passing the text as **Enter your username**: and **self** as parameters, whose default display will be at the top left position.

- In **RAP7**, we are creating an instance of **QFont** class and setting the QLabel object **mylbl1** font family as Calibri, font size as 10, and font-weight as Bold. For boldness control to be fine, we have set weight as 75.
- In **RAP8**, the QLabel object **mylbl1** is placed at position 14 pixels towards the right and 50 pixels below from (0,0).
- In **RAP9**, we are creating a QLabel object **mylbl2** to use in our GUI form and passing the text **Enter your password:** and self as **parameters**.
- In **RAP10**, we are creating an instance of **QFont** class and setting the QLabel object **mylbl2**, font family as Calibri, font size as 10, and font weight as Bold. For boldness control to be fine, we have set weight as 75.
- In **RAP11**, the QLabel object **mylbl2** is placed at position 14 pixels towards the right and 120 pixels below from (0,0).
- In **RAP12**, we are creating a QLineEdit object **mylineedit1** whose default display will be at the top left position.
- In **RAP13**, the QLineEdit object **mylineedit1** is placed at position 210 pixels towards the right and 50 pixels below from (0,0).
- In **RAP14**, we are creating a QLineEdit object **mylineedit2** whose default display will be at the top left position.
- In **RAP15**, the QLineEdit object **mylineedit2** is placed at position 210 pixels towards the right and 120 pixels below from (0,0).
- In **RAP16**, we are creating an instance of QPushButton object **mybtn** whose default display will be at the top left position, and passing a parameter self indicates that the pushbutton is part of the GUI form.
- In **RAP17**, the text for the QPushButton object **mybtn** is set as Confirm and will get displayed on the GUI form.

  In **RAP18**, the QPushButton object **mybtn** is placed at position 140 pixels towards the right and 180 pixels below from (0,0).

Absolute positioning is quite simple but there are some limitations, such as the follows:

- The widget's size and position will not be changing even if the GUI form will be resized. Refer to *Figure 2.3:*

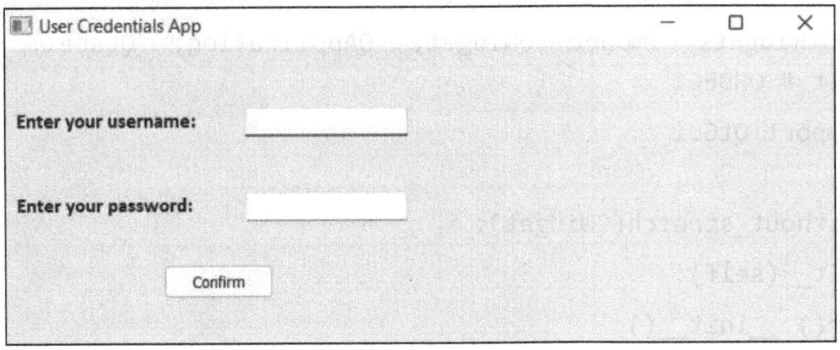

Figure 2.3: *Intact position of widgets on resizing*

We can see from *Figure 2.3*, that even on resizing the GUI form, the widget's size and position are still the same.

- If we are creating any application using absolute positioning, the layout may be different on various platforms.
- In some cases, there may be requirements of redesigning the form. In such cases, layout modification will be tedious and time-consuming.

The reader should understand the concepts of absolute positioning, before knowing about widgets placement using layout classes.

Widgets placement using layout classes

API of PyQt5 has a more elegant way of widgets positioning by providing layout classes which we will learn in subsequent sections.

QBoxLayout

Suppose in our application, there is a requirement to organize or arrange widgets either horizontally or vertically. In such cases, we will use **`QBoxLayout`** class. The two basic layout management classes for arranging the widgets either horizontally or vertically are **`QHBoxLayout`** and **`QVBoxLayout`**. First, we will see the code for arranging the widgets in a row, side-by-side, using **`QHBoxLayout`** with the usage of methods viz **`addStretch`**, **`addWidget`**, **`addLayout`**.

QHBoxLayout

In this section, we will see the code to arrange the widgets in a row, side-by-side using **`QHBoxLayout`**, without **`addstretch`**.

QHBoxLayout without addstretch

Observe the following code:

```
import sys
from PyQt5.QtWidgets import QWidget, QApplication, QLabel, QHBoxLayout,
QDesktopWidget # QHBEG1
from PyQt5 import QtGui

class HBox_without_stretch(QWidget):
    def __init__(self):
        super().__init__()
        self.display_widgets()
        self.setGeometry(0, 0, 398, 229)
        self.setWindowTitle('QHBoxLayout without stretch')# QHBEG2
        self.movecenter()
        self.show()

    def display_widgets(self):
        mylbl1 = QLabel('Label1:', self)
        myfont = QtGui.QFont()
        myfont.setFamily("Calibri")
        myfont.setPointSize(10)
        myfont.setBold(True)
        myfont.setWeight(75)
        mylbl1.setFont(myfont)

        mylbl2 = QLabel('Label2', self)
        myfont = QtGui.QFont()
        myfont.setFamily("Calibri")
        myfont.setPointSize(10)
        myfont.setBold(True)
        myfont.setWeight(75)
        mylbl2.setFont(myfont)
```

```
        # QHBoxlayout
        myhbox = QHBoxLayout()# QHBEG7
        myhbox.addWidget(mylbl1)# QHBEG8
        myhbox.addWidget(mylbl2)# QHBEG9
        self.setLayout(myhbox)# QHBEG10

    def movecenter(self):
        myfrm_gmtry = self.frameGeometry()# QHBEG3
        mycenter = QDesktopWidget().availableGeometry().center()# QHBEG4
        myfrm_gmtry.moveCenter(mycenter)# QHBEG5
        self.move(myfrm_gmtry.topLeft())# QHBEG6

if __name__ == '__main__':
    myapp = QApplication(sys.argv)
    mywindow = HBox_without_stretch()
    sys.exit(myapp.exec_())
```

Output:

The output can be seen in the following *Figure 2.4:*

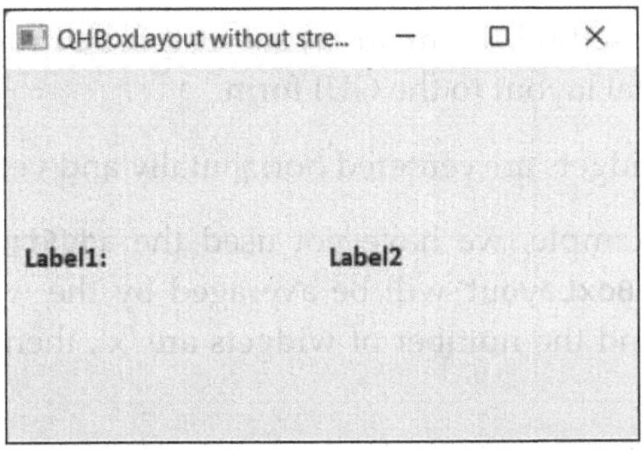

Figure 2.4: *Output of Chap2_Example2.py*

Note: The preceding code is covered in Program Name: Chap2_Example2.py

The preceding example depicts the example of **`QHBoxLayout`** with usage of **`addWidget`** and **`setLayout`** methods. Here, we have not used **`addStretch()`** method. In the above example, we created two Label widgets and arranged them horizontally. Moreover, a method is being called, to place the GUI form in the center of the screen. Let us learn these new concepts:

- In **QHBEG1**, first import the sys module for accessing the command line arguments. Then we will be importing from the class which creates desktop-style UIs of PyQt5 package, that is, **QtWidgets**, for creating an empty GUI and an application handler, that is, **QApplication**. In addition to it, we are also importing other widgets such as **QLabel**, **QHBoxLayout** and **QDesktopWidget**.
- In **QHBEG2**, we are setting the title of our GUI form, that is, window, as QHBoxLayout without stretch.
- From **QHBEG3** to **QHBEG6**, we are displaying the GUI form in the center of the screen.
- In **QHBEG3**, we are trying to get the location and size information of the GUI form using **frameGeometry** method that are stored in the **myfrm_gmtry** object.
- In **QHBEG4**, the monitor's screen center position is getting determined.
- In **QHBEG5**, the rectangular position of the GUI form is moved to the screen center.
- In **QHBEG6**, the current GUI form will move to the rectangle position (**myfrm_gmtry**) which is moved to the screen center resulting in the matching of the current GUI form center with the screen center, such that the GUI form will appear in the center.

  Just try to comment this line only. You will find that the GUI form will be placed at the top left of monitor screen.
- In **QHBEG7**, an instance of QHBoxLayout **myhbox** is created.
- In **QHBEG8**, label object **mylbl1** will be added to the box layout object **myhbox**.
- In **QHBEG9**, label object **mylbl2** will be added to the box layout object **myhbox**.
- In **QHBEG10**, we are setting the main layout of the GUI form. In other words, we are setting the horizontal layout to the GUI form.

We can see that the label widgets are centered horizontally and vertically in the GUI frame.

Moreover, in the above example, we have not used the **addStretch()** method, at all. So, the whole width of the **QHBoxLayout** will be averaged by the widgets. For example, if the **QHBoxLayout** width is 'a' and the number of widgets are 'x', then each widget width will be 'a/x'.

One important thing to observe is that on resizing the GUI form, the widgets size will also be re-sized, as shown in *Figure 2.5:*

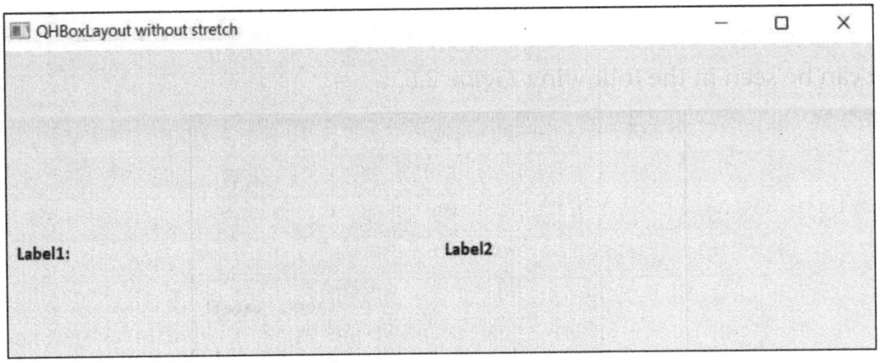

Figure 2.5: Resizing of GUI form

Now, we will look at another example of **QHBoxLayout**, but this time with **addStretch** method.

QHBoxLayout with addstretch

The syntax of **addStretch** is:

QHBoxLayout.addStretch(size)

Here, **size** can be an integer number say -1,0 or 1, …

So, an empty stretchable box can be created using **addStretch** and is a nice way for filling up the blank space.

We will only be adding the **addStretch()** method to **QHBoxLayout** instance object, changing the class name to **HBox_with_stretch** and changing the GUI form title, as shown below from the previous code example.

Observe the following code:

```
self.setWindowTitle('QHBoxLayout with addstretch')

# QHBoxlayout
        myhbox = QHBoxLayout()
        myhbox.addStretch() # added
        myhbox.addWidget(mylbl1)
        myhbox.addWidget(mylbl2)
        self.setLayout(myhbox)
```

Output:

The output can be seen in the following *Figure 2.6:*

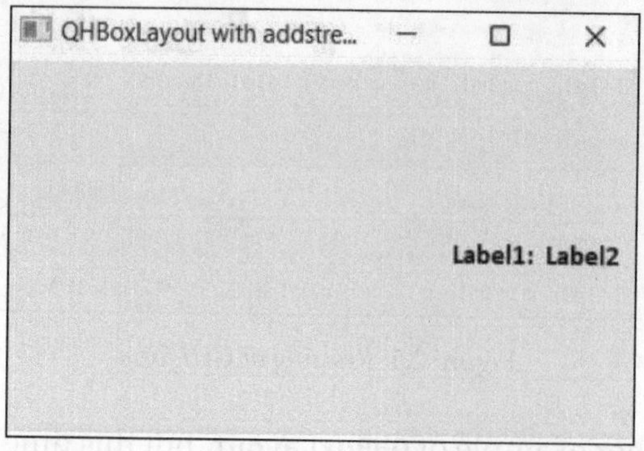

***Figure 2.6:** QHBoxLayout with addStretch*

Refer to *Figure 2.7* where we are indicating a double-sided arrow for the display of empty box when compared with *Figure 2.6*.

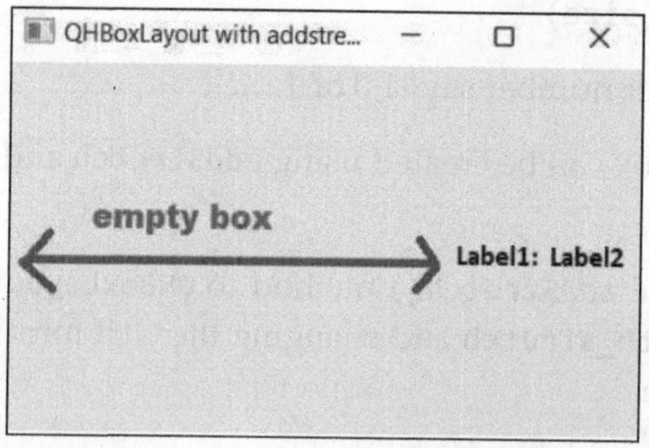

***Figure 2.7:** QHBoxLayout with addStretch displaying empty box*

Note: The complete code is covered in Program Name: Chap2_Example3.py

We can conclude the following points from above:

- The width of these widgets, that is, Label widget's width will be the original width and will not be the average whole width of **`QHBoxLayout`**.
- An empty stretchable box will be added in **`QHBoxLayout`** and stretched as long as it fills up the whole **`QHBoxLayout`**.

So, from the preceding figures, we understand that the width of the Label widgets is original and an empty box fills the remaining space.

Now, we shall **`addStretch`** before and after these two label widgets and see what output we shall see.

Observe the following code:

```
# QHBoxlayout
        myhbox = QHBoxLayout()
        myhbox.addStretch() # added
        myhbox.addWidget(mylbl1)
        myhbox.addWidget(mylbl2)
        self.setLayout(myhbox)
        myhbox.addStretch() # added
```

Output:

The output can be seen in the following *Figure 2.8:*

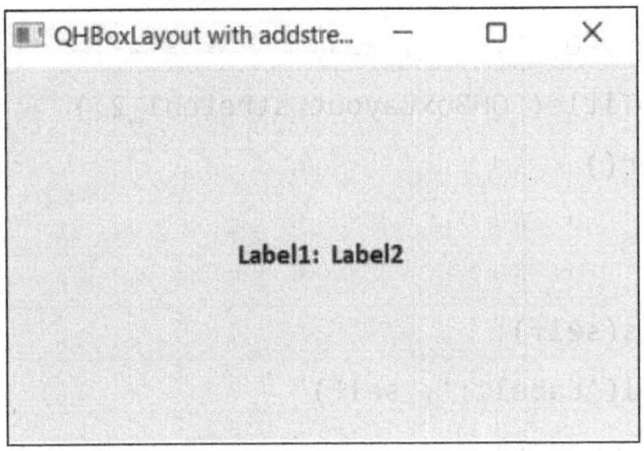

***Figure 2.8:** QHBoxLayout with addStretch at 2 places*

From *Figure 2.9,* we can conclude that the width of the two label widgets is original and remaining space is averaged by two empty boxes as depicted in the following figure:

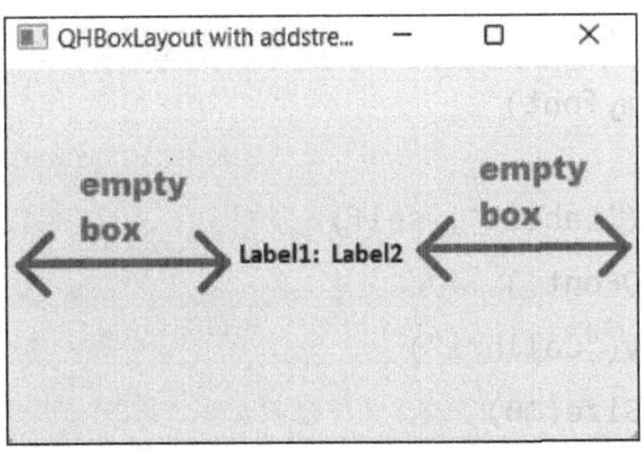

***Figure 2.9:** QHBoxLayout with empty boxes at 2 places*

Note: The complete code is covered in Program Name: Chap2_Example4.py

Now, we shall see the difference between **addStretch(1)** and **addStretch(2)**.

Observe the following code:

```
import sys

from PyQt5.QtWidgets import QWidget, QApplication, QLabel, QHBoxLayout,
QDesktopWidget

from PyQt5 import QtGui

class HBox_stretch1_2(QWidget):
    def __init__(self):
        super().__init__()
        self.display_widgets()
        self.setGeometry(0, 0, 398, 229)
        self.setWindowTitle('QHBoxLayout stretch1_2')
        self.movecenter()
        self.show()

    def display_widgets(self):
        mylbl1 = QLabel('Label1:', self)
        myfont = QtGui.QFont()
        myfont.setFamily("Calibri")
        myfont.setPointSize(10)
        myfont.setBold(True)
        myfont.setWeight(75)
        mylbl1.setFont(myfont)

        mylbl2 = QLabel('Label2', self)
        myfont = QtGui.QFont()
        myfont.setFamily("Calibri")
        myfont.setPointSize(10)
        myfont.setBold(True)
        myfont.setWeight(75)
        mylbl2.setFont(myfont)
```

```
        # QHBoxlayout
        myhbox = QHBoxLayout()
        myhbox.addStretch(1) # addstretch_1
        myhbox.addWidget(mylbl1)
        myhbox.addStretch(2) # addstretch_2
        myhbox.addWidget(mylbl2)
        self.setLayout(myhbox)

    def movecenter(self):
        myfrm_gmtry = self.frameGeometry()
        mycenter = QDesktopWidget().availableGeometry().center()
        myfrm_gmtry.moveCenter(mycenter)
        self.move(myfrm_gmtry.topLeft())

if __name__ == '__main__':
    myapp = QApplication(sys.argv)
    mywindow = HBox_stretch1_2()
    sys.exit(myapp.exec_())
```

Output:

The output can be seen in the following *Figure 2.10:*

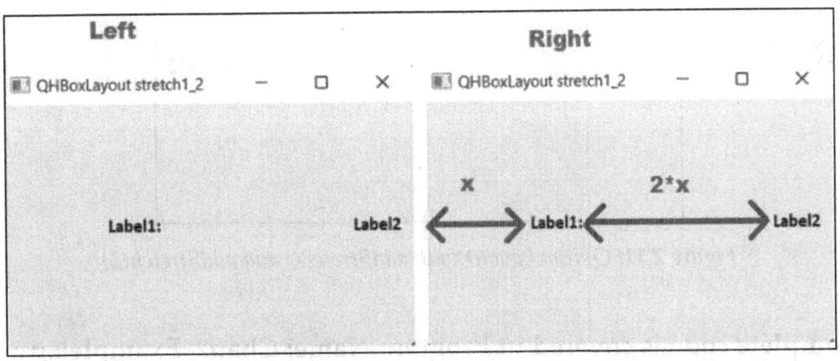

a) *b)*

***Figure 2.10:** Output of Chap2_Example5.py*
a) Output displaying the difference between addstretch(1) and addstretch(2) of Chap2_Example5.py
b) Output displaying with stretch factor 'x' between Label1: and Label2 of Chap2_Example5.py

Note: The preceding code is covered in Program Name: Chap2_Example5.py

We can clearly see from the output that:

- `myhbox.addStretch(1)`: An empty stretchable box will grow horizontally from the layout's left side moving rightwards. In the right image of *Figure 2.10*, it is denoted as **x**.
- `myhbox.addStretch(2)`: An empty stretchable box will be grown horizontally twice from the layout's left side moving rightwards. In the right image of *Figure 2.10*, it is denoted as **2*x**.

Now, observe the output for the following piece of code:

```
# QHBoxlayout
myhbox = QHBoxLayout()
myhbox.addStretch() # addstretch_0
myhbox.addWidget(mylbl1)
myhbox.addStretch(2) # addstretch_2
myhbox.addWidget(mylbl2)
self.setLayout(myhbox)
```

Output:

The output can be seen in the following *Figure 2.11:*

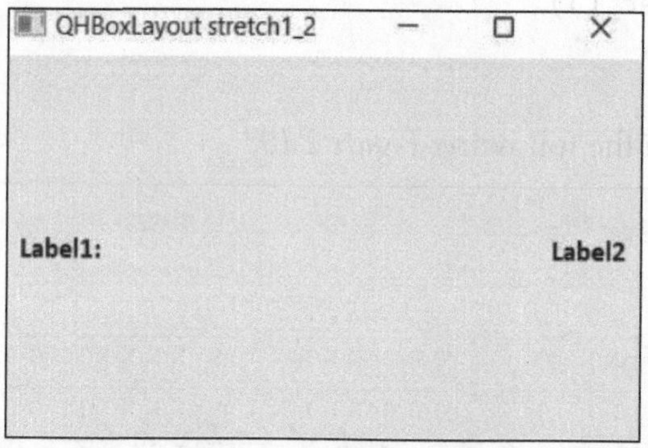

Figure 2.11: QHBoxLayout with addStretch() and addStretch(2)

Note: The complete code is covered in Program Name: Chap2_Example6.py

We can clearly see from the output that when the first stretch is 0, that is, `addStretch()` and then `addstretch(2)`, then the second empty box would not grow horizontally at all.

Now, we shall change the code as shown below:

```
# QHBoxlayout
  myhbox = QHBoxLayout()
  myhbox.addStretch(2) # addstretch_2
  myhbox.addWidget(mylbl1)
  myhbox.addStretch(1) # addstretch_1
  myhbox.addWidget(mylbl2)
  self.setLayout(myhbox)
```

Output:

The output can be seen in the following *Figure 2.12:*

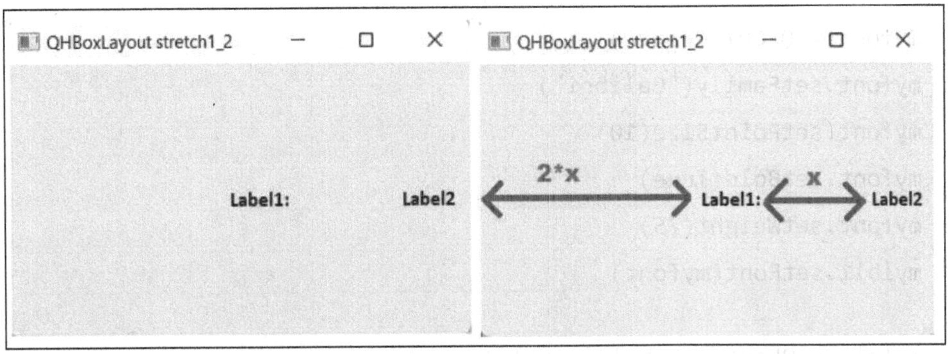

Figure 2.12: *QHBoxLayout with addStretch(2) and addStretch(1)*

Note: The complete code is covered in Program Name: Chap2_Example7.py

The first empty stretchable box will grow horizontally twice (2*x) from the layout's left side moving rightwards and then 'x' times.

QVBoxLayout

Now, let us learn how to arrange the same two label widgets vertically using QVBoxLayout.

Observe the following code:

```
import sys
from PyQt5.QtWidgets import QWidget, QApplication, QLabel, QVBoxLayout,
QDesktopWidget # QVBEG1
from PyQt5 import QtGui


class VBox_with_stretch(QWidget):
```

```
    def __init__(self):
        super().__init__()
        self.display_widgets()
        self.setGeometry(0, 0, 398, 229)
        self.setWindowTitle('QVBoxLayout with addstretch') # QVBEG2
        self.movecenter()
        self.show()

    def display_widgets(self):
        mylbl1 = QLabel('Label1:', self)
        myfont = QtGui.QFont()
        myfont.setFamily("Calibri")
        myfont.setPointSize(10)
        myfont.setBold(True)
        myfont.setWeight(75)
        mylbl1.setFont(myfont)

        mylbl2 = QLabel('Label2', self)
        myfont = QtGui.QFont()
        myfont.setFamily("Calibri")
        myfont.setPointSize(10)
        myfont.setBold(True)
        myfont.setWeight(75)
        mylbl2.setFont(myfont)

        # QHBoxlayout
        myvbox = QVBoxLayout() # QVBEG3
        myvbox.addStretch() # QVBEG4
        myvbox.addWidget(mylbl1) # QVBEG5
        myvbox.addWidget(mylbl2) # QVBEG6
        self.setLayout(myvbox) # QVBEG7
        myvbox.addStretch() # QVBEG8
```

```
    def movecenter(self):
        myfrm_gmtry = self.frameGeometry()
        mycenter = QDesktopWidget().availableGeometry().center()
        myfrm_gmtry.moveCenter(mycenter)
        self.move(myfrm_gmtry.topLeft())

if __name__ == '__main__':
    myapp = QApplication(sys.argv)
    mywindow = VBox_with_stretch()
    sys.exit(myapp.exec_())
```

Output:

The output can be seen in the following *Figure 2.13:*

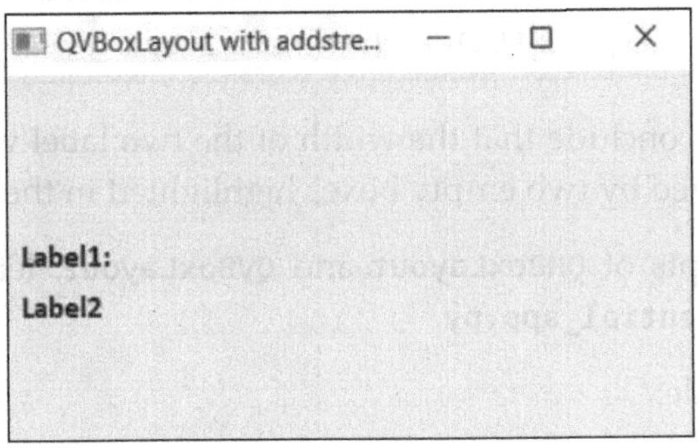

Figure 2.13: *Output of Chap2_Example8.py*

Note: The preceding code is covered in Program Name: Chap2_Example8.py

- In **QVBEG1**, first import the sys module for accessing the command line arguments. Then we will be importing from the class which creates desktop-style UIs of PyQt5 package .i.e. **QtWidgets**, for creating an empty GUI and an application handler, that is, **QApplication**. In addition to it, we are also importing other widgets such as **QLabel**, **QVBoxLayout** and **QDesktopWidget**.
- In **QVBEG2**, we are setting the title of our GUI form, that is, window as **QVBoxLayout** with addstretch.
- In **QVBEG3**, an instance of **QVBoxLayout myvbox** is created.
- In **QVBEG4**, we are adding the **addStretch()** method to **QVBoxLayout** instance object **myvbox**.
- In **QVBEG5**, label object **mylbl1** will be added to the box layout object **myvbox**.

- In **QVBEG6**, label object **mylbl2** will be added to the box layout object **myvbox**.
- In **QVBEG7**, we are setting the main layout of the GUI form. In other words, we are setting the vertical layout to the GUI form.
- In **QVBEG8**, we are again adding the **addStretch()** method to **QVBoxLayout** instance object **myvbox**.

Refer to *Figure 2.14:*

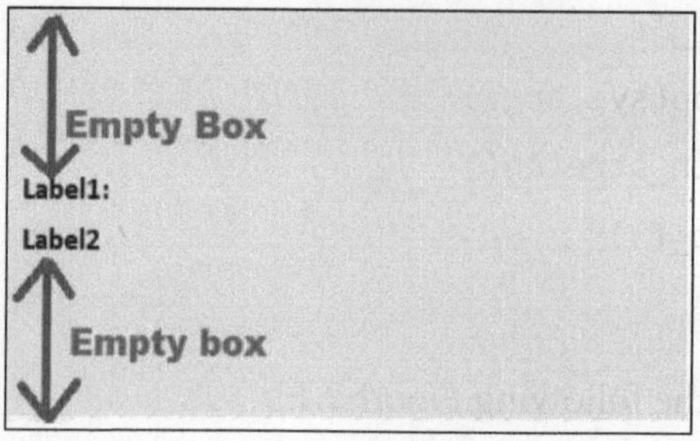

Figure 2.14: *QVBoxLayout with 2 empty boxes*

From *Figure 2.14,* we can conclude that the width of the two label widgets is original and the remaining space is averaged by two empty boxes highlighted in the figure of **QVBoxLayout**.

After learning the concepts of **QHBoxLayout** and **QVBoxLayout**, let us make an application similar to **run_user_credential_app.py**.

Observe the following code:

```
import sys
from PyQt5.QtWidgets import QWidget, QApplication, QLabel, QHBoxLayout,
QVBoxLayout, QDesktopWidget, QLineEdit, QPushButton # QBX1
from PyQt5 import QtGui

class BoxLayout_user_credential_App(QWidget):
    def __init__(self):
        super().__init__()
        self.display_widgets()
        self.setGeometry(0, 0, 398, 229)
        self.setWindowTitle('BoxLayout User Credential App') # QBX2
        self.movecenter()
        self.show()
```

```
def display_widgets(self):
    mylbl1 = QLabel('Enter your username:', self)
    myfont = QtGui.QFont()
    myfont.setFamily("Calibri")
    myfont.setPointSize(10)
    myfont.setBold(True)
    myfont.setWeight(75)
    mylbl1.setFont(myfont)

    mylbl2 = QLabel('Enter your password:', self)
    myfont = QtGui.QFont()
    myfont.setFamily("Calibri")
    myfont.setPointSize(10)
    myfont.setBold(True)
    myfont.setWeight(75)
    mylbl2.setFont(myfont)

    mylineedit1 = QLineEdit(self)
    mylineedit2 = QLineEdit(self)
    mybtn = QPushButton(self)
    mybtn.setText('Confirm')

    myhbox1 = QHBoxLayout() # QBX3
    myhbox1.setSpacing(60) # QBX4
    myhbox1.addStretch() # QBX5
    myhbox1.addWidget(mylbl1) # QBX6
    myhbox1.addWidget(mylineedit1) # QBX7
    myhbox1.addStretch() # QBX8

    # QBX9
    myhbox2 = QHBoxLayout()
    myhbox2.setSpacing(60)
    myhbox2.addStretch()
```

```
        myhbox2.addWidget(mylbl2)
        myhbox2.addWidget(mylineedit2)
        myhbox2.addStretch()

        # QBX10
        myhbox3 = QHBoxLayout()
        myhbox3.addStretch()
        myhbox3.addWidget(mybtn)
        myhbox3.addStretch()

        # QHBoxlayout
        myvbox = QVBoxLayout() # QBX11
        myvbox.addStretch() # QBX12
        myvbox.addLayout(myhbox1) # QBX13
        myvbox.addStretch() # QBX14
        myvbox.addLayout(myhbox2) # QBX15
        myvbox.addStretch() # QBX16
        myvbox.addLayout(myhbox3) # QBX17
        self.setLayout(myvbox) # QBX18

    def movecenter(self):
        myfrm_gmtry = self.frameGeometry()
        mycenter = QDesktopWidget().availableGeometry().center()
        myfrm_gmtry.moveCenter(mycenter)
        self.move(myfrm_gmtry.topLeft())

if __name__ == '__main__':
    myapp = QApplication(sys.argv)
    mywindow = BoxLayout_user_credential_App()
    sys.exit(myapp.exec_())
```

Output:

The output can be seen in the following *Figure 2.15:*

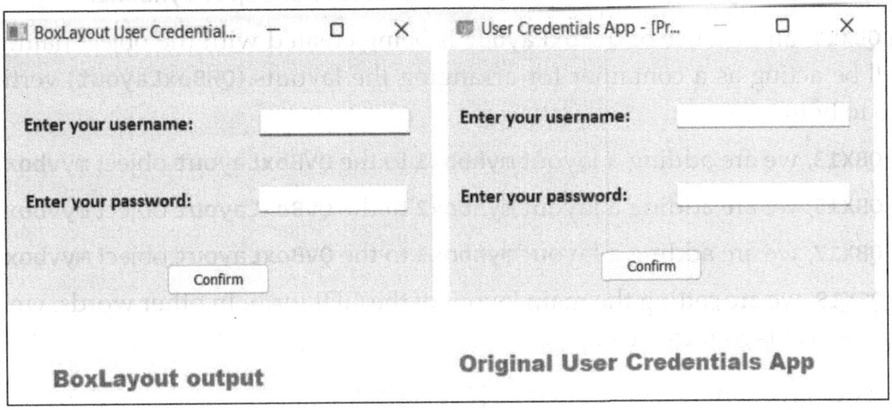

***Figure 2.15**: Output of Chap2_Example9.py*

Note: The preceding code is covered in Program Name: Chap2_Example9.py

- In **QBX1**, first import the sys module for accessing the command line arguments. Then we will be importing from the class which creates desktop-style UIs of PyQt5 package, that is, **QtWidgets** , for creating an empty GUI and an application handler, that is, **QApplication** . In addition to it, we are also importing other widgets like **QLabel**, **QHBoxLayout** ,**QVBoxLayout** , **QDesktopWidget**, **QLineEdit**, and **QPushButton**.
- In **QBX2**, we are setting the title of our GUI form, that is, window as **BoxLayout User Credential App**.
- In **QBX3**, an instance of **QHBoxLayout** is being created with an object name **myhbox1**.
- In **QBX4**, the spacing between the items when arranging horizontally is 60. It will take 60 as an argument. We are using the **setSpacing** method with the **QHBoxlayout** object.
- In **QBX5**, **QBX8**, **QBX12**, **QBX14** and **QBX16**, an empty stretchable box is created using **addStretch** for filling up the blank space.
- In **QBX6**, label object **mylbl1** will be added to the box layout object **myhbox1**.
- In **QBX7**, **lineEdit** object **mylineedit1** will be added to the box layout object **myhbox1**.
- In **QBX9**, an instance of **QHBoxLayout** is created with the object name **myhbox2**. The spacing between the items when arranged horizontally is 60. An empty stretchable box is created using **addStretch** for filling up the blank space. Label object **mylbl2** will be added to the box layout object **myhbox2**. **LineEdit** object **mylineedit2** will be added to the box layout object **myhbox2**.

- In **QBX10**, an instance of **QHBoxLayout** is created with an object name **myhbox3**. An empty stretchable box is created using **addStretch** for filling up the blank space. Push button object **mylbl2** will be added to the box layout object **myhbox2**.
- In **QBX11**, an instance of **QVBoxLayout** is being created with the object name **myvbox**. It will be acting as a container for arranging the layouts (**QHBoxLayout**) vertically from top to bottom.
- In **QBX13**, we are adding a layout **myhbox1** to the **QVBoxLayout** object **myvbox**.
- In **QBX15**, we are adding a layout **myhbox2** to the **QVBoxLayout** object **myvbox**
- In **QBX17**, we are adding a layout **myhbox3** to the **QVBoxLayout** object **myvbox**
- In **QBX18**, we are setting the main layout of the GUI form. In other words, we are setting the vertical layout to the GUI form.

This is all about layout management using **QBoxLayout**.

QGridLayout

Suppose in our application, there is a requirement to arrange widgets in a grid of rows and columns. In that case, we must know about **QGridLayout**. It is one of the most universal layout classes for arranging the widgets in pairs, where each widget will have a relative position, and will be arranged in a grid of rows and columns. Its application ranges from adding buttons, while creating a calculator app or making a virtual keypad and so on. The pair of coordinates for arranging the widgets and placing them on the cell should be zero based integer numbers. **QGridLayout** will leave the cell empty if no widgets are added to a given cell. We will use overloaded implementations of the **addWidget** method if we are adding widgets to a grid layout:

- **addWidget(self,QWidget, int row, int column)**: This method will add a widget at defined row and column.
- **addWidget(self,QWidget, int row, int column, int rowSpan, int columnSpan, alignment)**: This method will add a widget at defined row and column spanning multiple rows or columns or both. Alignment is an optional argument whose default value is 0, meaning that the entire cell will be filled by the widget.

Let us see some of the examples using QGridLayout.

Basic QGridLayout

Observe the following code:

```
import sys

from PyQt5.QtWidgets import QWidget, QApplication, QLabel, QGridLayout # GLEG1_1
```

```
from PyQt5 import QtGui

class GridLayout_Eg1(QWidget):
    def __init__(self):
        super().__init__()
        self.display_widgets()
        self.setGeometry(0, 0, 398, 229)
        self.setWindowTitle('Basic GridLayout example') #GLEG1_2
        self.show()

    def display_widgets(self):
        # writing the grid portion
        mygrid_layout = QGridLayout()# GLEG1_3
        self.setLayout(mygrid_layout)# GLEG1_4

        for outer in range(4):
            for lower in range(3):
                mylbl = QLabel('Label' + str(outer) + str(lower),self)# GLEG1_5
                myfont = QtGui.QFont()
                myfont.setFamily("Calibri")
                myfont.setPointSize(10)
                myfont.setBold(True)
                myfont.setWeight(75)
                mylbl.setFont(myfont)
                mygrid_layout.addWidget(mylbl, outer, lower)# GLEG1_6

if __name__ == '__main__':
    myapp = QApplication(sys.argv)
    mywindow = GridLayout_Eg1()
    sys.exit(myapp.exec_())
```

Output:

The output can be seen in the following *Figure 2.16:*

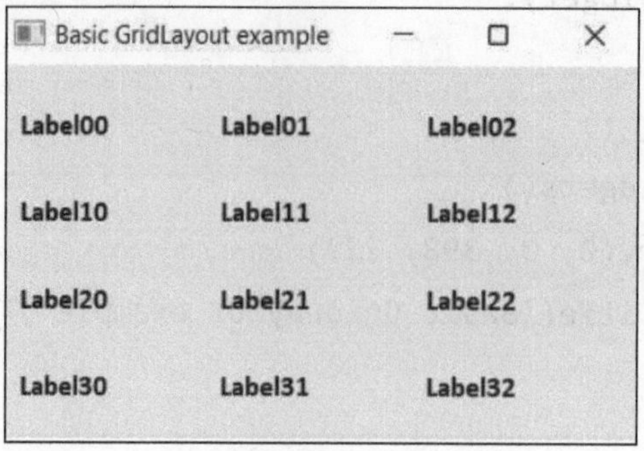

***Figure 2.16:** Output of Chap2_Example10.py*

Note: The preceding code is covered in Program Name: Chap2_Example10.py

- In **GLEG1_1**, first import the sys module for accessing the command line arguments. Then we will be importing from the class which creates desktop-style UIs of PyQt5 package, that is, **QtWidgets** , for creating an empty GUI and an application handler, that is, **QApplication**. In addition to it, we are also importing other widgets such as **QLabel** and **QGridLayout**.
- In **GLEG1_2**, we are setting the title of our GUI form, that is, window, as **Basic GridLayout example**.
- In **GLEG1_3**, an instance of **QGridLayout** is created with the object name as **mygrid_layout**.
- In **GLEG1_4**, we are setting the main layout of the GUI form. In other words, we are setting the Grid layout to the GUI form.
- In **GLEG1_5**, an instance of **QLabel** object **mylbl** is created, and setting **QLabel** object font family is Calibri, font size is 10, and font-weight is Bold. For boldness control to be fine, we have set weight as 75.
- In **GLEG1_6**, we are adding a **QLabel** widget at the defined row and column. The first row will be 0 and then the widget will be added to columns 0, 1, and 2. That is why we have appended the Label text with rows and columns for better identification to the reader.
- **GLEG1_5** and **GLEG1_6** will be repeated 11 times more than the initial count. Now, we will see another example of spanning in GridLayout.

QGridLayout span

In **QGridLayout** span, the default value of rowspan and columnspan is 1. If a positive value is mentioned, then the cell widget will extend to that value. If it is -1, then the extension will be done either to the right or bottom edge.

Observe the following code:

```
import sys
from PyQt5.QtWidgets import QWidget, QApplication, QLabel, QGridLayout, QPushButton # GLEG2_1
from PyQt5 import QtGui

class GridLayout_Eg2(QWidget):
    def __init__(self):
        super().__init__()
        self.display_widgets()
        self.setGeometry(0, 0, 398, 229)
        self.setWindowTitle('GridLayout with span')# GLEG2_2
        self.show()

    def display_widgets(self):
        # writing the grid portion
        mygrid_layout = QGridLayout()
        self.setLayout(mygrid_layout)

        mybtn1 = QPushButton("Row Spanning merging 2 rows")
        mygrid_layout.addWidget(mybtn1, 0,0, 2,1)# GLEG2_3

        mybtn2 = QPushButton("Column Spanning")
        mygrid_layout.addWidget(mybtn2, 2,0, 1,3)# GLEG2_4

        for outer in range(3,5):
            for lower in range(3,5):
                mylbl = QLabel('Label' + str(outer) + str(lower),self)# GLEG2_5
                myfont = QtGui.QFont()
```

```
            myfont.setFamily("Calibri")
            myfont.setPointSize(10)
            myfont.setBold(True)
            myfont.setWeight(75)
            mylbl.setFont(myfont)
            mygrid_layout.addWidget(mylbl, outer, lower)# GLEG2_6

if __name__ == '__main__':
    myapp = QApplication(sys.argv)
    mywindow = GridLayout_Eg2()
    sys.exit(myapp.exec_())
```

Output:

The output can be seen in the following *Figure 2.17:*

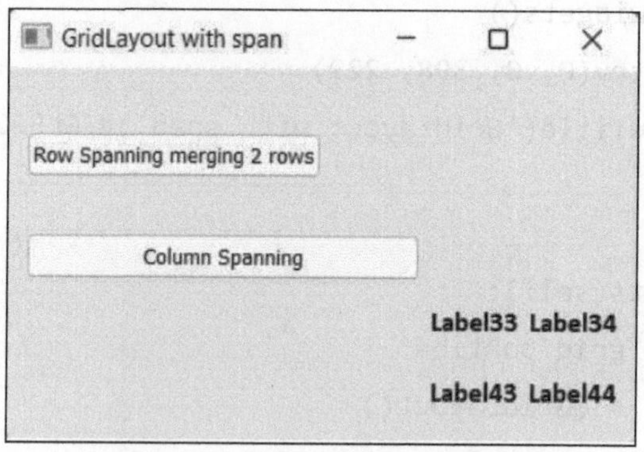

Figure 2.17: Output of Chap2_Example11.py

Note: The preceding code is covered in Program Name: Chap2_Example11.py

- In `GLEG2_1`, first import the sys module for accessing the command line arguments. Then, we will be importing from the class which creates desktop-style UIs of PyQt5 package, that is, `QtWidgets` , for creating an empty GUI and an application handler, that is, `QApplication` . In addition to it, we are also importing other widgets such as `QLabel`, `QGridLayout`, `QPushButton`.
- In `GLEG2_2`, we are setting the title of our GUI form, that is, window as `GridLayout with span`.
- In `GLEG2_3`, the `QPushButton` object `mybtn1` will be added at a defined row = 0 and column as 0 with `rowSpan` value as 2 and `columnSpan` value as 1.

- In **GLEG2_4**, the **QPushButton** object **mybtn2** will be added at a defined row = 2 and column as 0 with **rowSpan** value as 1 and **columnSpan** value as 3.
- In **GLEG2_5**, an instance of **QLabel** object **mylbl** is created and setting **QLabel** object font family as Calibri, font size as 10, font weight as Bold. For boldness control to be fine, we have set weight as 75.
- In **GLEG2_6**, we are adding **QLabel** widget at the defined row and column. The first row will be 3 and then the widget will be added to columns 3 and 4. That is why we have appended the Label text with rows and columns for better identification to the reader.

QGridLayout Stretch

Before writing the code, we will see methods: **setColumnStretch** and **setRowStretch**. These two methods generally focus on the stretch factor of column/row. More available space will be taken, based on the higher value of the stretch factor.

Observe the following code:

```
import sys
from PyQt5.QtWidgets import QWidget, QApplication, QTextEdit, QGridLayout #
GLEG3_1
from PyQt5 import QtGui

class GridLayout_Eg3(QWidget):
    def __init__(self):
        super().__init__()
        self.display_widgets()
        self.setGeometry(0, 0, 398, 229)
        self.setWindowTitle('GridLayout with stretch')# GLEG3_2
        self.show()

    def display_widgets(self):
        # writing the grid portion
        mygrid_layout = QGridLayout()
        self.setLayout(mygrid_layout)

        for outer in range(1,4):
            for lower in range(1,4):
```

```
                mytextedit = QTextEdit(self)# GLEG3_3
                mytextedit.setPlaceholderText(str(outer) + str(lower))# GLEG3_4
                mygrid_layout.addWidget(mytextedit, outer, lower)# GLEG3_5
            mygrid_layout.setColumnStretch(outer,outer+1)# GLEG3_6

if __name__ == '__main__':
    myapp = QApplication(sys.argv)
    mywindow = GridLayout_Eg3()
    sys.exit(myapp.exec_())
```

Output:

The output can be seen in the following *Figure 2.18:*

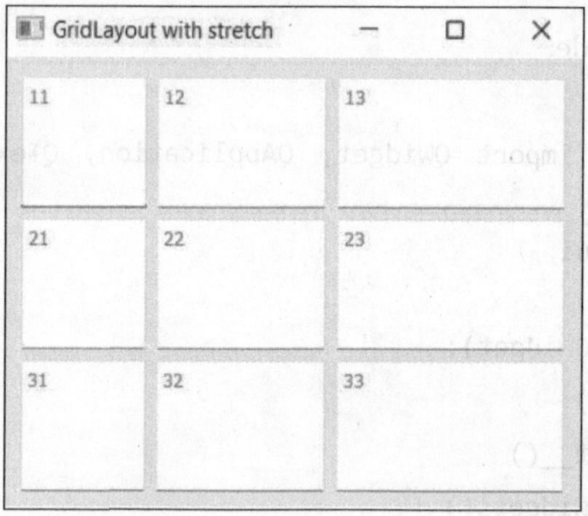

Figure 2.18: Output of Chap2_Example12.py

Note: The preceding code is covered in Program Name: Chap2_Example12.py

- In **GLEG3_1** , first import the sys module for accessing the command line arguments. Then we will be importing from the class which creates desktop-style UIs of PyQt5 package, that is, **QtWidgets** , for creating an empty GUI and an application handler, that is, **QApplication**. In addition to it, we are also importing other widgets such as **QTextEdit**, and **QGridLayout**.
- In **GLEG3_2**, we are setting the title of our GUI form, that is, window, as **GridLayout with stretch**.
- In **GLEG3_3**, an instance of **QTextEdit** is created with the object name as **mytextedit**.

- In **GLEG3_4**, the texteditor placeholder text will be a concatenation of outer and lower and will be displayed as grayed-out text.
- In **GLEG3_5**, we are adding **QTextEdit** widget at a defined row and column. The first row will be 1 and then the widget will be added to columns 1,2 and 3.
- In **GLEG3_6**, the **setColumnStretch** factor will take the first argument as outer and 2nd as outer+1. So, value will be (1,2). Therefore, column width order will be more for 3rd column, then 2nd and finally the 1st one as shown in the output. The rows stretch factor will be set to 1, 2 and 3.

Now, let us learn how to develop the same User Credential App using **QGridLayout**.

Observe the following code:

```
import sys
from PyQt5.QtWidgets import QWidget, QApplication, QLabel, QGridLayout,
QPushButton, QLineEdit , QHBoxLayout
from PyQt5 import QtGui


class GridLayout_User_Credential_App(QWidget):
    def __init__(self):
        super().__init__()
        self.display_widgets()
        self.setGeometry(0, 0, 398, 229)
        self.setWindowTitle('GridLayout with User Credential App')
        self.show()


    def display_widgets(self):
        # writing the grid portion
        mygrid_layout = QGridLayout()
        self.setLayout(mygrid_layout)


        mylbl1 = QLabel('Enter your username:',self)
        mylbl1.setMinimumWidth(161)
        myfont = QtGui.QFont()
        myfont.setFamily("Calibri")
        myfont.setPointSize(10)
        myfont.setBold(True)
```

```
        myfont.setWeight(75)
        mylbl1.setFont(myfont)
        mygrid_layout.addWidget(mylbl1, 1, 0, 1, 2)

        mylbl2 = QLabel('Enter your password:',self)
        mylbl2.setMinimumWidth(161)
        myfont = QtGui.QFont()
        myfont.setFamily("Calibri")
        myfont.setPointSize(10)
        myfont.setBold(True)
        myfont.setWeight(75)
        mylbl2.setFont(myfont)
        mygrid_layout.addWidget(mylbl2, 3, 0, 1, 2)

        mylineEdit1 = QLineEdit(self)
        mylineEdit1.setMinimumWidth(161)
        mygrid_layout.addWidget(mylineEdit1, 1, 2,1,2)
        mygrid_layout.setColumnStretch(1,2)

        mylineEdit2 = QLineEdit(self)
        mylineEdit2.setMinimumWidth(161)
        mygrid_layout.addWidget(mylineEdit2, 3, 2,1,2)

        myhbox = QHBoxLayout()
        myhbox.addStretch()
        mybtn1 = QPushButton("Confirm")
        myhbox.addWidget(mybtn1)
        myhbox.addStretch()

        mygrid_layout.addLayout(myhbox,4,1,1,3)

if __name__ == '__main__':
    myapp = QApplication(sys.argv)
```

```
    mywindow = GridLayout_User_Credential_App()
    sys.exit(myapp.exec_())
```

Output:

The output can be seen in the following *Figure 2.19:*

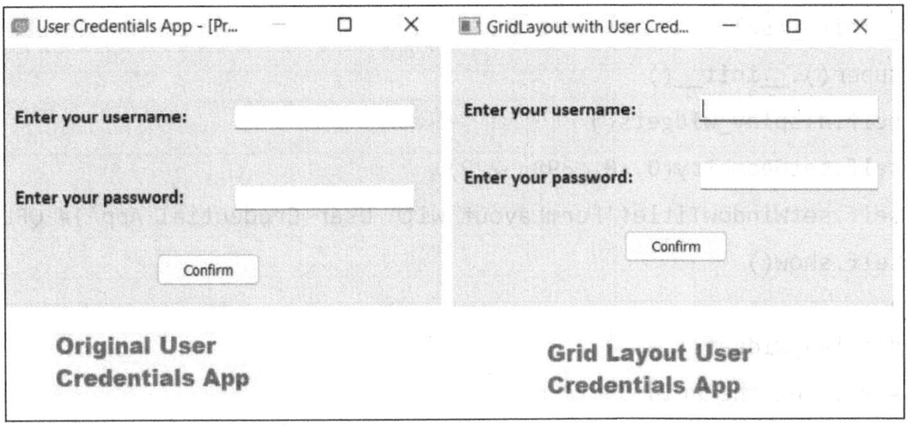

***Figure 2.19**: Output of Chap2_Example13.py*

Note: The preceding code is covered in Program Name: Chap2_Example13.py

QFormLayout

Whenever there is a requirement to create an application in 2-column form where each row consists of a label (first column) associated with an entry field (second column), then we can use **`QFormLayout`**. An important overloaded method which is most commonly used in **`QFormLayout`**, will be the **`addRow()`** method, which is described as follows:

- **`addRow(QLabel, QWidget)`**: This method will add a row containing the label and its widget in the second column.
- **`addRow(QWidget)`**: This method will add a row containing the widget spanning 2 columns and stretching it to a GUI form.
- **`addRow(QLayout)`**: This method will add a specified layout spanning both columns, or we can say that it will be used for nesting the layouts.
- **`addRow(QLabel, QLayout)`**: This method will add a row containing the label and its child layout in the second column.

Let us create the same user credential app using **`QFormLayout`** this time.

Observe the following code:

```
import sys
```

```
from PyQt5.QtWidgets import QWidget, QApplication, QLabel, QFormLayout,
QPushButton,QHBoxLayout, QLineEdit , QHBoxLayout # QFL_1
from PyQt5 import QtGui

class FormLayout_User_Credential_App(QWidget):
    def __init__(self):
        super().__init__()
        self.display_widgets()
        self.setGeometry(0, 0, 398, 229)
        self.setWindowTitle('FormLayout with User Credential App')# QFL_2
        self.show()

    def display_widgets(self):
        # writing the grid portion
        myfrm_layout = QFormLayout()

        mylbl1 = QLabel('Enter your username:',self)
        mylbl1.setMinimumWidth(161)
        myfont = QtGui.QFont()
        myfont.setFamily("Calibri")
        myfont.setPointSize(10)
        myfont.setBold(True)
        myfont.setWeight(75)
        mylbl1.setFont(myfont)

        mylbl2 = QLabel('Enter your password:',self)
        mylbl2.setMinimumWidth(161)
        myfont = QtGui.QFont()
        myfont.setFamily("Calibri")
        myfont.setPointSize(10)
        myfont.setBold(True)
        myfont.setWeight(75)
        mylbl2.setFont(myfont)
```

```
        mylineEdit1 = QLineEdit(self)
        mylineEdit1.setMinimumWidth(161)
        mylineEdit2 = QLineEdit(self)
        mylineEdit2.setMinimumWidth(161)

        myhbox = QHBoxLayout()
        myhbox.addStretch()
        mybtn1 = QPushButton("Confirm")
        myhbox.addWidget(mybtn1)
        myhbox.addStretch()
        myfrm_layout.addRow(mylbl1, mylineEdit1)# QFL_3
        myfrm_layout.addRow(mylbl2, mylineEdit2)# QFL_4
        myfrm_layout.addRow(myhbox)# QFL_5

        self.setLayout(myfrm_layout)# QFL_6

if __name__ == '__main__':
    myapp = QApplication(sys.argv)
    mywindow = FormLayout_User_Credential_App()
    sys.exit(myapp.exec_())
```

Output:

The output can be seen in the following *Figure 2.20:*

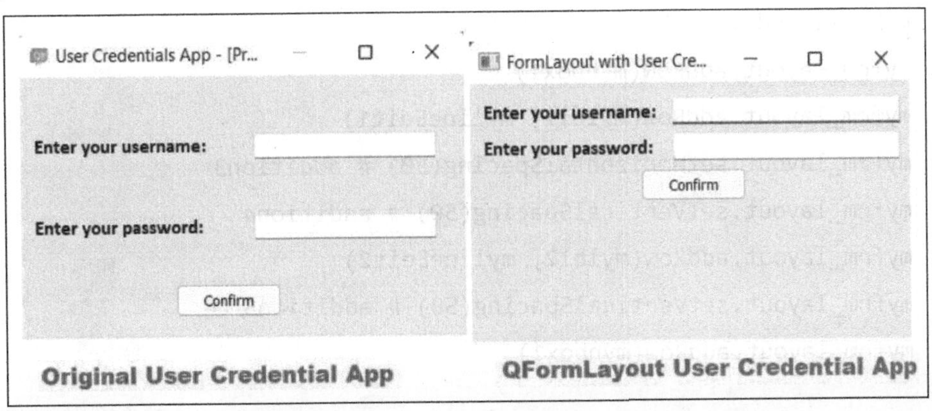

***Figure 2.20**: Output of Chap2_Example14.py*

Note: The preceding code is covered in Program Name: Chap2_Example14.py

- In **QFL_1**, first import the sys module for accessing the command line arguments. Then we will be importing from the class which creates desktop-style UIs of PyQt5 package, that is, **QtWidgets**, for creating an empty GUI and an application handler, that is, **QApplication**. In addition to it, we are also importing other widgets such as **QLabel**, **QFormLayout**, **QPushButton**, **QLineEdit**.
- In **QFL_2**, we are setting the title of our GUI form, that is, window, as **FormLayout with User Credential App**.
- In **QFL_3**, we are adding a row containing label object **mylbl1** in the first column and **QLineEdit** object **mylineEdit1** in 2nd column respectively.
- In **QFL_4**, we are adding a row containing label object **mylbl2** in the first column and **QLineEdit** object **mylineEdit2** in 2nd column respectively.
- In **QFL_5**, we are adding a row containing **QHBoxLayout** object.
- In **QFL_6**, we are setting the main layout of GUI form. In other words, we are setting the **QFormLayout** to the GUI form.

Now, from QFormLayout code, we can see that the space between the 2 QLabel or 2 **QLineEdit** widgets is very less. The same happens between **QLabel** or **QLineEdit** widgets too. So, in such cases, we need to provide spacing. We will be providing vertical spacing between the widgets using the **setVerticalSpacing** method and horizontal spacing using the **setHorizontalSpacing** method.

We will modify the previous code by introducing the concept of Vertical and Horizontal spacer.

Note: The complete code is covered in Program Name: Chap2_Example15.py

```
myhbox1 = QHBoxLayout() # addition1
myhbox1.addStretch() # addition2
myfrm_layout.addRow(myhbox1)
myfrm_layout.addRow(mylbl1, mylineEdit1)
myfrm_layout.setHorizontalSpacing(50) # addition3
myfrm_layout.setVerticalSpacing(50) # addition4
myfrm_layout.addRow(mylbl2, mylineEdit2)
myfrm_layout.setVerticalSpacing(50) # addition5
myfrm_layout.addRow(myhbox1)
```

Output:

The output can be seen in the following *Figure 2.21:*

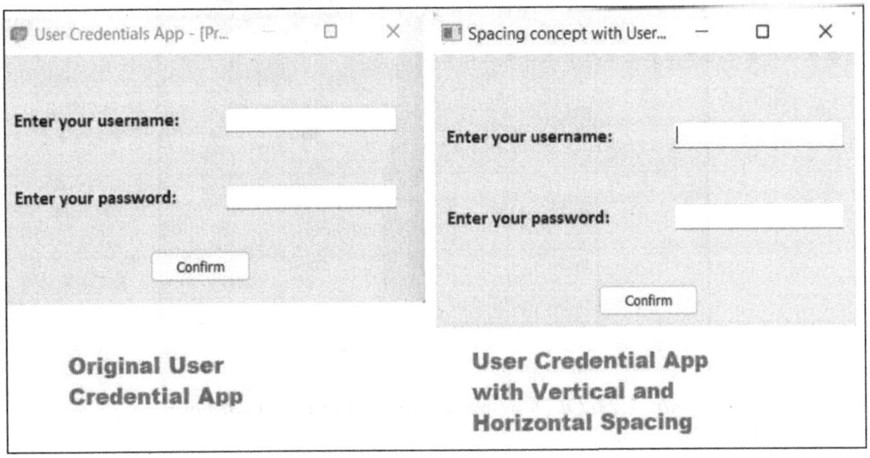

***Figure 2.21:** O/P of vertical and horizontal spacing approach and original user credentials app*

Let us see this Python snippet.

- In **addition1**, an instance of QHBoxLayout object **myhbox1** is created.
- In **addition2**, an empty stretchable box is created for the **myhbox1** object using **addStretch** for filling up the blank space.
- In **addition3**, the space between the widgets lying side by side (horizontally only) will be 50. **setHorizontalSpacing** takes an integer value as an argument.
- In **addition4** and **addition5**, the space between the widgets lying out vertically (only) will be 50. **setVerticalSpacing** takes an integer value as an argument.

Now, the most important observation of all these concepts about widgets placement which we saw till now, is that we can easily manage using Qt Designer, as shown in *Figure 2.22:*

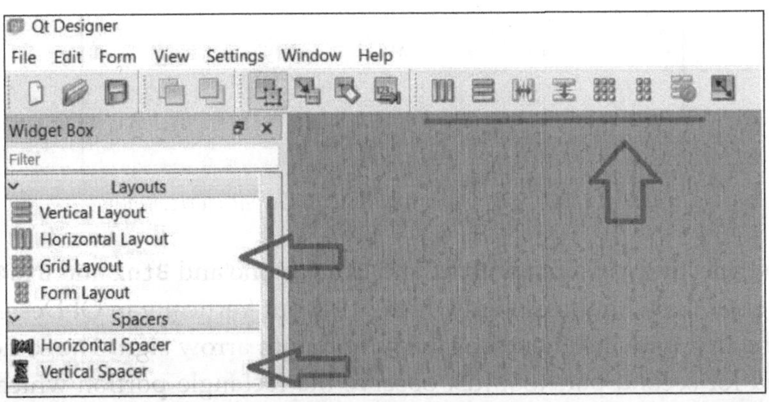

***Figure 2.22:** Qt Designer View of Layout, Spacers in Widget Box and toolbar controls*

Let us show their usage with the help of figures, by playing with **default GUI form**. This is inarguably one of the best ways to learn. Refer to *Figure 2.23* containing the default GUI form:

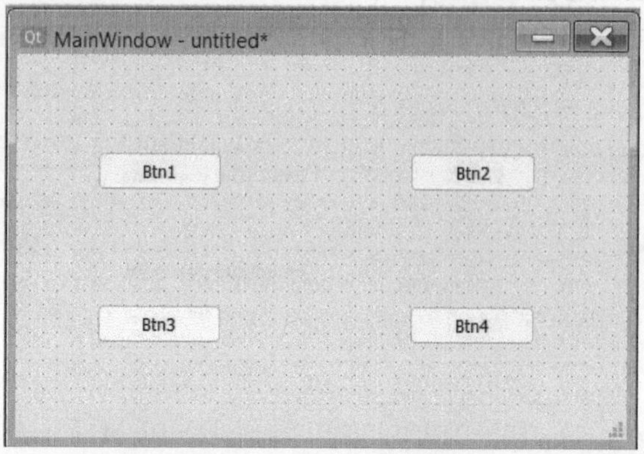

Figure 2.23: *Qt Designer toolbar with Default GUI Form*

Now, we will be selecting in pairs say **Btn1** and **Btn2** as one and **Btn3** and **Btn4** as another. As displayed in *Figure 2.24* with arrow sign which is Layout Horizontally in Qt Designer, we will be first selecting the first pair and then click the button with arrow sign. The same methodology will be repeated for second pair too. Just observe the rectangle portion which are treated as pairs. The result after performing these activities are displayed in the following figure:

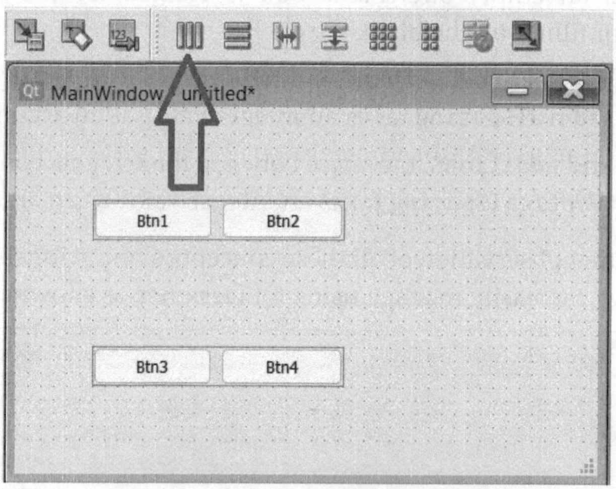

Figure 2.24: *Qt Designer toolbar with Layout Horizontally*

Now, we will be selecting in pairs say **Btn1** and **Btn3** as one and **Btn2** and **Btn4** as another. As displayed in *Figure 2.25* with arrow sign which is Layout Vertically in Qt Designer, we will be first selecting the first pair and then click the button with arrow sign. The same methodology will be repeated for second pair too. Just observe the rectangle portion which are treated as pairs. The result after performing these activities are displayed in the following figure:

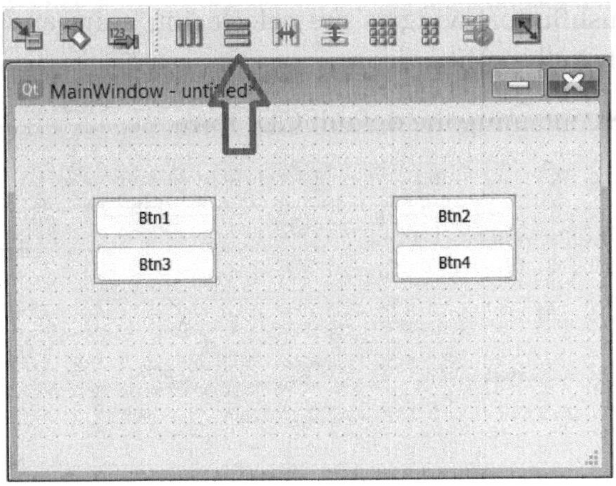

Figure 2.25: Qt Designer toolbar with Layout Vertically

Just observe the outputs when **QPushButton** widget, in pairs, are being selected and corresponding Toolbar icons are being pressed (highlighted with arrow sign against each feature), as shown in *Figure 2.26:*

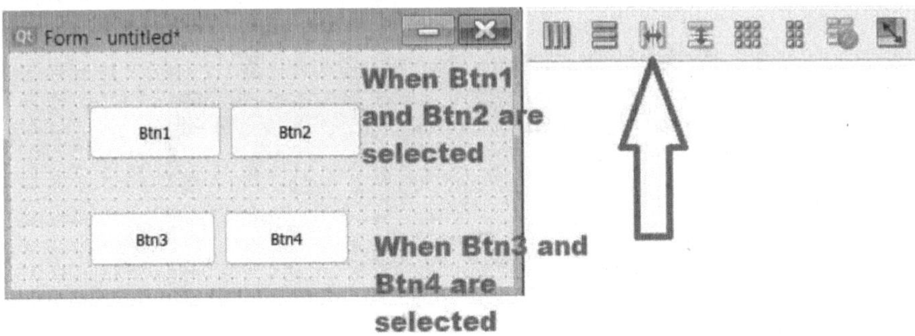

Figure 2.26: Qt Designer toolbar with lay out horizontally in Splitterfrom default GUI form

In *Figure 2.27,* the **QPushButton** widgets are selected in pairs and stretched horizontally by clicking **Lay Out Horizontally** in splitter icon:

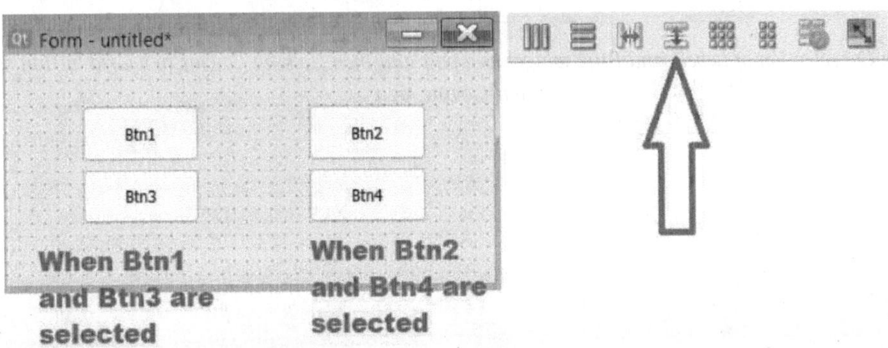

Figure 2.27: Qt Designer toolbar with Lay Out Vertically in Splitterfrom Default GUI form

In *Figure 2.27,* the QPushButton widgets are selected in pairs and stretched vertically by clicking **Lay Out Vertically** in the splitter icon.

Now refer to *Figure 2.28* containing the default GUI form:

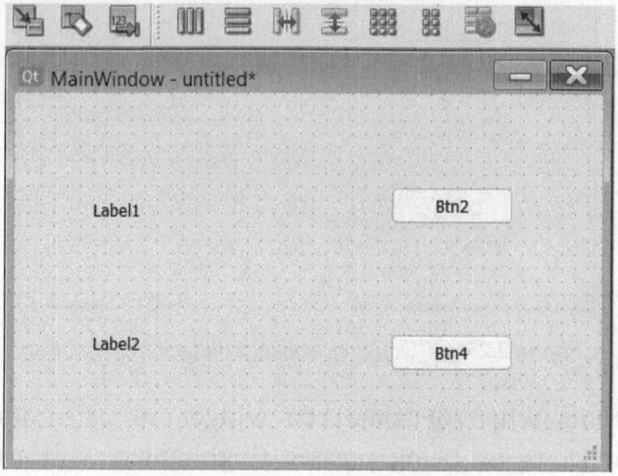

Figure 2.28: *Qt designer toolbar with layout in a grid transformation from default GUI form*

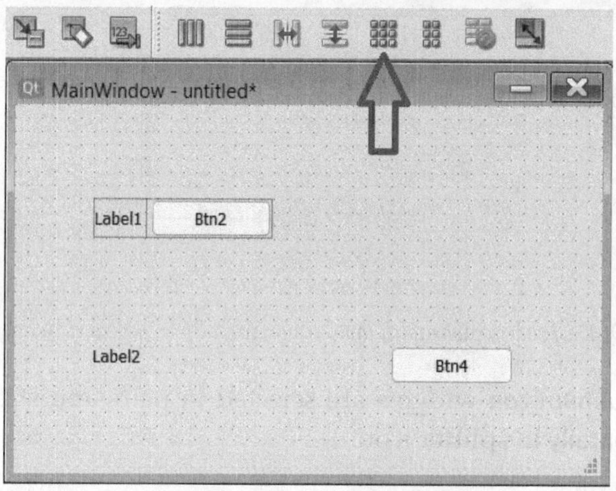

Figure 2.29: *On selection of Label1 and Btn2 widget as a pair and then clicking Layout in a Grid button as displayed with arrow sign*

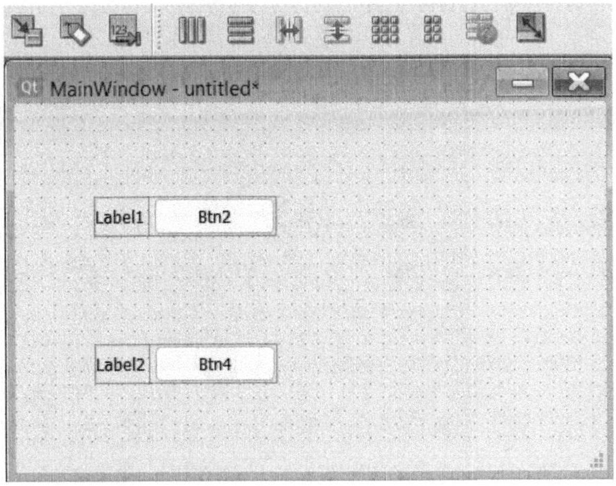

Figure 2.30: On selection of Label2 and Btn4 widget as a pair and then clicking Layout in a Grid button as displayed with arrow sign

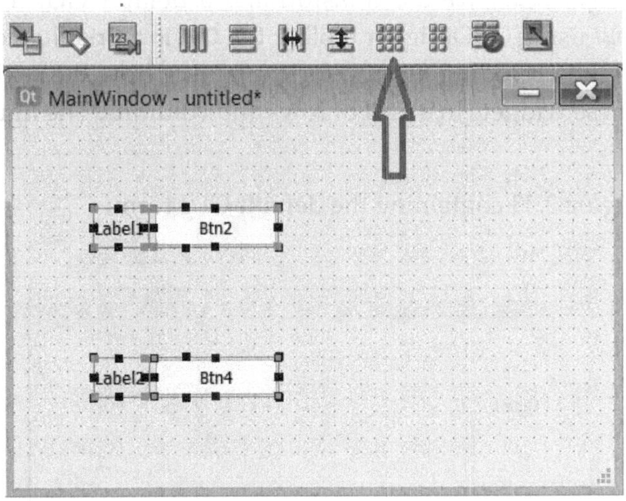

Figure 2.31: On selecting both pairs and then clicking Layout in a Grid button as displayed with arrow sign

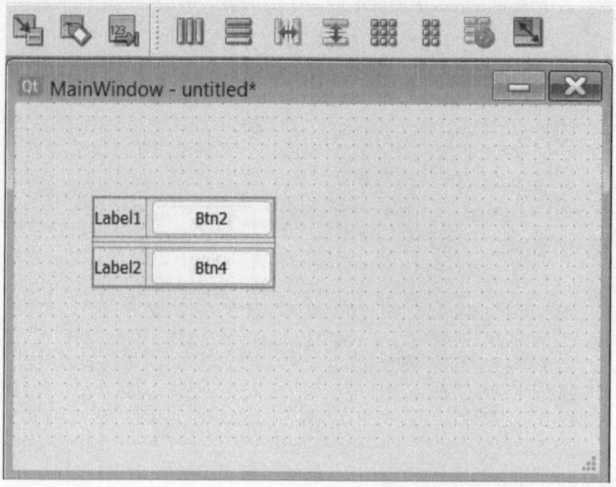

Figure 2.32: *Final layout form as displayed using grid transformation in Qt Designer*

From *Figure 2.28* to *Figure 2.32* we are transforming a default GUI form by arranging the widgets in a *Grid layout* using Qt Designer toolbar **Lay Out in a Grid**. Just observe the steps that we have described in the preceding figures, for explaining how the widgets are used in pair and then laying out these widgets in a grid of rows and columns. The figure with arrow marks are self-explanatory.

Let us now go over *Figure 2.33* containing the default GUI form:

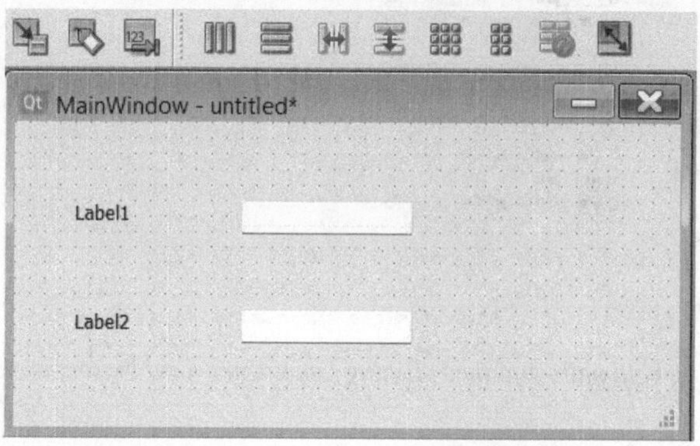

Figure 2.33: *Qt Designer toolbar with layout in a form layout transformation from default GUI form*

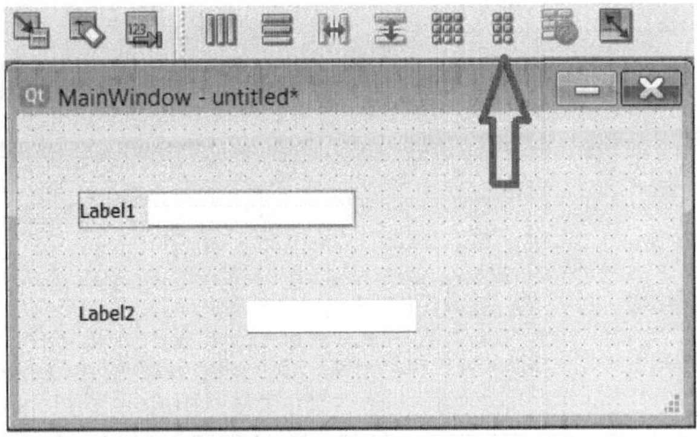

Figure 2.34: On selection of Label1 and Line Edit1 widget as a pair and then clicking Lay Out in a Form Layout button as displayed with arrow sign

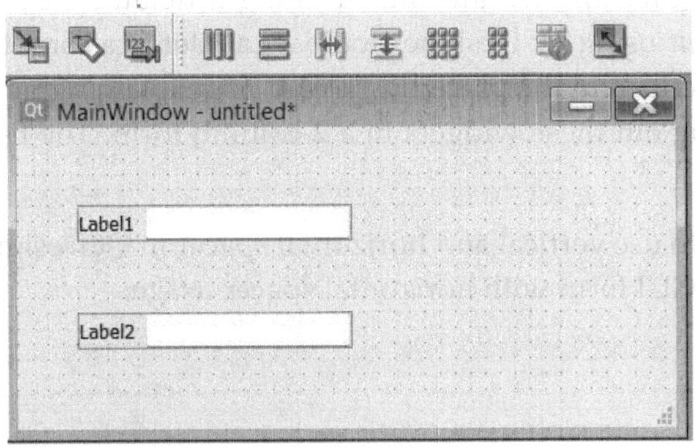

Figure 2.35: On selection of Label2 and Line Edit2 widget as a pair and then clicking Lay Out in a Form Layout button as displayed with arrow sign

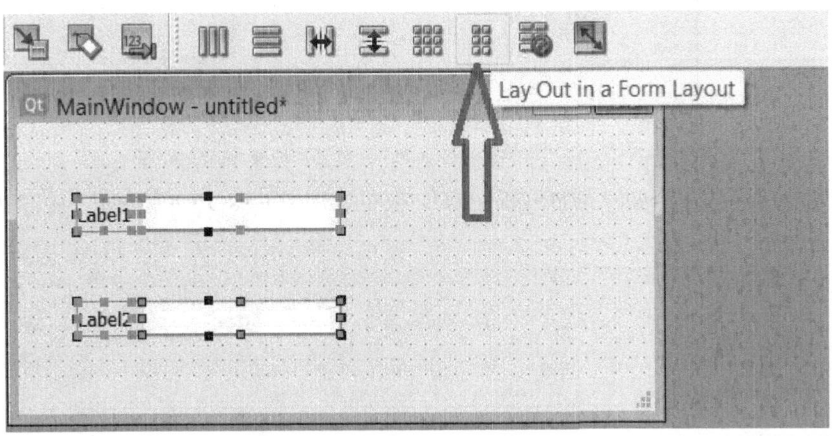

Figure 2.36: On selecting both pairs and then clicking Layout in a Form Layout button as displayed with arrow sign

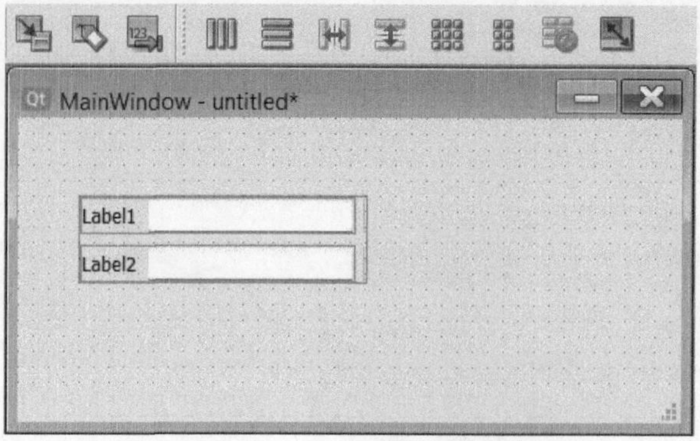

Figure 2.37: Final layout form as displayed using form layout transformation in Qt Designer

From *Figure 2.33 to Figure 2.37,* we are transforming a default GUI form by arranging the widgets in a *Form layout* using Qt Designer toolbar **Lay Out in a Form Layout**. Just observe the steps that we have described in the preceding figure, for explaining how the widgets are used in pairs and then laying out these widgets in a 2-column form. The figure with arrow marks are self-explanatory.

Now, we will see how to use vertical and horizontal spacer in Qt Designer. Refer to *Figure 2.38* containing the default GUI form with horizontal spacer usage:

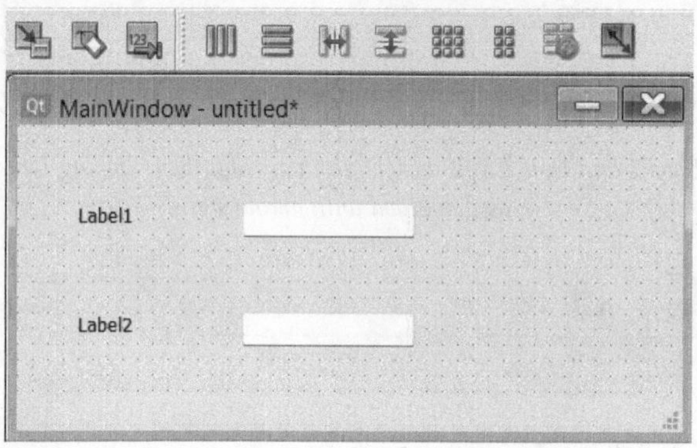

Figure 2.38: *Qt Designer form displaying horizontal spacer usage from Default GUI form*

Figure 2.39: Qt Designer form inserting horizontal spacer as shown using arrow on first pair of Label1 and Line Edit1 widget after performing Lay Out in a Grid transformation

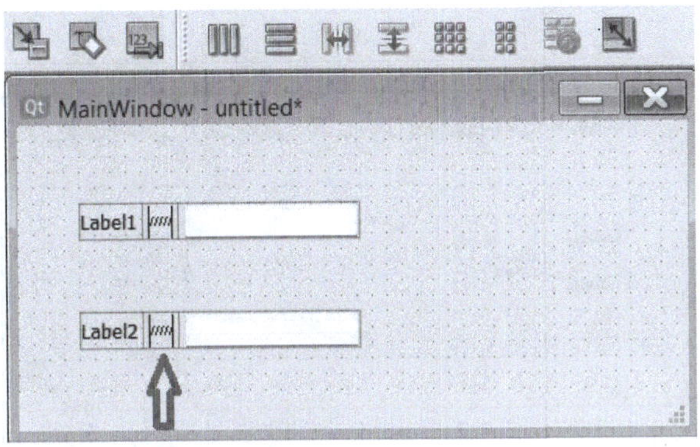

Figure 2.40: Qt Designer form inserting horizontal spacer as shown using arrow on second pair of Label1 and Line Edit1 widget after performing Lay Out in a Grid transformation

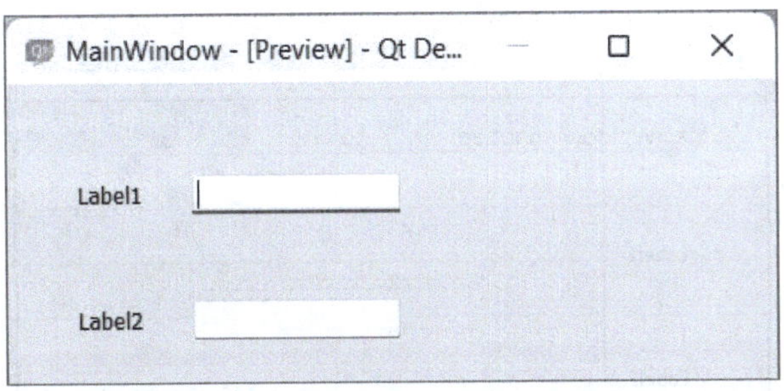

Figure 2.41: Final layout form as displayed using horizontal spacer usage by pressing Ctrl + R

From *Figure 2.38 to Figure 2.41*, we can see the usage of a **horizontal spacer** from the widget box on a default GUI form. By default, the widgets pair **`QLabel`** and **`QLineEdit`** are arranged in a grid of rows and columns. Then, a horizontal spacer is introduced between the widgets thus indicating the usage of a horizontal spacer. Finally, by pressing *Ctrl + R*, we can view the final output of the GUI form.

Refer to *Figure 2.42* containing the default GUI form with vertical spacer usage:

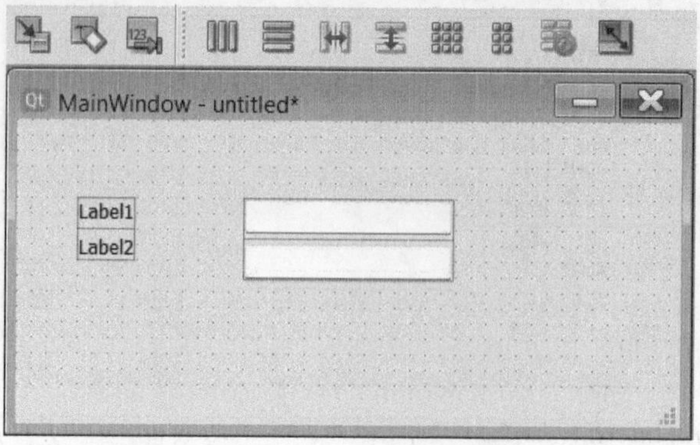

Figure 2.42: *Qt Designer form displaying vertical spacer usage from Default GUI Form*

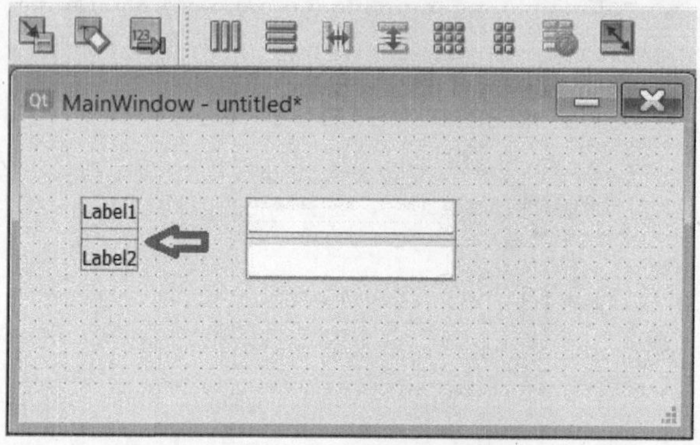

Figure 2.43: *Qt Designer form inserting vertical spacer as shown using arrow on first pair of Label1 and Label2 widget after performing Lay Out in a Grid transformation*

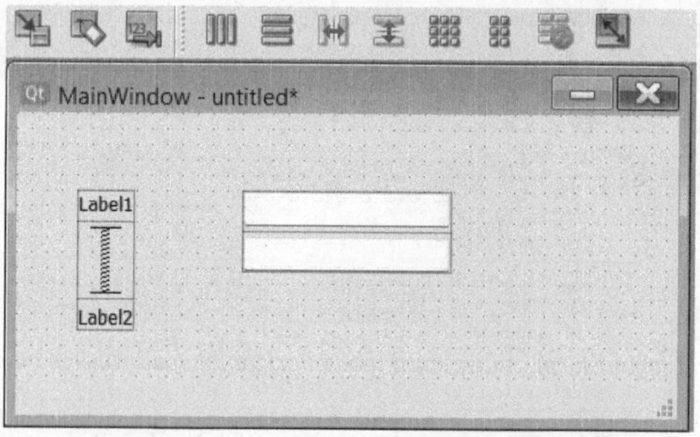

Figure 2.44: *Qt Designer after stretching Label1 and Label2 pair as they are arranged in a vertical layout*

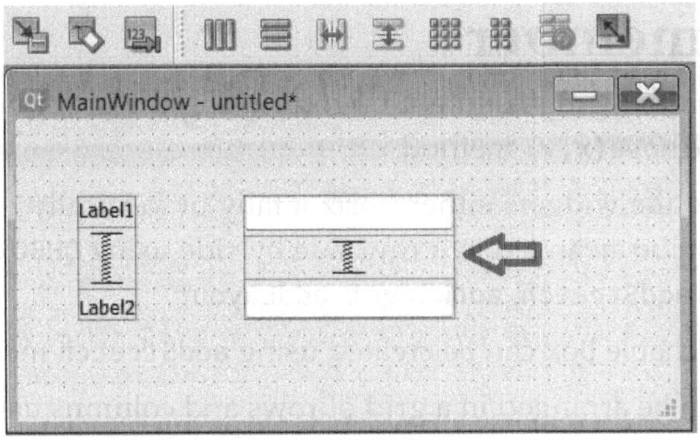

***Figure 2.45:** Qt Designer with Line Edit1 Line Edit2 widget stretched vertically after introducing vertical spacer between them as shown using arrow*

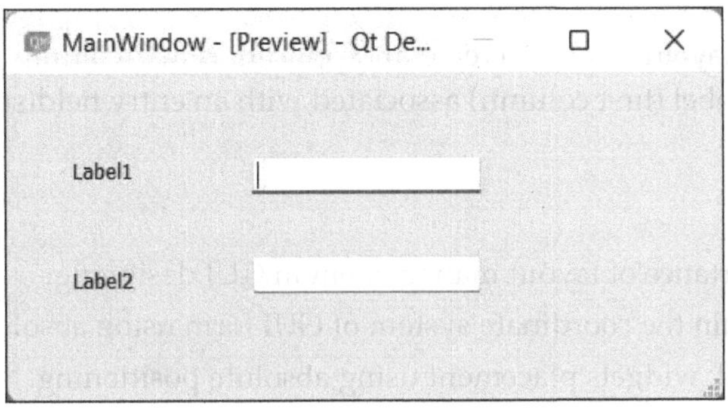

***Figure 2.46:** Final layout form as displayed using vertical spacer usage in Qt Designer by pressing Ctrl + R*

From *Figure 2.42 to Figure 2.46*, the widgets pair of **`QLabel`** and **`QLineEdit`** are arranged by introducing vertical spacer between them and are stretched to the heights mentioned. Finally, by pressing *Ctrl + R*, we can see the final output of the GUI form.

Conclusion

In this chapter, we learned how to arrange the widgets using absolute positioning and layout classes. We saw different approaches of creating " User Credential App " application using absolute positioning, **`QBoxLayout`**, **`QGridLayout`** and **`QFormLayout`** class.

This chapter is important to understand, since in forthcoming chapters, we will be displaying multiple applications using all these concepts. We will write the code on how to arrange the widgets by applying drag and drop of widgets from Widget Box and using toolbar icons to arrange the layouts for creating our application.

Points to remember

- We can position the widgets in a GUI form using the absolute positioning approach with help of the `move(x,y)` method.
- We can arrange the widgets either horizontally or vertically using **`QBoxLayout`** class. The widgets can be arranged in a row side by side using **`QHBoxLayout`** with the usage of methods viz **`addStretch`**, **`addWidget`**, **`addLayout`**.
- An empty stretchable box can be created using **`addStretch`** method.
- The widgets can be arranged in a grid of rows and columns using **`QGridLayout`**.
- The default value of rowspan and columnspan is 1 in **`QGridLayout`** span.
- **`setColumnStretch`** and **`setRowStretch`** will generally focus on the stretch factor of column/row.
- Using **`QFormLayout`**, we can create an application in 2-column form where each row consists of a label (first column) associated with an entry field(second column).

Questions

1. Enlist the importance of layout management in GUI designing.
2. Draw and explain the coordinate system of GUI form using absolute positioning.
3. Explain in detail, widgets placement using absolute positioning.
4. Explain in detail the placement of the widget using layout classes.
5. Explain the following:
    a. QBoxLayout
    b. QHBoxLayout
    c. QHBoxLayout with addstretch
    d. QVBoxLayout
    e. QGridLayout
    f. QFormLayout

Join our book's Discord space

Join the book's Discord Workspace for Latest updates, Offers, Tech happenings around the world, New Release and Sessions with the Authors:

https://discord.bpbonline.com

CHAPTER 3

Getting Insights of Events, Signals and Slots

Introduction

PyQt5, a Python framework for desktop application development, relies on the concept of events, signals, and slots to create interactive user interfaces. Events are fundamental to this system, representing user actions (like button clicks or keyboard input) and system events. Signals act as intermediaries, informing the application when a particular event occurs. Meanwhile, slots are functions or methods connected to signals, defining the application's response to those events. By linking signals to slots, developers can precisely control how their applications react to user interactions and other events, ultimately enabling the creation of dynamic, responsive, and user-friendly desktop applications in Python. This understanding is crucial for both beginners and experienced PyQt5 developers, empowering them to build applications that seamlessly adapt to user actions and system changes.

Structure

In this chapter, we will discuss the following topics:

- Introduction to Events, Signals and Slots
- Usage of Toolbar icons in Qt Designer
- Signal slot examples in Qt Designer

Objectives

After reading this chapter, the reader will get to know about Events, Signals, and Slots in PyQt5, and creating useful desktop applications using these concepts. Firstly, we shall see a GUI form application creation in Qt Designer by tracking the mouse movements. We will change the background color of the **QPushButton** widget by tracking the left and right mouse clicks. Various examples will be shown of how a signal is linked to a slot, in order to create a simple user interface application by toying with **QPushButton** widget. Finally, we shall see how connections can be created with an object, signals, and slots for layouts and widgets, which can be connected using Edit Signals / Slots with various case study examples. So, in this chapter, we will be dealing exclusively with various events, signals, and slot concepts. Moreover, we will be learning signal / slot editor usage in Qt Designer.

Introduction to Events, Signals, and Slots

Any GUI application created using widgets will act as an event source. In response to at least one event, every widget is designed in such a way that it will emit a signal. To explain in simpler terms, when user interaction with the widget will occur, then the notifications will pop out from the widgets. However, it is not a rule. In addition, it may also send data about what happened. To perform any action, as the signal itself is not enough, it must be connected to a slot. In a GUI application, the slot must be connected to a signal. Any function or method can be used in a GUI application as a slot. We can also say that it is used for the signal receiver. There are various built-in slots by many PyQt5 widgets, which we will learn while creating applications.

Let us first see the most common event that every widget may experience. It is related to the mouse. Let us try to use our mouse, prompting some action to perform on either, by using left click, right-click, hover, and so on?

We are creating a GUI form using Qt Designer with the file name **MouseEvents_Eg1.ui** as shown in the following *Figure 3.1*:

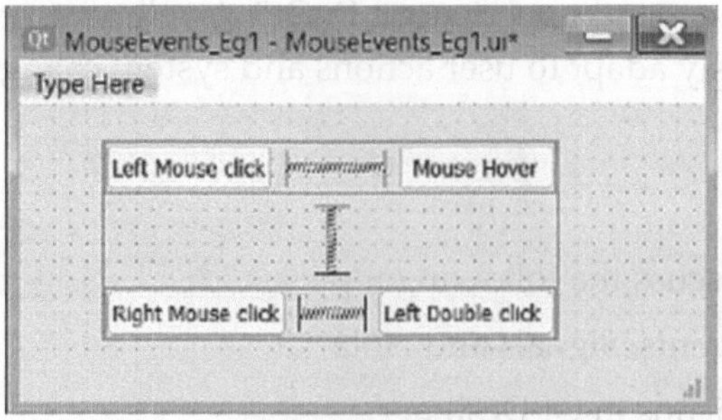

Figure 3.1: *Qt Designer file: MouseEvents_Eg1.ui*

Note: The above .ui file is covered in Path: MouseEvents_Eg1_files/MouseEvents_Eg1.ui

We will then convert this **.ui** file into a Python **.py** file using the following command:

pyuic5 MouseEvents_Eg1.ui -o MouseEvents_Eg1.py

Note: The .ui and .py files of every example discussed in the chapter, will be available in the code bundle. Only the Python code of the file name preceding run_ will be displayed with comments at the important line for discussion.

Another Python file has been created with the name **run_MouseEvents_Eg1.py** as follows:

```
import sys
from PyQt5.QtWidgets import QMainWindow, QApplication  # RME_1
from MouseEvents_Eg1 import *# RME_2
from PyQt5.QtCore import Qt


class MyMainWindow(QMainWindow):
    def __init__(self):
        super().__init__()
        self.myui = Ui_MouseEvents_Eg1()
        self.myui.setupUi(self)
        self.setMouseTracking(True)# RME_3
        self.myui.hover_mouse_btn_2.leaveEvent = lambda e: self.myui.hover_
        mouse_btn_2.setStyleSheet("background-color : blue")  # RME_4
        self.myui.hover_mouse_btn_2.enterEvent = lambda e: self.myui.hover_
        mouse_btn_2.setStyleSheet("background-color : violet")  # RME_5
        self.show()


    def mousePressEvent(self, e): # RME_6
        if e.button() == Qt.LeftButton:# RME_7
            self.myui.lm_click_btn_2.setStyleSheet("background-color :
            green")# RME_8


        if e.button() == Qt.RightButton:# RME_9
```

```
            self.myui.rm_click_btn_2.setStyleSheet("background-color : red")#
            RME_10

    def mouseDoubleClickEvent(self, e):# RME_11
        if e.button() == Qt.LeftButton:# RME_12
            self.myui.left_double_click_btn_2.setStyleSheet("background-color
            : yellow")# RME_13

if __name__ == '__main__':
    myapp = QApplication(sys.argv)
    mywindow = MyMainWindow()# RME_14
    sys.exit(myapp.exec_())
```

Output:

The output can be seen in *Figures 3.2 to 3.6* with different cases below:

Case-1: When mouse is getting entered in Button with text "Mouse Hover"

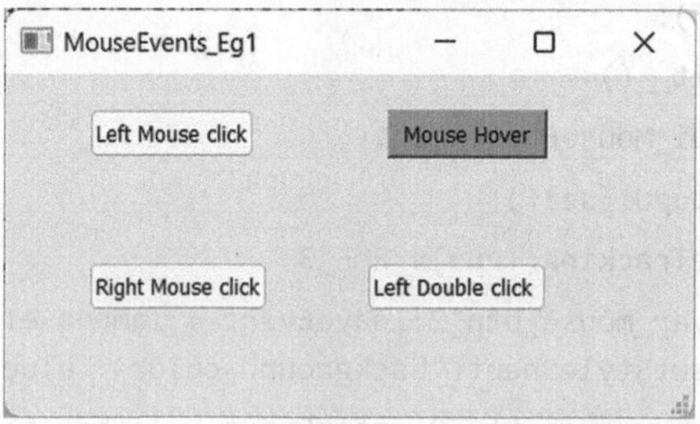

***Figure 3.2**: Case-1 Output of MouseEvents_Eg1_files/run_MouseEvents_Eg1.py*

Case-2: When mouse is leaving in Button with text "Mouse Hover"

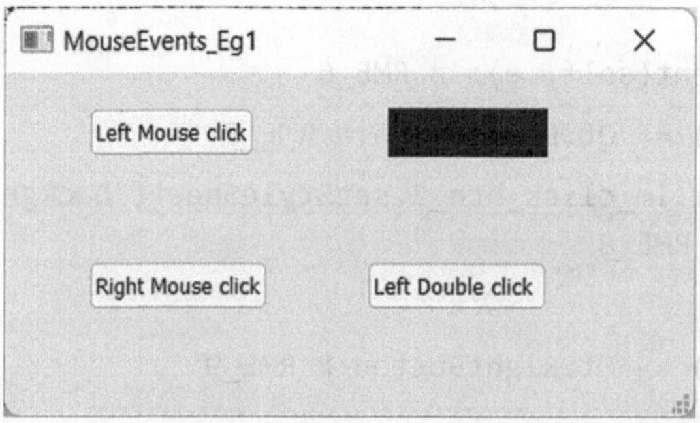

***Figure 3.3**: Case-2 Output of MouseEvents_Eg1_files/run_MouseEvents_Eg1.py*

Case-3: When Button with text "Left Mouse Click" is clicked

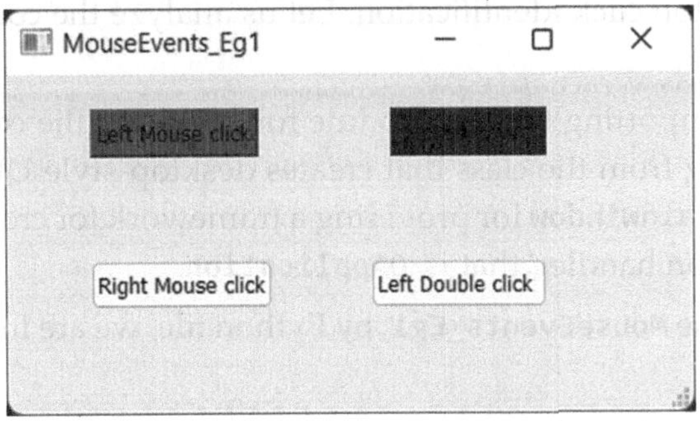

Figure 3.4: Case-3 Output of MouseEvents_Eg1_files/run_MouseEvents_Eg1.py

Case-4: When Button with text "Right Mouse Click" is clicked

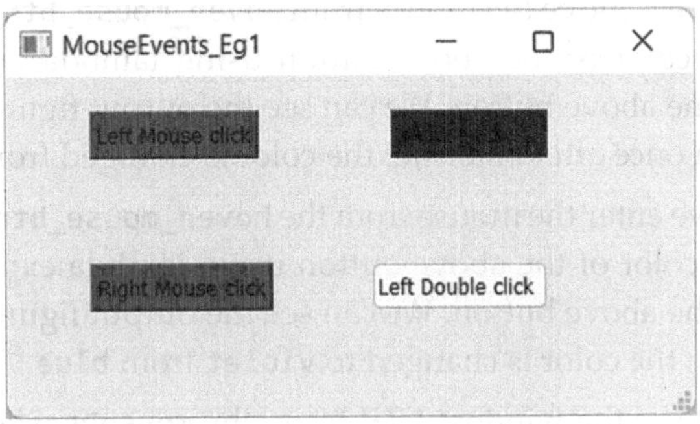

Figure 3.5: Case-4 Output of MouseEvents_Eg1_files/run_MouseEvents_Eg1.py

Case-5: When Button with text "Left Double Click" is clicked by Left mouse button twice

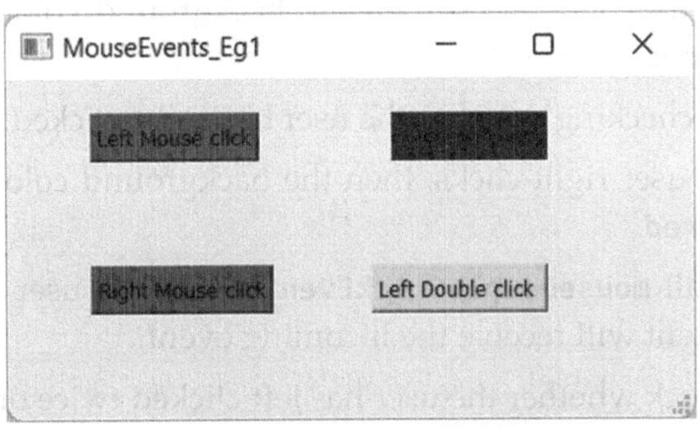

Figure 3.6:: Case-5 Output of MouseEvents_Eg1_files/run_MouseEvents_Eg1.py

Note: The preceding code is covered in Program Name: MouseEvents_Eg1_files/run_MouseEvents_Eg1.py

In the above example, we are displaying the background color of buttons to different colors, based on the mouse button click identification. Let us analyze the code and try to understand the process.

- In **RME_1**, after importing the **sys** module for accessing the command line arguments, we are importing from the class that creates desktop-style UIs of **PyQt5** package, that is, **QtWidgets**, **QMainWindow** for providing a framework for creating new GUI interfaces and an application handler, that is, **QApplication**.
- In **RME_2**, from the **MouseEvents_Eg1.py** Python file, we are importing all the members of a module.
- In **RME_3**, if we want to trigger the mouse events on a window by pressing the mouse, then the above statement will be executed. That is why **self.setMouseTracking(True)** is executed.
- In **RME_4**, when we remove the mouse from **hover_mouse_btn_2** button, we are setting the background color of the above button using lambda expression as **blue**, using **leaveEvent** on the above button. We can see the output figure when the mouse leaves the above button once after entering; the color is changed from **violet** to **blue**.
- In **RME_5**, when we enter the mouse from the **hover_mouse_btn_2** button, we are setting the background color of the above button using lambda expression as **violet**, using **enterEvent** on the above button. We can see the output figure when the mouse enters the above button; the color is changed to **violet** from **blue**.
- In **RME_6**, on clicking the window GUI form, the **mousePressEvent** event handler will be called, which will receive the incoming event using an argument.
- In **RME_7**, we are checking whether the user has left-clicked.
- In **RME_8**, if the user left-clicks, then the background color of the **lm_click_btn_2** button will turn **green**.
- In **RME_9**, we are checking whether the user has right-clicked.
- In **RME_10**, if the user right-clicks, then the background color of the **rm_click_btn_2** button will turn **red**.
- In **RME_11**, we call **mouseDoubleClickEvent** when the user clicks the window form twice and argument will receive the incoming event.
- In **RME_12**, we check whether the user has left clicked twice or not.
- In **RME_13**, if the use left-clicks twice, then the background color of the **left_double_click_btn_2** button will turn **yellow**.
- In **RME_14**, an instance of **MyWindow** class **mywindow** is created.

This is just one example. We will study many more as we progress with the chapter. Let us now concentrate on understanding the concepts of signals and slots.

QObject class will be deriving **PyQt** Widget, and each widget in response to one or more events, will emit **Signal**. To perform an action, this **Signal** will be connected to **Slot**. The **Slot** can be a function/method which will be callable.

A widget emitting a signal is done using the following most convenient way:

```
widget.signal.connect(slot_function/slot_method)
```

or

```
QtCore.QObject.connect(widget,

QtCore.SIGNAL('signalname'),slot_function/slot_method)
```

Just imagine the widget to be an instance of a **QPushbutton** say **btn1**. Consider the signal to be clicked; that is when the button is clicked, it must be connected to a slot function/method, say **mydef_slot**. This can be achieved by 2 approaches:

```
btn1.clicked.connect(mydef_slot)
```

or

```
QtCore.QObject.connect(btn1, QtCore.SIGNAL("clicked()"), mydef_slot)
```

But there is no support for the **connect()** method of **QObject** class in PyQt5, in order to have a connection between signal and slot.

Let us see a simple example in Qt Designer, where the details of file names are as shown in *Table 3.1:*

S No.	Qt Designer file name (.ui)	Converting the Qt Designer file name to Python file (.py)	Creating another Python file and importing the converted Python file from Qt Designer
1.	`Signal_Slot_Eg2.ui`	`Signal_Slot_Eg2.py`	`run_ Signal_Slot_Eg2.py`

Table 3.1: *Table depicting file names of Signal_Slot_Eg2*

The Qt Designer file is shown in the following *Figure 3.7:*

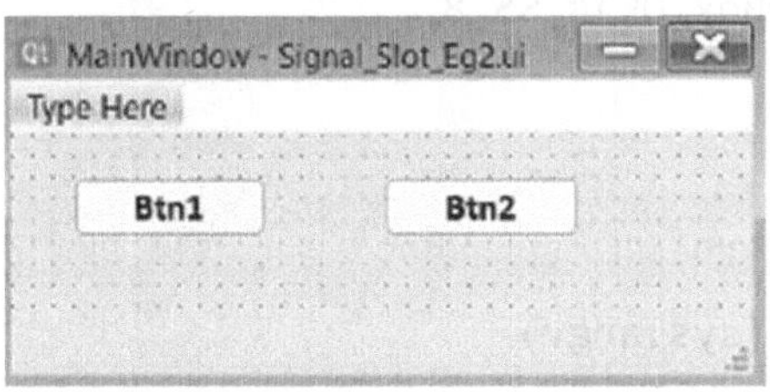

Figure 3.7: *Qt Designer file: Signal_Slot_Eg2.ui*

Note: The above .ui file is covered in Path: Signal_Slot_Eg2_files/Signal_Slot_Eg2.ui

In this example, we will be performing a click operation on two buttons and displaying some information to the user in a message form.

Consider the following code of **run_Signal_Slot_Eg2.py**:

```
import sys
from PyQt5.QtWidgets import QMainWindow, Qapplication, QmessageBox  # SS_1
from Signal_Slot_Eg2 import *# SS_2

class MySignalSlot_Window(QmainWindow):
    def __init__(self):
        super().__init__()
        self.myui = Ui_MainWindow()
        self.myui.setupUi(self)
        self.myui.mybtn1.clicked.connect(self.mymethod_btn1)# SS_3
        self.myui.mybtn2.clicked.connect(self.mymethod_btn2)# SS_4
        self.show()

    def mymethod_btn1(self):# SS_5
        QmessageBox.information(self, "Button 1", "Button1 is clicked",
QmessageBox.Ok, QmessageBox.Ok)# SS_6
        return

    def mymethod_btn2(self):# SS_7
        QmessageBox.information(self, "Button 2", "Button2 is clicked",
QmessageBox.Ok, QmessageBox.Ok)# SS_8
        return

if __name__ == '__main__':
    myapp = Qapplication(sys.argv)
    mywindow = MySignalSlot_Window()# SS_9
    sys.exit(myapp.exec_())
```

Output:

The output can be seen in *Figure 3.8 and 3.9* with different cases below:

Case-1: When button with text "Btn1" is clicked

Figure 3.8: *Case-1 Output of Signal_Slot_Eg2_files/ Signal_Slot_Eg2.py*

Case-2: When button with text "Btn2" is clicked

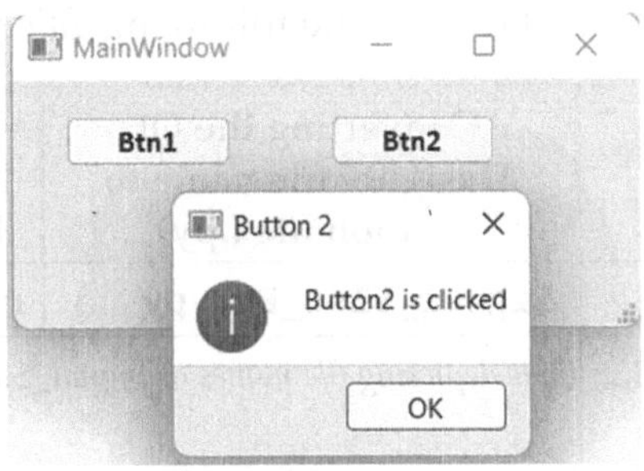

Figure 3.9: *Case-2 Output of Signal_Slot_Eg2_files/ Signal_Slot_Eg2.py*

Note: The preceding code is covered in Program Name: Signal_Slot_Eg2_files/Signal_Slot_Eg2.py

Let us understand the code with reference to the tag mentioned:

- In **SS_1**, after importing the **sys** module for accessing the command line arguments, we are importing from the class, which creates desktop-style UIs of PyQt5 package, that is, **QtWidgets**, **QMainWindow** for providing a framework for creating new GUI interfaces, and an application handler, that is, **QApplication**. In addition to it, we are also importing a widget for creating dialogs, which is **QMessageBox**.
- In **SS_2**, from the **Signal_Slot_Eg2.py** Python file, we are importing all the module members.
- In **SS_3**, the widget is **mybtn1**. The signal is clicked and connected to the slot, and a signal is emitted. In other words, when the **mybtn1** button is clicked (click **event | signal**), **mymethod_btn1** (slot) will be invoked.

- In **SS_4**, the widget is **mybtn2**. The signal is clicked and connected to the slot. Here, if the signal emits, the **mymethod_btn2** method will be called.
- In **SS_5**, a custom slot **mymethod_btn1** is created, which will accept the clicked signal from **mybtn1**.
- In **SS_6**, a message is being displayed. On clicking the **Btn1** button, as shown in the output figure, the informative text **Button1** pops on a new window.
- In **SS_7**, a custom slot **mymethod_btn2** is created, which will accept the clicked signal from **mybtn2**.
- In **SS_8**, a message is being displayed. On clicking the **Btn2** button, as shown in the output figure, the informative text **Button2** pops on a new window.
- In **SS_9**, an instance of **MySignalSlot_Window** class **mywindow** is created.

Many signals are being supported in PyQt5 and not just clicked signals, which we have seen just now. Let us view another example of signal and slot.

The details of the file names are as shown in the following *Table 3.2*:

S No.	Qt Designer file name (.ui)	Converting the Qt Designer file name to Python file (.py)	Creating another Python file and importing the converted Python file from Qt Designer
1	**Signal_Slot_Eg3.ui**	**Signal_Slot_Eg3.py**	**run_ Signal_Slot_Eg3.py**

Table 3.2: *Table depicting file names of Signal_Slot_Eg3*

The Qt Designer file is shown in the following *Figure 3.10:*

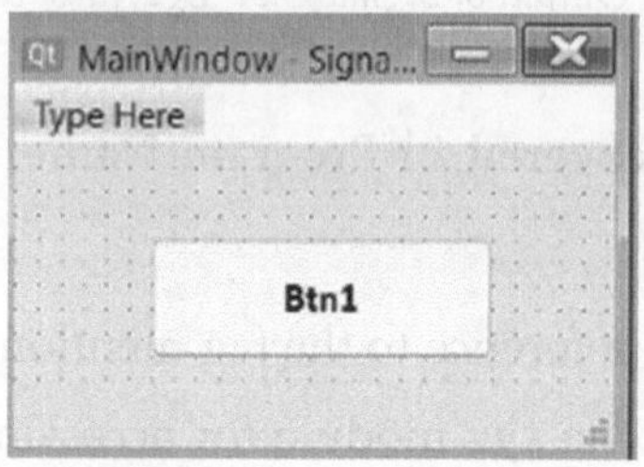

Figure 3.10: *Qt Designer File: Signal_Slot_Eg3.ui*

Note: The above .ui file is covered in Path: Signal_Slot_Eg3_files/Signal_Slot_Eg3.ui

In this example, we will be viewing the toggled state of the button, where the signals can also send the data, thereby revealing some information about what is happening.

Consider the following code of **run_Signal_Slot_Eg3.py**:

```
import sys
from PyQt5.QtWidgets import QMainWindow, QApplication# SS2_1
from Signal_Slot_Eg3 import * # SS2_2


class MySignalSlot2_Window(QMainWindow):
    def __init__(self):
        super().__init__()
        self.myui = Ui_Signal_Slot_Eg3()
        self.myui.setupUi(self)
        self.myui.mybtn1.setCheckable(True)# SS2_3
        self.myui.mybtn1.setStyleSheet("background-color : green")# SS2_4
        self.myui.mybtn1.clicked.connect(self.mymethod_btn1)# SS2_5
        self.myui.mybtn1.clicked.connect(self.mymethod_btn2)# SS2_6
        self.show()

    def mymethod_btn1(self):# SS2_7
        print("Clicked")# SS2_8

    def mymethod_btn2(self,checked):# SS2_9
        print("Checked?", checked)# SS2_10


if __name__ == '__main__':
    myapp = QApplication(sys.argv)
    mywindow = MySignalSlot2_Window()# SS2_11
    sys.exit(myapp.exec_())
```

Output:

The output can be seen in *Figure 3.11:*

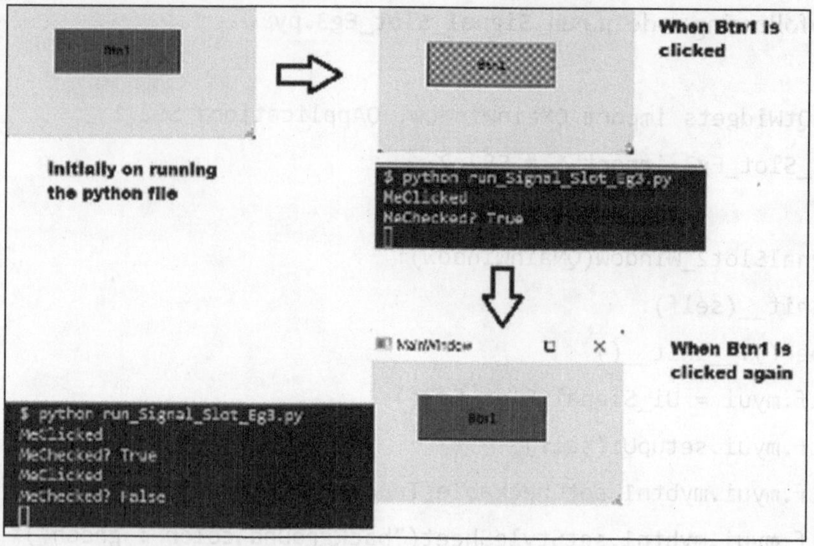

Figure 3.11: Output of Signal_Slot_Eg3_files/ Signal_Slot_Eg3.py

Note: The preceding code is covered in Program Name: Signal_Slot_Eg3_files/Signal_Slot_Eg3.py

Let us analyze the code.

- In **`SS2_1`**, after importing the **`sys`** module for accessing the command line arguments, we are importing from the class that creates desktop-style UIs of PyQt5 package, that is, **`QtWidgets`**, **`QMainWindow`** for providing a framework for creating new GUI interfaces, and an application handler, that is, **`QApplication`**.
- In **`SS2_2`**, from the **`Signal_Slot_Eg3.py`** Python file, we are importing all the members of a module.
- In **`SS2_3`**, when we explore the Property Editor of **`Btn1`**, we will find that the above property is **False**.

Refer to the following *Figure 3.12:*

Figure 3.12: Checkable property of button widget

- The **`checkable`** property is unchecked. So, by using this property, we can make the button widget checkable. So, it is set as **True**.
- In **`SS2_4`**, we are set the background color of the above button as **`green`**.

- In **SS2_5**, when the **mybtn1** button is clicked (click **event | signal**), **mymethod_btn1** (slot) will be invoked.
- In **SS2_6**, when the **mybtn1** button is clicked (click **event | signal**) **mymethod_btn2** (slot) will be invoked.
- In **SS2_7**, the **mymethod_btn1** method contains the default argument self only. This slot method has actually disregarded checkable/toggled data.
- In **SS2_8**, when the **mybtn1** button will be clicked, then **MeClicked** message will be displayed as shown in the figure output. Intentionally, the background color of the **mybtn1** button was set to **green** initially. After clicking, just observe the **mybtn1** button.
- In **SS2_9**, the **mymethod_btn2** method contains the default argument self and the checked argument.
- In **SS2_10**, when the **mybtn1** button will be clicked again, then **MeChecked?** message will be displayed, along with the status value of the checkable, which will be either **True/False** as shown in the output. On clicking the button first, the checked value was **True** and on clicking again it changed to **False**.
- In **SS2_11**, an instance of **MySignalSlot2_Window** class **mywindow** is created.

In the above example, we have connected two slots to a signal that clicked and responded to different signal versions simultaneously on our slots. Moreover, the message has been displayed in the console instead of the message box. All these approaches are being followed so that adjustments can be made anytime while coding for displaying the information to the user.

As we saw from the above example of receiving the data, we can store the data for the current widget state in a variable. This is just an exercise for practice.

Now, we shall see signals and slots in Qt Designer.

Till now, we have seen the creation of the slot method manually, which was reacting to the signal. However, now, with the help of Qt Designer, we will see how signal and slot will be used with the objects, which will either send a signal or receive a signal. There are some inbuilt methods inside PyQt5 that we can use. But before that, we must see some toolbar icons in Qt Designer, which will be used commonly.

Usage of Toolbar icons in Qt Designer

Refer to *Figure 3.13*:

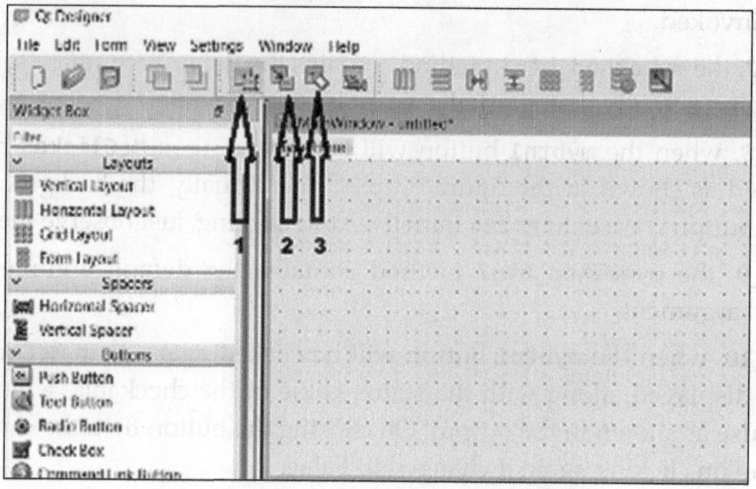

Figure 3.13: Some Toolbar Icons of Qt Designer

Figure 3.13 displays some toolbar icons with labels as 1, 2 and 3, as follows:

1. **Edit widget**: Edit widget is a default mode where we can perform multiple operations such as selection of widgets on a GUI form by dragging and dropping from **Widget Box**. Further, we can edit the objects on a GUI form or, with the help of Property Editor apply layouts to widgets, apply spacers, and so on.
2. **Edit Signals/Slots**: In **Edit Signals/Slots**, connections can be created with an object, and signals and slots for layouts and widgets can be connected. If the above icon is clicked, **Widget Box** is disabled, and on clicking on the Edit widgets, the **Widget Box** will be enabled again. With the help of the simple signals and slots mechanism in Qt, the objects in a GUI form can be connected.
3. **Edit Buddies**: In **Edit** Buddies, we are starting the connections at label widgets as the widgets in a GUI form will be similar to the editing mode of signals and slots. Here, each `label` widget providing a shortcut should be connected with an input widget like `QTextEdit` or `QLineEdit`. It is important to know that for each label, only one buddy connection can be defined.

Next to **Edit** buddies, is the **Edit Tab Order** (one highlighted in a transparent rectangular box), which will be used if there is a requirement to set the order for focusing widgets on pressing the *Tab* key as per ease of requirement.

All the above-discussed toolbar icons will be available under the **Edit** menu bar in Qt Designer.

Now, we shall see some useful applications with some widget objects.

Signal slot examples in Qt Designer

Consider the following Qt Designer file shown in *Figure 3.14:*

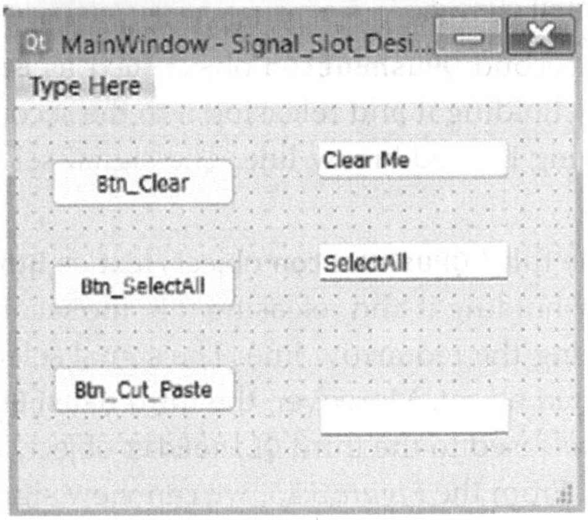

Figure 3.14: *Signal_Slot_Designer1.ui*

Note: The above .ui file is covered in Path: Signal_Slot_Designer_Files/Signal_Slot_Designer1.ui

In the above designer file, we use three **QPushButton** objects and three **QLineEdit** objects:

- Using the first **QPushButton** object, we are clearing the text present in the first **QLineEdit**, which is **Clear Me**.
- Using the second **QPushButton** object, we select the text present in the second **QLineEdit**, which is **SelectAll**.
- Using the third **QPushButton** object, we will remove the text in the second **QLineEdit** and paste the text in the third **QLineEdit**. So, the text will be **SelectAll**.

Let us see how we are doing this using Qt Designer:

1. Just click the **Edit Signals and Slots** Toolbar icon. The moment this icon is clicked, Widget Box will be disabled, and we can configure signals and slots.
2. We will see that the widget items that can be connected are highlighted the moment the mouse cursor moves over them. For the connection to be connected, we need to release the mouse button when we see a red arrow connecting the widgets. After that, only configuration of signals and slots will be left.
3. In this Qt Designer file, we are first selecting the **QPushButton** object (text as **Btn_Clear**) and then moving the mouse cursor by holding it and releasing it to **QLineEdit** object (text as **Clear Me**) after viewing the red arrow line. We are configuring the clicked signal

for **`QPushButton(Sender)`** object and a clear slot for **`QLineEdit(Receiver)`** object. The same can be viewed in the **signal/slot editor**. The object which sends the signal is the sender and the object which receives the signal is a Receiver. So, the *clear* method slot is reacting to the signal *clicked*.

4. Then we select the second **`QPushButton`** object (text as **Btn_SelectAll**) and then move the mouse cursor by holding it and releasing it to the second **`QLineEdit`** object (text as **SelectAll**) after viewing the red arrow line. The signal selected is *clicked* by the signal and slot as *selectAll*.
5. Finally, we select the third **`QPushButton`** object (text as **Btn_Cut_Paste**) and then move the mouse cursor by holding it and releasing it to the second **`QLineEdit`** object (text as **SelectAll**) after viewing the red arrow line. The signal selected is *clicked* by the signal, and the slot is selected as *cut*. Moreover, the third **`QPushButton`** **Btn_Cut_Paste** will be again selected and released to the third **`QLineEdit`** object. The signal selected is *clicked* and the slot *as paste*. From the *Figure 3.15*, we can view signals and slots:

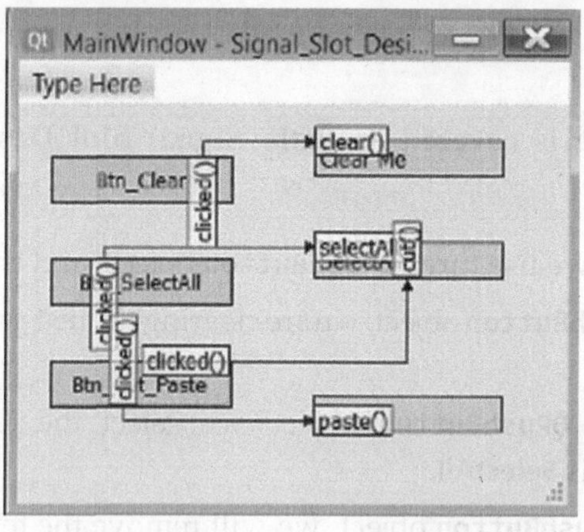

***Figure 3.15:** Signal and slots connection in Signal_Slot_Designer1.ui*

6. The same can be viewed in **Signal/Slot Editor**, as shown in *Figure 3.16:*

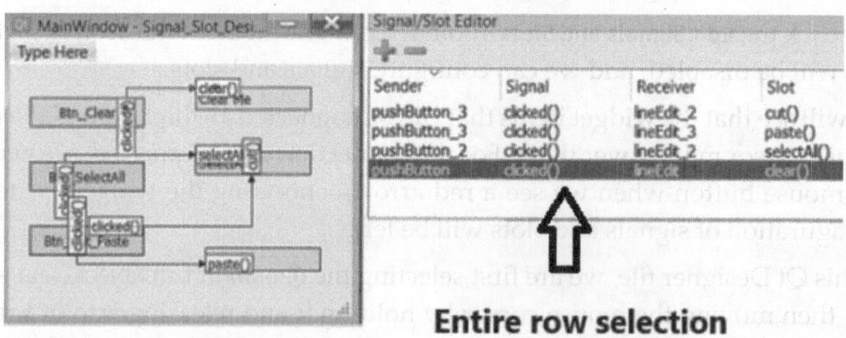

***Figure 3.16:** Signal/Slot Editor details in Signal_Slot_Designer1.ui file*

7. In *Figure 3.16*, we can see that the entire row is selected as displayed by the arrow, highlighting the widgets and signal/slot connections in the GUI form in pink color. From **Signal/Slot Editor**, we can view the entire widgets selected as Sender or Receiver in the GUI form with signals and slot details. So, let us run the above **.ui** file by pressing *Ctrl + R*. On running, the GUI form is shown in *Figure 3.17:*

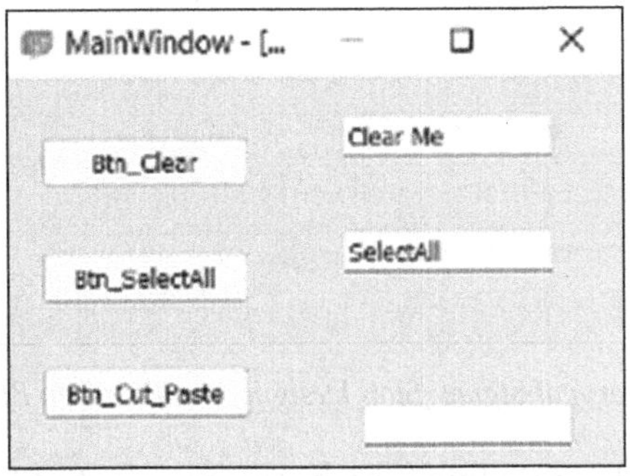

Figure 3.17: *Run Time GUI Form of Signal_Slot_Designer1.ui file*

8. Let us click **Btn_Clear** button and visualize the output, as shown in *Figure 3.18:*

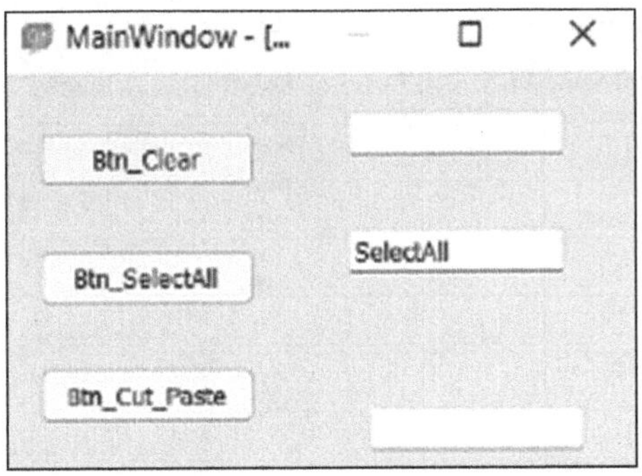

Figure 3.18: *Run Time GUI Form of Signal_Slot_Designer1.ui file when Btn_Clear button is clicked*

9. Now, on clicking **Btn_SelectAll** button, the **SelectAll** text in second **QLineEdit** object will be selected as shown in *Figure 3.19:*

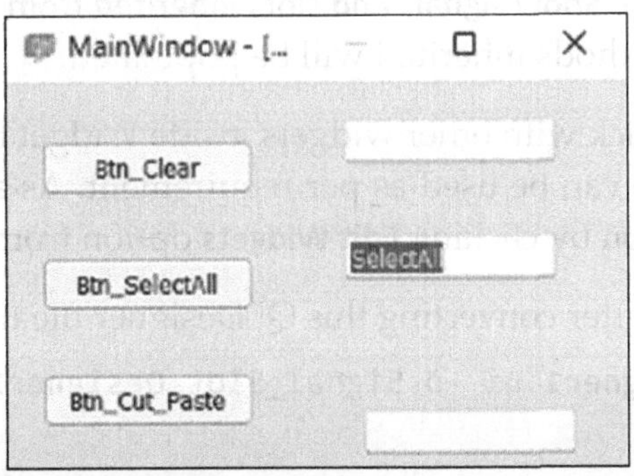

Figure 3.19: *Run Time GUI Form of Signal_Slot_Designer1.ui file when Btn_SelectAll button is clicked*

10. Now, on clicking the **`Btn_Cut_Paste`** button, the **`SelectAll`** text from second **`QLineEdit`** object will be cut and pasted into the third **`QLineEdit`** object, as shown in *Figure 3.20:*

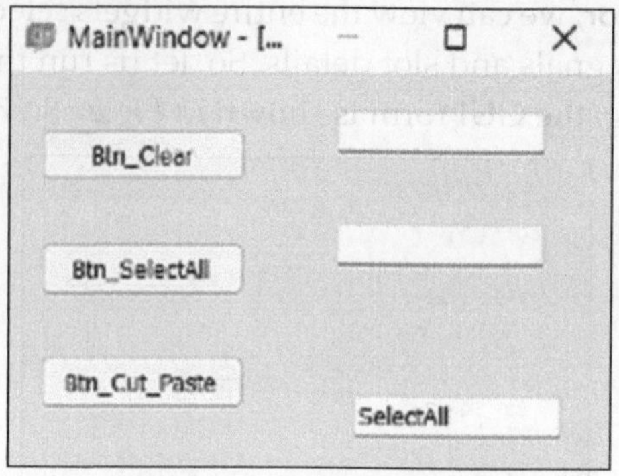

***Figure 3.20:** Run Time GUI Form of Signal_Slot_Designer1.ui file when Btn_Cut_Paste button is clicked*

11. There are other signals and slots which can be selected by using **`QPushButton`** widget and **`QLineEdit`** widget, as shown in *Figure 3.21:*

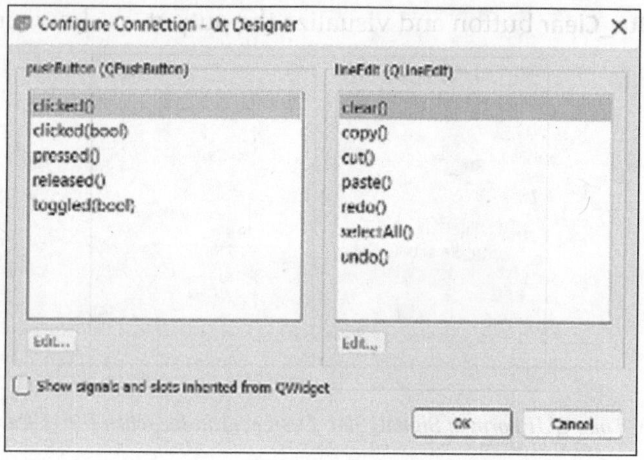

***Figure 3.21:** Signals and slots selection of QPushButton and QLineEdit widget*

12. If the user checks the **Show signals and slots inherited from QWidget** option, then all the signals and slots methods inherited will be populated.

We can perform the same trick with other widgets inside Widget box and see what the signals and slots are having, which can be used as per requirement. As already stated, we can come out of **Edit Signals/Slots** option by clicking **Edit Widgets** option from toolbar icon.

Let us see the Python code after converting this Qt Designer file using the command:

```
pyuic5 Signal_Slot_Designer1.ui -o Signal_Slot_Designer1.py
```

Signal_Slot_Designer1.py

```
from PyQt5 import QtCore, QtGui, QtWidgets

class Ui_MainWindow(object):
    def setupUi(self, MainWindow):
        MainWindow.setObjectName("MainWindow")
        MainWindow.resize(333, 260)
        self.centralwidget = QtWidgets.QWidget(MainWindow)
        self.centralwidget.setObjectName("centralwidget")
        self.pushButton = QtWidgets.QPushButton(self.centralwidget)
        self.pushButton.setGeometry(QtCore.QRect(20, 30, 111, 28))
        self.pushButton.setObjectName("pushButton")
        self.lineEdit = QtWidgets.QLineEdit(self.centralwidget)
        self.lineEdit.setGeometry(QtCore.QRect(180, 20, 113, 22))
        self.lineEdit.setObjectName("lineEdit")
        self.lineEdit_2 = QtWidgets.QLineEdit(self.centralwidget)
        self.lineEdit_2.setGeometry(QtCore.QRect(180, 80, 113, 22))
        self.lineEdit_2.setObjectName("lineEdit_2")
        self.pushButton_2 = QtWidgets.QPushButton(self.centralwidget)
        self.pushButton_2.setGeometry(QtCore.QRect(20, 90, 111, 28))
        self.pushButton_2.setObjectName("pushButton_2")
        self.lineEdit_3 = QtWidgets.QLineEdit(self.centralwidget)
        self.lineEdit_3.setGeometry(QtCore.QRect(180, 170, 113, 22))
        self.lineEdit_3.setText("")
        self.lineEdit_3.setObjectName("lineEdit_3")
        self.pushButton_3 = QtWidgets.QPushButton(self.centralwidget)
        self.pushButton_3.setGeometry(QtCore.QRect(20, 150, 111, 28))
        self.pushButton_3.setObjectName("pushButton_3")
        MainWindow.setCentralWidget(self.centralwidget)
        self.menubar = QtWidgets.QMenuBar(MainWindow)
        self.menubar.setGeometry(QtCore.QRect(0, 0, 333, 26))
```

```
        self.menubar.setObjectName("menubar")
        MainWindow.setMenuBar(self.menubar)
        self.statusbar = QtWidgets.QStatusBar(MainWindow)
        self.statusbar.setObjectName("statusbar")
        MainWindow.setStatusBar(self.statusbar)

        self.retranslateUi(MainWindow)
        self.pushButton.clicked.connect(self.lineEdit.clear)
        self.pushButton_2.clicked.connect(self.lineEdit_2.selectAll)
        self.pushButton_3.clicked.connect(self.lineEdit_2.cut)
        self.pushButton_3.clicked.connect(self.lineEdit_3.paste)
        QtCore.QMetaObject.connectSlotsByName(MainWindow)

    def retranslateUi(self, MainWindow):
        _translate = QtCore.QCoreApplication.translate
        MainWindow.setWindowTitle(_translate("MainWindow","MainWindow"))
        self.pushButton.setText(_translate("MainWindow", "Btn_Clear"))
        self.lineEdit.setText(_translate("MainWindow", "Clear Me"))
        self.lineEdit_2.setText(_translate("MainWindow", "SelectAll"))
        self.pushButton_2.setText(_translate("MainWindow", "Btn_SelectAll"))
        self.pushButton_3.setText(_translate("MainWindow", "Btn_Cut_Paste"))
```

If we observe the rectangular portion highlighted in the preceding code **Signal_Slot_Designer1.py** file, we will find that the signal clicked is connected to the **QPushButton** object names with **QLineEdit** object slots like **clear**, **selectAll**, **cut** and **paste**. These are all automatically generated codes with the usage of signals and slots. Hopefully, the concept of signals and slots using Qt Designer is clear. We shall see one more example.

Consider the following Qt Designer file in *Figure 3.22:*

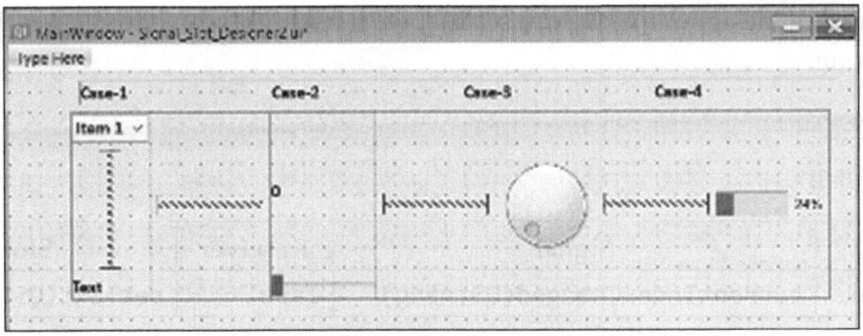

Figure 3.22: Signal_Slot_Designer2.ui

Note: The above .ui file is covered in Path: Signal_Slot_Designer_Files/Signal_Slot_Designer2.ui.

Now, we shall see the signal and slot connections of the above designer file, as shown in *Figure 3.23:*

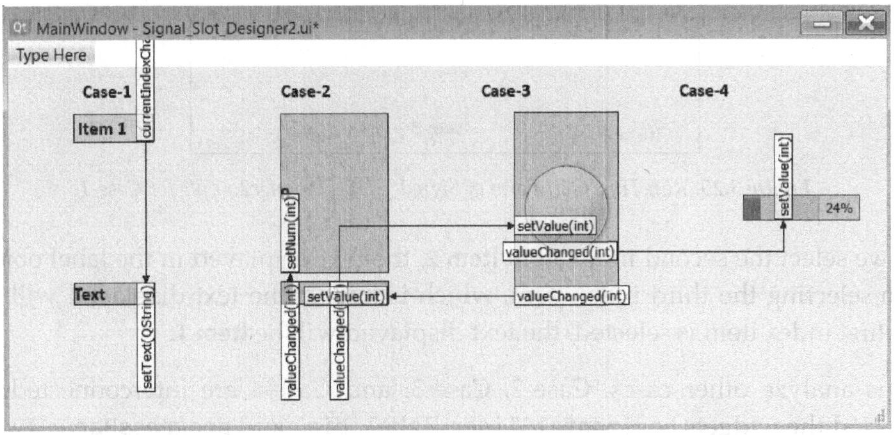

Figure 3.23: Signal and slots connection in Signal_Slot_Designer2.ui

Let us view the **Signal/Slot Editor** details in the above designer file, in the following *Figure 3.24*:

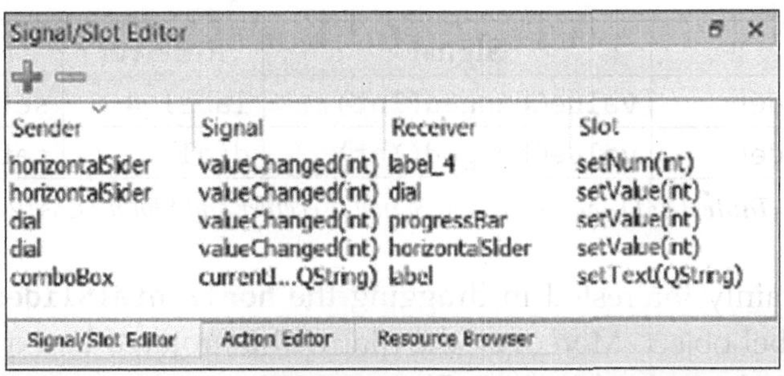

Figure 3.24: Signal/Slot Editor details in Signal_Slot_Designer2.ui file

From the preceding designer file, we can see that we have highlighted four cases. Let us discuss each, one by one.

Case-1:

Refer to *Table 3.3:*

Sender	Signal	Receiver	Slot
comboBox	currentIndexChanged(QString)	label	setText(QString)

***Table 3.3:** Details of Sender, Signal, Receiver and Slot for Case-1*

In Case-1, we are trying to get the text of the current index of the selected item from the **comboBox** object and displaying that text in the label object, as shown in *Figure 3.25:*

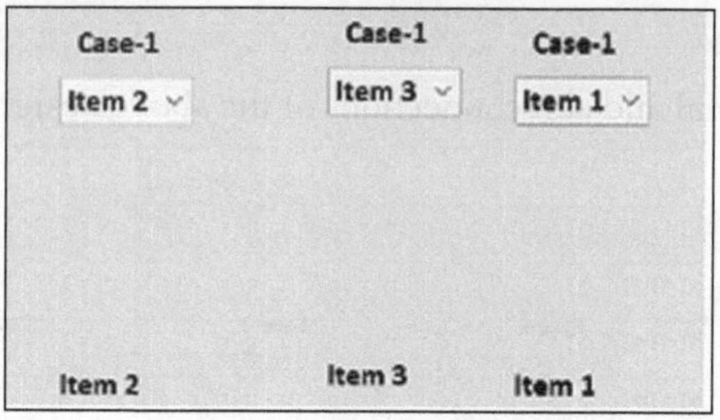

***Figure 3.25:** Run Time GUI Form of Signal_Slot_Designer2.ui file for Case-1*

So, when we select the second index item **Item 2**, the text displayed in the label object will be **Item 2**. On selecting the third index item, which is **Item 3**, the text displayed will be **Item 3**. When the first index item is selected, the text displayed will be **Item 1**.

Now let us analyze other cases. Case-2, Case-3, and Case-4 are interconnected. We have interconnected the widgets **horizontalSlider**, **label**, **dial** and **progressBar**.

Case-2:

Refer to *Table 3.4:*

Sender	Signal	Receiver	Slot
horizontalSlider	valueChanged(Int)	label_4	setNum(int)
horizontalSlider	valueChanged(Int)	dial	setValue(Int)

***Table 3.4:** Details of Sender, Signal, Receiver and Slot for Case 2*

In Case-2, we are mainly interested in dragging the **horizontalSlider** and displaying the integer value in a label object. Moreover, the dial will be rotated based on the movement of **horizontalSlider**. Refer to the following *Figure 3.26:*

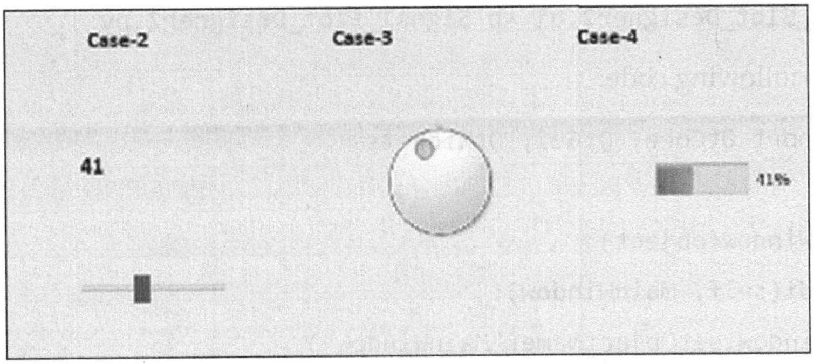

Figure 3.26: *Run Time GUI Form of Signal_Slot_Designer2.ui file for Case-2*

We move the **`horizontalSlider`** and a value is chosen by the user. This will result in a display of value on a **`label`** object, and based on the value selected, the slider position is displayed. It is also important to know that, by changing the value for the **`dial`** object, the **`progressBar`** value is set due to Case-4.

Case-3:

Refer to *Table 3.5:*

Sender	Signal	Receiver	Slot
`Dial`	`valueChanged(Int)`	`horizontalSlider`	`setValue(Int)`
`Dial`	`valueChanged(Int)`	`progressBar`	`setValue(Int)`

Table 3.5: *Details of Sender, Signal, Receiver and Slot for Case-3*

Refer to the following *Figure 3.27:*

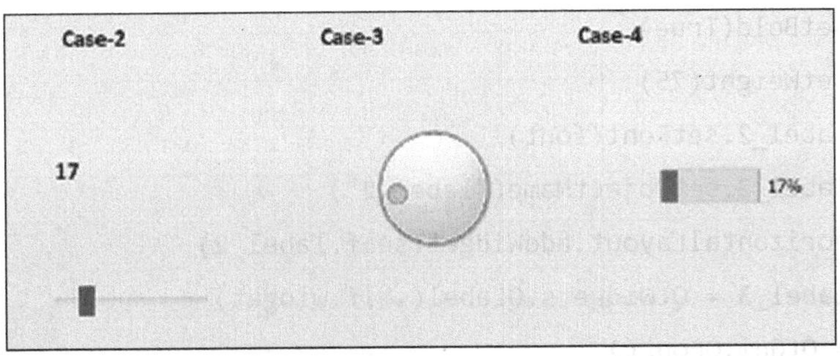

Figure 3.27: *Run Time GUI Form of Signal_Slot_Designer2.ui file for Case-3 and Case-4*

When the slider value of dial object is changed, we can see the effect of value in **`label`**, **`horizontalSlider`** and **`progressBar`** objects.

Let us see the Python code after converting this Qt Designer file using the command:

```
pyuic5 Signal_Slot_Designer2.ui -o Signal_Slot_Designer2.py
```

Just observe the following code:

```
from PyQt5 import QtCore, QtGui, QtWidgets


class Ui_MainWindow(object):
    def setupUi(self, MainWindow):
        MainWindow.setObjectName("MainWindow")
        MainWindow.resize(840, 277)
        self.centralwidget = QtWidgets.QWidget(MainWindow)
        self.centralwidget.setObjectName("centralwidget")
        self.widget = QtWidgets.QWidget(self.centralwidget)
        self.widget.setGeometry(QtCore.QRect(70, 10, 751, 23))
        self.widget.setObjectName("widget")
        self.horizontalLayout = QtWidgets.QHBoxLayout(self.widget)
        self.horizontalLayout.setContentsMargins(0, 0, 0, 0)
        self.horizontalLayout.setObjectName("horizontalLayout")
        self.label_2 = QtWidgets.QLabel(self.widget)
        font = QtGui.QFont()
        font.setFamily("Calibri")
        font.setPointSize(10)
        font.setBold(True)
        font.setWeight(75)
        self.label_2.setFont(font)
        self.label_2.setObjectName("label_2")
        self.horizontalLayout.addWidget(self.label_2)
        self.label_3 = QtWidgets.QLabel(self.widget)
        font = QtGui.QFont()
        font.setFamily("Calibri")
        font.setPointSize(10)
        font.setBold(True)
        font.setWeight(75)
        self.label_3.setFont(font)
```

```
self.label_3.setObjectName("label_3")
self.horizontalLayout.addWidget(self.label_3)
self.label_5 = QtWidgets.QLabel(self.widget)
font = QtGui.QFont()
font.setFamily("Calibri")
font.setPointSize(10)
font.setBold(True)
font.setWeight(75)
self.label_5.setFont(font)
self.label_5.setObjectName("label_5")
self.horizontalLayout.addWidget(self.label_5)
self.label_6 = QtWidgets.QLabel(self.widget)
font = QtGui.QFont()
font.setFamily("Calibri")
font.setPointSize(10)
font.setBold(True)
font.setWeight(75)
self.label_6.setFont(font)
self.label_6.setObjectName("label_6")
self.horizontalLayout.addWidget(self.label_6)
self.widget1 = QtWidgets.QWidget(self.centralwidget)
self.widget1.setGeometry(QtCore.QRect(60, 40, 751, 181))
self.widget1.setObjectName("widget1")
self.horizontalLayout_2 = QtWidgets.QHBoxLayout(self.widget1)
self.horizontalLayout_2.setContentsMargins(0, 0, 0, 0)
self.horizontalLayout_2.setObjectName("horizontalLayout_2")
self.verticalLayout = QtWidgets.QVBoxLayout()
self.verticalLayout.setObjectName("verticalLayout")
self.comboBox = QtWidgets.QComboBox(self.widget1)
font = QtGui.QFont()
font.setFamily("Calibri")
font.setPointSize(10)
```

```
font.setBold(True)
font.setWeight(75)
self.comboBox.setFont(font)
self.comboBox.setObjectName("comboBox")
self.comboBox.addItem("")
self.comboBox.addItem("")
self.comboBox.addItem("")
self.verticalLayout.addWidget(self.comboBox)
spacerItem = QtWidgets.QSpacerItem(20, 40, QtWidgets.QSizePolicy.
Minimum, QtWidgets.QSizePolicy.Expanding)
self.verticalLayout.addItem(spacerItem)
self.label = QtWidgets.QLabel(self.widget1)
font = QtGui.QFont()
font.setFamily("Calibri")
font.setPointSize(10)
font.setBold(True)
font.setWeight(75)
self.label.setFont(font)
self.label.setObjectName("label")
self.verticalLayout.addWidget(self.label)
self.horizontalLayout_2.addLayout(self.verticalLayout)
spacerItem1 = QtWidgets.QSpacerItem(48, 20, QtWidgets.QSizePolicy.
Expanding, QtWidgets.QSizePolicy.Minimum)
self.horizontalLayout_2.addItem(spacerItem1)
self.verticalLayout_2 = QtWidgets.QVBoxLayout()
self.verticalLayout_2.setObjectName("verticalLayout_2")
self.label_4 = QtWidgets.QLabel(self.widget1)
font = QtGui.QFont()
font.setFamily("Calibri")
font.setPointSize(10)
font.setBold(True)
font.setWeight(75)
self.label_4.setFont(font)
```

```
self.label_4.setObjectName("label_4")
self.verticalLayout_2.addWidget(self.label_4)
self.horizontalSlider = QtWidgets.QSlider(self.widget1)
self.horizontalSlider.setOrientation(QtCore.Qt.Horizontal)
self.horizontalSlider.setObjectName("horizontalSlider")
self.verticalLayout_2.addWidget(self.horizontalSlider)
self.horizontalLayout_2.addLayout(self.verticalLayout_2)
spacerItem2 = QtWidgets.QSpacerItem(78, 20, QtWidgets.QSizePolicy.
Expanding, QtWidgets.QSizePolicy.Minimum)
self.horizontalLayout_2.addItem(spacerItem2)
self.dial = QtWidgets.QDial(self.widget1)
self.dial.setObjectName("dial")
self.horizontalLayout_2.addWidget(self.dial)
spacerItem3 = QtWidgets.QSpacerItem(78, 20, QtWidgets.QSizePolicy.
Expanding, QtWidgets.QSizePolicy.Minimum)
self.horizontalLayout_2.addItem(spacerItem3)
self.progressBar = QtWidgets.QProgressBar(self.widget1)
self.progressBar.setProperty("value", 24)
self.progressBar.setObjectName("progressBar")
self.horizontalLayout_2.addWidget(self.progressBar)
MainWindow.setCentralWidget(self.centralwidget)
self.menubar = QtWidgets.QMenuBar(MainWindow)
self.menubar.setGeometry(QtCore.QRect(0, 0, 840, 26))
self.menubar.setObjectName("menubar")
MainWindow.setMenuBar(self.menubar)
self.statusbar = QtWidgets.QStatusBar(MainWindow)
self.statusbar.setObjectName("statusbar")
MainWindow.setStatusBar(self.statusbar)
self.retranslateUi(MainWindow)
self.comboBox.currentIndexChanged['QString'].connect(self.label.setText)
self.horizontalSlider.valueChanged['int'].connect(self.label_4.setNum)
self.horizontalSlider.valueChanged['int'].connect(self.dial.setValue)
self.dial.valueChanged['int'].connect(self.progressBar.setValue)
```

```
        QtCore.QMetaObject.connectSlotsByName(MainWindow)

    def retranslateUi(self, MainWindow):
        _translate = QtCore.QCoreApplication.translate
        MainWindow.setWindowTitle(_translate("MainWindow", "MainWindow"))
        self.label_2.setText(_translate("MainWindow", "Case-1"))
        self.label_3.setText(_translate("MainWindow", "Case-2"))
        self.label_5.setText(_translate("MainWindow", "Case-3"))
        self.label_6.setText(_translate("MainWindow", "Case-4"))
        self.comboBox.setItemText(0, _translate("MainWindow", "Item 1"))
        self.comboBox.setItemText(1, _translate("MainWindow", "Item 2"))
        self.comboBox.setItemText(2, _translate("MainWindow", "Item 3"))
        self.label.setText(_translate("MainWindow", "Text"))
        self.label_4.setText(_translate("MainWindow", "0"))
```

Note: The preceding code is covered in Program Name: Signal_Slot_Designer_Files/ Signal_Slot_Designer2.py

Just observe the rectangular box of the above Python code file where there is the generation of automatic code based on the signal and slot connection between the widgets.

With the help of Qt Designer signal and slots, we can perform many functions. It is recommended to explore the other widgets of Qt Designer, as it is difficult to cover all the signals and slot connections of the widgets in this book. From the next chapter, we will learn the categories of widgets in a Widget Box of Qt Designer in detail.

Conclusion

In this chapter, we have learned an in-depth understanding of events, signals, and slots in PyQt5 and demonstrated their practical application in creating desktop applications. The user has learned how to develop useful GUI form applications using Qt Designer and track mouse movements to trigger events such as changing the background color of a **QPushButton** widget. Through numerous examples, the concept of linking signals to slots has been illustrated, enabling the creation of simple user interface applications using the **QPushButton** widget.

Additionally, the chapter explored the creation of connections between Objects, signals, and slots for layouts and widgets, highlighting their versatility in Edit Signals/Slots. The presented case study examples further reinforce the knowledge and skills acquired throughout the chapter, which will empower the user to leverage these concepts effectively in their own PyQt5 projects.

Points to remember

- Events serve as notifications that something has occurred. A button click is an example of an event.
- Objects emit signals to notify other objects that something has happened. For instance, when a button object is clicked, a signal may be emitted.
- When a signal is emitted, functions called slots are activated. For instance, when a button object is clicked, a slot may be called.
- Signals and slots can be connected/disconnected to each other at any time.
- Edit widgets, Signals/Slots, and Buddies are all important Qt Designer elements that can assist designers in developing user interfaces that are more effective and efficient.
- Users may edit widgets to change their characteristics in the user interface. When changing the size, color, or other characteristics of widgets, this can be helpful.
- The use of buddies allows users to synchronize two widgets at all times. For example, the text in the text box will always be displayed in the label if a text box and a label is connected using this method.

Questions

1. Explain the role of events, signals, and slots for GUI designing in Qt Designer.
2. Explain signal/slot Editor usage in Qt Designer.
3. Show and explain the GUI form using Qt Designer for mouse operation.
4. Explain the following with their usage in GUI designing:
    a. Edit Widgets
    b. Edit Signals/Slots
    c. Edit Buddies
5. Explain the toolbar icons of Qt Designer and highlight their importance in GUI designing.
6. Write a short note on Edit Tab Order in Qt Designer.
7. Explain signal and slot connections in Qt Designer with some case studies.

Join our book's Discord space

Join the book's Discord Workspace for Latest updates, Offers, Tech happenings around the world, New Release and Sessions with the Authors:

https://discord.bpbonline.com

CHAPTER 4

Getting Insights of Button Widgets in Qt Designer

Introduction

In this chapter, we shall see our next anticipated topic for discussion, revolving around Button widgets in Qt Designer. The different buttons present in Qt Designer include **Push Button**, **Tool Button**, **Radio Button**, **Check Box**, **Command Link Button**, and **Dialog Button Box**. We will be discussing all these widgets in detail, including their description, importance and useful properties, methods/functions, and signals with examples. Our entire flow of discussion will not only be restricted to this chapter, and the same pattern will be followed in the explanation of other widgets of Qt Designer in the remaining chapters. All these button types will be available, as shown in the following *Figure 4.1*, in the Widget Box where the user can select any of the widgets under button types of Qt Designer and drag and drop in a GUI form. Please refer to the following figure:

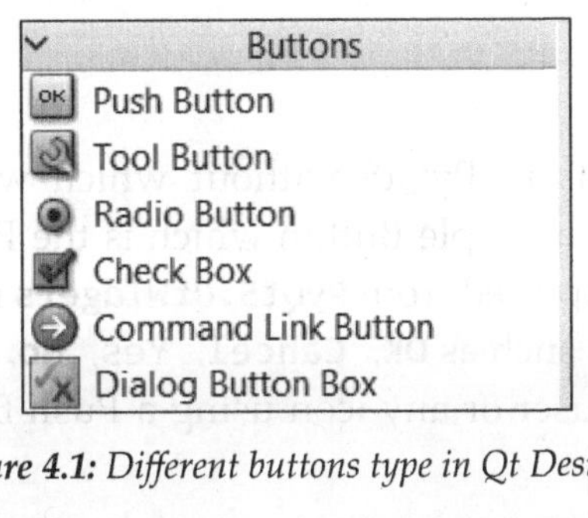

***Figure 4.1:** Different buttons type in Qt Designer*

Now, without any further delay, let us learn about different Button widgets. These Button widgets will come into handy when the user wants to interact with the GUI form widgets and waits for some kind of feedback. Icons or text can be displayed in PyQt5 using these Button widgets. The base class for Button widgets is **`QAbstractButton`** which provides checkable (toggle) buttons and Push Buttons support.

Structure

In this chapter, we will discuss the following topics:

- Push Button
- Tool Button
- Radio Button
- Check Box
- Command Link Button
- Dialog Button Box
- Common properties for Button widgets

Objectives

After reading this chapter, the reader will get to know about Button widgets, which are commonly used for creating interactive user interfaces. The primary objective of this chapter is to understand their properties, functionality, and customization options. By exploring the features and settings related to Button widgets, we can effectively design and implement user-friendly interfaces in our Qt applications. Qt Designer offers a number of different Button widgets, including **`CheckBox`**, **`PushButton`**, **`ToolButton`**, **`Radio Button`**, **`Command Link Button`** and so on. We shall explore description, properties, important methods, important signals and an application example with output display of each Button widget in detail. The important properties of **`QObject`**, **`QWidget`** and **`QAbstractButton`** are covered with images at the end as an add-on information. The same concept of common properties will be applicable for all further chapters.

Push Button

One of the most used widgets in PyQt5 without which we cannot imagine creating an application, is none other than a simple Button which is the Push Button. **`QPushButton`** class which represents a Button is imported from **`PyQt5.QtWidgets`** module. We have seen different buttons in various applications such as **`OK`**, **`Cancel`**, **`Yes`**, **`No`**, **`Help`** and so on. Generally, we can display simple text to the user or any icon using a Push Button. Its shape is rectangular.

Just remember, whenever we need to prompt some action to be done in the background of application using some click operation, the first widget which comes to your mind must be the Push Button.

Important properties

There are multiple properties that will be discussed. Just drag and drop a simple Push Button from Widget Box. Under **Property Editor**, we will see different properties which are headed under **QObject**, **QWidget**, **QAbstractButton**, and **QPushButton**. For all Qt objects, **QObject** class is the base class. Under this, we have the **objectName** property where some name is provided by the user. The name may be changed based on the requirement.

Note: It is important to know that properties for QObject, QWidget and QAbstractButton classes are common to all Button types, except the Dialog Button Box widget. Under this Dialog Button Box widget, we have the properties for QObject and QWidgetclasses only. In fact, every widget in Qt Designer will have the properties for QObject and QWidgetclasses.

The properties common for different Button widgets, that is, QObject, QWidget and QAbstractButton class are discussed at the end of this chapter.

Apart from the properties of these 3 classes, there are some other properties of the **QPushButton** widget, as can be seen in the following *Figure 4.2*:

***Figure 4.2:** Other QPushButton Properties apart from properties of 3 classes (QObject, QWidget and QAbstractButton)*

autoDefault

This property will enable the **autoDefault** Button property in a **QPushButton** widget. If the parent is **QDialog** for buttons, then this property default value is **True**. Otherwise, it is **False**. Auto-default button may have a larger size as it is drawn with some extra frames of 3 pixels or more.

default

From this property, we can decide whether **QPushButton** widget has a **default** Button property or not. It is disabled by default.

When the user presses *Enter* button from keyboard, the dialog's **default** button will automatically be pressed when this property will be enabled, that is, set to True but with an exception. If the **autoDefault** button is present and has *focus*, then this **autoDefault** button is pressed. If there is an **autodefault** button but no **default** button, then pressing *Enter* will press an **autodefault** button that has focus. If no button has focus, then pressing *Enter* will press the next **autodefault** button in the focus chain. We can see the behavior of the **default** button only in dialogs. From the keyboard, we can use a spacebar for clicking buttons when it has focus. If the property is set to False on the current **default** button, then a new **default** button will be automatically assigned the next time the **QPushButton** widget in the dialog will receive focus.

flat

This property will decide whether to raise the button border or not. It is unchecked by default. Unless the button is pressed, most styles will not paint the background when checked.

Important methods

Some important methods of **QPushButton** widget are as follows:

- **isChecked()**: Using this method, we will get the **QPushButton** widget Boolean state.
- **setCheckable()**: Using this method, we can distinguish the pressed and released state of the **QPushButton** widget when set to True.
- **text()**: Using this method, we will get the text from the **QPushButton** widget.
- **setText()**: Using this method, the text will be assigned to the **QPushButton** widget.
- **setDefault()**: Using this method, the **QPushButton** widget will be set as default.
- **setIcon()**: Using this method, an icon will be assigned to the **QPushButton** widget.
- **setEnabled()**: On using this method, if set to False, the signal will not be emitted from the **QPushButton** widget as it will be disabled.
- **toggle()**: From this method, there will be a change of state in the **QPushButton** widget as it will toggle between checkable states.

Important signals

The signals which can be used with this **QPushButton** widget, are shown in the following figure:

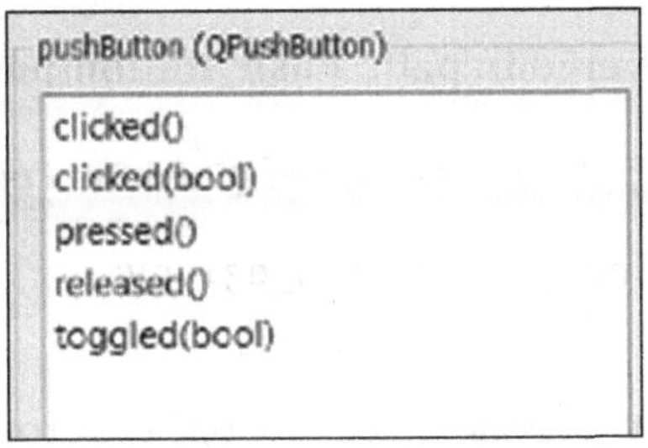

Figure 4.3: Signals in QPushButton widget in Qt Designer

- **`pressed()`**: This signal will be emitted when the left mouse button in **`QPushButton`** widget is pressed.
- **`released()`**: This signal will be emitted when the left mouse button in **`QPushButton`** widget is released.
- **`clicked()`**: This signal will be emitted when the **`QPushButton`** widget is clicked.
- **`toggled()`**: This signal will be emitted when the **`QPushButton`** widget state is changed.

Now, we shall see an example of the **`QPushButton`** widget where we see its usage of properties, methods, and signals.

The details of the file names are given in the following table:

S No.	Qt Designer File Name (.ui)	Converting the QtDesigner file name to Python file (.py)	Creating another Python file and importing the converted Python file from Qt Designer
1	**`pushbutton_eg1.ui`**	**`pushbutton_eg1.py`**	**`run_pushbutton_eg1.py`**

Table 4.1: Details of the file names

The Qt Designer file is shown in the following figure:

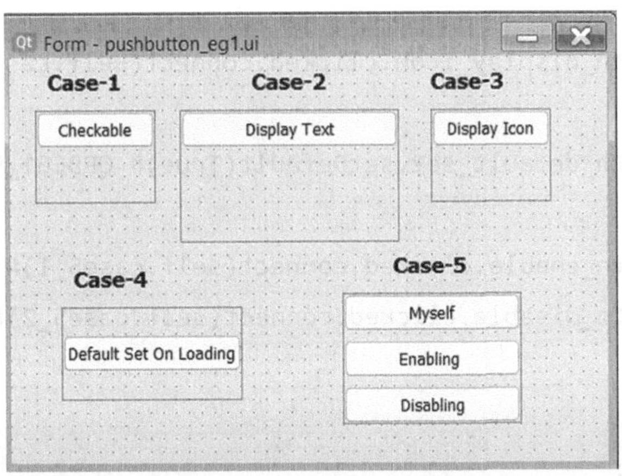

Figure 4.4: Qt Designer file: pushbutton_eg1.ui

Note: The above .ui file is covered in path: Push_Button/pushbutton_eg1.ui.

In this code, we are discussing 5 different cases of **QPushButton** widgets.

Consider the following code of **run_pushbutton_eg1.py**:

```
import sys
from PyQt5.QtWidgets import QMainWindow, QApplication  # QPBEG1_1
from pushbutton_eg1 import * # QPBEG1_2
from PyQt5.QtCore import Qt
from PyQt5.QtGui import QPixmap,QIcon# QPBEG1_3

class MyPushButton_Example(QMainWindow):
    def __init__(self):
        super().__init__()
        self.myui = Ui_Form()
        self.myui.setupUi(self)
        # Case1
        self.myui.btn_checkable.setCheckable(True) # QPBEG1_4
        self.myui.btn_checkable.toggle()# QPBEG1_5
        self.myui.btn_checkable.clicked.connect(self.case1)# QPBEG1_6
        # Case2
        self.myui.btn_displaytxt.clicked.connect(lambda: self.case2(self.myui.
        btn_displaytxt))# QPBEG1_7
        # Case3
        self.myui.btn_display_icon.clicked.connect(self.case3)# QPBEG1_8
        # Case4
        self.myui.btn_default_set.setDefault(True)# QPBEG1_9
        # Case5
        self.myui.btn_enable.clicked.connect(self.case5_1)# QPBEG1_10
        self.myui.btn_disable.clicked.connect(self.case5_2)# QPBEG1_11
        self.show()

    def case1(self):
```

```
        if self.myui.btn_checkable.isChecked():# QPBEG1_12
            self.myui.mylbl1.setText("I am checked")
        else:
            self.myui.mylbl1.setText("I am unchecked")

    def case2(self, mybtn):
        self.myui.mylbl2.setText("Text name is: " + mybtn.text())# QPBEG1_13

    def case3(self):
        display_icon_image = "E:/my_pythonbook/PyQt5/Chapter_4/Push_Button/
        help-contents copy.png"# QPBEG1_14
        try:
            with open(display_icon_image):
                self.myui.btn_display_icon.setIcon(QIcon(QPixmap(display_icon_
                image)))# QPBEG1_15
                self.myui.mylbl3.setPixmap(QPixmap(display_icon_image))
        except FileNotFoundError:
            print("Wrong image selection")

    def case5_1(self):
        self.myui.btn_myself.setEnabled(True)# QPBEG1_16
    def case5_2(self):
        self.myui.btn_myself.setEnabled(False)# QPBEG1_17

if __name__ == '__main__':
    myapp = QApplication(sys.argv)
    mywindow = MyPushButton_Example()# QPBEG1_18
    sys.exit(myapp.exec_())
```

Output:

The output here can be seen in the following multiple scenarios:

Case-1

When **Checkable** Button is clicked, there will be display of "**I am unchecked**" message in the **QLabel** widget as shown in *Figure 4.5:*

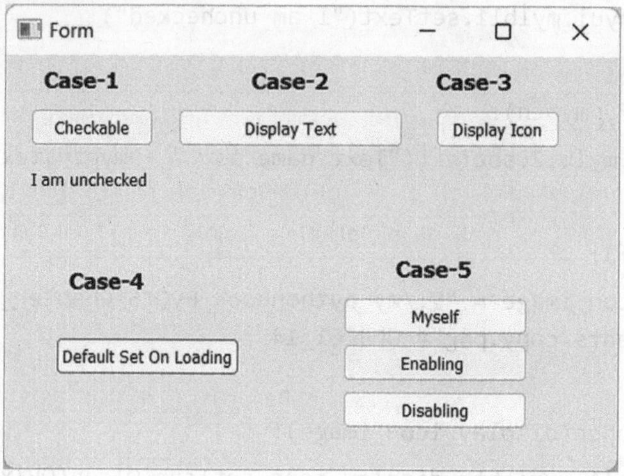

***Figure 4.5:** Output for Case-1 of run_pushbutton_eg1.py when checkable button is clicked*

On clicking of **Checkable** Button again, there will be display of "**I am checked**" message in the **QLabel** widget as shown in *Figure 4.6:*

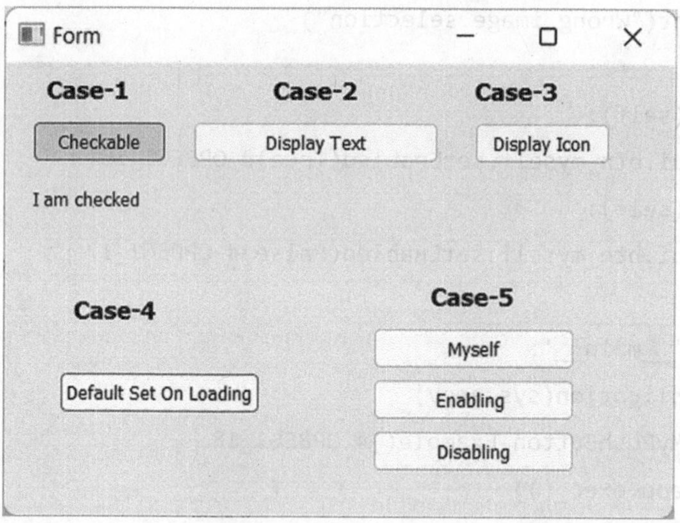

***Figure 4.6:** Output for Case-1 of run_pushbutton_eg1.py when checkable button is clicked again*

Case-2

When **Display Text** Button is clicked, there will be display of **Text name is: Display text** message in the `QLabel` widget:

Refer to the following figure:

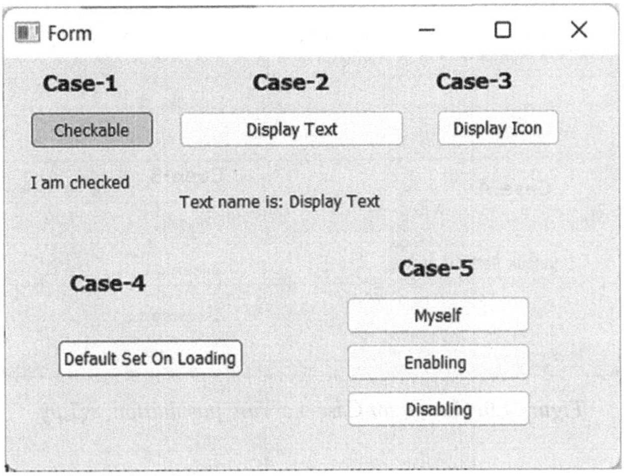

Figure 4.7: Output for Case-2 of run_pushbutton_eg1.py

Case-3

When you click the **Display Icon** Button, the icon will be displayed in both the **`button`** and **`label`** widget. Refer to the following figure:

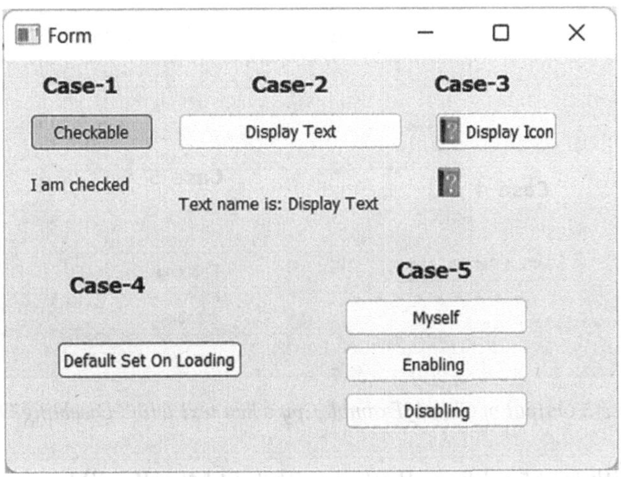

Figure 4.8: Output for Case-3 of run_pushbutton_eg1.py

Case-4

Default Set on Loading Button is focused on loading of GUI, as shown in the following *Figure 4.9:*

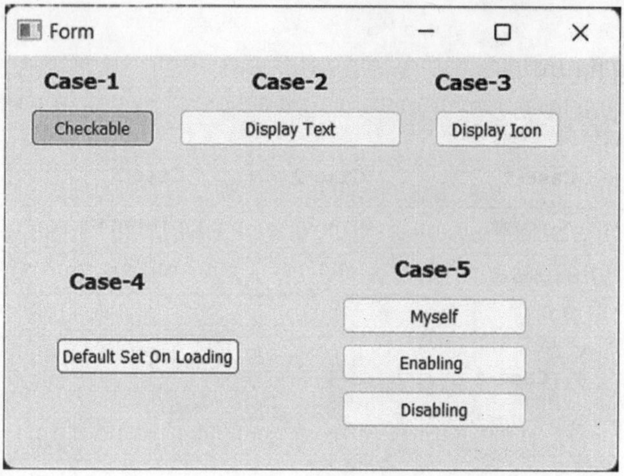

***Figure 4.9:** Output for Case-4 of run_pushbutton_eg1.py*

Case-5:

On clicking button with text **Disabling**, Button with text **Myself** will be disabled, as shown in the following *Figure 4.10:*

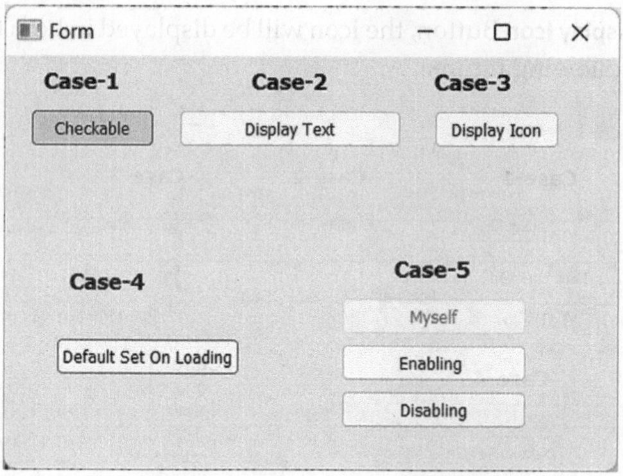

***Figure 4.10**: Case-5 Output of Chap4_Example1.py when text with "Disabling" button is clicked*

On clicking button with text **Enabling** , Button with text **Myself** will be enabled, as shown in the following *Figure 4.11:*

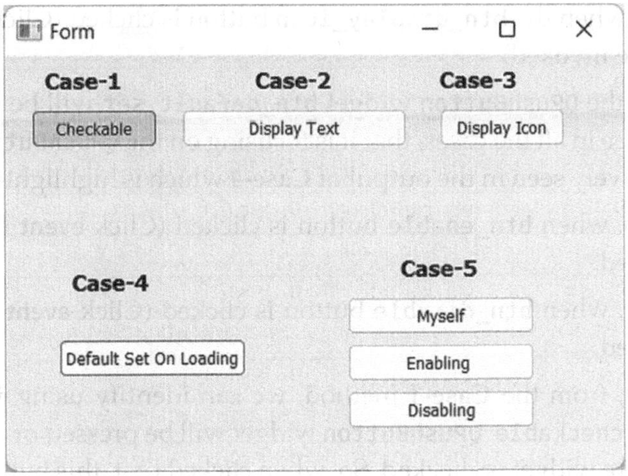

Figure 4.11: *Case-5 Output of Chap4_Example1.py when text with "Enabling" button is clicked*

Note: The preceding code is covered in Program Name: Push_Button/ run_pushbutton_eg1.py.

Let us understand important steps in the code:

- In **QPBEG1_1**, after importing the sys module for accessing the command line arguments, we are importing from the class which creates desktop-style UIs of **PyQt5** package, that is, **QtWidgets**, **QMainWindow** for providing a framework for creating new GUI interfaces and an application handler, that is, **QApplication**.
- In **QPBEG1_2**, from **pushbutton_eg1.py** Python file, we are importing all the members of a module.
- In **QPBEG1_3**, from the **PyQt5** package, we are importing from the class which contains graphical controls, that is, **QtGui**, **QPixMap** which provides the image's off-screen representation and **QIcon** class for the display of either small, large, active, or disabled pixmaps from the set of pixmaps.
- In **QPBEG1_4** and **QPBEG1_5**, our aim is to convert the **btn_checkableQPushButton** widget into a toggle button. So, first, we are setting the checkable state of this button widget to True for distinguishing its pressed and released state and then we are enabling this button widget for toggling.
- In **QPBEG1_6**, when **btn_checkable** button is clicked (Click **event | signal**) **Case-1** (slot) will be invoked.
- In **QPBEG1_7**, when **btn_displaytxt** button is clicked (Click **event | signal**) **Case-2** (slot) will be invoked by passing the argument as the **btn_displaytxtQPushButton** widget.

- In **QPBEG1_8**, when the **btn_display_icon** button is clicked (Click **event | signal**) **Case-3** (slot) will be invoked.
- In **QPBEG1_9**, the **QPushButton** widget **btn_default_set** will be set as default. That is why we can see in all the cases, that it is focusing on the **QPushButton** widget. The same can be exclusively seen in the output of **Case-4** which is highlighted in rectangular box.
- In **QPBEG1_10**, when **btn_enable** button is clicked (Click **event | signal**) **case5_1** (slot) will be invoked.
- In **QPBEG1_11**, when **btn_disable** button is clicked (Click **event | signal**) **case_2** (slot) will be invoked.
- In **QPBEG1_12**, from the **Case-1** method, we can identify using **isChecked()** method whether **btn_checkable QPushButton** widget will be pressed or released. Initially, this **btn_checkable** widget is checked. So, when clicked first, this button widget will toggle from checked to unchecked state and the message **I am unchecked** will be displayed. On clicking again, the message **I am checked** will be displayed.
- In **QPBEG1_13**, we are setting the text of the **mylbl2** widget with the text of **btn_displayQPushButton** widget text which is "**Displaytext**". So, on clicking the **btn_display** button, we will get the message in the **mylbl2** widget as the **Text name is: Display text.**
- In **QPBEG1_14**, we are storing the path of the **.png** extension file in an object variable **display_icon_image** (The path may be changed in your file system. You can write as per need).
- In **QPBEG1_15**, the icon will be displayed in **btn_display_icon** and **mylbl3** widgets after clicking the **btn_display_icon** button using the **setIcon()** method where an icon will be displayed as it will take **QPixmap** object as an argument for any image file. Also, using the **setPixmap** method, we are displaying an icon in the **QLabel** widget object too.
- In **QPBEG1_16**, on clicking **btn_enable** button, **btn_myself** button object will be set as enabled as we are using **setEnabled()** method and the argument passed is True.
- In **QPBEG1_17**, on clicking **btn_disable** button, **btn_myself** button object will be set as disabled as we are using **setEnabled()** method and argument passed is False.
- In **QPBEG1_18**, an instance of **MyPushButton_Example** class **mywindow** is created.

The concept of the **QPushButton** widget should be clear by now. We shall see our next widget which is the Tool Button widget.

Tool Button

Often, there comes a requirement for selecting commands or actions by providing quick access buttons. In such cases, we will be using Tool Buttons which are most commonly used in the `QToolBar` widget. We generally see an icon itself instead of text in a Tool Button widget.

Important properties

Apart from the properties of 3 classes (**`QObject`**, **`QWidget`** and **`QAbstractButton`**), there are some other properties of the **`QToolButton`** widget, and they are explained as follows:

popupMode

Refer to the following *Figure 4.12:*

Figure 4.12: *Image depicting popupMode property of QToolButton widget in Qt Designer*

Using this property, a menu containing a menu set or some action list will be described as well as how it will pop up for Tool Buttons. There are 3 constants:

- **DelayedPopup:** Here, the menu will be displayed on first pressing and then holding the Tool Button widget down for some time duration. One of the common examples we see is the usage of the back button in the web browser where a menu depicting the current history list will be displayed, if the user will press and then hold the button down. This is the default value to be displayed.
- **MenuButtonPopup:** If we use this constantly, then a special arrow is displayed in the Tool Button widget indicating that a menu is present and will be displayed on pressing the arrow part of the button.
- **InstantPopup:** If we use this constantly, then the menu will be displayed instantly with no delay on pressing the Tool Button widget.

toolButtonStyle

Refer to the following *Figure 4.13:*

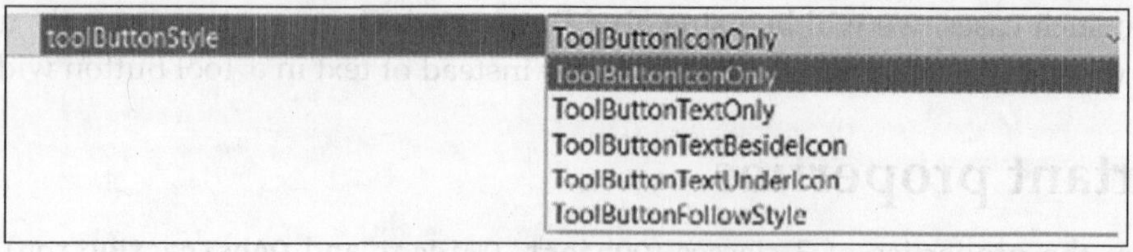

Figure 4.13: *Image depicting toolButtonStyle property of QToolButton widget in Qt Designer*

This property of the `QToolButton` widget will decide what to display on the Tool Button: whether text only or icon only or text beside the icon or text below the icon. We can see that the default value is **ToolButtonIconOnly**. If there is a requirement to follow the system settings, then set the above property with **ToolButtonFollowStyle**. The rest of the selections are self-explanatory.

autoRaise

Refer to the following figure:

Figure 4.14: *Image depicting autoRaise property of QToolButton widget in Qt Designer*

Using this property, we can enable the **autoRaise**. It is disabled, by default.

arrowType

Refer to the following *Figure 4.15:*

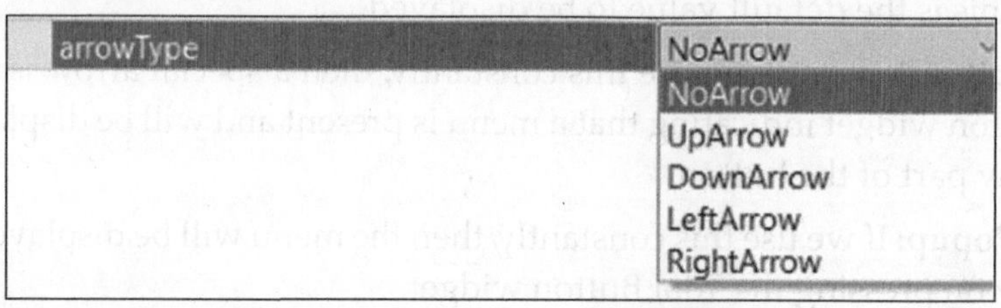

Figure 4.15: *Image depicting arrowType property of QToolButton widget in Qt Designer*

On using this property, there is a choice available for the user whether to display an arrow instead of an icon.

Important methods

Some of the important methods of **QToolButton** widget are as follows:

- **setAutoRaise()**: Using this method, we can check or uncheck the **autoRaise** feature of **QToolButton** widget.
- **setPopupMode()**: Using this method, we can describe the popup menu way with the **QToolButton** widget.
- **setToolButtonStyle()**: Using this method, we can set the display style of the **QToolButton** widget, that is, whether to display either text only or icon only or text beside the icon or text below the icon.
- **setMenu()**: Using this method, based on the **QToolButton** widget's popup Mode, the given menu can be associated with the **QToolButton** widget.

Important signals

The signals are similar to the **QPushButton** widget. In addition to it, we have triggered signal which will be fired only if we add some **QActionconnected** to the **QToolButton** widget using **addAction()** method, that is, when action is triggered, signal will be emitted. Refer to the following *Figure 4.16:*

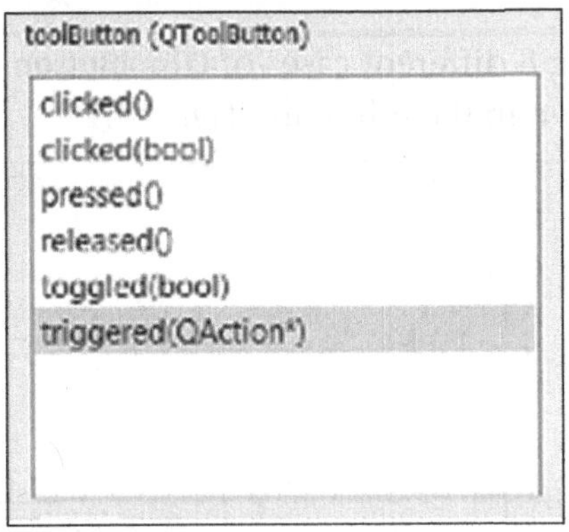

Figure 4.16: *Signals in QToolButton widget in Qt Designer*

This **QToolButton** widget is widely seen in day/today various applications like creating a Notepad, Wordpad, Paint and so on.

Let us create one simple application to understand this **QToolButton** widget.

The details of the file names are given in the following *Table 4.2*:

S No.	Qt Designer File Name (.ui)	Converting the QtDesigner file name to Python file (.py)	Creating another Python file and importing the converted Python file from Qt Designer
1	`toolbutton_eg1.ui`	`toolbutton_eg1.py`	`run_toolbutton_eg1.py`

Table 4.2: *Details of the file names*

The Qt Designer file **`toolbutton_eg1.ui`** is shown in the following figure:

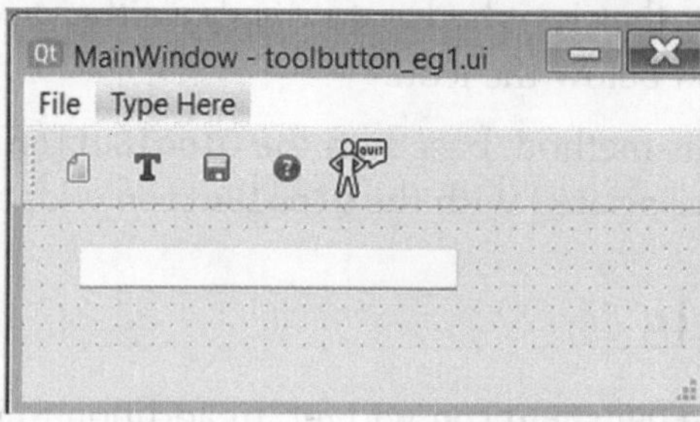

Figure 4.17: *Qt Designer file :toolbutton_eg1.ui*

Note: The above .ui file is covered in Path: Tool_Button/toolbutton_eg1.ui.

In this code, we are discussing 8 different cases of **QToolButton** widgets. The **Action Editor** of the above designer file is shown in the following *Figure 4.18:*

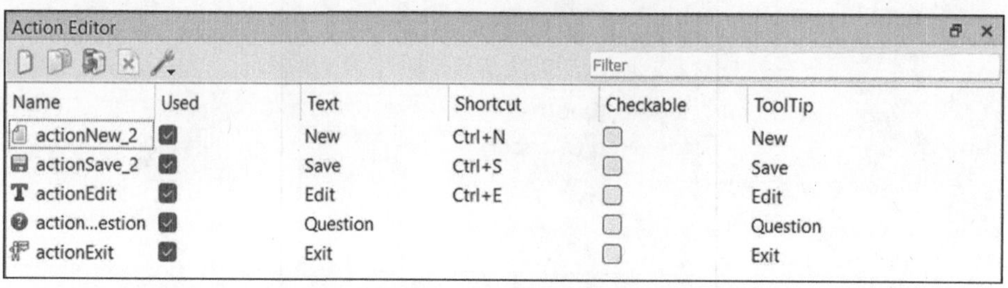

Figure 4.18: *Action Editor depicting QAction for toolbutton_eg1.ui*

Consider the following code of **`run_toolbutton_eg1.py:`**

```
import sys
from PyQt5.QtWidgets import QMainWindow, QApplication, QAction, QToolButton#
QTBEG1_1
from toolbutton_eg1 import *# QTBEG1_2
from PyQt5 import QtGui, QtCore
from PyQt5.QtCore import Qt
```

```
class MyToolButton_Example(QMainWindow):
    def __init__(self):
        super().__init__()
        self.myui = Ui_MainWindow()
        self.myui.setupUi(self)

        # Case-1
        self.myui.actionNew_2.setCheckable(True) # QTBEG1_3
      self.myui.actionNew_2.setStatusTip("New text will be displayed")# QTBEG1_4

        # Case-2
        self.myui.actionEdit.setCheckable(False)# QTBEG1_5
      self.myui.actionEdit.setStatusTip("Edit text will be displayed")# QTBEG1_6

        # Case-3
        self.myui.actionSave_2.setStatusTip("Save text will be displayed")#
        QTBEG1_7
        # Case-4
        self.myui.actionQuestion.setStatusTip("Question text will be
        displayed")# QTBEG1_8

        # addition of one toolButton using code

        # Case-5
        self.mytb_btn1 = QAction(QtGui.QIcon("C:/Users/SAURABH/Desktop/python
        course/search.gif"),"Search",self)# QTBEG1_9
        self.mytb_btn1.setStatusTip("Search text will be displayed")# QTBEG1_10
        self.myui.toolBar.addAction(self.mytb_btn1)# QTBEG1_11
        self.myui.toolBar.actionTriggered[QAction].connect(self.mydisplay)#
        QTBEG1_12

        # Case-6
```

```
        self.mytb_btn2 = QToolButton()# QTBEG1_13
        self.mytb_btn2.setCheckable(True)# QTBEG1_14
        self.mytb_btn2.setChecked(False)# QTBEG1_15
        self.mytb_btn2.setArrowType(Qt.LeftArrow)# QTBEG1_16
        self.mytb_btn2.setAutoRaise(True)# QTBEG1_17
        self.mytb_btn2.setToolButtonStyle(Qt.ToolButtonIconOnly)# QTBEG1_18
        self.mytb_btn2.clicked.connect(self.myshowDetail)# QTBEG1_19
        self.myui.toolBar.addWidget(self.mytb_btn2)# QTBEG1_20

        # Case-7
        self.mytb_btn3 = QToolButton()# QTBEG1_21
        self.mytb_btn3.setIcon(QtGui.QIcon("C:/Users/SAURABH/Desktop/python
        course/globe-green.png")) # QTBEG1_22
        self.mytb_btn3.setIconSize(QtCore.QSize(30,30))# QTBEG1_23
        self.mytb_btn3.setPopupMode(QToolButton.MenuButtonPopup)# QTBEG1_24
        self.myui.toolBar.addWidget(self.mytb_btn3)# QTBEG1_25

        # Case-8
        self.myui.actionExit.triggered.connect(self.exit)# QTBEG1_26
        self.show()

    def mydisplay(self, mytxt):# QTBEG1_27
        self.myui.lineEdit.setText(mytxt.text())# QTBEG1_28


    def exit(self):
        sys.exit()# QTBEG1_29


    def myshowDetail(self):
        if self.mytb_btn2.isChecked(): # QTBEG1_30
            self.myui.lineEdit.setText("Display...1")
        else:
            self.myui.lineEdit.setText("Display...2")# QTBEG1_31
```

```
if __name__ == '__main__':
    myapp = QApplication(sys.argv)
    mywindow = MyToolButton_Example()# QTBEG1_32
    sys.exit(myapp.exec_())
```

Output:

The output here can be seen in multiple scenarios.

Case-1: On clicking New QAction icon or pressing Ctrl+N

Refer to the following figure where Toolbutton image icon "**New**" is being clicked:

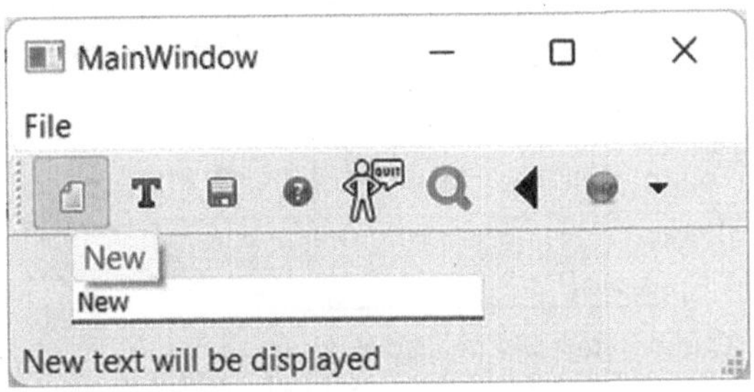

Figure 4.19: Case-1 Output for run_toolbutton_eg1.py

Case-2: On clicking EditQAction icon or pressing Ctrl+E

Refer to the following figure where Toolbutton image icon "**Edit (T)**" is being clicked:

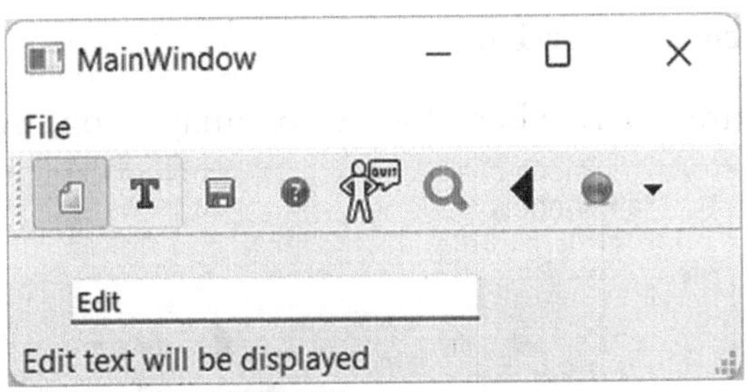

Figure 4.20: Case-2 Output for run_toolbutton_eg1.py

Case-3: On clicking Save QAction icon or pressing Ctrl+S

Refer to the following figure where Toolbutton image icon "**Save**" is being clicked:

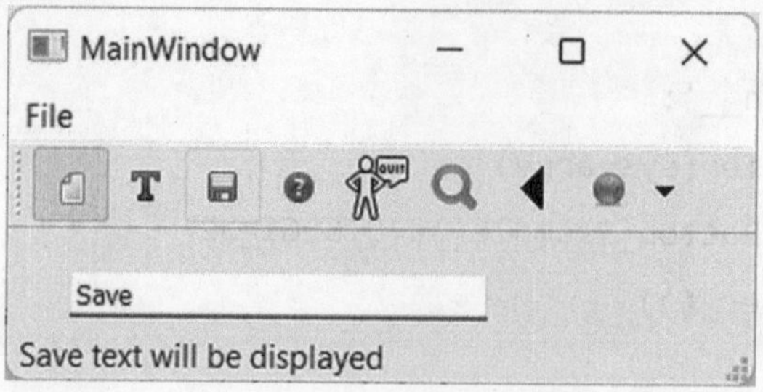

Figure 4.21: Case-3 Output for run_toolbutton_eg1.py

Case-4: On clicking Question QAction icon

Refer to the following figure where Toolbutton image icon "**Question (?)**" is being clicked:

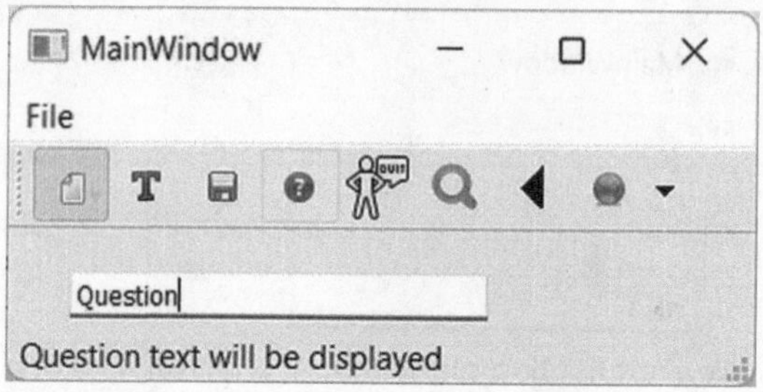

Figure 4.22: Case-4 Output for run_toolbutton_eg1.py

Case-5: On clicking ExitQAction icon

This will exit the entire application on clicking the Toolbutton image icon "**Quit**".

Case-6: On clicking Search QAction Icon

Refer to the following figure where where Toolbutton image icon "**Search**" is being clicked:

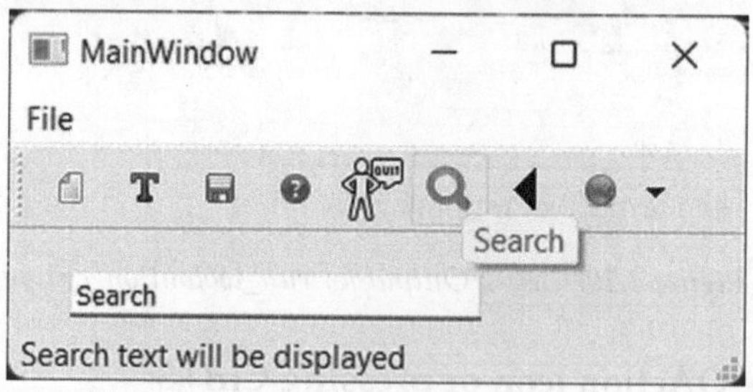

Figure 4.23: Case-6 Output for run_toolbutton_eg1.py

Case-7: On clicking Left Arrow QToolButton

Refer to the following figure:

When left arrow `QToolButton` is clicked first time.

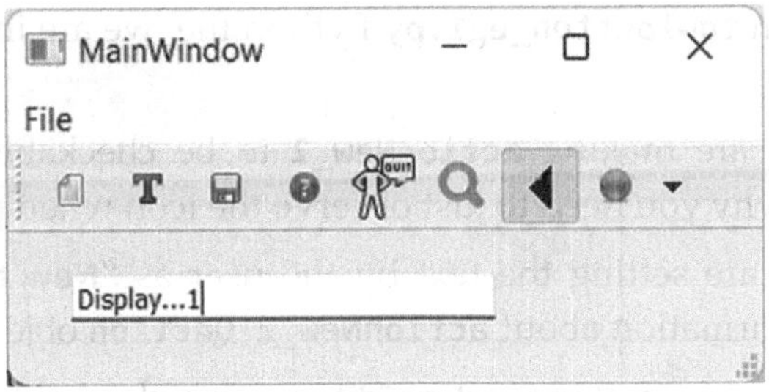

Figure 4.24: *Case-7 Output for run_toolbutton_eg1.py when Toolbutton image icon with arrow is clicked first time*

When left arrow **QToolButton** is clicked next time.

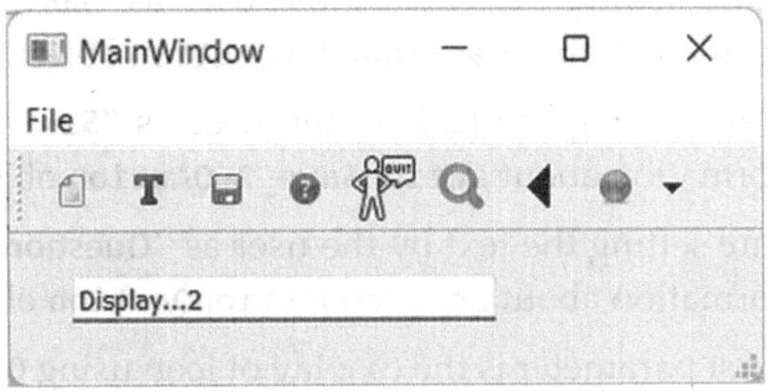

Figure 4.25: *Case-7 Output for run_toolbutton_eg1.py when Toolbutton image icon with arrow is clicked next time*

Case-8: QToolButton with MenuButtonPopupMode

Refer to the following figure which display the Toolbutton image icon with **MenuButtonPopup** Mode:

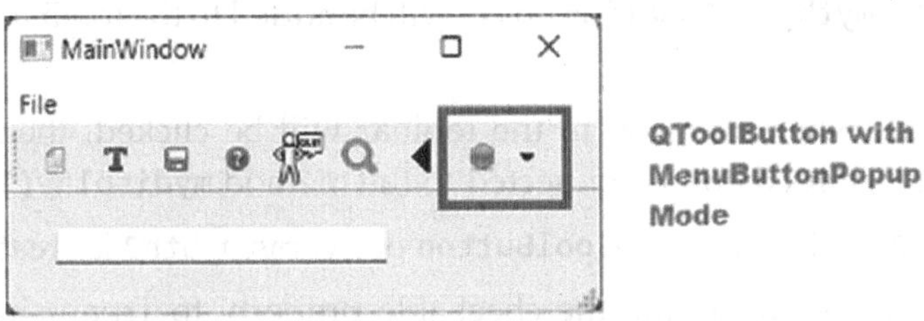

Figure 4.26: *Case-8 Output for run_toolbutton_eg1.py*

Note: The preceding code is covered in Program Name: Tool_Button/run_toolbutton_eg1.py.

- In **QTBEG1_1**, after importing the **sys** module for accessing the command line arguments, we are importing from class which creates desktop style UIs of PyQt5 package, that is, **QtWidgets**, **QMainWindow**, an application handler, that is, **QApplication**, **QAction** class for describing abstract user interfaces and **QToolButton** widget.

- In **QTBEG1_2**, from **toolbutton_eg1.py** Python file, we are importing all the members of a module.
- In **QTBEG1_3**, we are making **actionNew_2** to be checkable using **setCheckable()** method. That is why you need to just observe the icon when pressed as seen in **Case-1**.
- In **QTBEG1_4**, we are setting the text by the user as "**New text will be displayed**" for providing the information about **actionNew_2 QAction** object.
- In **QTBEG1_5**, we are making **actionEdit** as non-checkable using **setCheckable()** method. That is why you need to just observe the icon when pressed, as seen in **Case-2**. This is done to explain the difference between icons of first 2 cases.
- In **QTBEG1_6**, we are setting the text by the user as "**Edit text will be displayed**" for providing the information about **actionEditQAction** object.
- In **QTBEG1_7**, we are setting the text by the user as "**Save text will be displayed**" for providing the information about **actionSave_2 QAction** object as seen in **Case-3**.
- In **QTBEG1_8**, we are setting the text by the user as "**Question text will be displayed**" for providing the information about **actionQuestionQAction** object as seen in **Case-4**.
- In **QTBEG1_9**, the first parameter is the display of icon using **QIcon** method. The second parameter is the string which is "**Search**" and finally the parent for the action will be the current main window, and that is why it is passing self as a reference as third argument.
- In **QTBEG1_10**, we are setting the text by the user as "**Search text will be displayed**" for providing the information about **mytb_btn1QAction** object.
- In **QTBEG1_11**, **mytb_btn1QAction** object will be added to the toolbar using **addAction()** method.
- In **QTBEG1_12**, when any icon in the toolbar will be clicked, then **actionTriggered** signal will be emitted and is connected to the method **mydisplay()**as seen in **Case-6**.
- In **QTBEG1_13**, an instance of **QToolButton** object **mytb_btn2** is created.
- In **QTBEG1_14**, we are setting the checkable property to True using **setCheckable()** method of **mytb_btn2** object.
- In **QTBEG1_15**, initially **mytb_btn2** object is unchecked.
- In **QTBEG1_16**, we are displaying an arrow as **LeftArrow** for **mytb_btn2** object.
- In **QTBEG1_17**, the **autoRaise** property is set as True for **mytb_btn2** object.
- In **QTBEG1_18**, the display style of **QToolButton mytb_btn2** object is set as **ToolButtonIconOnly**.
- In **QTBEG1_19**, when **mytb_btn2** object is clicked (click **event | signal**) **myshowDetail** (slot) will be invoked.

- In **QTBEG1_20**, we are adding the **mytb_btn2** object into the toolbar using **addWidget()** method.
- In **QTBEG1_21**, an instance of **QToolButton** object **mytb_btn3** is created.
- In **QTBEG1_22**, we are adding an icon to **mytb_btn3** object.
- In **QTBEG1_23**, the size of an icon is set as with width and height both set as 30,30.
- In **QTBEG1_24**, the popup menu way with **mytb_btn3** object is described as **MenuButtonPopup**. Just observe in **Case-8**.
- In **QTBEG1_25**, we are adding the **mytb_btn3** object into the toolbar as seen in **Case-8**.
- In **QTBEG1_26**, we are closing an application when triggered signal is emitted when **actionExitQAction** object is clicked as seen in **Case-5**.
- In **QTBEG1_27**, **mydisplay()** method contains an additional parameter as **mytxt**.
- In **QTBEG1_28**, we are displaying the text of **QAction** object when clicked on the toolbar into the **QLineEdit** widget. We can observe the output from Cases 1,2,3,4 and 6. Also, using shortcuts, the text can be displayed for Case-1,2 and 3.
- In **QTBEG1_29**, we are closing an application and will be executed when **actionExitQAction** object is clicked.
- In **QTBEG1_30**, we are checking whether **mytb_btn2** object is checked or not.
- In **QTBEG1_31**, Display…1 will be first displayed and then Display…2 on the input widget as initially we are first checking and then unchecking. Observe the output in **Case-7**.
- In **QTBEG1_32**, an instance of **MyToolButton_Example** class **mywindow** is created.

Radio Button

This widget will mainly be used when we need to select only one option from multiple options of a GUI form. We can provide some text label with any selectable button. If any of the **QRadioButton** widget is selected, then there will be deselection of the previously selected button since it is auto-exclusive by default. We mostly used the above widget with **QButtonGroup** or **QGroupBox**.

Important properties

It contains properties of 3 classes:

- **QObject**
- **QWidget**
- **QAbstractButton**

Important methods

Some important methods are as follows:

- **`isChecked()`**: Using this method, Boolean value will be returned if the **`QRadioButton`** widget is selected.
- **`setChecked()`**: Using this method, we can select/deselect the **`QRadioButton`** widget based on the Boolean value passed.
- **`text()`**: Using this method, we can retrieve the text of **`QRadioButton`** widget.
- **`setText()`**: From the name we can guess that using this method, will set the text of **`QRadioButton`** widget.
- **`setIcon()`**: Using this method, an icon will be displayed with **`QRadioButton`** widget.

Important signals

The signals are similar to **`QPushButton`** widget. Refer to *Figure 4.27:*

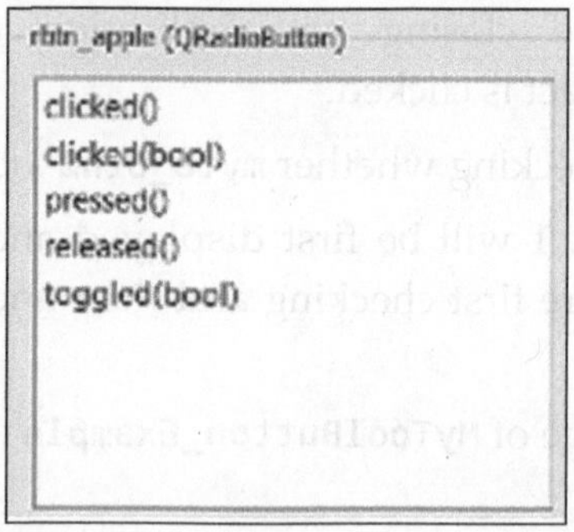

***Figure 4.27:** Signals in QRadioButton widget in Qt Designer*

Let us create one simple application to understand this **`QRadioButton`** widget. The details of file names are as shown in the following *Table 4.3:*

S No.	Qt Designer File Name (.ui)	Converting the QtDesigner file name to Python file (.py)	Creating another Python file and importing the converted Python file from Qt Designer
1	**`radiobutton_eg1.ui`**	**`radiobutton _eg1.py`**	**`run_radiobutton_eg1.py`**

***Table 4.3:** Details of the file names*

The Qt Designer file **radiobutton_eg1.ui** is shown in the following figure:

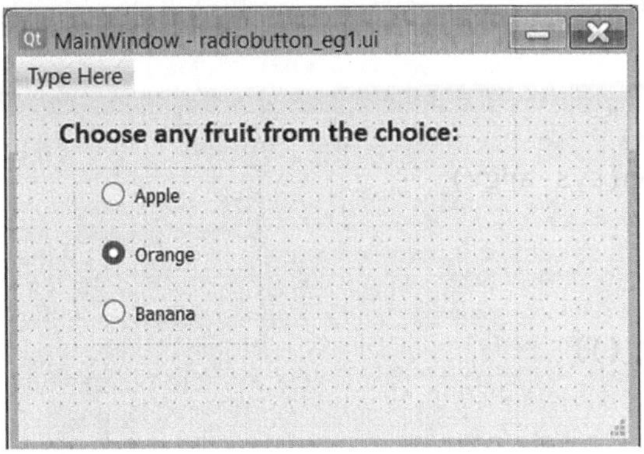

Figure 4.28: Qt Designer file: radiobutton_eg1.ui

Note: The above .ui file is covered in Path: Radio_Button/radiobutton_eg1.ui.

Consider the following code of **run_radiobutton_eg1.py:**

```
import sys
from PyQt5.QtWidgets import QMainWindow, QApplication
from radiobutton_eg1 import * # RBEG1_1

class MyForm(QMainWindow):
    def __init__(self):
        super().__init__()
        self.ui = Ui_MainWindow()
        self.ui.setupUi(self)
        self.ui.rbtn_apple.toggled.connect(lambda:self.myselfcheck(self.
        ui.rbtn_apple)) # RBEG1_2
        self.ui.rbtn_orange.toggled.connect(lambda:self.myselfcheck(self.
        ui.rbtn_orange)) # RBEG1_3
        self.ui.rbtn_banana.toggled.connect(lambda:self.myselfcheck(self.
        ui.rbtn_banana)) # RBEG1_4
        self.show()

    def myselfcheck(self, myradiobutton): # RBEG1_5
        if myradiobutton.isChecked(): # RBEG1_6
```

```
                self.ui.lbldisplay.setText(myradiobutton.text() + " is selected")
                # RBEG1_7


if __name__=="__main__":
    app = QApplication(sys.argv)
    w = MyForm()
    w.show()
    sys.exit(app.exec_())
```

Output:

Refer to the following *Figure 4.29:*

Case-1: Default output initially on executing the code

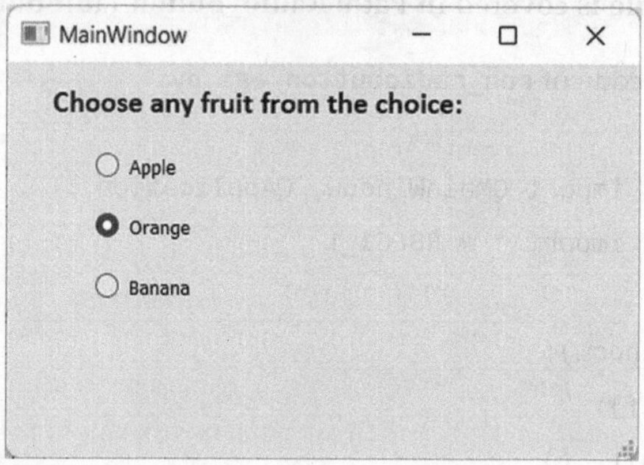

Figure 4.29: *Case-1 Output of run_radiobutton_eg1.py*

Case-2: When radiobutton with text as Apple is clicked

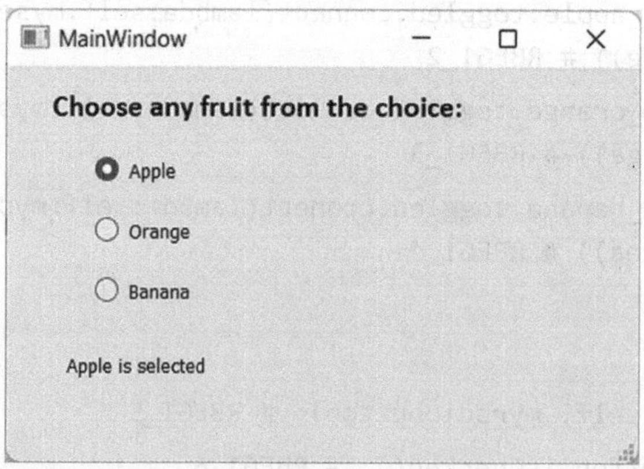

Figure 4.30: *Case-2 Output of run_radiobutton_eg1.py*

Case-3: When radiobutton with text as Orange is clicked

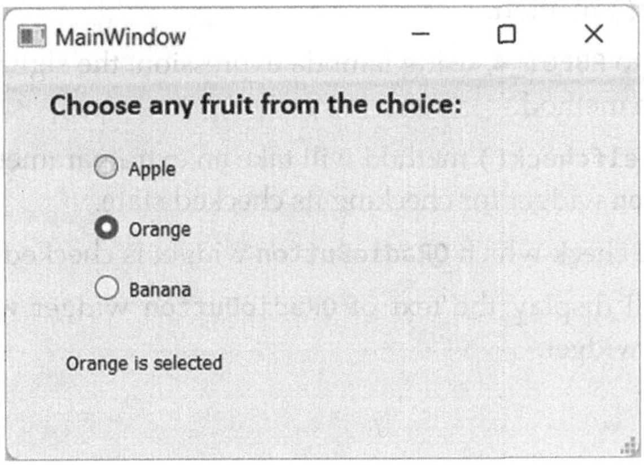

Figure 4.31: Case-3 Output of run_radiobutton_eg1.py

Case-4: When radiobutton with text as Banana is clicked

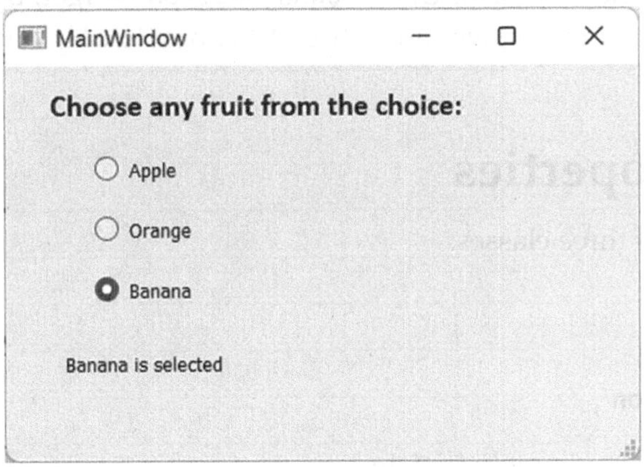

Figure 4.32: Case-4 Output of run_radiobutton_eg1.py

Note: The preceding code is covered in Program Name: Radio_Button/run_radiobutton_eg1.py.

Let us understand the code:

- In **RBEG1_1**, from **radiobutton_eg1.py** Python file we are importing all the members of a module.
- In **RBEG1_2**, we are connecting the toggled signal of **QRadioButton** widget **rbtn_apple** to **myselfcheck()** method.
- In **RBEG1_3**, we are connecting the toggled signal of **QRadioButton** widget **rbtn_orange** to **myselfcheck()** method.

- In **RBEG1_4**, we are connecting the toggled signal of **QRadioButton** widget **rbtn_banana** to **myselfcheck()** method.
- From **RBEG1_2** to **RBEG1_4**, using lambda expression, the signal source is passed as an argument to the method.
- In **RBEG1_5**, **myselfcheck()** method will take an extra parameter which acts as sender for **QRadioButton** widget for checking its checked state.
- In **RBEG1_6**, will check which **QRadioButton** widget is checked.
- In **RBEG1_7**, will display the text of **QRadioButton** widget which is checked in the **QLabel** display widget.

Check Box

Whenever there is a requirement to use a selectable button and select more than one option, then we shall choose **QCheckBox** widget from Widget Box. The appearance of this widget is a rectangular box before the text label. Unlike **QRadioButton** widget, by default, this widget is not mutually exclusive. However, we can restrict the choice to only one of the items by adding to the **QButtonGroup**.

Important properties

It contains properties of three classes:

- **QObject**
- **QWidget**
- **QAbstractButton**

There is one more property, namely tristate.

tristate

This property when set to True, will make the **QCheckBox** widget behave as a tri-state checkbox. The default state is False.

Important methods

Some important methods are as follows:

- **`isChecked()`**: Using this method, Boolean value will be returned if the **`QCheckBox`** widget is selected.
- **`setChecked()`**: Using this method, we can select/deselect the **`QCheckBox`** widget based on the Boolean value passed.
- **`text()`**: Using this method, we can retrieve the text of **`QCheckBox`** widget.
- **`setText()`**: Using this method, will set the text of **`QCheckBox`** widget.
- **`setIcon()`**: Using this method, an icon will be displayed with **`QCheckBox`** widget.
- **`setTriState()`**: When Boolean value is passed as True, we are adding third state to **`QCheckBox`** widget which is neither True or False.

Important signals

The signals are similar to **`QPushButton`** widget. In addition to it, we have **`stateChanged(int)`** signal, which will return the **`QCheckBox`** widget's check state. Refer to *Figure 4.33:*

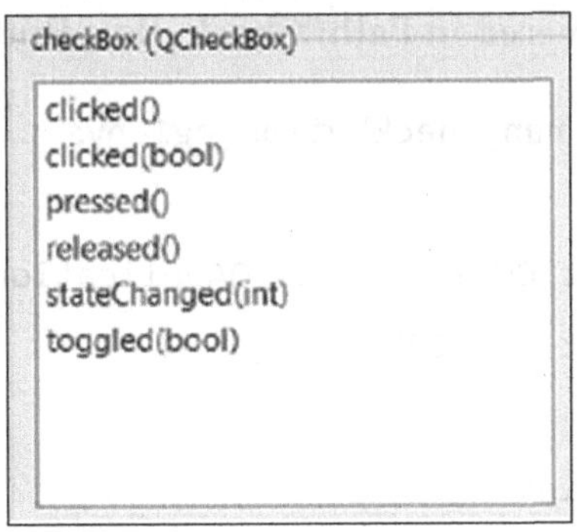

***Figure 4.33:** Signals in QCheckBox widget in Qt Designer*

Let us create one simple application to understand this **`QCheckBox`** widget. The details of the file names are as shown in the following *Table 4.5*:

S No.	Qt Designer File Name (.ui)	Converting the QtDesigner file name to Python file (.py)	Creating another Python file and importing the converted Python file from Qt Designer
1	**`checkbutton_eg1.ui`**	**`checkbutton _eg1.py`**	**`run_checkbutton_eg1.py`**

***Table 4.5:** Details of the file names*

The Qt Designer file **checkbutton_eg1.ui** is shown in the following figure:

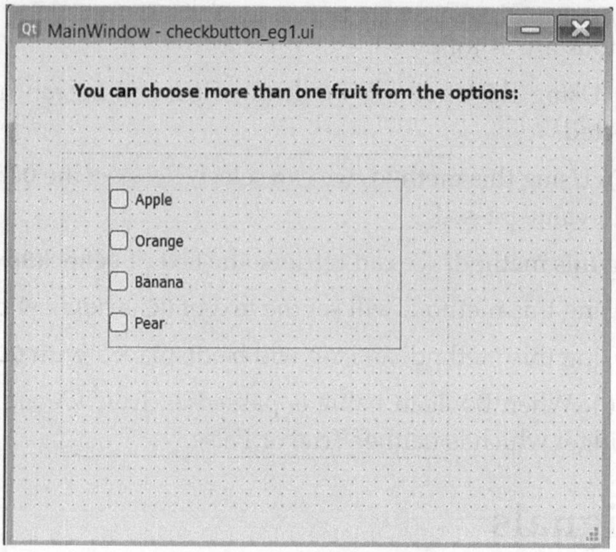

Figure 4.34: Qt Designer file: checkbutton_eg1.ui

Note: The above .ui file is covered in Path: Check_Box_Button/checkbutton_eg1.ui.

Consider the following code of **run_checkbutton_eg1.py**:

```
import sys
from PyQt5.QtWidgets import QMainWindow, QApplication
from checkbutton_eg1 import * # CBEG1_1

class MyCheckButton(QMainWindow):
    def __init__(self):
        super().__init__()
        self.ui = Ui_MainWindow()
        self.ui.setupUi(self)
        self.myfruits = {'apple':0, 'orange':0, 'banana':0, 'pear':0} # CBEG1_2
        self.ui.chk_Apple.stateChanged.connect(lambda:self.myselfcheck(self.
        ui.chk_Apple)) # CBEG1_3
        self.ui.chk_Orange.stateChanged.connect(lambda:self.myselfcheck(self.
        ui.chk_Orange)) # CBEG1_4
        self.ui.chk_Banana.stateChanged.connect(lambda:self.myselfcheck(self.
        ui.chk_Banana)) # CBEG1_5
```

```
        self.ui.chk_Pear.stateChanged.connect(lambda:self.myselfcheck(self.
        ui.chk_Pear)) # CBEG1_6
        self.show()

    def myselfcheck(self, mychkbutton): # CBEG1_7
        if self.ui.chk_Apple.text() == "Apple" :  # CBEG1_8
            if self.ui.chk_Apple.isChecked(): # CBEG1_9
                self.myfruits['apple'] = 1
            else:
                self.myfruits['apple'] = 0

            self.mydisplay()

        if self.ui.chk_Orange.text() == "Orange" :# CBEG1_10
            if self.ui.chk_Orange.isChecked(): # CBEG1_11
                self.myfruits['orange'] = 1
            else:
                self.myfruits['orange'] = 0
            self.mydisplay()

        if self.ui.chk_Banana.text() == "Banana" :# CBEG1_12
            if self.ui.chk_Banana.isChecked(): # CBEG1_13
                self.myfruits['banana'] = 1
            else:
                self.myfruits['banana'] = 0
            self.mydisplay()

        if self.ui.chk_Pear.text() == "Pear" :# CBEG1_14
            if self.ui.chk_Pear.isChecked(): # CBEG1_15
                self.myfruits['pear'] = 1
            else:
                self.myfruits['pear'] = 0
```

```
            self.mydisplay()

    def mydisplay(self):
        checkedfruits =', '.join([mykey for mykey in self.myfruits.keys() if
        self.myfruits[mykey]== 1]) # CBEG1_16
        self.ui.lbl1.setText("You selected: " + checkedfruits) # CBEG1_17

if __name__=="__main__":
    app = QApplication(sys.argv)
    w = MyCheckButton()
    w.show()
    sys.exit(app.exec_())
```

Output:

Refer to the following *Figure 4.35:*

Case-1: Default output initially on executing the code

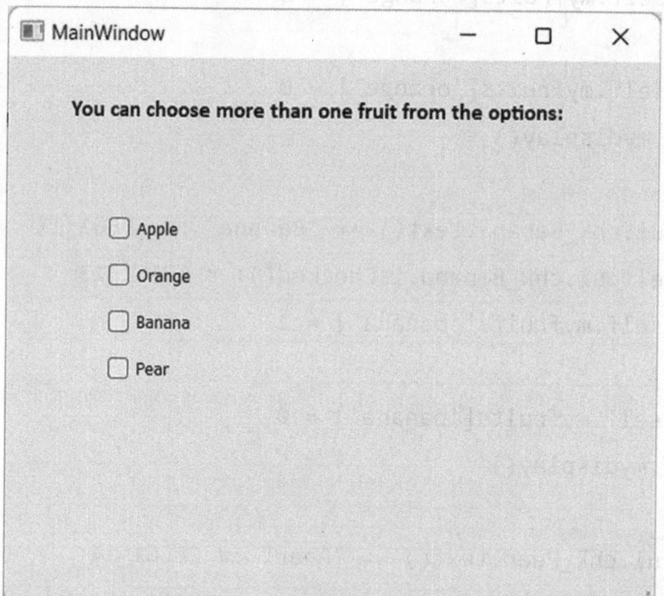

Figure 4.35*: Case-1 Output of Check_Box_Button/checkbutton_eg1.ui*

Case-2: When "1" Checkbox button is selected

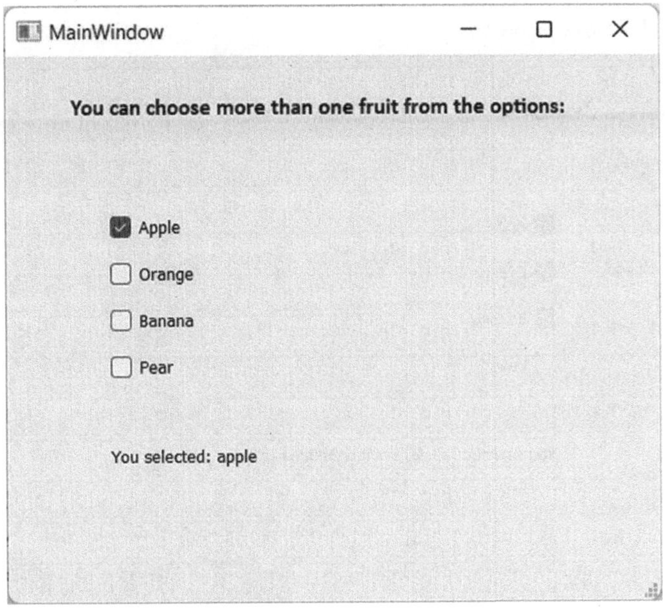

***Figure 4.36**: Case-2 Output of Check_Box_Button/checkbutton_eg1.ui*

Case-3: When "2" Checkbox button is selected

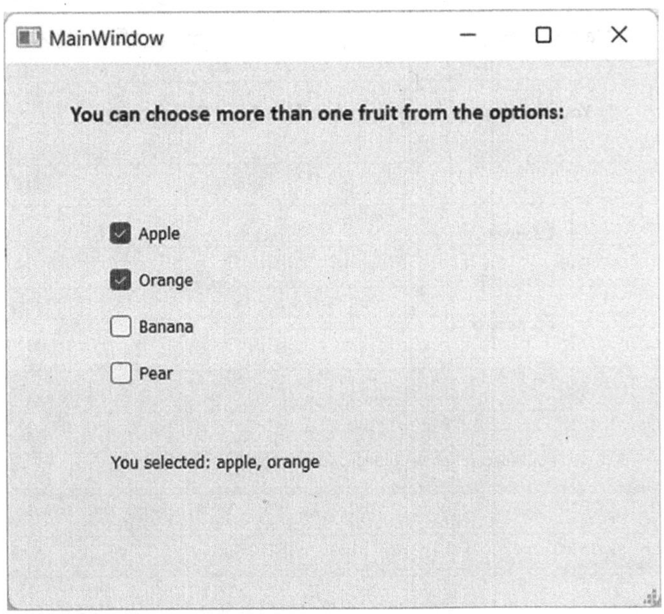

***Figure 4.37**: Case-3 Output of Check_Box_Button/checkbutton_eg1.ui*

Case-4: When "3" Checkbox button is selected

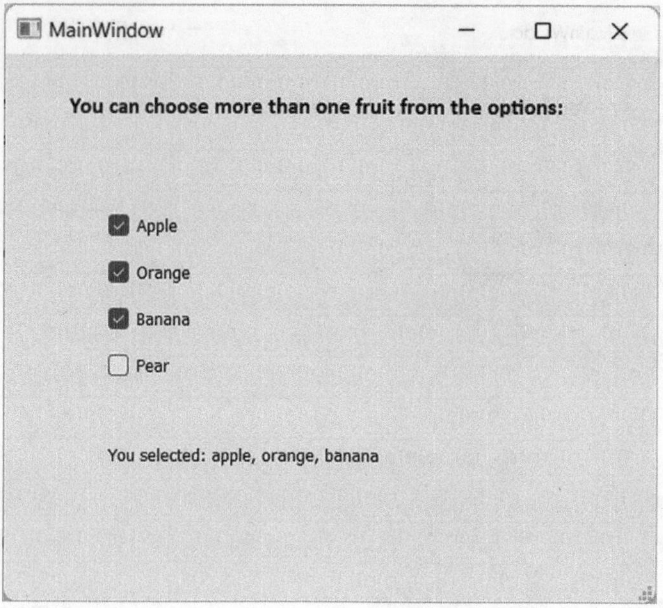

Figure 4.38: *Case-3 Output of Check_Box_Button/checkbutton_eg1.ui*

Case-5: When "4" Checkbox button is selected

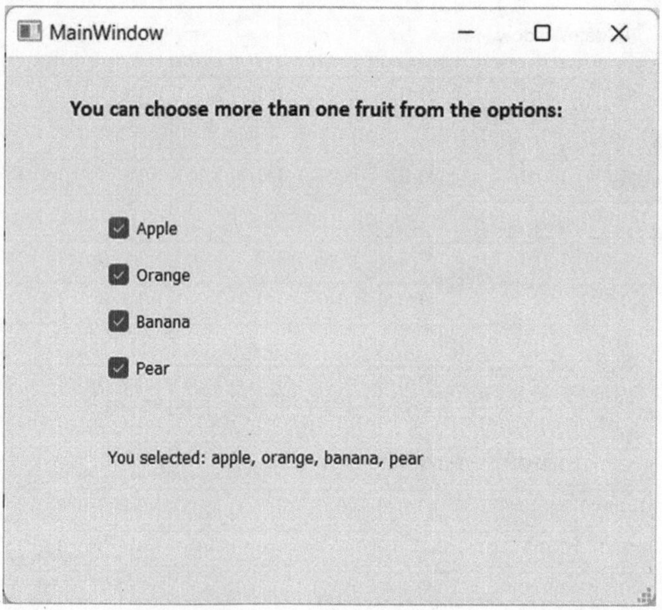

Figure 4.39: *Case-5 Output of Check_Box_Button/checkbutton_eg1.ui*

Note: The preceding code is covered in Program Name: Check_Box_Button/run_checkbutton_eg1.py

Let us understand the code:

- In **CBEG1_1**, from **checkbutton_eg1.py** Python file, we are importing all the members of a module.
- In **CBEG1_2**, a dictionary object **myfruits** is created with 4 pairs of key and values.
- In **CBEG1_3**, we are connecting the **stateChanged** signal of **QCheckBox** widget **chk_Apple** to **myselfcheck()** method.
- In **CBEG1_4**, we are connecting the **stateChanged** signal of **QCheckBox** widget **chk_Orange** to **myselfcheck()** method.
- In **CBEG1_5,** we are connecting the **stateChanged** signal of **QCheckBox** widget **chk_Banana** to **myselfcheck()** method.
- In **CBEG1_6**, we are connecting the **stateChanged** signal of **QCheckBox** widget **chk_Pear** to **myselfcheck()** method.
- From **CBEG1_3**to **CBEG1_6**, using lambda expression, the signal source is passed as an argument to the method.
- In **CBEG1_7**, **myselfcheck()** method will take an extra parameter **mychkbutton** which acts as sender for **QCheckBoxwidget** for checking its checked state.
- In **CBEG1_8** and **CBEG1_9**, if **QCheckBox** widget **chk_Apple** is checked, then we are changing the value of key '**apple**' to 1 else it will be 0.
- In **CBEG1_10** and **CBEG1_11**, if **QCheckBox** widget **chk_Orange** is checked, then we are changing the value of key '**orange**' to 1 else it will be 0.
- In **CBEG1_12** and **CBEG1_13**, if **QCheckBox** widget **chk_Banana** is checked, then we are changing the value of key '**banana**' to 1 else it will be 0.
- In **CBEG1_14** and **CBEG1_15**, if **QCheckBox** widget **chk_Pear** is checked, then we are changing the value of key '**pear**' to 1 else it will be 0.
- In **CBEG1_16**, all the items in an iterable here, which we have used as a list comprehension, will be taken up and joined as one single string. Here, we are checking the value for each key item of a dictionary object **myfruits** as 1. If found **True**, it will be appended one by one and will be finally joining as one string.
- In **CBEG1_17**, we are displaying the checked state of each **QCheckBox** widget into a **QLabel** widget **lbl1**.

Command Link Button

This widget was first introduced in Windows Vista and is a control widget. The appearance allows for a descriptive text which is similar to that of **`QPushButton`** widget in addition to the normal text and carries an arrow icon, which may indicate opening of a new GUI form or page or perform any task.

Important properties

It contains properties of 3 classes:

- **`QObject`**
- **`QWidget`**
- **`QAbstractButton`**

Interestingly, it also contains **`default`** and **`autodefault`** property of **`QPushButton`** (already discussed) and description.

Using this property, we are setting a descriptive text on the button displayed on the smaller font, thus complementing the label text. Refer to the following figure:

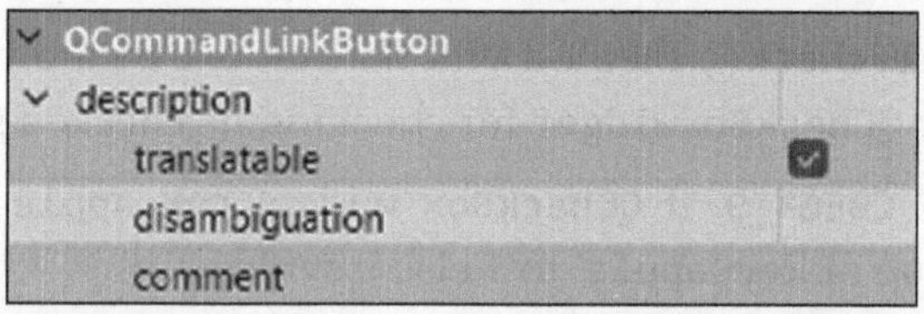

Figure 4.40: Description property of QCommandLinkButton widget in Qt Designer

Important methods

Generally, there is an empty action list in **`QCommandLinkButton`** widget. However, we can add action/actions or insert action to the menu of **`QCommandLinkButton`** widget. We will learn it through an example. The most commonly used method is **`setDescription()`**.

setDescription

We are setting the descriptive text of **`QCommandLinkButton`** widget using this method and is usually displayed in a smaller font than the primary text.

Important signals

The signals are similar to **QPushButton** widget.

Let us create one simple application to understand this **QCommandLinkButton** widget.

The details of the file names are as shown in the following *Table 4.6*:

S No.	Qt Designer File Name (.ui)	Converting the QtDesigner file name to Python file (.py)	Creating another Python file and importing the converted Python file from Qt Designer
1	**commandlinkbutton_eg1.ui**	**commandlinkbutton_eg1.py**	**run_commandlinkbutton_eg1.py**

Table 4.6: *Details of the file names*

The **Qt Designer** file **commandlinkbutton_eg1.ui** is shown in the following figure:

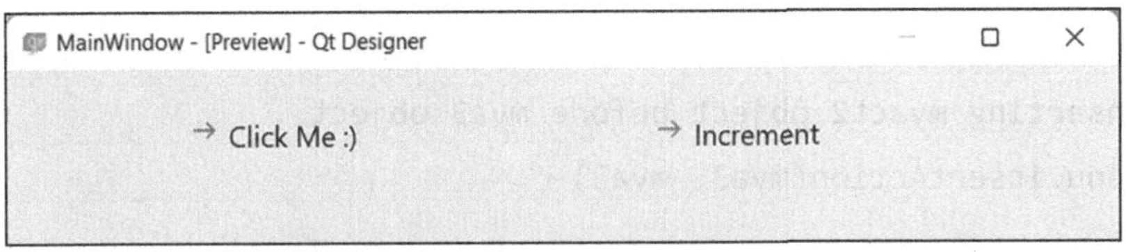

Figure 4.41: *Qt Designer file commandlinkbutton_eg1.ui*

Note: The above .ui file is covered in Path: Command_Link_Button/run_commandlinkbutton_eg1.ui.

Note: From now on, we will be describing some specific portions in the code (which will be new to the reader) using comments .i.e. the code lines which are new to the readers and are not explored till now.

Consider the following code of **run_commandlinkbutton_eg1.py**.

```
import sys
from PyQt5.QtWidgets import QMainWindow, QApplication, QAction, QMenu
from commandlinkbutton_eg1 import *


class MyCommandlinkButton(QMainWindow):
    def __init__(self):
        super().__init__()
        self.ui = Ui_MainWindow()
```

```
        self.ui.setupUi(self)

        # Creating 2 QActions object
        mya1 = QAction("First Action", self)
        mya3 = QAction("Third Action", self)
        # Creating QMenu object
        mymenu = QMenu()
        # adding 2 actions as a list to menu object
        mymenu.addActions([mya1, mya3])

        # Creating another QAction
        mya2 = QAction("Second Action", self)

        # inserting myact2 object before mya3 object
        mymenu.insertAction(mya3, mya2)

        # we are setting menu object to the command link button
        self.ui.clb_btn1.setMenu(mymenu)
        # initially counter is set as 0
        self.mycount = 0

        # connecting clicked signal of command link button object to slot
        myincrement(passing
        # my count as a parameter) and we are using lambda expression
        self.ui.clb_btn2.clicked.connect(lambda: self.myincrement(self.
        mycount))

        self.show()

    def myincrement(self,mycount): # taking mycount as another parameter
        self.mycount +=1# incrementing the counter by one.
        self.ui.mylbl2.setText("Text Description: : " + str(self.mycount)) #
        displaying the counter value to label object
```

```
if __name__=="__main__":
    app = QApplication(sys.argv)
    w = MyCommandlinkButton()
    w.show()
    sys.exit(app.exec_())
```

Output:

Refer to the following *Figure 4.42:*

Case-1: On clicking text with Click Me:)

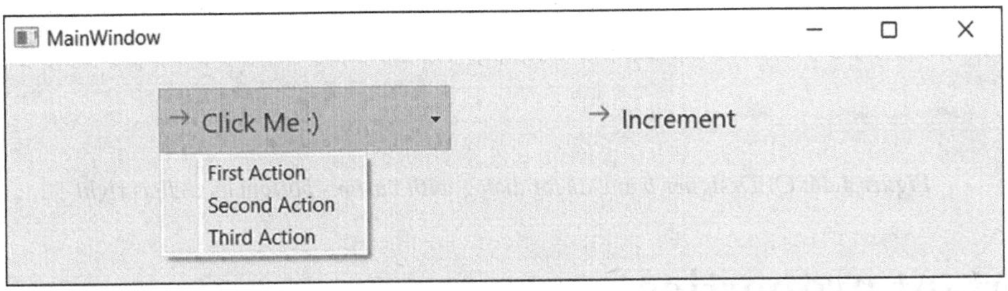

***Figure 4.42**: Case-1 Output of Command_Link_Button/run_commandlinkbutton_eg1.py*

Case-2: On clicking text with Increment commandlinkbutton object once

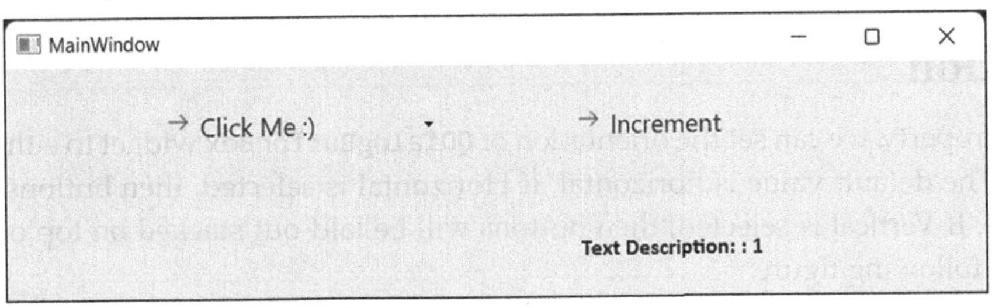

***Figure 4.43**: Case-2 Output of Command_Link_Button/run_commandlinkbutton_eg1.py*

Note: The preceding code is covered in Program Name: Command_Link_Button/run_commandlinkbutton_eg1.py.

Dialog Button Box

Whenever there is a requirement to use standard buttons (like **OK**, **Cancel**, **Ignore**, **Yes**, **No** and so on) in a layout automatically on a GUI form, then we can go for **`QDialogButtonBox`** widget. We can also create buttons and add them to the button box. But this will be a tedious process. We can see that even in Qt Designer, there are options for selecting a template as shown in the following figure:

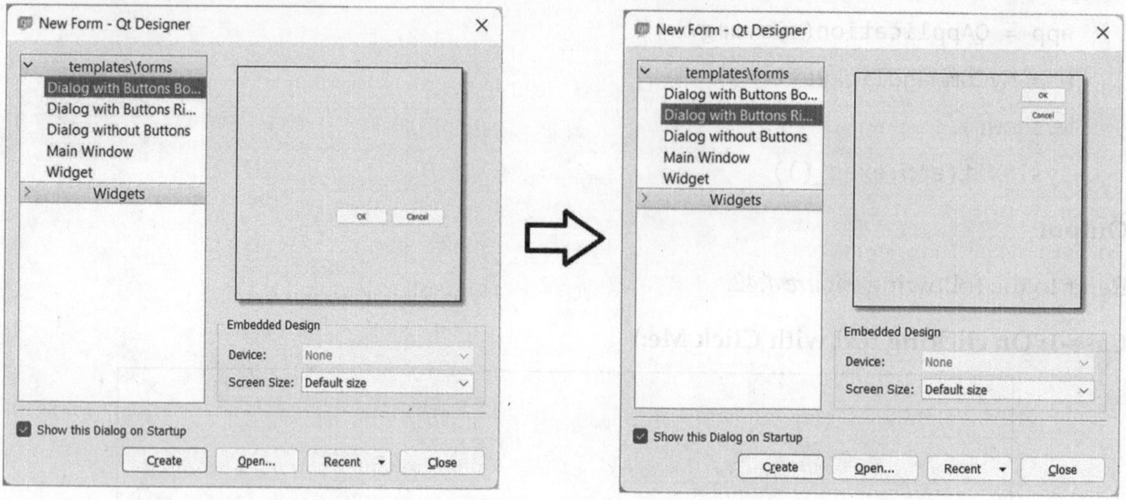

Figure 4.44: Qt Designer template for dialog with buttons bottom as well as right

Important properties

Apart from the properties of 2 classes (`QObject` and `QWidget`), there are some other properties of `QDialogButtonBox` widget, which will be discussed as follows.

orientation

Using this property, we can set the orientation of `QDialogButtonBox` widget to either **Horizontal** or **Vertical**. The default value is horizontal. If Horizontal is selected, then buttons will be laid side by side. If Vertical is selected, then buttons will be laid out stacked on top of each other. Refer to the following figure:

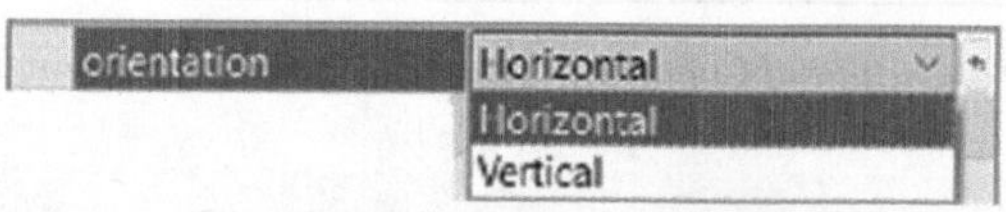

Figure 4.45: Image depicting orientation property of QDialogButtonBox in Qt Designer

standardButtons

From a list of standard buttons, we can choose any of them based on our application. This returns the enum value of standard buttons corresponding to the given button. By default, **Ok** and **Cancel** standard buttons are checked and will be displayed in a GUI form, when drag and dropped from Widget Box. Refer to the following figure:

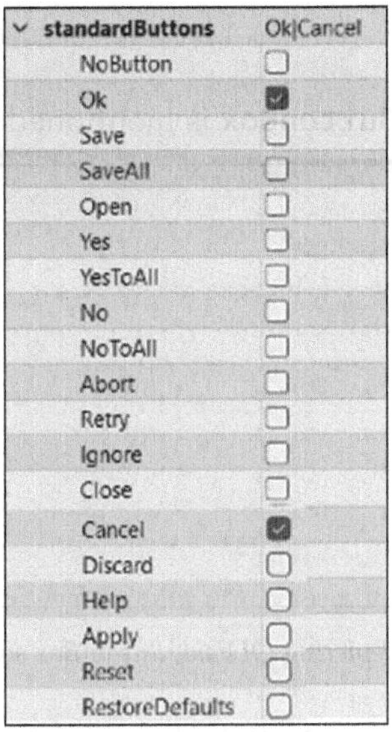

Figure 4.46: *Image depicting standardButtons property of QDialogButtonBox in Qt Designer*

centerButtons

When checked, the buttons in the **`QDialogButtonBox`** widget will be centered. It is unchecked by default. This property will determine whether the buttons in the button box object are centered horizontally or not. This property can be used to create dialog boxes that are more visually appealing.

Important methods

The various important methods are:

- **`addButton` (button)**: Using this method, standard button can be added to the **`QDialogButtonBox`** widget if valid. Zero will be returned and will not be added to the **`QDialogButtonBox`** widget if button is invalid.
- **`addButton` (button, role)**: Using this method, the button can be added to the **`QDialogButtonBox`** widget with role specified. The button will not be added when the role is invalid. Already added button will be removed and with a new role will be added again.
- **`setOrientation` (Orientation)**: Using this method, we can set the orientation of the **`QDialogButtonBox`** widget to either horizontal or vertical.
- **`setStandardButtons` (buttons)**: Using this method, we can set the collection of standard Buttons in the **`QDialogButtonBox`** widget.

Important signals

The important signals of **QDialogButtonBox** is mentioned in the figure below.

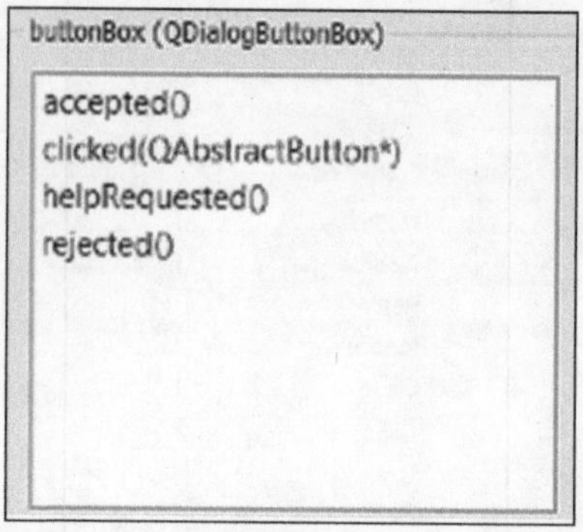

Figure 4.47: Image depicting QDialogButtonBox signals in Qt Designer

accepted(): When the user clicks on a button that accepts the dialog , then this signal will be emitted. This include buttons such as **Ok**, **Yes** or **Save**.

rejected(): When the user clicks on a button that rejects the dialog , then this signal will be emitted. This include buttons such as **Cancel**, **No** or **Close**.

clicked(QABstractButton*):When the user clicks on any button in the buttonbox, then this signal will be emitted. It takes a parameter which is a pointer to the button that was clicked.

helpRequested: When the user clicks on a button that has the *HelpRole* role, then this signal will be emitted. This include buttons such as **Help**, **?** or **More Information**.

Let us create one simple application to understand this **QCommandLinkButton** widget.

The details of file names are as shown in the following table:

S No.	Qt Designer File Name (.ui)	Converting the QtDesigner file name to Python file (.py)	Creating another Python file and importing the converted Python file from Qt Designer
1	**dialogbuttonbox_eg1.ui**	**dialogbuttonbox _eg1.py**	**run_dialogbuttonbox _eg1.py**

Table 4.7: Details of the file names

The Qt Designer file **dialogbuttonbox_eg1.ui** is shown in the following figure:

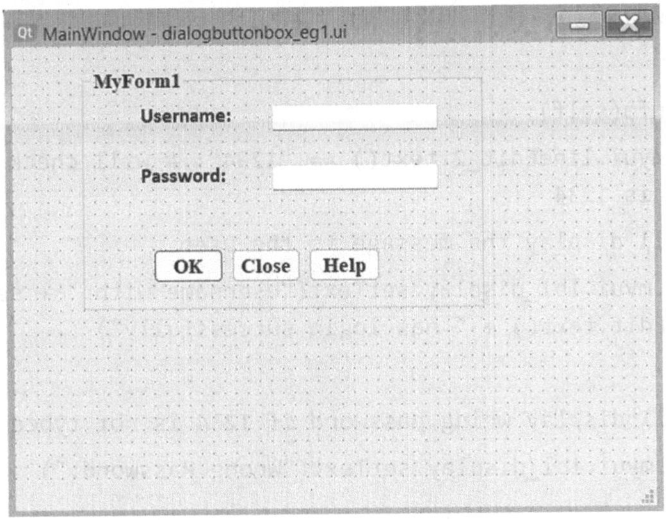

Figure 4.48: Qt Designer file :dialogbuttonbox_eg1.ui

Note: The above .ui file is covered in Path: Dialog_Button/run_dialogbuttonbox_eg1.ui.

Consider the following code of **run_dialogbuttonbox_eg1.py:**

```
import sys
from PyQt5.QtWidgets import QMainWindow, QApplication
from dialogbuttonbox_eg1 import *
import webbrowser# importing webbrowser module

class MyDialogButtonBox(QMainWindow):
    def __init__(self):
        super().__init__()
        self.myui = Ui_MainWindow()
        self.myui.setupUi(self)
         # will act when OK button is clicked and displayinfo method is executed
        self.myui.buttonBox.accepted.connect(self.displayinfo)
        # will act when close button is clicked and will close the GUI form
        self.myui.buttonBox.rejected.connect(self.close)
        # will act when help button is clicked
        self.myui.buttonBox.helpRequested.connect(lambda: webbrowser.
        open("https://auth0.com/blog/username-password-authentication/"))
```

```
        self.show()

    def displayinfo(self):
        if self.myui.lineEdit_2.text() == "1234": # will check whether
        password is 1234
            # will display the message to the user
            self.myui.lbl_display.setText("Username with " + self.myui.
            lineEdit.text() + " has login successfully")
        else:
            # will display wring password if 1234 is not typed
            self.myui.lbl_display.setText("Wrong Password:")

if __name__=="__main__":
    app = QApplication(sys.argv)
    w = MyDialogButtonBox()
    w.show()
    sys.exit(app.exec_())
```

Output:

The output can be seen in the following figure:

Case-1: When wrong password is entered and Ok button is clicked.

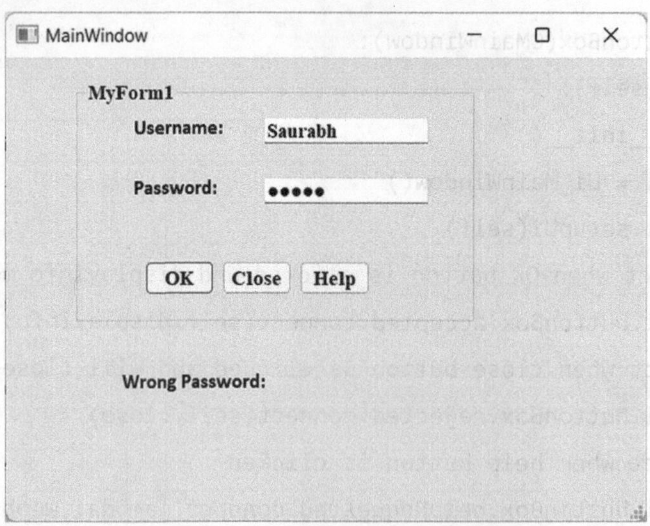

Figure 4.49: Case-1 Output of Dialog_Button/ run_dialogbuttonbox_eg1.py

Case-2: When correct password is entered and Ok button is clicked.

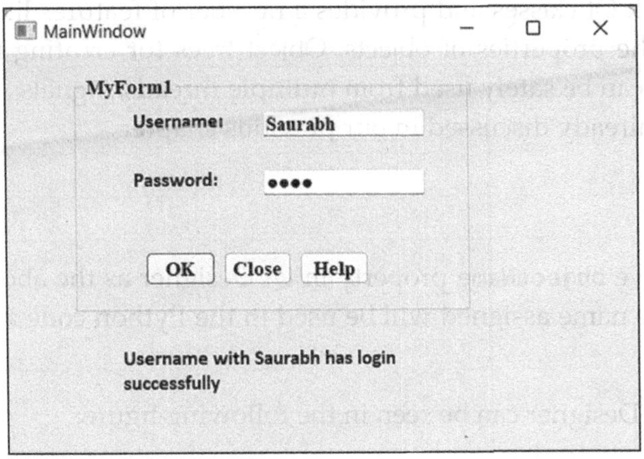

***Figure 4.50**: Case-2 Output of Dialog_Button/ run_dialogbuttonbox_eg1.py*

Case-3: When Close button is clicked, GUI form is closed.

Case-4: When Help button is clicked and if internet is connected, then the above page with link https://auth0.com/blog/username-password-authentication/ will be opened

Note: The preceding code is covered in Program Name: Dialog_Button/run_dialogbuttonbox_eg1.py

Common properties for Button widgets

We will be discussing each property of Button widgets which are common among each other. Here, we will drag **Push Button** widget from the Widget Box into the GUI form and will select and explain the properties which are common among Button widgets. When we will be using the term widget, just imagine that we are talking about **Push Button** widget. But the same may be applied to other widgets too. Refer to the following figure:

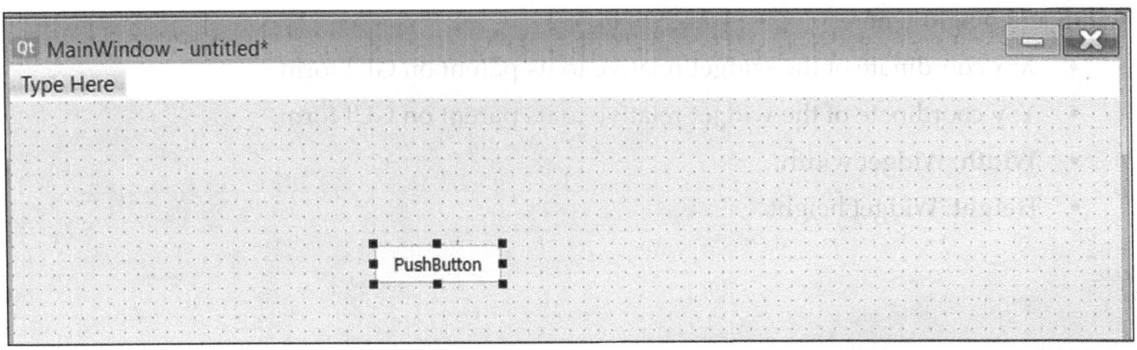

***Figure 4.51**: Image depicting only Push Button Widget on a GUI form*

Let us go over **`QObject`** which are common for all the widgets of Qt Designer. The **`QObject`** is the base class for all Qt classes and provides a number of features like Property system for getting and setting the properties of objects, Object trees for creating hierarchies of objects, Threading as objects can be safely used from multiple threads, signals , slots , event handling etc. which will have already discussed in our previous chapter.

objectName

Every widget will have **`objectName`** property in Qt Designer as the above property will hold the widget name. The name assigned will be used in the Python code as we have seen in our previous examples.

Property image in Qt Designer can be seen in the following figure:

Figure 4.52: Image depicting objectName property in Qt Designer

enabled

As the name suggests, it decides whether the widget will be enabled or not. It is checked in Qt Designer by default for every widget.

Property image in Qt Designer can be seen in the following figure:

Figure 4.53: Image depicting enabled property in Qt Designer

geometry

Relative to its parent, this property holds the widget's geometry. In Qt Designer, we have x, y, width and height where:

- **X**: x coordinate of the widget relative to its parent on GUI form.
- **Y**: y coordinate of the widget relative to its parent on GUI form.
- **Width**: Widget width.
- **Height**: Widget height.

Property image in Qt Designer can be seen in the following figure:

geometry	[(300, 60), 93 x 28]
X	300
Y	60
Width	93
Height	28

Figure 4.54: Image depicting geometry property

sizePolicy

This property which got from the class **`QSizePolicy`** will tell the widget's willingness to be resized, meaning either stretch or shrink in various ways. Generally, **`QSizePolicy`** contains 2 stretch factors and 2 independent size policy which can be retrieved using **`horizontalPolicy()`**, **`verticalPolicy()`**, **`horizontalStretch()`** and **`verticalStretch()`** functions. We can use **`setHeightForWidth()`** function for indication of widget's **`sizeHint()`** whether it is width-dependent or not. The **`horizontalStretch()`** and **`verticalStretch()`** will return the horizontal and vertical stretch factor of **`sizePolicy()`** respectively.

Different sizing types when constructing either horizontal or vertical **`SizePolicy`** are shown in the following table:

S No.	Constant	Value	Details
1	Fixed	`0`	Widget's size is fixed and can never be grown or shrink, that is, it cannot be stretched and remains at its **`sizeHint()`**.
2	Minimum	`GrowFlag`	Here, **`sizeHint()`** is smallest possible widget size and can grow bigger if necessary.
3	Maximum	`ShrinkFlag`	Here, **`sizeHint()`** is maximum possible widget size and can shrink if necessary.
4	Preferred	`GrowFlag | ShrinkFlag`	Here, **`sizeHint()`** can be best preferred which can either grow or shrink if necessary.
5	MinimumExpanding	`GrowFlag |ExpandFlag`	Here, the widget makes use of extra space for getting as much possible space as the **`sizeHint()`** is minimal and sufficient.

S No.	Constant	Value	Details
6	Expanding	**`GrowFlag | ShrinkFlag|ExpandFlag`**	Here, the widget makes use of extra space for getting as much possible space as the **`sizeHint()`** is of sensible size, but widget can be shrunk if necessary and can be useful.
7	Ignored	**`GrowFlag | ShrinkFlag|IgnoredFlag`**	Here, the widget will get as much space as possible as **`sizeHint()`** is ignored.

Table 4.8: *Different sizing types when constructing either horizontal or vertical SizePolicy*

These components will be present as a comboBox item in Qt Designer. Property image in Qt Designer can be seen in the following figure:

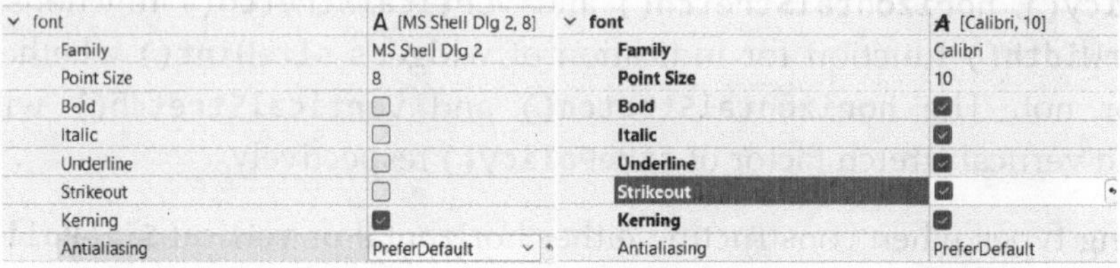

Figure 4.55: *Image depicting sizePolicy property in Qt Designer*

minimumSize

From the name, we can guess that this property will hold the minimum size of the widget. The default value will have size with value as 0 for both width and height. The minimum permissible height is restricted to this default value.

Property image in Qt Designer can be seen in the following figure:

Figure 4.56: *Image depicting minimumSize property in Qt Designer*

maximumSize

From the name, we can guess that this property will hold the maximum size of the widget. The default value will have size with value as **16777215** for both **width** and **height**. The maximum permissible width is restricted to this default value.

Property image in Qt Designer can be seen in the following figure:

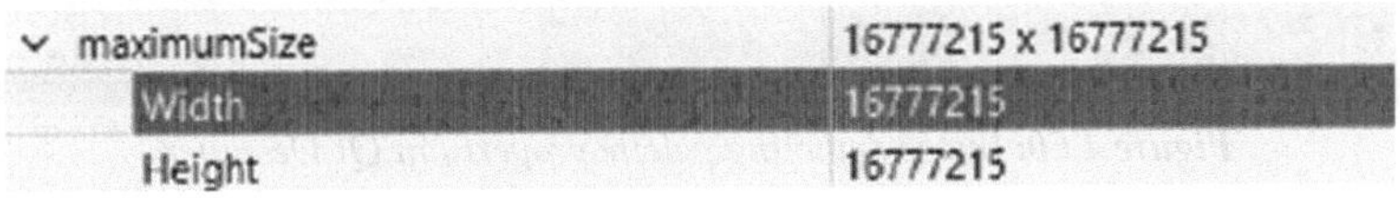

***Figure 4.57:** Image depicting maximumSize property in Qt Designer*

sizeIncrement

This property will hold the widget size increment whose default values will be 0 for both width and height. **`baseSize()`** will be kept as basis and the size increment will be done vertically and horizontally in terms of **`sizeIncrement.height()`** pixels and **`sizeIncrement.width()`** pixels respectively.

Property image in Qt Designer can be seen in the following figure:

***Figure 4.58:** Image depicting sizeIncrement property in Qt Designer*

baseSize

This property will hold the widget base size whose default values will be 0 for both width and height. Here, proper widget size will be calculated on defining **`sizeIncrement()`** by the widget.

Property image in Qt Designer can be seen in the following figure:

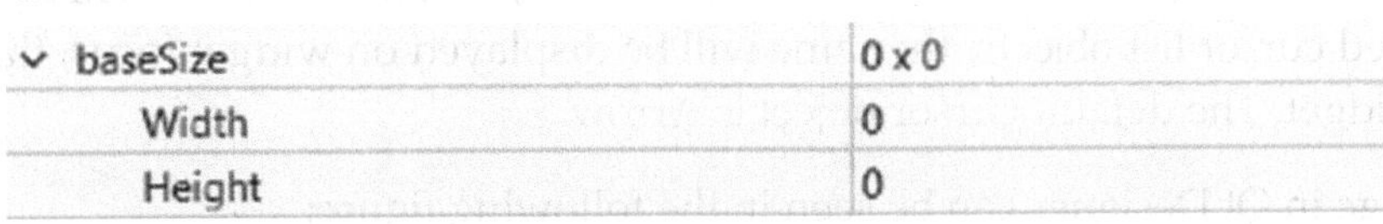

***Figure 4.59:** Image depicting baseSize property in Qt Designer*

palette

There are 3 color groups under this palette property namely Active, Disabled, and Inactive. The Active group will have keyboard focus for the window, Inactive group is for other windows; and as for Disabled group, from the name itself, we can guess that it is for widgets which are disabled and are often called grayed out. Active and inactive groups mostly look the same in most styles, while the color groups for each widget state are contained under **`QPalette`** class.

Property image in Qt Designer can be seen in the following figure:

Figure 4.60: Image depicting palette property in Qt Designer

font

This property will be used to set the font for the widget. We can set the **Family**, **Point Size** and make the text **Bold**, **Italic**, **Underline** the text, **Strikeout** the text, spacing between the letters using kerning and making the text look readable and smoother on the screen.

Property image in Qt Designer can be seen in the following figure:

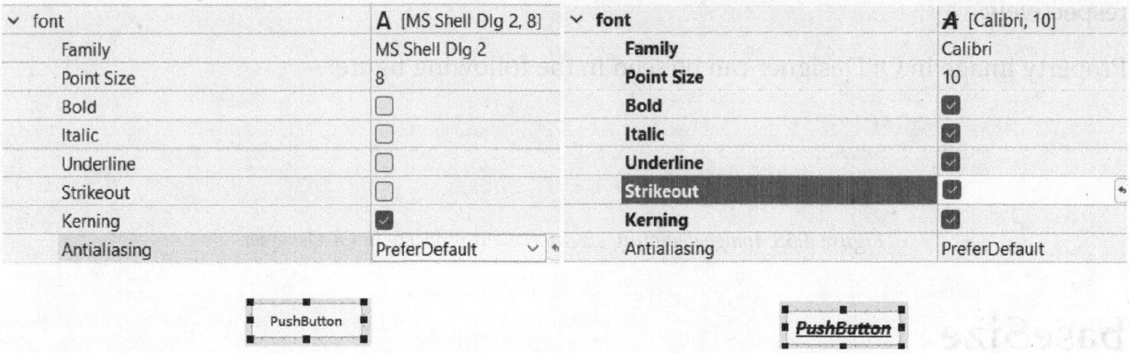

Figure 4.61: Image depicting font property in Qt Designer

cursor

This property will hold the cursor of the widget, that is, whatever cursor will be chosen from the pre-defined cursor list objects, the same will be displayed on widget focus, that is, when it is over the widget. The default cursor object is Arrow.

Property image in Qt Designer can be seen in the following figure:

Figure 4.62: Image depicting cursor property in Qt Designer

mouseTracking

From this property, we can enable/disable the **`mouseTracking`** for the widget. It is disabled by default and while the mouse is moved when at least one mouse button is pressed, the mouse move events are received by the widget. When enabled, the mouse move events are received by the widget irrespective of whether buttons pressed or not.

Property image in Qt Designer can be seen in the following figure:

Figure 4.63: *Image depicting mouseTracking property in Qt Designer*

tabletTracking

From this property, we can enable / disable the **`tabletTracking`** for the widget. It is disabled by default. When at least one stylus button is being pressed or there is contact connected between the stylus and tablet, the tablet move events are received by the widget. When it is enabled, the tablet move events are received by the widget even on hovering in close proximity.

Property image in Qt Designer can be seen in the following figure:

Figure 4.64: *Image depicting tabletTracking property in Qt Designer*

focusPolicy

This property defines the keyboard focus acceptance on the widget. There are different types of **`focusPolicy`**:

- **NoFocus:** The keyboard focus is not at all accepted on the widget.
- **TabFocus:** The keyboard focus acceptance on the widget is done by tabbing.
- **ClickFocus:** The keyboard focus acceptance on the widget is done by clicking.
- **StrongFocus:** The keyboard focus acceptance on the widget is done by both tabbing and clicking.
- **WheelFocus:** When the wheel of a mouse is moved, then the widget will accept focus.

Property image in Qt Designer can be seen in the following figure:

Figure 4.65: *Image depicting focusPolicy property in Qt Designer*

contextMenuPolicy

This property depicts the display of context menu by the widget. The default value of this property is **`DefaultContextMenu`**. We can set the other values as **`NoContextMenu`**, **`ActionsContextMenu`**, **`CustomContextMenu`** and **`PreventContextMenu`**.

Property image in Qt Designer can be seen in the following figure:

Figure 4.66: Image depicting contextMenu property in Qt Designer

acceptDrops

This property allows enabling of drop events for the widget. Default value is unchecked, that is, set as False and when checked, that is, value set to True, drop events will be enabled for the widget.

Property image in Qt Designer can be seen in the following figure:

Figure 4.67: Image depicting acceptDrops property in Qt Designer

toolTip

This property will hold the **toolTip** of a widget which contains a default empty string. The behavior of tooltip can be controlled by intercepting the `event()` function and catching the **toolTip** event. `setTooltip()` method can be used for displaying the text in rich text format on a widget.

Property image in Qt Designer can be seen in the following figure:

Figure 4.68: Image depicting ToolTip property in Qt Designer

toolTipDuration

From the name, we can guess that it will hold the **toolTipDuration** of a widget. The default value is -1 and the duration is mostly calculated based on the toolTip length. The unit will be in milliseconds. So, value of 1000 set in Qt Designer will be 1 sec.

Property image in Qt Designer can be seen in the following figure:

Figure 4.69: Image depicting toolTipDuration property in Qt Designer

statusTip

This property will hold the **statusTip** of a widget which contains a default empty string. Property image in Qt Designer can be seen in the following figure:

Figure 4.70: Image depicting statusTip property in Qt Designer

whatsThis

This property generally displays **whatsThis** help text of a widget, which contains a default empty string. We can set the help text of a widget using **`setWhatsThis()`** method.

Property image in Qt Designer can be seen in the following figure:

Figure 4.71: Image depicting whatsThis property in Qt Designer

accessibleName

This property contains a default empty string which will display the name of the widget when seen by assistive technologies like screenreaders.

Property image in Qt Designer can be seen in the following figure:

Figure 4.72: Image depicting accessibleName property in Qt Designer

accessibleDescription

This property contains a default empty string which will display the description of the widget when seen by assistive technologies.

Property image in Qt Designer can be seen in the following figure:

Figure 4.73: Image depicting accessibleDescription property in Qt Designer

layoutDirection

This property will hold the widget's layout direction, whose default value will be from **LeftToRight**. The other values chosen can be either RightToLeft or LayoutDirectionAuto.

Property image in Qt Designer can be seen in the following figure:

Figure 4.74: Image depicting layoutDirection property in Qt Designer

autoFillBackground

This property will fill the widget background automatically. The default value is unchecked. When checked, the widget's background will be filled by **QPalette** color before paint event is invoked.

Property image in Qt Designer can be seen in the following figure:

Figure 4.75: Image depicting autoFillBackground property in Qt Designer

stylesheet

This property will display the **styleSheet** of the widget. We can customize the textual description as per widget's style. This property contains a default string. For details, refer Qt style sheets document.

Property image in Qt Designer can be seen in the following figure:

Figure 4.76: Image depicting stylesheet property in Qt Designer

locale

This property will display the **locale** of a widget. We can set the language and country. Formatting is done using widget's **locale** if there is display of date or number by the widget.

Property image in Qt Designer can be seen in the following figure:

***Figure 4.77:** Image depicting locale property in Qt Designer*

inputMethodHints

This property is pertinent for input widgets which specifically hints what input method the widget should have. Its default value is **ImhNone**. The input method operation depends on many flags which can be set. If only numbers need to be entered, then the user can check **ImhPreferNumbers**. In addition to it, upper case letters should also be allowed, and then user may check **ImhPreferUppercase**.

Property image in Qt Designer can be seen in the following figure:

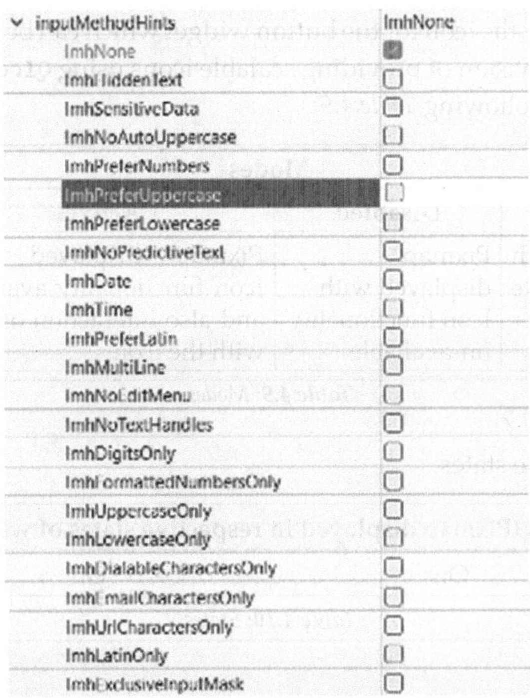

***Figure 4.78:** Image depicting inputMethodHints property in Qt Designer*

Let us now learn **`QAbstractButton`** which are common for all the Button widgets of Qt designer, except Dialog Button box.

text

This property will display the text on the Button widgets. An empty string is returned if the button widget text does not contain any text. A shortcut is created automatically if an ampersand character is present in the text, as the shortcut key will be that character which follows '&'. So, there are chances that the previous shortcut will be cleared or overwritten. If 2 '&&' are used, then 1 '&' will be displayed.

Property image in Qt Designer can be seen in the following figure:

***Figure 4.79:** Image depicting text property in Qt Designer*

icon

This property will display the icon for the button widget which can be adjusted using **`iconSize`** property. There is the provision of providing scalable icons using **`QIcon`** class in different states and modes. Refer to the following *Table 4.9:*

Modes			
Normal	**Disabled**	**Active**	**Selected**
Pixmap displayed with Icon functionality available and *non-* interaction of user with the icon	Pixmap displayed with Icon functionality un-available	Pixmap displayed with Icon functionality available and also interaction of user with the icon	Pixmap displayed with Icon selected

***Table 4.9:** Modes*

The table below shows the states:

States (Pixmap displayed in respective states of widget)	
On	Off

***Table 4.10:** States*

Property image in Qt Designer can be seen in the following figure:

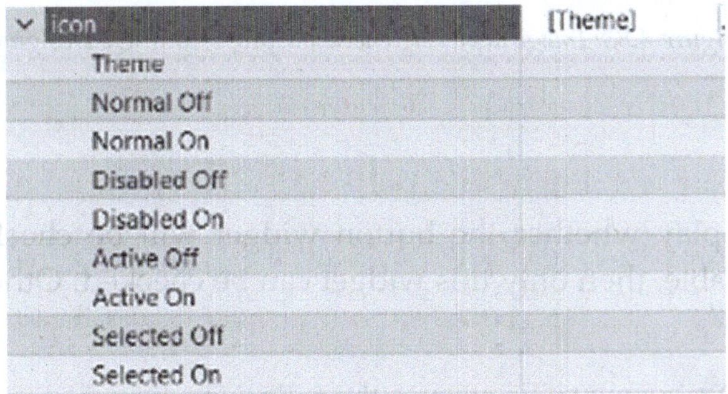

Figure 4.80: Image depicting icon property in Qt Designer

iconSize

We can set the width and height of the icon size from this property. The default size is 20*20.

Property image in Qt Designer can be seen in the following figure:

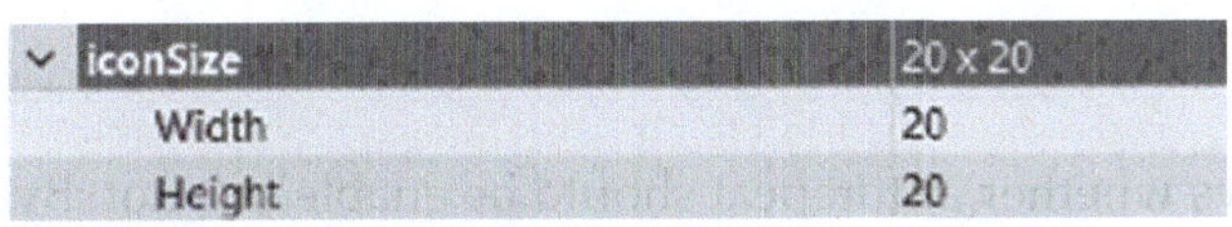

Figure 4.81: Image depicting iconSize property in Qt Designer

shortcut

This property will display the mnemonic which is associated to the button widget.

Property image in Qt Designer can be seen in the following figure:

Figure 4.82: Image depicting shortcut property in Qt Designer

checkable

This property will display whether the button widget will be checkable or not.

Property image in Qt Designer can be seen in the following figure:

***Figure 4.83:** Image depicting checkable property in Qt Designer*

checked

This property will display whether the button widget will be checked or not. When the button widget is checkable, then only this widget can be checked. Otherwise, by default, it is unchecked.

Property image in Qt Designer can be seen in the following figure:

***Figure 4.84:** Image depicting checked property in Qt Designer*

autoRepeat

This property displays whether autorepeat should be enabled or not. By default, it is disabled and when it is checked the signals **`pressed()`**, **`released()`** and **`clicked()`** will be emitted.

Property image in Qt Designer can be seen in the following figure:

***Figure 4.85:** Image depicting autoRepeatproperty in Qt Designer*

autoExclusive

Except for the radio-buttons widget, this property is off by default and when enabled, the buttons which are checkable behave in the same exclusive button group, such that when one button is checked, it will uncheck the previous one as at any time only a single button can be checked. It will have no effect on buttons that belongs to a button group.

Property image in Qt Designer can be seen in the following figure:

***Figure 4.86:** Image depicting autoExclusive property in Qt Designer*

autoRepeatDelay

This property will define the auto-repetition initial delay in milliseconds before activation of auto-repetition when **autoRepeat** is enabled. The default value set is 300 msecs.

Property image in Qt Designer can be seen in the following figure:

Figure 4.87: *Image depicting autoRepeatDelay property in Qt Designer*

autoRepeatInterval

This property will define the auto-repetition interval length in milliseconds when **autoRepeat** is enabled. It is set as 100msec by default.

Property image in Qt Designer can be seen in the following figure:

Figure 4.88: *Image depicting autoRepeatInterval property in Qt Designer*

Note: Please visit the official documentation page https://doc.qt.io/qtforpython-5 and explore different widgets.

Conclusion

In this chapter, we have learned in-depth understanding of Button widgets in Qt Designer. Button widgets are widely used for creating interactive user interfaces, and their properties, functionality, and customization options have been thoroughly explained. By exploring the features and settings related to Button widgets, the user can effectively design and implement user-friendly interfaces in their Qt Applications. Qt Designer offers a variety of Button widgets, including **CheckBox**, **Push Button**, **Tool Button**, **Radio Button**, and **Command Link Button**, each serving a specific purpose. Moreover, we have seen different Dialog Button Box present in Qt Designer. The chapter explores the description, properties, important methods, and signals associated with each button widget. Additionally, an application example with an output display is provided to illustrate the practical implementation of Button widgets. Furthermore, the chapter covers the important properties of **QObject**, **QWidget**, and **QAbstractButton**, which are relevant to Button widgets. These properties are supplemented with images to enhance understanding.

In the next chapter, we will learn about **Item Views** in Qt Designer, which are commonly used for creating interactive user interfaces. We will learn how data will be presented in the form of list, hierarchical tree structures and tabular representations.

Points to remember

- A push button widget is a rectangle button that, when clicked, does a certain operation. It can be used to do a number of things, such open a file, close a window, or submit a form, and it can have text or an icon.
- A small, rectangular button known as a Tool Button widget is used to access a particular tool or feature. In toolbars, Tool Buttons are frequently utilized, and they can be used for a range of tasks like cutting, pasting, or zooming in and out.
- A rectangular button that can be used to pick one or more alternatives is known as a check button widget. A checkbox is checked when it is clicked, and it is unchecked when it is clicked again. Check boxes are frequently used to let users choose from a variety of options, such as the languages or functionality they want to use.
- A Radio Button widget is a circular button that enables users to choose one item from a list of choices. All other Radio Buttons in the group are deselected when a Radio Button is clicked, which selects it. Radio Buttons are frequently used to let users choose just one option, like the font size or the background color.
- A rectangle button that triggers an action when pressed, is known as a Command Link Button widget. While it resembles a Push Button, its look is distinct. Command Link Buttons are frequently used to make it clear to users what will happen when they click the button.
- Give buttons a description in the text. The text should make it crystal obvious as to what will happen when the button is clicked.
- For buttons, use icons. In addition to helping to identify the function of the button, icons can improve the visual appeal of buttons.
- Group similar buttons together. Users will find it simpler to locate the buttons they require as a result.

  For buttons, stick to a consistent look. This will contribute to your application having a cohesive look and feel.

Questions

1. Explain important properties of Push Button in Qt Designer tool.
2. Explain the importance of **`autoDefault`**, **`default`**, and **`flat`** functions in the Push Button.
3. Differentiate between the **`isChecked()`** and **`setCheckable()`** function.
4. Differentiate between the **`text()`** and **`setText()`** function.
5. Explain any two important signals of the Push Button widget.
6. Write short notes on the Tool Button widget in the Qt Designer system.
7. Explain any two important properties of the Tool Button widget in the Qt Designer system.
8. Explain the **`popupMode`** property along with its constants.
9. Draw and explain **`toolButtonStyle`** property.
10. Explain the use of **`autoRaise`** and **`arrowType`** property in the Tool Button widget of the Qt Designer system.
11. Explain the important methods of the **`QToolButton`** widget.
12. Explain the use of Radio Button in GUI designing.
13. Explain the signals in the **`QRadioButton`** widget.
14. Explain the use of Check Box in GUI designing.
15. Explain the important methods of the **`QCheckBox`** widget.
16. Describe the function of the **`QCommandLinkButton`** widget in Qt Designer.
17. State the usefulness of **`QDialogButtonBox`** in Qt Designer.
18. Explain the important properties of the **`QDialogButtonBox`** widget in Qt Designer.

CHAPTER 5

Getting Insights of Item Views in Qt Designer

Introduction

After discussing button widgets, we shall now move on to our next topic, which is about Item Views in Qt Designer. There has to be some approach for accessing, managing, and displaying the data to the user. So, based on the software design pattern of **Model-View-Controller (MVC)**, PyQt5 utilizes the same architecture of Model/View. The data from the data source will be accessed by the model and will provide data to the view. This view will present the items stored in a model and reflect the changes to the data in the model. The data editing in the model will be handled by the delegate, who will also be responsible for items drawn in the view. You may visit the website at **https://doc.qt.io**, where a plethora of information on PyQt5 functions and properties is provided.

Our main focus in this chapter will be on learning about `QListView`, `QTreeView`, `QTableView`, and `QColumnView`. We will be focusing on properties and some useful methods. All these widgets are available under **Item Views** in Qt Designer, as shown in the following figure. The user can select any of the widgets under **Item Views** and drag and drop in a GUI form. Please refer to the following figure:

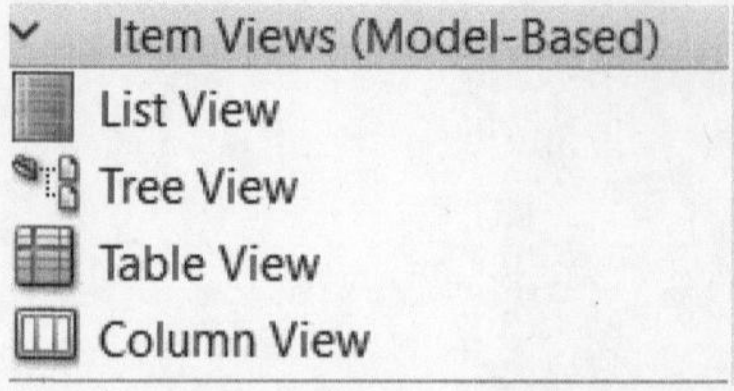

***Figure 5.1:** Different Item Views (ModelBased) in Qt Designer*

The base class for these widgets is an abstract class **`QAbstractItemView`,** which provides support for header management and item selection. We have already seen **`QObject`** and **`QWidget`** classes when dealing with Button type widgets. The same applies to **Item Views** widgets, too. There are other classes we will be discussing about, such as **`QFrame`**, **`QAbstractScrollArea`,** and **`QAbstractItemView`** class, which will be discussed at the end of this chapter. Moreover, we will also discuss **`QStandardItemModel`** at the end, which provides a standard item-based approach for working with the model.

Structure

In this chapter, we will learn the following topics:

- List view
- Tree view
- Table view
- Column view

Objectives

After reading this chapter, the reader will get to know about **Item Views** in Qt Designer, which are commonly used for creating interactive user interfaces. The primary objective of this chapter is to help you understand their properties, functionality, and customization options. Understanding and using the many widget classes and components offered by the Qt framework for displaying and manipulating data in a tabular or list-based manner is the primary goal of discussing **Item View** widgets in Qt Designer. Qt Designer's **Item View** widgets, such as **`QTableView`**, **`QTreeView`**, and **`QListView`**, are effective tools for presenting data in an organized and ordered way.

Data presentation

Item View widgets can be used to present data in a graphical and user-friendly manner. Users can use these widgets to display data in simple list formats (**`QListView`**), hierarchical tree structures (**QTreeView**), or rows and columns (**QTableView**). Data editing and manipulation are capabilities that are already built into **Item View** widgets. The user can add, remove, or alter objects to interact with the data shown in the widgets and can also design behaviors and set properties for these activities using Qt Designer. Since the user can alter their appearance and behavior and may also design unique user interfaces suited to their requirements, item views are entirely adjustable. The Model-View architecture, a key Qt idea for separating data representation (model) from the visual display (view) and user interaction (delegate), is also introduced to the user. The user may better understand the ideas of models, views, and delegates as well as how they interact by learning about item view widgets. The important properties of **QFrame**, **QAbstractScrollArea,** and **QAbstractItemView** are covered with images at the end as add-on information.

List view

It is one of the Model/View frameworks of PyQt5. In the **QListView** class, we can store the items as an icon collection or as a non-hierarchical list. There will be a display of items in a **listview** using either **ListMode** or **IconMode**, and the current view mode is determined using **viewMode()**. In a **QListView**, widget items can be spaced/laid or can be rendered as small or large icons.

Important properties

Let us check some important properties.

movement

This property describes the movement of items in a **QListView** widget. There are three options:

- If the user selects **Static**, there will be no movement of items.
- If the user selects **Free**, there will be drag and drop of items to any position in the **QListView** widget.
- If the user selects **Snap**, there will be a drag and drop of items to the notional grid positions denoted by the **gridSize** parameter.

Refer to the following *Figure 5.2:*

***Figure 5.2:** Image depicting movement property of QListView widget in Qt Designer*

flow

Using this property, we can set the direction for the layout of the items. By default, the items are laid out in the **QListView** widget from top to bottom. Items can also be laid out from left to right. Refer to the following *Figure 5.3:*

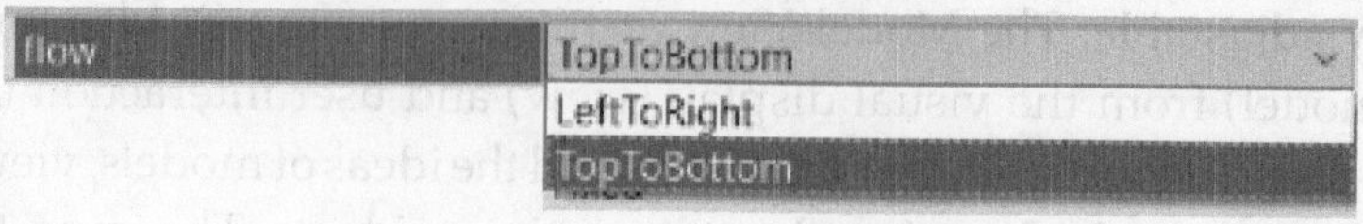

Figure 5.3: *Image depicting flow property of QListView widget in Qt Designer*

isWrapping

We can set the items layout wrapping when checked, using this property. Default value is **False**. Refer to the following *Figure 5.4:*

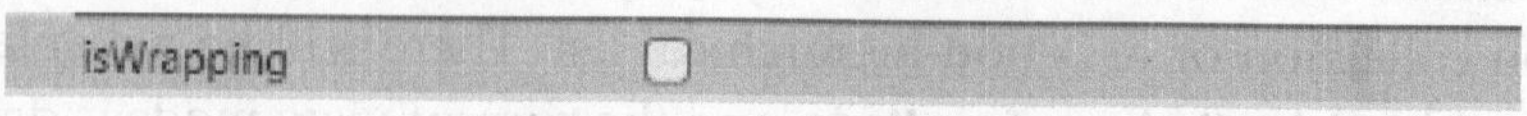

Figure 5.4: *Image depicting isWrapping property of QListView widget in Qt Designer*

resizeMode

Using this property, we can decide the layout of the items again by resizing of **QListView** widget. By default, the value is Fixed, that is, on resizing of **QListView** widget, the items will not be laid out, whereas they will be laid out again when set to **Adjust**. Refer to the following *Figure 5.5:*

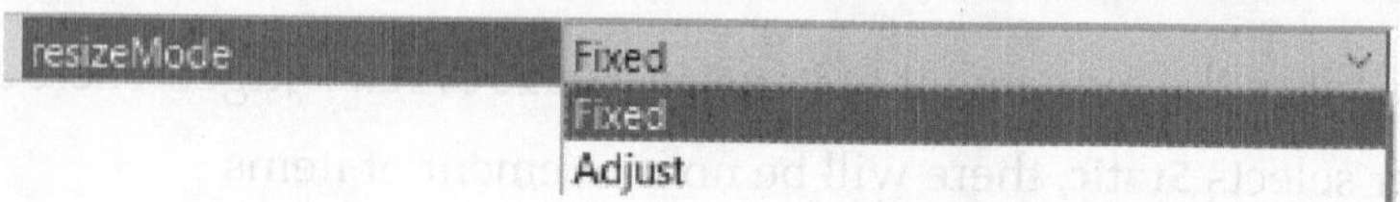

Figure 5.5: *Image depicting resizeMode property of QListView widget in Qt Designer*

layoutMode

Using this property, we can determine if the items' layout should be delayed or happen immediately. So, the items' layout happens all at once when set to **SinglePass** or in batches of **batchSize** items when set to **Batched**. Refer to the following *Figure 5.6:*

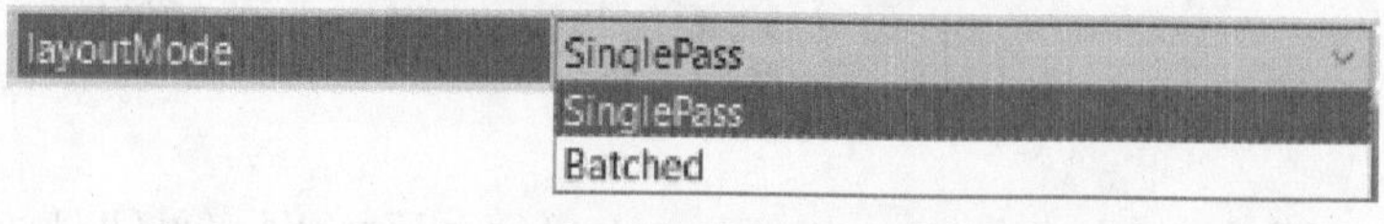

Figure 5.6: *Image depicting layoutMode property of QListView widget in Qt Designer*

spacing

Whenever there is a requirement to pad an empty space size around an item, we can use this property. By default, its value is set to **0**. Refer to the following *Figure 5.7:*

***Figure 5.7:** Image depicting spacing property of QListView widget in Qt Designer*

gridSize

We can set the grid size using this property, by setting the width and height in which items are laid out. The default value of width and height is **0** indicating no grid. Refer to the following *Figure 5.8:*

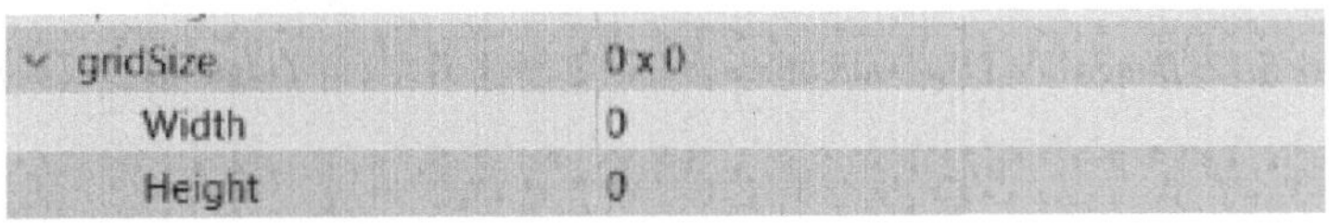

***Figure 5.8:** Image depicting gridSize property of QListView widget in Qt Designer*

viewMode

The view mode of **`QListView`** widget is set using this property. When set to **ListMode**, drag and drop is disabled, as the default movement will be Static. When set to **IconMode**, drag and drop is enabled, as the default movement will be Free. Refer to the following *Figure 5.9:*

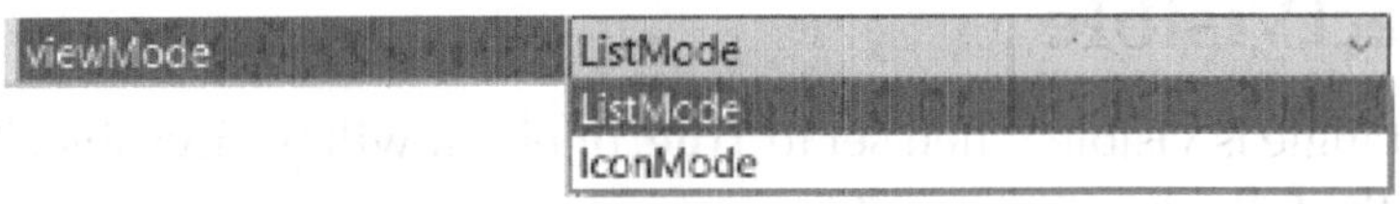

***Figure 5.9:** Image depicting viewMode property of QListView widget in Qt Designer*

modelColumn

This property will set the visibility of the column in the model. The default value is **0**, indicating the display of the first column in the model. Refer to the following *Figure 5.10:*

***Figure 5.10:** Image depicting modelColumn property of QListView widget in Qt Designer*

uniformItemSizes

When set to **True**, all the items in the **QListView** widget will have the same size. The default value is **False**. Refer to the following *Figure 5.11:*

***Figure 5.11:** Image depicting uniformItemSizes property of QListView widget in Qt Designer*

batchSize

When the **layoutMode** value is set to batch, in each batch, we can set the number of items. The default value is set to **100**. Refer to the following *Figure 5.12:*

***Figure 5.12:** Image depicting batchSize property of QListView widget in Qt Designer*

wordWrap

The item text is wrapped at word breaks as needed if this parameter is set to **True**. Refer to the following *Figure 5.13:*

***Figure 5.13:** Image depicting wordWrap property of QListView widget in Qt Designer*

selectionRectVisible

The selection rectangle is visible when set to **True**, or else it will be invisible. The default value is **False**. Refer to the following *Figure 5.14:*

***Figure 5.14:** Image depicting selectionRectVisible property of QListView widget in Qt Designer*

Important methods of QAbstractItemView base class

Let us now check some important methods:

- **setModel(model)**: We can set the view model when this method is called.
- **setItemDelegate(delegate)**: We can set an item delegate for the model/view framework of the view.

- `setIconSize(size)`: The icon size can be set using this method.
- `setDragEnabled(bool)`: When the bool value is set as **True**, we can drag the items around in the view.
- `setAcceptDrops(bool)`: When the bool value is set as **True**, we can drop the items into the view.
- `setAlternatingRowColors(bool)`: The view background will be drawn with alternating colors when the bool value is **True**.
- `setCurrentIndex(index)`: Using this method, the item at the index specified will be set as the current item.
- `update(index)`: The area at the specified index will be updated.
- `clearSelection()`: Here, all the selected items will be deselected.
- `selectAll()`: All the items in the view will be selected.

Important signal of QAbstractItemView base class

In all the above signals listed, the signal will be emitted when:

- `pressed(index)`: An item at the index is pressed using the mouse button.
- `entered(index)`: The item at the index is entered by the mouse cursor. Mouse tracking is turned on for use.
- `activated(index)`: The user activates the item at the index.
- `clicked(index)`: An item in the view is clicked with the left mouse button as specified by the index.
- `doubleClicked(index)`: An item in the view is double-clicked by the mouse button as specified by the index.

Now, we shall see an example of a `ListView` widget.

The details of the file names are as follows:

S No.	Qt Designer file name (.ui)	Converting the QtDesigner file name to Python file (.py)	Creating another Python file and importing the converted Python file from Qt Designer
1.	`listView_eg1.ui`	`listView_eg1.py`	`run_listView_eg1.py`

Table 5.1: *Details of file names*

The Qt Designer file is shown in the following figure:

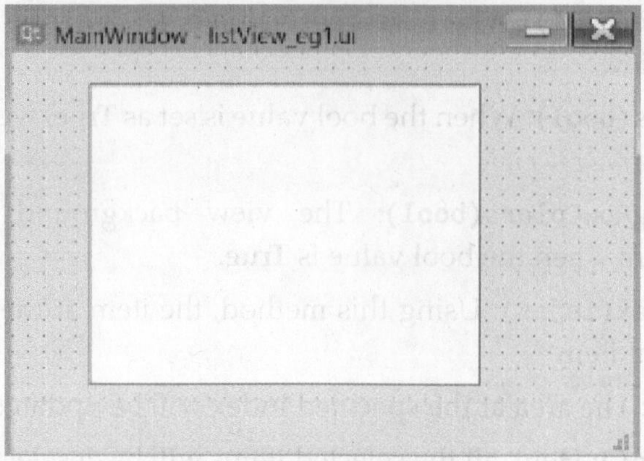

Figure 5.15: Qt Designer file: listView_eg1.ui

Note: The above .ui file is covered in Path: ListView/listview_eg1.ui

Consider the following code of **run_listView_eg1.py:**

```
import sys
from PyQt5.QtWidgets import QMainWindow, QApplication
from PyQt5.QtGui import QStandardItemModel
from listView_eg1 import *

class MyListView(QMainWindow):
    def __init__(self):
        super().__init__()
        self.ui = Ui_MainWindow()
        self.ui.setupUi(self)
        self.myfruits = ['apple', 'orange', 'banana', 'pear'] # creating a
        list object
        # creating an object of one of the model/view class for storing custom
        data.
        model = QStandardItemModel()
        # A view is set up to display the items in the listView object
        self.ui.mylV1.setModel(model)
        # iterating each elements of the myfruits list object
```

```
        for i in self.myfruits:
            # QStandardItem provides the items in a QStandardItemModel
            item = QtGui.QStandardItem(i)
            # adding items to the model using appendRow
            model.appendRow(item)
        self.show()


if __name__=="__main__":
    app = QApplication(sys.argv)
    w = MyListView()
    w.show()
    sys.exit(app.exec_())
```

Output:

The output can be seen in the following *Figure 5.16*:

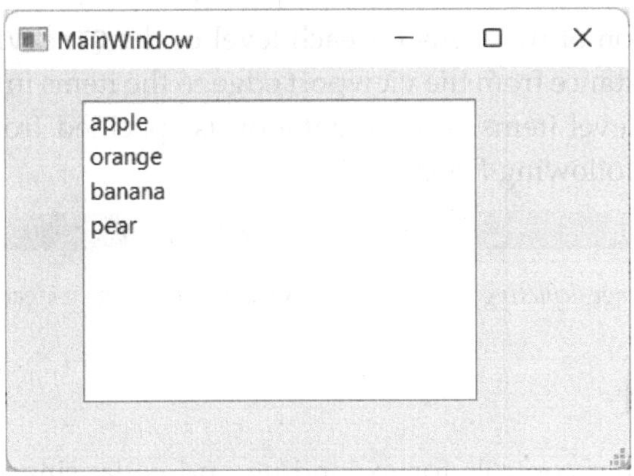

***Figure 5.16:** Output of ListView/ run_listview_eg1.py*

Note: The preceding code is covered in program name: ListView/run_listview_eg1.py

From the above code, we can view that we are displaying fruit items row-wise on a **`listView`** widget.

Tree view

One of the parts of Qt's Model / View framework creates a tree representation of items from the model. In order to display data provided by models descended from the **`QAbstractItemModel`** class, **QTreeView** implements the interfaces described by the **QAbstractItemView** class. The model/view architecture ensures that as the model changes, the tree view's contents are updated. A tree view's default model/view implementation is offered by the **QTreeView** class.

Important properties

Let us now check some important properties.

autoExpandDelay

During a drag-and-drop operation, the delay time is specified in milliseconds before items in a **QTreeView** widget are opened using this property. The default value is **-1**, indicating the disabling of the auto-expansion property. Refer to the following *Figure 5.17:*

***Figure 5.17:** Image depicting autoExpandDelay property of QTreeView widget in Qt Designer*

indentation

We can set the indentation of the items for each level of the **QTreeView** widget, measured in pixels. The horizontal distance from the viewport edge to the items in the first column specifies the indentation for top-level items. The indentation is specified from their parent items for child items. Refer to the following *Figure 5.18:*

***Figure 5.18:** Image depicting indentation property of QTreeView widget in Qt Designer*

rootIsDecorated

We can determine whether controls for expanding and collapsing top-level items are to be displayed or not. The controls will not be displayed for top-level items if unchecked and make a single-level tree structure appear like a simple list of items. The default is checked. Refer to the following *Figure 5.19:*

***Figure 5.19:** Image depicting rootIsDecorated property of QTreeView widget in Qt Designer*

uniformRowHeights

When checked, all the items in the **QTreeView** widget will have the same height. The first item in the view provides the height. When data changes on that item, it is updated automatically.

By default, it is unchecked. Refer to the following *Figure 5.20:*

***Figure 5.20:** Image depicting uniformRowHeights property of QTreeView widget in Qt Designer*

itemsExpandable

The default value is checked and this property will decide whether the user can interactively expand and collapse items. Refer to the following *Figure 5.21:*

***Figure 5.21:** Image depicting itemsExpandable property of QTreeView widget in Qt Designer*

sortingEnabled

The default value is unchecked. If set to **True**, then sorting will be enabled for the **`QTreeView`** widget, else it will be disabled. Refer to the following *Figure 5.22:*

***Figure 5.22:** Image depicting sortingEnabled property of QTreeView widget in Qt Designer*

animated

The Tree view will animate the expansion and collapsing of branches when set to **True**. When unchecked, there will be immediate expansion and collapsing of branches without a display of animation. Refer to the following *Figure 5.23:*

***Figure 5.23:** Image depicting animated property of QTreeView widget in Qt Designer*

allColumnsShowFocus

The default value is unchecked, meaning only one column will show focus. When checked, all columns will show focus. Refer to the following *Figure 5.24:*

***Figure 5.24:** Image depicting allColumnsShowFocus property of QTreeView widget in Qt Designer*

wordWrap

The item text is wrapped when necessary, at word breaks, if this attribute is **True**. It is unchecked by default, that is, set as **False**. Refer to the following *Figure 5.25:*

Figure 5.25: *Image depicting wordWrap property of QTreeView widget in Qt Designer*

headerHidden

The header is hidden when checked, or else it is displayed when unchecked. The default value is set as **False**. Refer to the following *Figure 5.26:*

Figure 5.26: *Image depicting headerHidden property of QTreeView widget in Qt Designer*

expandsOnDoubleClick

The default value is set to **True,** and from the name, we can understand that the items can be expanded or collapsed by double-clicking. Refer to the following *Figure 5.27:*

Figure 5.27: *Image depicting expandsOnDoubleClick property of QTreeView widget in Qt Designer*

Now, we shall see an example of the tree view widget.

The details of the file names are as follows:

S No.	Qt Designer file name (.ui)	Converting the QtDesigner file name to Python file (.py)	Creating another Python file and importing the converted Python file from Qt Designer
1	`TreeView_eg1.ui`	`TreeView_eg1.py`	`run_TreeView_eg1.py`

Table 5.2: *Details of file names*

The Qt Designer file is shown in the following *Figure 5.28:*

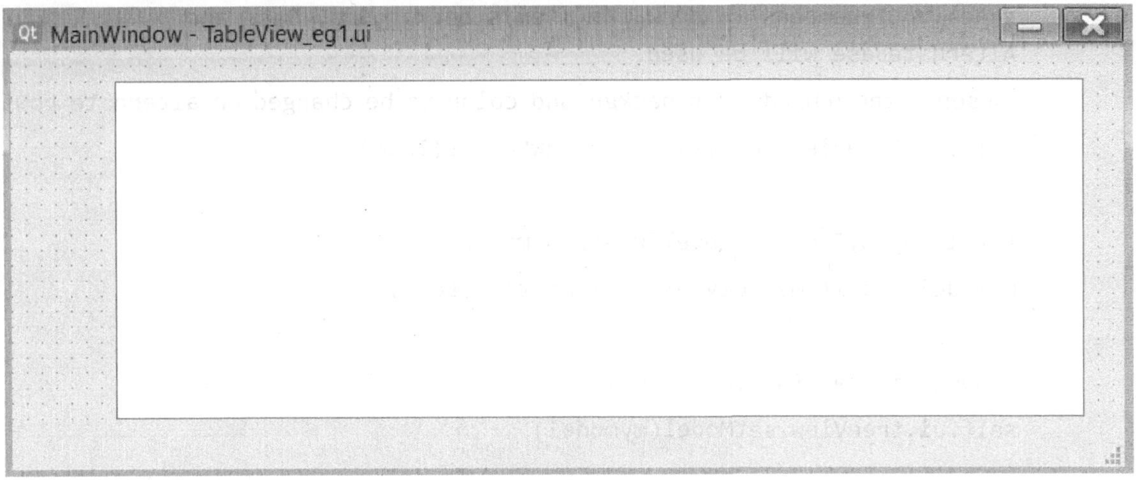

Figure 5.28: *Qt Designer file: TreeView_eg1.ui*

Note: The above .ui file is covered in Path: TreeView/TreeView_eg1.ui

Consider the following code of **run_TreeView_eg1.py:**

```
import sys
from PyQt5.QtWidgets import QMainWindow, QApplication
from PyQt5.QtCore import Qt
from PyQt5.QtGui import QStandardItemModel
from TreeView_eg1 import *

class MyTreeView(QMainWindow):
    # setting object Name, Contact_Number, City, Profession
    # with values as    0      1              2         3
    Name, Contact_Number, City, Profession = range(4)

    def __init__(self):
        super().__init__()
        self.ui = Ui_MainWindow()
        self.ui.setupUi(self)
        # set to False means making a single level tree structure appear like
        a simple list of items
        self.ui.treeView.setRootIsDecorated(False)
```

```
        # set to Truemeans To draw the item's background, Base and
        AlternateBase will be used.
      # observe the output with background color to be changed on alternate rows
        self.ui.treeView.setAlternatingRowColors(True)

        # calling myTreeViewModelCreation method
        mymodel = self.myTreeViewModelCreation(self)

        # model is set for the Treeview
        self.ui.treeView.setModel(mymodel)

        # filling Data on passing Name, Contact_Number, City and Profession
        headers
        # by calling myaddition method
        self.myaddition(mymodel, 'Divya', '9857611111','Delhi','Scientist')
        self.myaddition(mymodel, 'Sargam', '9857622222','Kolkata','HouseWife')
        self.myaddition(mymodel, 'Sugandh', '9857633333','Aligarh','Engineer')
        self.myaddition(mymodel, 'Munnu', '9857644444','Mumbai','Cricketer')
        self.show()

    def myTreeViewModelCreation(self, myparent):
        # creating a new item model with the initial rows = 0, initial columns
        = 4 and specified parent
        mymodel = QStandardItemModel(0, 4, myparent)

        #setHeaderData(): Sets the data in the header for the provided
        section(0, 1, 2 and 3)
        #with the specified orientation as Horizontal to the
        # given value (Name, Contact_Number, City and Profession).
```

```
        # if the header's data is updated , it will be returning True
        mymodel.setHeaderData(0, Qt.Horizontal, "Name")
        mymodel.setHeaderData(1, Qt.Horizontal, "Contact_Number")
        mymodel.setHeaderData(2, Qt.Horizontal, "City")
        mymodel.setHeaderData(3, Qt.Horizontal, "Profession")

        # returning the item model
        return mymodel

    def myaddition(self,mymodel, myname, mycontactnumber, mycity, myprofession):
        # insertRow for displaying the data
        mymodel.insertRow(0)
        # index(): gives the QModelIndex associated with the item
        # setData(): set the specified value (which are passed as arguments)
        # to the item's data for the given role.
        # ----> Also, setData() is in charge of changing the details
        # information of a role related to a QModelIndex.
        mymodel.setData(mymodel.index(0, self.Name), myname)
        mymodel.setData(mymodel.index(0, self.Contact_Number), mycontactnumber)
        mymodel.setData(mymodel.index(0, self.City), mycity)
        mymodel.setData(mymodel.index(0, self.Profession), myprofession)

if __name__=="__main__":
    app = QApplication(sys.argv)
    w = MyTreeView()
    w.show()
    sys.exit(app.exec_())
```

Output:

The output can be seen in the following *Figure 5.29:*

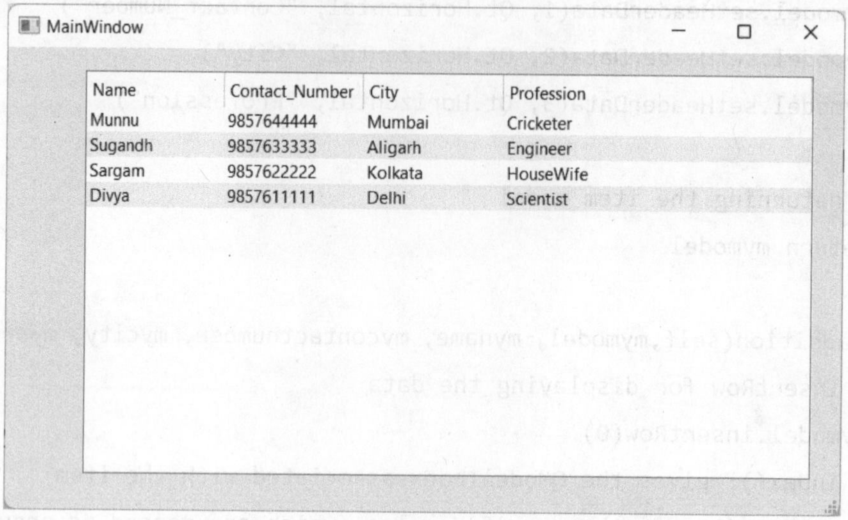

Figure 5.29: *Output of TreeView/ run_TreeView_eg1.py*

Note: The preceding code is covered in the program name: TreeView/run_TreeView_eg1.py

From the above code, we see that we are adding the data to the **`Treeview`** object using code.

Table view

A table view is implemented to display items from a model using **`QTableView`**. It is one of the Model/View frameworks of PyQt5. To show data provided by models derived from the **`QAbstractItemModel`** class, **`QTableView`** implements the interfaces defined by the **`QAbstractItemView`** class. The **`QTableView`** widget from PyQt5 will be used to build spreadsheets and tables. The rows and columns will be creating the Tables. Cells are formed where rows and columns intersect. The **`TableView`** widget allows editing and interaction with each cell. The table view receives instructions on how to populate and format the table cells from the **`rowCount()`**, **`columnCount()`**, and **`data()`** methods for the item model.

Important properties

Let us now check some important properties.

showGrid

This property will decide whether the grid is to be displayed or not. The grid will be drawn when checked, or else there will be no grid. The default value is set to **True**. Refer to the following *Figure 5.30:*

Figure 5.30: *Image depicting showGrid property of QTableView widget in Qt Designer*

gridStyle

The pen style is set for drawing the grid using the **`gridStyle`** property. From the list of options shown in the following *Figure 5.31*, the user may choose any option:

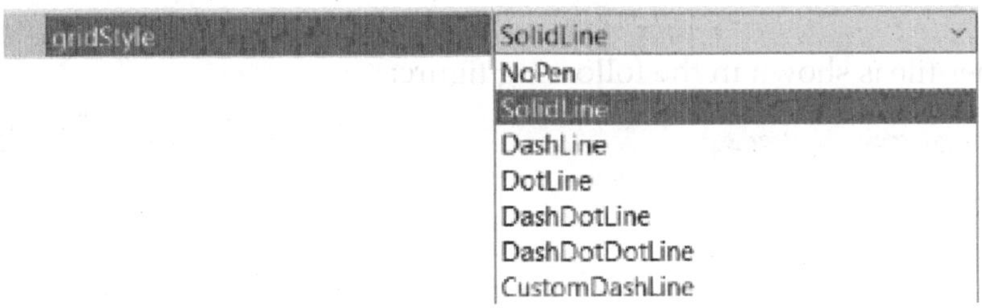

Figure 5.31: *Image depicting gridStyle property of QTableView widget in Qt Designer*

sortingEnabled

The default value is unchecked, which means sorting is disabled for the **`QTableView`** widget. When checked, the sorting will be enabled. Refer to the following *Figure 5.32:*

Figure 5.32: *Image depicting sortingEnabled property of QTableView widget in Qt Designer*

wordWrap

The default value is **True** indicating that the item text will be wrapped at necessary word breaks, and otherwise not. Refer to the following *Figure 5.33:*

Figure 5.33: *Image depicting wordWrap property of QTableView widget in Qt Designer*

cornerButtonEnabled

The default value is **True,** indicating that the top-left corner button will be enabled. When clicked, all the cells in the **QTableView** widget will be selected. Refer to the following *Figure 5.33:*

Figure 5.34*: Image depicting cornerButtonEnabled property of QTableView widget in Qt Designer*

Now, we shall see an example of **Table View** widget.

The details of the file names are as follows:

S No.	Qt Designer file name (.ui)	Converting the QtDesigner file name to Python file (.py)	Creating another Python file and importing the converted Python file from Qt Designer
1.	**TableView_eg1.ui**	**TableView_eg1.py**	**run_TableView_eg1.py**

Table 5.3: *Details of filenames*

The Qt Designer file is shown in the following figure:

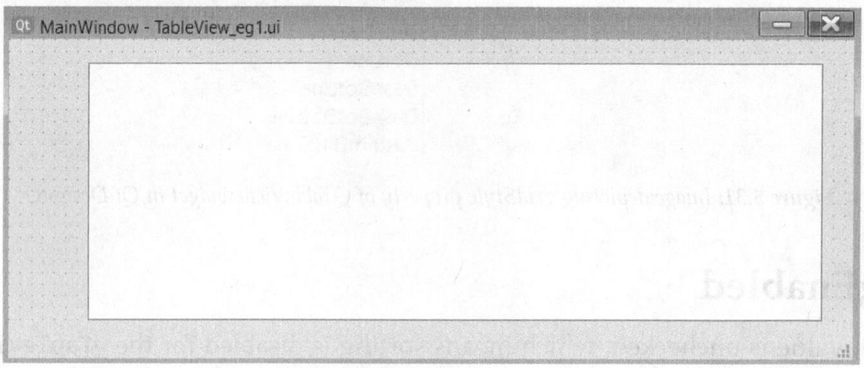

Figure 5.35*: Qt Designer file: TableView_eg1.ui*

Note: The above .ui file is covered in path: TableView/TableView_eg1.ui

Consider the following code of **run_TableView_eg1.py:**

```
import sys

from PyQt5.QtWidgets import QMainWindow, QApplication

from PyQt5.QtCore import Qt, QAbstractTableModel# using QAbstractTableModel

from PyQt5.QtGui import QStandardItemModel

from TableView_eg1 import *
```

```
class MyTableView(QMainWindow):

    def __init__(self):
        super().__init__()
        self.ui = Ui_MainWindow()
        self.ui.setupUi(self)
        #creating a 2-D list
        mydata = [
          [11, 12, 13, 14],
          [15, 16, 17, 18],
          [19, 20, 21, 22],
          [23, 24, 25, 26]
        ]
        self.model = MyTableModel(mydata) # calling a custom model MyTableModel
        and passing mydata as a parameter into the constructor
         # model is set for the Tableview
        self.ui.tableView.setModel(self.model)

# creating a custom model for interfacing between data object and view
class MyTableModel(QAbstractTableModel):
    def __init__(self, mydata):
            super().__init__()
            self._data = mydata

    # data is returned for given table locations and parameters index and role
    are passed
    def data(self, index, role):
        if role == Qt.DisplayRole: # for returning string
            # The table location for which the information is currently being
            requested
            # is given by the index parameter
            # The row and column numbers in the view are provided by the
            # functions .row() ---> (indexing into the outer list)
```

```
            # and.column(indexing into the sub-list) ---> (), respectively.
            # in the form of nested list , data is stored
            return self._data[index.row()][index.column()]

    # number of rows is returned
    def rowCount(self, index):
        # outer list length is returned.
        return len(self._data)

    # number of columns is returned
    def columnCount(self, index):
        # first sub list is taken .that is no. of elements in inner list and
        the length is being returned
        # if all rows are of an equal length , then only it will work
        return len(self._data[0])

if __name__=="__main__":
    app = QApplication(sys.argv)
    w = MyTableView()
    w.show()
    sys.exit(app.exec_())
```

Output:

The output can be seen in the following *Figure 5.36:*

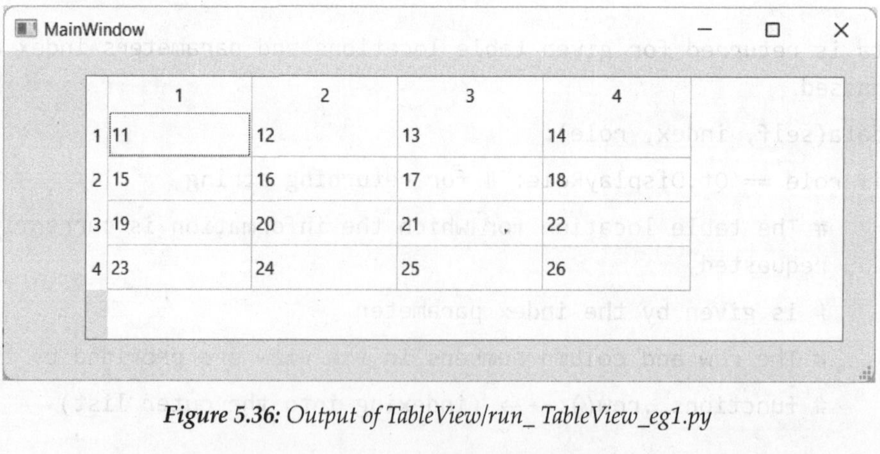

***Figure 5.36:** Output of TableView/run_ TableView_eg1.py*

Note: The preceding code is covered in program name: TableView/run_TableView_eg1.py

In the above code, we can see the display of values using a simple data structure by using a custom class **`MyTableModel`**.

Column view

One of the parts of Qt's Model/View framework illustrates a model in many **`QListViews`**, one for each tree hierarchy. Moreover, it is coined as list cascading. In order to display data provided by models derived from the **`QAbstractItemModel`** class, **`QColumnView`** implements the interfaces described by the **`QAbstractItemView`** class.

Important properties

Let us now check some important properties.

resizeGripsVisible

This property will decide whether resize grips are experienced by list views or not. The default value is set to **True**. Refer to the following *Figure 5.37:*

Figure 5.37: *Image depicting resizeGripsVisible property of QColumnView widget in Qt Designer*

Now, we shall see an example of a **`ColumnView`** widget.

The details of the file names are as follows:

S No.	Qt Designer file name (.ui)	Converting the Qt Designer file name to Python file (.py)	Creating another Python file and importing the converted Python file from Qt Designer
1.	`ColumnView_eg1.ui`	`ColumnView_eg1.py`	`run_ColumnView_eg1.py`

Table 5.4: *Details of filenames*

The Qt Designer file is shown in the following figure:

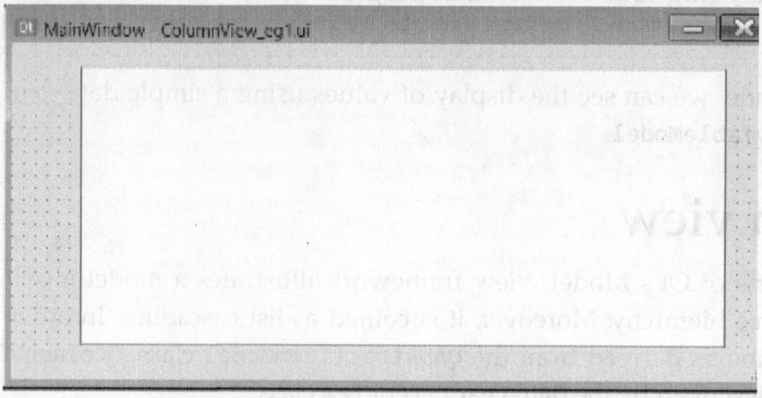

Figure 5.38: Qt Designer file: ColumnView_eg1.ui

Note: The above .ui file is covered in Path: ColumnView/ColumnView_eg1.ui

Consider the following code of **`run_ColumnView_eg1.py`:**

```
import sys
from PyQt5.QtWidgets import QMainWindow, QApplication, QFileSystemModel#
importing QFileSystemModel
from ColumnView_eg1 import *
from PyQt5.QtCore import QDir

class MyColumnView(QMainWindow):
    def __init__(self):
        super().__init__()
        self.ui = Ui_MainWindow()
        self.ui.setupUi(self)

        # creating an object of QFileSystemModel() class
        self.myfile = QFileSystemModel()

        # serTootPath(): Installs a file system watcher on it and changes the
        directory
        # that the model is watching to newPath. The model will update if files
        # or directories in this directory change.
```

```
        self.myfile.setRootPath(QDir.rootPath())
        print(QDir.rootPath()) # returns the root directory's absolute path.
        print(QDir.homePath()) # returns the user's home directory's absolute
        path.
        print(QDir.currentPath()) # provides the current directory of the
        application's absolute path.

        for dirname in (QDir.rootPath(), QDir.homePath(), QDir.currentPath()):
            # model is set for the Columnview
            self.ui.columnView.setModel(self.myfile)

            # setRootIndex: Sets the item at the specified index as the root
            item.
            self.ui.columnView.setRootIndex(self.myfile.index(dirname))
        self.show()

if __name__=="__main__":
    app = QApplication(sys.argv)
    w = MyColumnView()
    w.show()
    sys.exit(app.exec_())
```

Output:

The output can be seen in the following *Figure 5.39:*

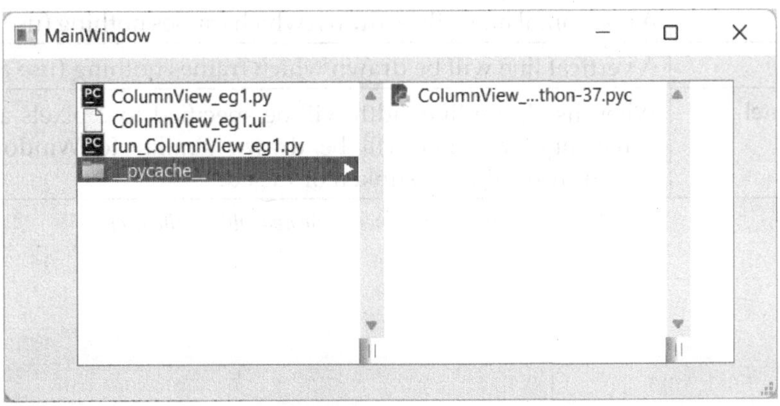

***Figure 5.39**: Output of ColumnView/ run_ColumnView_eg1.py*

Note: The preceding code is covered in program name: ColumnView/run_ColumnView_eg1.py

In the above code, the views have a **rootIndex** that instructs them which portion of the model to display, and the **QFileSystemModel** has a **rootPath** that specifies the root from which the files will be monitored.

QFrame

The widgets base class, which can have a frame, is provided by **QFrame** class. A frame shape and a shadow style that will be used to distinguish the frame from neighboring widgets, visually, make up the frame style. We shall now delve into their important properties.

frameShape

This property will set the available **frameShape** value to the user from the frame style. Users may choose any of the frame shapes from the available list. The default value is **StyledPanel** in Qt Designer, and then drag and drop any **ItemView** widget in a GUI form. Different frame shapes value available to the user are as follows:

S No.	Frame shapes availability	Description
1	**NoFrame**	Nothing will be drawn.
2	**Box**	A box will be drawn around its contents.
3	**Panel**	A panel will be drawn for making the appearance of contents either sunken or raised.
4	**StyledPanel**	A rectangular panel will be drawn with a look depending on the current GUI style with an appearance either as sunken or raised.
5	**HLine**	A horizontal line will be drawn which frames nothing (use as a separator)
6	**VLine**	A vertical line will be drawn which frames nothing (use as a separator)
7	**WinPanel**	When used, the linewidth will be specified to 2 pixels and using this, a rectangular panel will be drawn similar to Windows 2000 with appearance either as sunken or raised.

***Table 5.5:** Different frame shapes value available to the user*

The property image in Qt Designer is shown in the following figure:

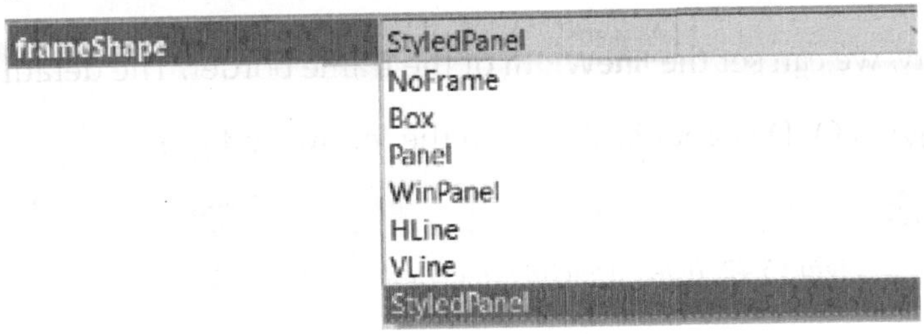

Figure 5.40: Image depicting frameShape property in Qt Designer

frameShadow

In order to give a 3D effect to frames, the shadow type can be set using this property. User may choose any of the following from the availability, which is **Plain, Raised,** or **Sunken**:

S No.	frameShadow availability	Description
1.	**Plain**	There is no 3-D effect, and when drawn with the WindowTextcolor palette, the frame and contents seem level with the surroundings.
2.	**Raised**	Draws a 3D raised line using the light and dark colors in the current color group, giving the appearance that the frame and its contents are raised.
3.	**Sunken**	Draws a 3D raised line using the light and dark colors in the current color group, giving the appearance that the frame and its contents are sunken. The default value is sunken in Qt Designer when dragging and dropping any `ItemView` widget in a GUI form.

Table 5.6: frameShadow availability

The property image in Qt Designer is shown in the following figure:

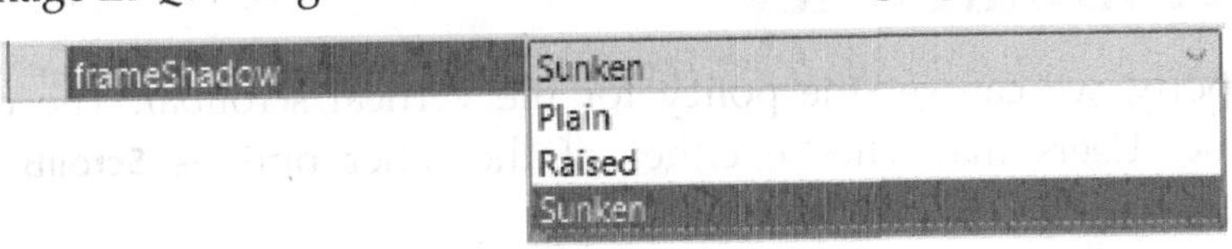

Figure 5.41: Image depicting frameShadow property in Qt Designer

lineWidth

Using this property, we can set the **lineWidth** of the frame border. The default value is **1**.

The property image in Qt Designer is shown in the following figure:

***Figure 5.42:** Image depicting lineWidth property in Qt Designer*

midLineWidth

Using this property, we can determine how wide that extra line must be in the middle of the frame. To create a distinctive 3D effect, a third color is used. The default value is **0**.

The property image in Qt Designer is shown in the following figure:

***Figure 5.43:** Image depicting midLineWidth property in Qt Designer*

You may go through various combinations of line width and frame styles from **https://doc.qt.io**

QAbstractScrollArea

In **QAbstractScrollArea** class (common for all the model-based item views widgets of Qt Designer), there is a viewport (area contents providing a central widget) that is scrolled. There is a vertical and horizontal scroll bar next to the viewport. The viewport expands when a scrollbar is hidden to cover the available space and shrinks when it is visible again to make its room.

verticalScrollBarPolicy

Using this property, we can set the policy for the vertical scrollbar. The default value is **ScrollBarAsNeeded**. Users may choose either of the other options **ScrollBarAlwaysOff** and **ScrollBarAlwaysOn**.

The property image in Qt Designer is shown in the following figure:

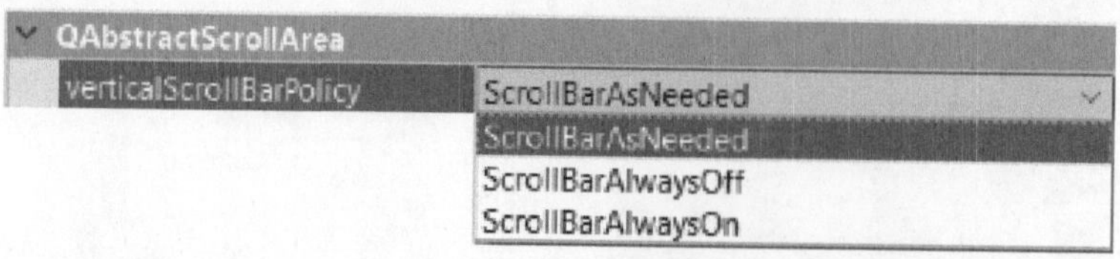

***Figure 5.44:** Image depicting verticalScrollBarPolicy property in Qt Designer*

horizontalScrollBarPolicy

Using this property, we can set the policy for the horizontal Scrollbar. The default value is **ScrollBarAsNeeded**. User may choose either of the other options **ScrollBarAlwaysOff** and **ScrollBarAlwaysOn** as well.

The property image in Qt Designer is shown in the following figure:

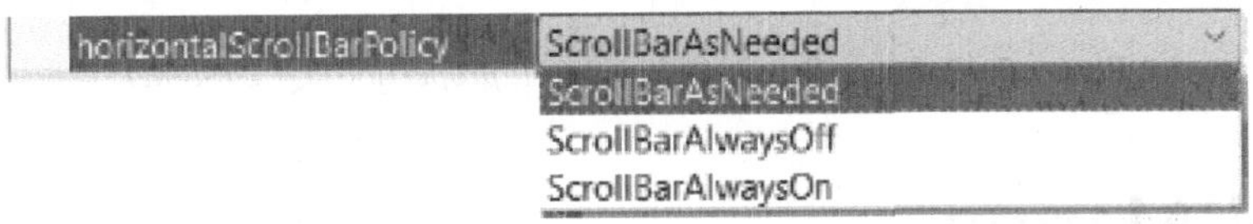

***Figure 5.45**: Image depicting horizontalScrollBarPolicy property in Qt Designer*

sizeAdjustPolicy

Using this property, we can set the policy on how the scroll area size changes when the view port size is changed. The default value is **AdjustIgnored**. Refer to the following *Table 5.7:*

S No.	Different sizeAdjustPolicy constants	Description
1	**AdjustIgnored**	The scroll area will not alter its earlier behavior as it will not make adjustments.
2	**AdjustToContents**	The scroll area will continuously change to fit the viewport.
3	**AdjustToContentsOnFirstShow**	The first time the scroll area is displayed, it will adjust to its viewport.

***Table 5.7:** Different sizeAdjustPolicy constants*

The property image in Qt Designer is shown in the following figure:

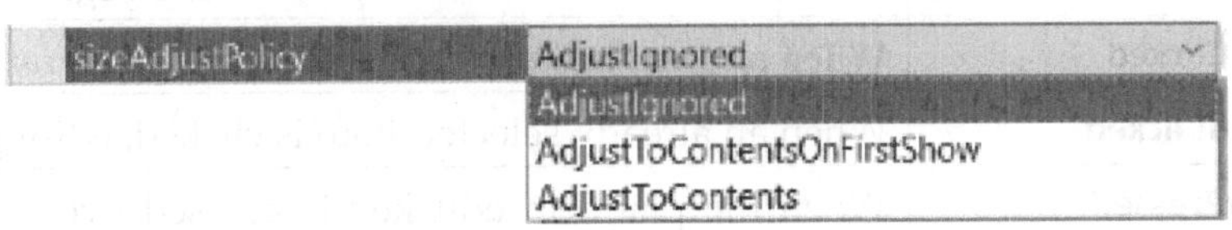

***Figure 5.46**: Image depicting sizeAdjustPolicy property in Qt Designer*

QAbstractItemView

The **`QAbstractItemView`** class (common for all the model based item views widgets of Qt Designer) gives item view class's fundamental capabilities.

autoScroll

This property is set to **True** by default and the **`QAbstractItemView`** widget will automatically scroll its contents if the user moves it within 16 pixels of the viewport edge.

The property image in Qt Designer is shown in the following figure:

Figure 5.47: *Image depicting autoScroll property in Qt Designer*

autoScrollMargin

The area size will be set using this property when auto-scrolling is enabled. The default value is 16 pixels.

The property image in Qt Designer is shown in the following figure:

Figure 5.48: *Image depicting autoScrollMargin property in Qt Designer*

editTriggers

When checked, actions of **`QAbstractItemView`** widget will initiate item editing. **Doubleclicked** and **EditKeyPressed** are checked by default and are combined using the OR operator. Different constants are shown in the following *Table 5.8*:

S No.	Different editTriggers constants	Description
1	**NoEditTriggers**	No editing is allowed.
2	**CurrentChanged**	When the current item changes, editing begins.
3	**DoubleClicked**	When an item is double-clicked, editing begins.
4	**SelectedClicked**	When an already selected item is clicked, editing begins.
5	**EditKeyPressed**	When the platform edit key is pressed over an item, editing begins.
6	**AnyKeyPressed**	When any key is pressed over an item, editing begins.
7	**AllEditTriggers**	All aforementioned actions begin editing.

Table 5.8: *Different editTriggers constants*

The property image in Qt Designer is shown in the following figure:

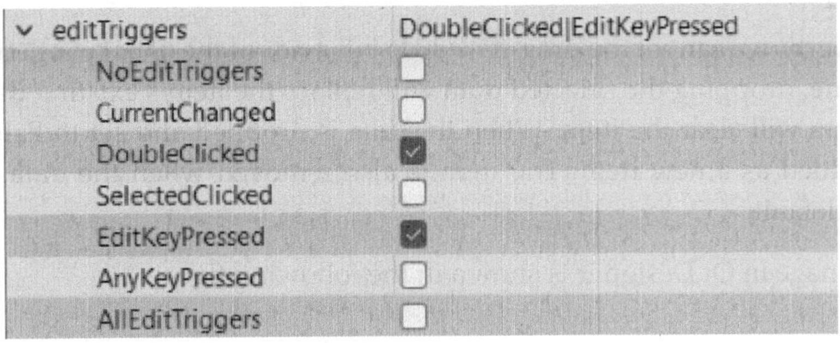

***Figure 5.49**: Image depicting editTriggers property in Qt Designer*

tabKeyNavigation

When set, item navigation with tab and back tab is enabled.

The property image in Qt Designer is shown in the following figure:

***Figure 5.50**: Image depicting tabKeyNavigation property in Qt Designer*

showDropIndicator

When set, the drop indicator is visible in **`QAbstractItemView`** widget while dragging and dropping objects.

The property image in Qt Designer is shown in the following figure:

***Figure 5.51**: Image depicting showDropIndicator property in Qt Designer*

dragEnabled

When set, the **`QAbstractItemView`** widget supports dragging of its own items.

The property image in Qt Designer is shown in the following figure:

***Figure 5.52**: Image depicting dragEnabled property in Qt Designer*

dragDropOverwriteMode

Using this property, we can set the drag-and-drop behavior of the **QAbstractItemView** widget. When set to **True**, dropping the selected data will replace the item's existing data, whereas on moving, the data will clear the item. When the data is dropped and set to **False**, the selected data will be added as a new item. The item is also removed when the data is moved. It is unchecked by default.

The property image in Qt Designer is shown in the following figure:

Figure 5.53*: Image depicting dragDropOverwriteMode property in Qt Designer*

dragDropMode

This property explains various drag-and-drop actions that the **QAbstractItemView** widget can take.

Different constants are shown in the following *Table 5.9*:

S No.	Different dragDropMode constants	Description
1	**NoDragDrop**	Dragging or dropping is not supported.
2	**DragOnly**	Dragging of its own items are supported by **QAbstractItemView** widget.
3	**DropOnly**	Dropping is supported by **QAbstractItemView** widget.
4	**DragDrop**	Both dragging and dropping is supported by **QAbstractItemView** widget.
5	**InternalMove**	Only move operations are accepted and not copy from itself by **QAbstractItemView** widget.

Table 5.9*: Different dragDropMode constants*

The property image in Qt Designer is shown in the following figure:

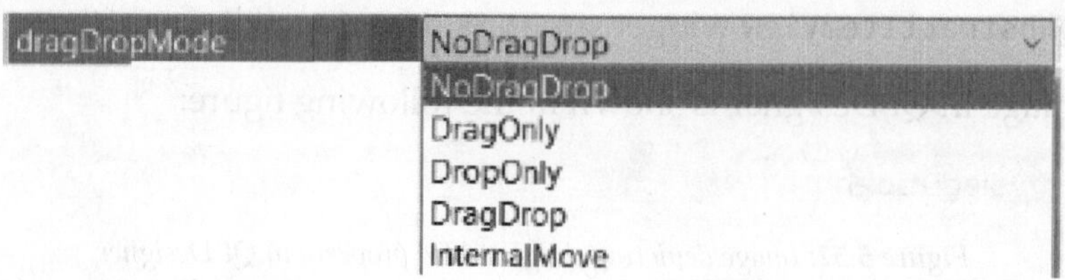

Figure 5.54*: Image depicting dragDropOverwriteMode property in Qt Designer*

defaultDropAction

Using this property, we can set the default drop action used in the **QAbstractItemView** widget. When the supported actions support **CopyAction** and the property is not set, the drop action is **CopyAction.**

The property image in Qt Designer is shown in the following figure:

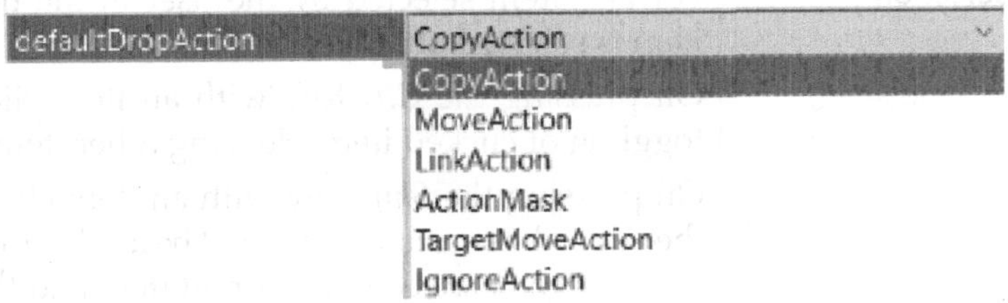

***Figure 5.55:** Image depicting defaultDropAction property in Qt Designer*

alternatingRowColors

When set to **True**, using Base and **AlternateBasecolor**, the item background will be drawn. If set to **False** using Base color, which is the default value, only the item background will be drawn.

The property image in Qt Designer is shown in the following figure:

***Figure 5.56:** Image depicting alternatingRowColors property in Qt Designer*

selectionMode

Using this property, the user can decide whether to select one item or many items and in many item selections, whether continuous range of items must be selected or not. Refer to the following *Table 5.10:*

S No.	Different selectionMode constants	Description
1	**NoSelection**	There is no selection of items.
2	**SingleSelection**	Any item that was already picked by the user is unselected when they select an item. By pressing down the *Ctrl* key while clicking the selected item, the user can deselect the item.

S No.	Different selectionMode constants	Description
3	**MultiSelection**	Any item selected by the user in a usual way, the selection status is toggled for that item leaving the other items alone. On dragging the mouse over multiple items, they can be toggled.
4	**ExtendedSelection**	For any item selected by the user in the usual way, a new item is selected after clearing the selection. On pressing the *Ctrl* Key with an item click, there will be toggling of clicked items, leaving other items untouched. On pressing the *Shift* Key with an item click, depending on the clicked item state, there will be a selection or no selection for all items between the current item and the clicked item. On dragging the mouse multiple items, selection can be done.
5	**ContiguousSelection**	For any item selected by the user in a usual way, a new item is selected after clearing the selection. On pressing *Shift* Key with an item click, depending on the clicked item state, there will be selection or no selection for all items between the current item and the clicked item.

Table 5.10: Different selectionMode constants

The property image in Qt Designer is shown in the following figure:

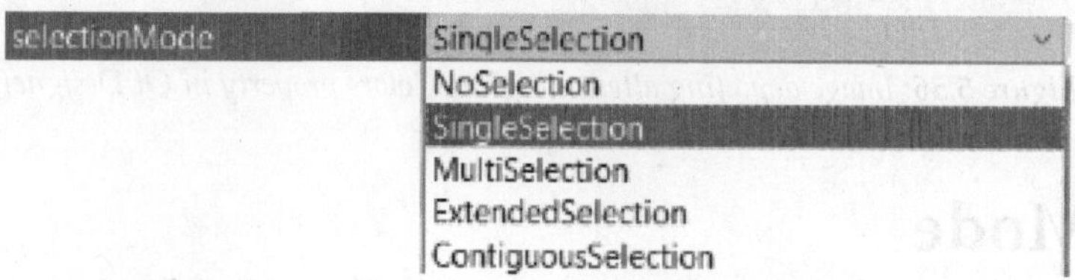

***Figure 5.57:** Image depicting selectionMode property in Qt Designer*

selectionBehavior

`QAbstractItemView` widget will set the selection behavior using this property. Different constants are as shown in the following *Table 5.11:*

S No.	Different selectionBehavior constants	Description
1	**SelectItems**	Single item will be selected.
2	**SelectRows**	Items with only rows will be selected.
3	**SelectColumns**	Items with only columns will be selected.

Table 5.11: Different selectionBehavior constants

The property image in Qt Designer is shown in the following figure:

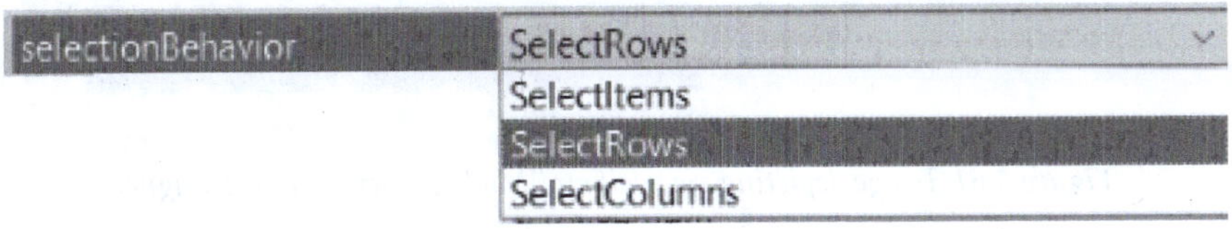

Figure 5.58: Image depicting selectionBehavior property in Qt Designer

iconSize

Using this property, the item size icons will be set.

The property image in Qt Designer is shown in the following figure:

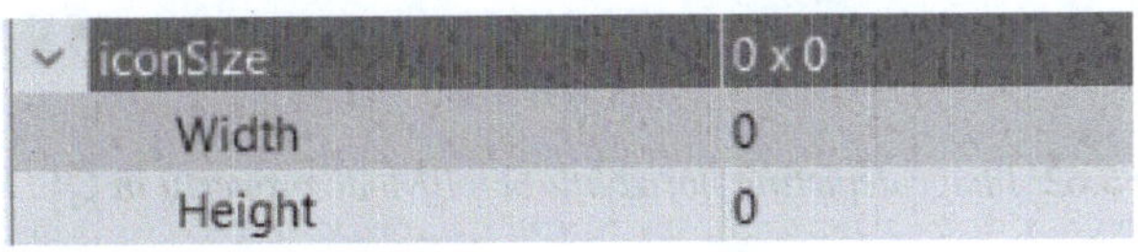

Figure 5.59: Image depicting iconSize property in Qt Designer

textElideMode

This property will set the position of **QAbstractItemView** widget in elided text whose default value is **ElideRight**.

The property image in Qt Designer is shown in the following figure:

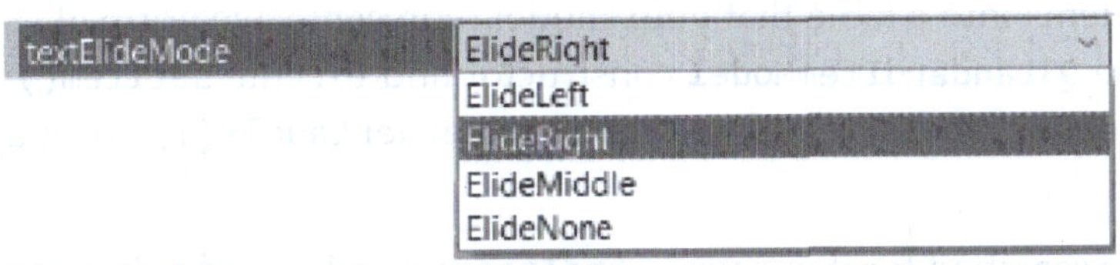

Figure 5.60: Image depicting textElideMode property in Qt Designer

verticalScrollMode

This property will set the scrolling of **QAbstractItemView** widget item contents in the vertical direction. Scrolling can be performed either per item or per pixel.

The property image in Qt Designer is shown in the following figure:

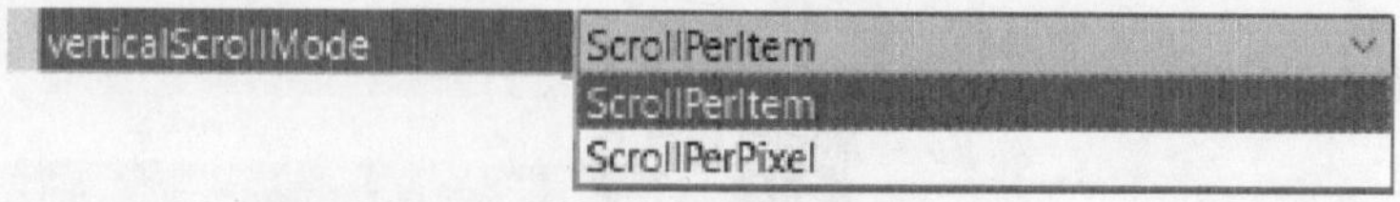

***Figure 5.61:** Image depicting verticalScrollMode property in Qt Designer*

horizontalScrollMode

This property will set the scrolling of **QAbstractItemView** widget item contents in the horizontal direction. Scrolling can be performed either per item or per pixel.

The property image in Qt Designer is shown in the following figure:

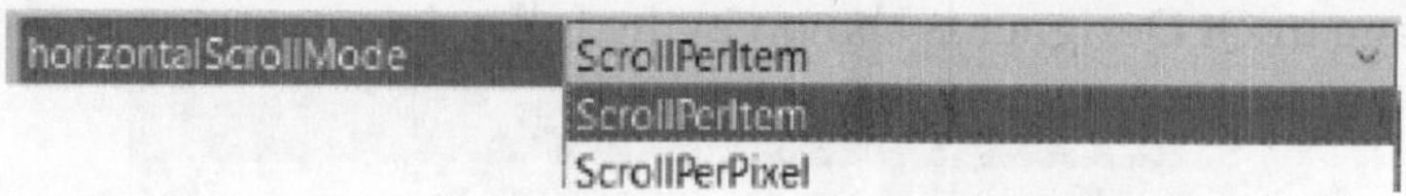

***Figure 5.62:** Image depicting horizontalScrollMode property in Qt Designer*

QStandardItemModel

It is a Model/View Class and a component of the Model/View Framework in PyQt5. **QStandardItem** provides the items in a **QStandardItemModel**. Data is provided by this model in any view which supports the interface such as **QListView**, **QTableView** and **QTreeView**.

Typically, we start with an empty **QStandardItemModel** and use **appendRow()** method to add items to the model and **item()** method to access individual items when you want a list or tree. To arrange items into a table that your model represents, we normally supply the table's dimensions to the **QStandardItemModel** constructor and execute **setItem()**. With the help of **setHorizontalHeaderLabels()** and **setVerticalHeaderLabels(),** we may set the header labels of our model.

The model can be searched for items using **findItems()** and sorted using **sort()** methods.

To remove all elements from the model, we can use the **clear()** method.

Please refer to the link **https://doc.qt.io** for more information. Examples are already demonstrated while explaining different views.

Conclusion

In this chapter, we learned about in-depth understanding of Item view widgets, including **QTableView**, **QTreeView**, and **QListView** which have proven to be effective tools for presenting data in an ordered and structured way. List formats, hierarchical tree structures, and tabular representations are just a few of the alternatives they provided for data presentation. These widgets are efficient in presenting data in a graphical and user-friendly manner. Additionally, data editing and modification features are included in item view widgets. Users can quickly add, remove, or change items to interact with the data displayed. The user interface is made more interactive by allowing users to specify behaviors and change parameters for these actions using Qt Designer. Additionally, the Model-View architecture, a crucial Qt concept, was presented in this chapter. The user became familiar with models, views, and delegates as well as learned how to interact by learning item view widgets. The Model-View architecture can be used to build and implement applications with the use of this information. The chapter concluded with more details, illustrated with useful illustrations, on key **`QFrame`**, **`QAbstractScrollArea`**, and **`QAbstractItemView`** features. In conclusion, the goal of this chapter on item view widgets in Qt Designer to explain the qualities, features, and customization possibilities was successfully attained.

Points to remember

- Item views are powerful tools for presenting data in a table-like format.
- Because item views are so completely adjustable, user can alter their appearance and behavior to suit your particular requirements.
- A fundamental Qt idea for separating data representation (model) from the visual display (view) and user interaction (delegate) is the Model-View architecture.
- The model/view architecture is the foundation of item views. Thus, the model, the view, and the delegate are three distinct elements that work together to show data. The data is provided by the model, shown by the view, and interacted with by the user is handled by the delegate.
- Items can be viewed in a wide variety of ways. **`QTableView`**, **`QListView`**, and **`QTreeView`** are the most popular varieties. Data can be shown with these widgets in a tree, table, or list format accordingly.
- **`QTreeView`**: This tree view widget uses a hierarchical manner to present data.
- **`QTableView`**: This table view widget uses a tabular layout to present data.
- **`QListView`**: This list view widget uses a list format to display data.
- **`QColumnView`**: This widget displays data in a columnar format for displaying a variety of data types, including strings, integers, and dates.

Questions

1. Describe Item Views in Qt Designer.
2. Explain the following:
   a. **`QListView`**

b. `QTreeView`
c. `QTableView`
d. `QColumnView`
e. Describe `QFrame`, `QAbstractScrollArea`, and `QAbstractItemView`

3. State the function of the list view widget in Qt Designer.
4. List and explain the important properties QListView widget.
5. Explain the following:
   a. `resizeMode`
   b. `layoutMode`
   c. `spacing`
   d. `gridSize`
   e. `viewMode`
   f. `wordWrap`
6. State the function of the tree view widget in Qt Designer.
7. State the function of the table view widget in Qt Designer.
8. Explain the important properties of the table view widget in Qt Designer.
9. State the function of the column view widget in Qt Designer.
10. Explain the important properties of the column view widget in Qt Designer.
11. Explain the following:
    a. `autoExpandDelay`
    b. `indentation`
    c. `rootIsDecorated`
    d. `uniformRowHeights`

CHAPTER 6

Getting Insights of Item Based Widgets in Qt Designer

Introduction

In the previous chapter, we discussed different item views in PyQt5. In this chapter, we will focus on **Item Widgets**. Our primary focus in this chapter will be on learning about **List Widget**, **Tree Widget**, and **Table Widget**. We will be focusing on properties and some useful methods. All these widgets are available under **Item Widgets** in Qt Designer, as shown in the following *Figure 6.1*, where the user can select any of the widgets under **Item Widgets** and drag and drop in a GUI form.

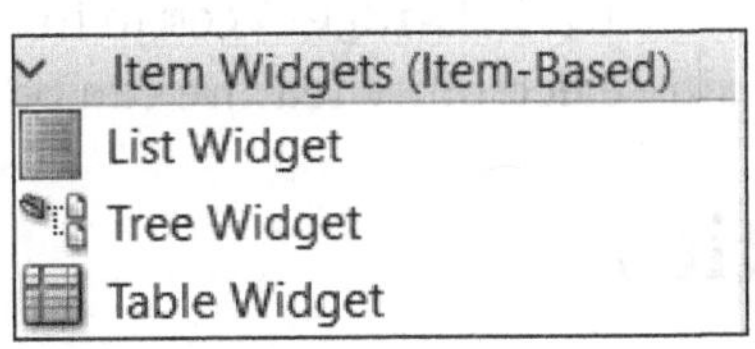

***Figure 6.1:** Different Item Widgets (Item Based) in Qt Designer*

We have already seen about `QObject` and `QWidget` classes when we were dealing with button type widgets. The same applies to **Item Widgets** too. We have already discussed other classes about `QFrame`, `QAbstractScrollArea`, and `QAbstractItemView` class in the previous chapter. The **Item Widgets** have all these range of properties. But the default values may differ from widget to widget. Now, we shall be discussing 3 item widgets and their properties.

Structure

In this chapter, we will discuss the following topics:

- List widget
- Tree widget
- Table widget

Objectives

After reading this chapter, the reader will get to know about **Item Widgets** in Qt Designer which are commonly used for creating interactive user interfaces. The primary objective of this chapter is to understand their properties, functionality, customization options and to gain a thorough knowledge of how to create and operate item-based widgets within the Qt Designer environment. After completion of this chapter, user will be able to create dynamic, interactive user interfaces using the power of item-based widgets. They will discover different features and characteristics to personalize the look and behavior of widgets viz **List Widget**, **Tree Widget** and **Table Widget**. To facilitate user interaction and implement functionality, readers will learn how to manage the events and signals connected to item-based widgets. The reader will be well-equipped to develop complex yet user-friendly interfaces in Qt Designer utilizing item-based widgets. In the end, solved examples of **Item Widgets** will be well discussed along with the comments at mandate places for better understanding of the code.

List widget

List widget is a classic item-based interface for adding and removing items. It has a list view similar to the one supplied by **QListView**, provided by the convenience class **QListWidget**. An item-based interface to add or delete items from a list is the **QListWidget** class. The list's items are all **QListWidgetItem** objects. Each **QListWidgetItem** in the list is managed by **QListWidget** using an internal model. The multi-selectability feature can be set for the **QListWidget** object.

Important properties

We have already seen the different **QListView** properties in the previous chapter. The same properties apply here too. Apart from these properties, we shall discuss **QListWidget** properties.

currentRow

The current item's row is set using this property. The row may also be selected depending on the active selection mode. Default value is **-1**. Refer to the following figure:

Figure 6.2: Image depicting currentRow property of QListWidget in Qt Designer

sortingEnabled

The default value is unchecked and when set to true, this property will decide that sorting is enabled for the list. Refer to the following figure:

Figure 6.3: Image depicting sortingEnabled property of QListWidget in Qt Designer

Important methods

Let us now go over some important methods:

- **clear()**: All the items from the **QListWidget** object will be removed as it will be permanently deleted.
- **insertItem(row, item)**: The **QListWidgetItem** object will be inserted at the position specified by the row (integer).
- **addItem()**: Either a **QListWidgetItem** object or string will be added to the **QListWidget** object.
- **addItems(labels)**: Items with a list of strings will be inserted at the end of the **QListWidget** object.
- **setCurrentItem(item, command)**: Programmatically, we can set the currently selected item to the **QListWidgetItem** object with/without the usage of selection flags, that is, using the command parameter.
- **sortItems([order=Qt.AscendingOrder])**: **QListWidget** items will be arranged according to the specified order.

Important signals

Some signals are as follows:

- **currentItemChanged()**: The signal is emitted whenever the current item changes of the **QListWidget** object.
- **itemClicked()**: The signal is emitted whenever an item in the **QListWidget** object is clicked.

Now, we shall see an example of **QListWidget**.

The details of the file names are given in the following *Table 6.1:*

S No.	Qt Designer File Name (.ui)	Converting the QtDesigner file name to Python file (.py)	Creating another Python file and importing the converted Python file from Qt Designer
1	`listWidget_eg1.ui`	`listWidget_eg1.py`	`run_listWidget_eg1.py`

***Table 6.1:** Details of file names*

The Qt Designer file is shown in the following figure:

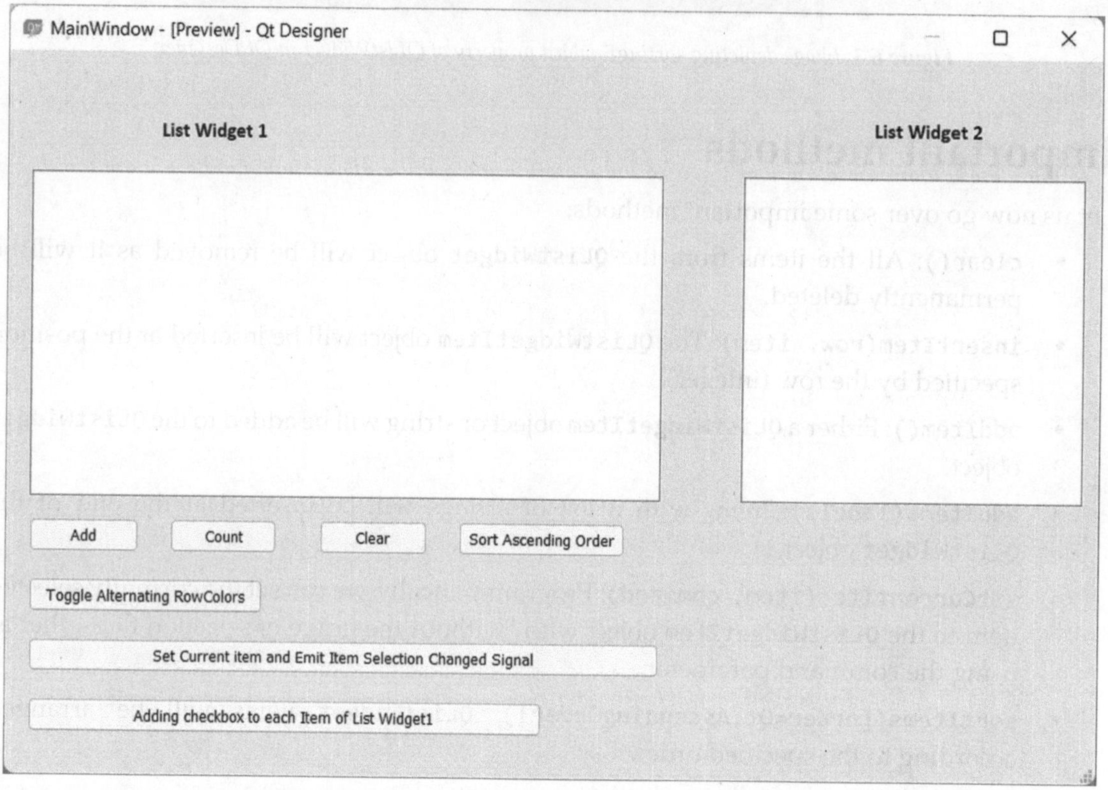

***Figure 6.4**: Qt Designer file: ListWidget/listWidget_eg1.ui*

Note: The above .ui file is covered in Path: ListWidget/listWidget_eg1.ui

Consider the following code of **`run_listWidget_eg1.py`**:

```
import sys
from PyQt5.QtWidgets import QMainWindow,QAbstractItemView, QApplication,QList-
WidgetItem,QCheckBox,QHBoxLayout,QLabel,QWidget, QMessageBox
from PyQt5.QtGui import QPalette, QColor
```

```
from listWidget_eg1 import *

class MyListWidget(QMainWindow):
    def __init__(self):
        super().__init__()
        self.myui = Ui_MainWindow()
        self.myui.setupUi(self)
        self.myui.lw_Add.clicked.connect(self.btn1)
        self.myui.lw_Count.clicked.connect(self.btn2)
        self.myui.lw_Clear.clicked.connect(self.btn3)
        self.myui.lw_SortAsc.clicked.connect(self.btn4)
        self.myui.lw_Toggle.clicked.connect(self.btn5)
        self.myui.lw_SetCurrentItem.clicked.connect(self.btn6)
        self.myui.lw_AddCheckBox.clicked.connect(self.btn7)
        self.myui.lw1.setDragEnabled(True) # allowing dragenabled property of
        lw1 to be True
        self.myui.lw2.setDragEnabled(False)# allowing dragenabled property of
        lw2 to be False
        self.myui.lw1.setDragDropMode(QAbstractItemView.DragDrop) # setting
        dag drop mode of lw1
        self.myui.lw1.setAcceptDrops(False)# allowing acceptDrops property of
        lw1 to be False
        self.myui.lw2.setAcceptDrops(True)# allowing acceptDrops property of
        lw2 to be True
        self.show()

        # Add items to the list widget
        for loop in range(5):
            item = QListWidgetItem()
            item.setText("    Itemmno: {}".format(loop+1))
            self.myui.lw1.addItem(item)

    def btn1(self):
```

```
        # creating an instance of QListWidgetItem
        item = QListWidgetItem()
        # setting the text
        item.setText("    Itemmno: {}".format(self.myui.lw1.count()+1))
        # adding it to the listWidget using addItem method
        self.myui.lw1.addItem(item)

        # Add multiple items to the list widget
        mylist_items = ["     Zeeshan", "      Vicky", "     Abdul"]
        for list_item in mylist_items:
            myinst_item = QListWidgetItem()
            myinst_item.setText(list_item)
            self.myui.lw1.addItem(myinst_item)

    def btn2(self):
        QMessageBox.information(None, 'Item Count Title', "The number of items
        in the list is {}".format(self.myui.lw1.count()))

    def btn3(self):
        # clearing all the listWidget items
        self.myui.lw1.clear()

    def btn4(self):
        # Sorting the listWidget items in ascending order
        self.myui.lw1.sortItems(QtCore.Qt.AscendingOrder)

    def btn5(self):
        # Enable alternate row colors
        self.myui.lw1.setAlternatingRowColors(True)
        mypalette = self.myui.lw1.palette()
        mypalette.setColor(QPalette.AlternateBase, QColor("lightgray"))
```

```
        self.myui.lw1.setPalette(mypalette)

    def btn6(self):
        myselect_item = self.myui.lw1.item(4) # Selecting 5th item of the list
        self.myui.lw1.setCurrentItem(myselect_item) # will set the current
        item of the listWidget

        # Emitting the itemSelectionChanged signal
        self.myui.lw1.itemSelectionChanged.emit() # signal will be emitted
        when the selection of items in the list widget is changed


    def btn7(self):
        #Create a checkbox for each ListWidget item
        for myitm in range(self.myui.lw1.count()):
            myitem = self.myui.lw1.item(myitm)
            mycheck_box = QCheckBox()
            self.myui.lw1.setItemWidget(myitem, mycheck_box)


if __name__=="__main__":
    app = QApplication(sys.argv)
    w = MyListWidget()
    w.show()
    sys.exit(app.exec_())
```

Output:

Default case on running initially

Refer to the following figure:

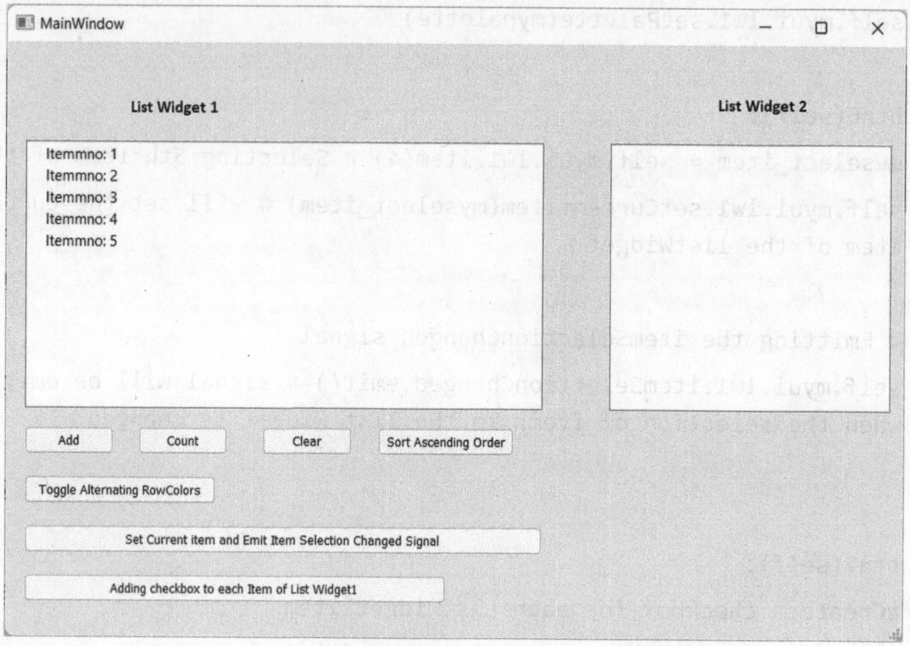

***Figure 6.5**: Default output of ListWidget/run_ listWidget_eg1.py*

Case 1: On pressing Add button

Refer to the following figure:

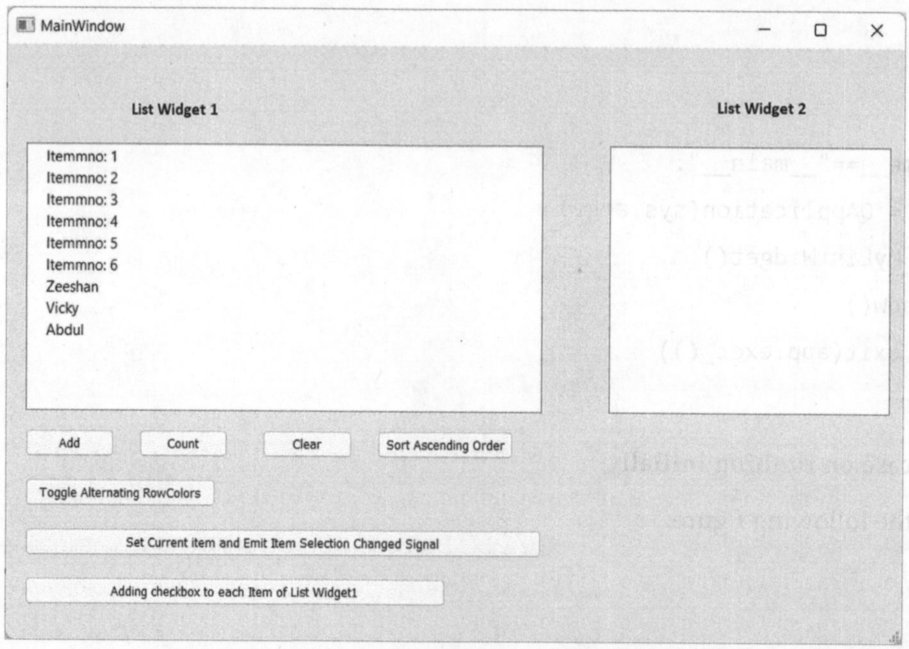

***Figure 6.6**: Case 1 Output of ListWidget/run_ listWidget_eg1.py*

Case 2: On pressing Count button

Refer to the following figure:

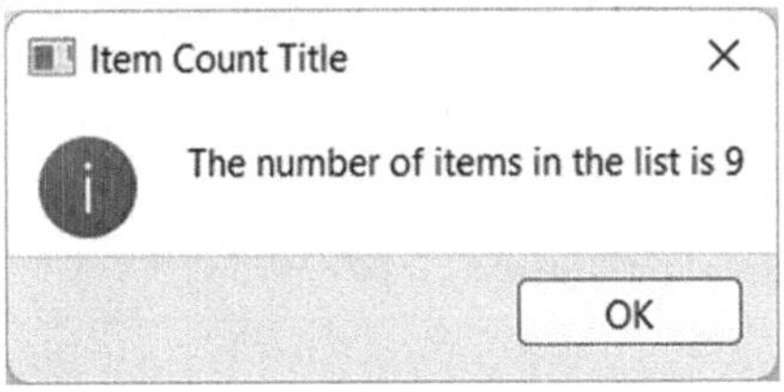

Figure 6.7: *Case-2 Output of ListWidget/run_ listWidget_eg1.py*

Case 3: On pressing Sort Ascending Order button

Refer to the following figure:

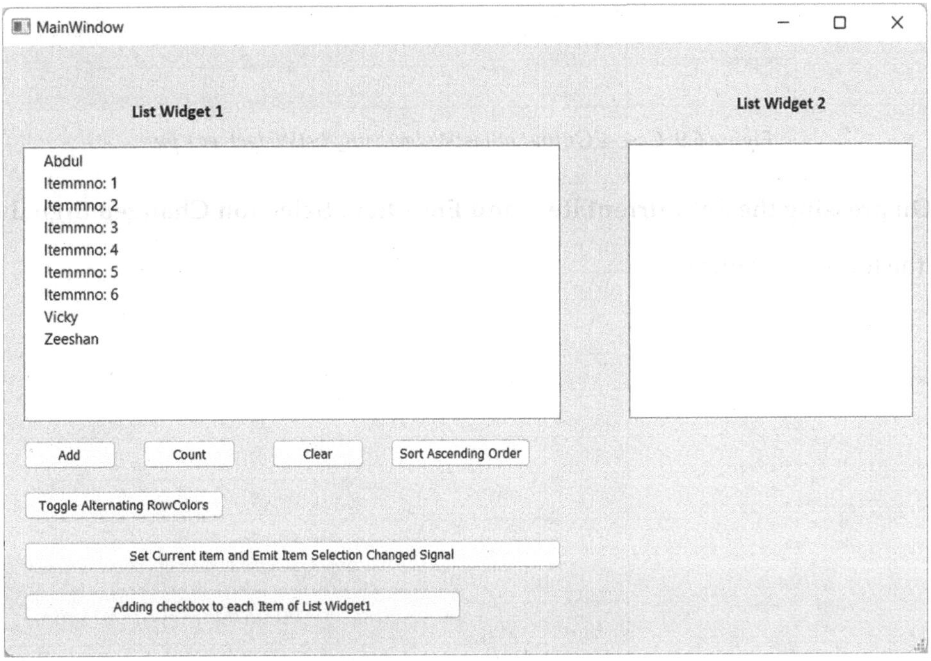

Figure 6.8: *Case-3 Output of ListWidget/run_ listWidget_eg1.py*

Case 4: On pressing Toggle Alternating RowColors button

Refer to the following figure:

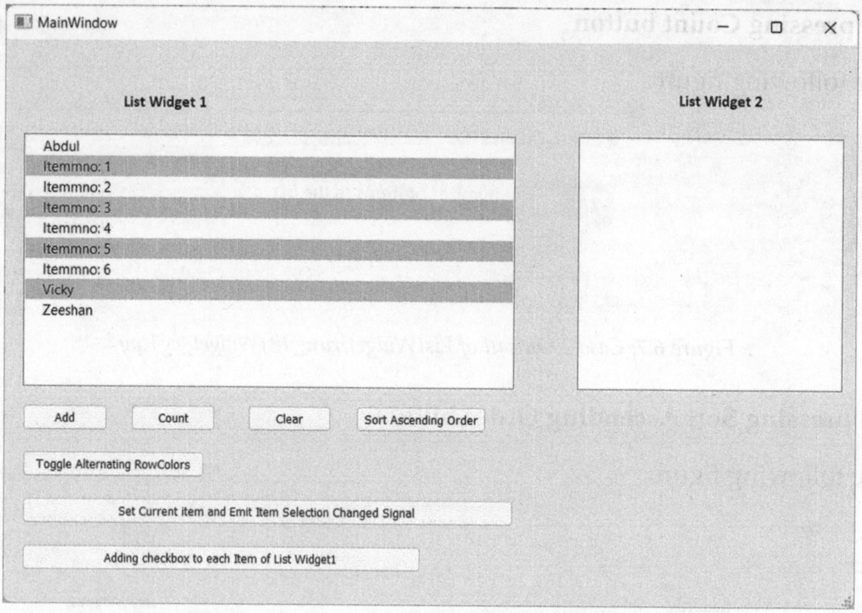

***Figure 6.9**: Case-4 Output of ListWidget/run_ listWidget_eg1.py*

Case 5: On pressing the Set Current item and Emit Item Selection Changed Signal button

Refer to the following figure:

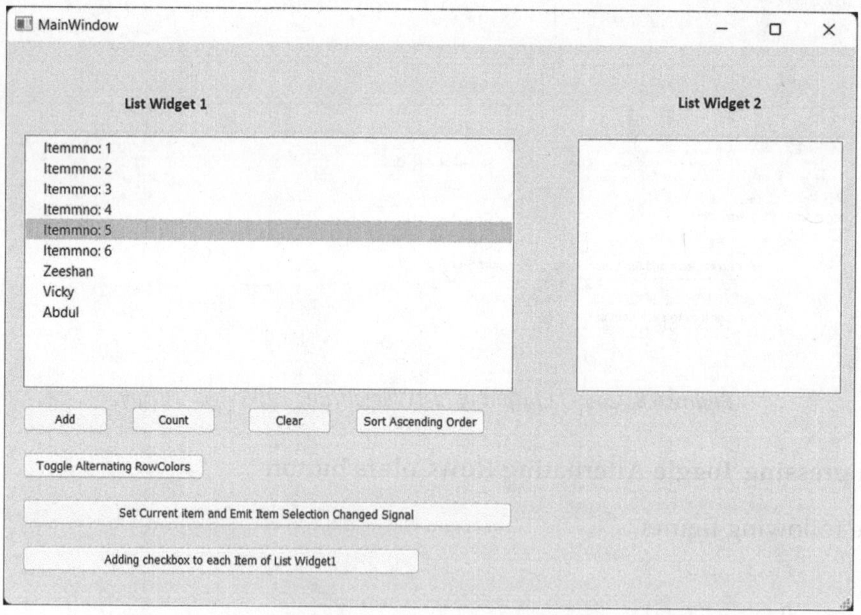

***Figure 6.10**: Case-5 Output of ListWidget/run_ listWidget_eg1.py*

Case 6: On pressing the Adding checkbox to each Item of List Widget1 button

Refer to the following figure:

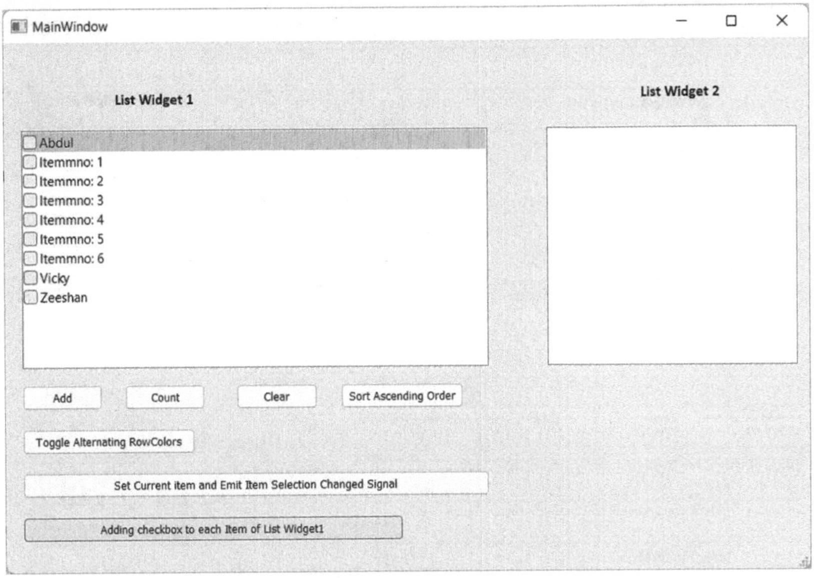

***Figure 6.11**: Case-6 Output of ListWidget/run_ listWidget_eg1.py*

Case 7: On pressing Clear button

Refer to the following figure:

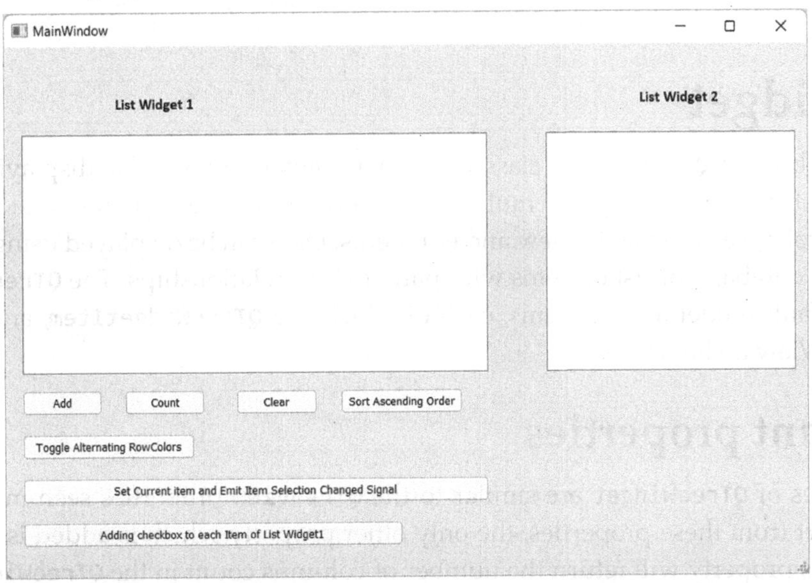

***Figure 6.12**: Case-7 Output of ListWidget/run_ listWidget_eg1.py*

Case 8: Drag and Drop from lw1 to lw2 only

Refer to the following figure:

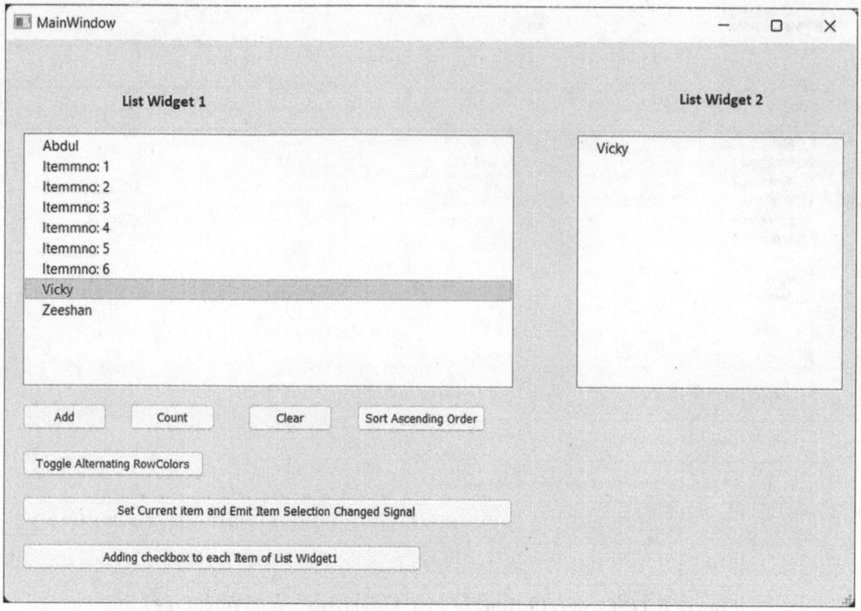

Figure 6.13: Case-8 Output of ListWidget/run_ listWidget_eg1.py

Note: The preceding code is covered in Program Name: ListWidget/run_ listWidget_eg1.py

Tree widget

The PyQt5 library's **`QTreeWidget`** class offers a **`treeView`** widget for displaying data in a hierarchical structure. It supports multiple columns and custom items, and the user can expand and collapse branches to view and edit items. Data can be displayed using it, including a file system, database, or list of items with parent-child relationships. The **`QTreeWidget`** class utilizes a default model to hold items, each of which is a **`QTreeWidgetItem`**, and is based on Qt's Model/View architecture.

Important properties

The properties of **`QTreeWidget`** are similar to the **`QTreeView`** properties seen in the previous chapter. Apart from these properties, the only other property which is added is **`columnCount`** property. This property will return the number of columns count in the **`QTreeWidget`**. Default value is set to 1. We can also set the column count by using the **`setColumnCount(count)`** method. Refer to the following figure:

Figure 6.14: Image depicting columnCount property of QTreeWidget in Qt Designer

Important methods

Let us now go over some important methods:

- **`clear()`**: All the items from the **`QTreeWidget`** object will be removed as it will be permanently deleted.
- **`addTopLevelItem(item)`**: A top-level item can be added to the **`QTreeWidget`** object using this method. The **`QTreeWidgetItem`** or one of its subclass can be the item parameter.
- **`currentItem()`**: The current item in the **`QTreeWidget`** object (the one that is selected and has focus) is returned by this method.
- **`selectedItems()`**: This method will return a list of all selected non-hidden items in the **`QTreeWidget`** object.
- **`setHeaderLabels(labels)`**: This method is used to set the header labels (list of strings) for each column of the **`QTreeWidget`** object.
- **`sortItems(column,order)`**: This function uses the specified column and orders to sort the items in the **`QTreeWidget`** object. The order parameter is a **`Qt.SortOrderenum`** (**`Qt.AscendingOrder`** or **`Qt.DescendingOrder`**), and the column parameter is an integer that specifies the column to sort by.
- **`takeTopLevelItem(index)`**: This method is used to remove an item from the **`QTreeWidget`** object at the specified index parameter and return it. Otherwise, it will return **`None`**. The index parameter is the index of the item to be removed.
- **`setColumnCount(columns)`**: The number of columns displayed in the **`QTreeWidget`** object is specified using this method.

Important signals

Some signals are as follows:

- **`itemActivated(item,column)`**: When an item is activated (double-clicked or pressed when the *Enter* key is pressed), this signal is emitted. The item parameter is the activated item and the column parameter is the column of the item.
- **`itemChanged(item,column)`**: When an item's data has been changed, this signal is emitted. The item parameter is the changed item and the column parameter is the column of the item.

- **`itemClicked(item,column)`**: When an item is clicked, this signal is emitted. The item parameter is the clicked item and the column parameter is the column of the item.
- **`itemCollapsed(item)`**: When an item is collapsed (its children are hidden), this signal is emitted. The item parameter is the collapsed item.
- **`itemDoubleClicked(item,column)`**: When an item is double-clicked, this signal is emitted. The item parameter is the double-clicked item and the column parameter is the column of the item.
- **`itemEntered(item,column)`**: When the mouse-cursor enters an item, this signal is emitted. The item parameter is the entered item and the column parameter is the column of the item.
- **`itemExpanded(item)`**: This signal is emitted when an item is expanded (its children are shown). The item parameter is the expanded item.
- **`itemPressed(item,column)`**: When an item is pressed, this signal is emitted. The item parameter is the pressed item and the column parameter is the column of the item.

Now, we shall see an example of **`QTreeWidget`**.

The details of the file names are as shown in the following *Table 6.2*:

S No.	Qt Designer File Name (.ui)	Converting the Qt Designer file name to Python file (.py)	Creating another Python file and importing the converted Python file from Qt Designer
1	`treeWidget_eg1.ui`	`treeWidget_eg1.py`	`run_treeWidget_eg1.py`

***Table 6.2:** Details of file names*

The Qt Designer file is shown in the following figure:

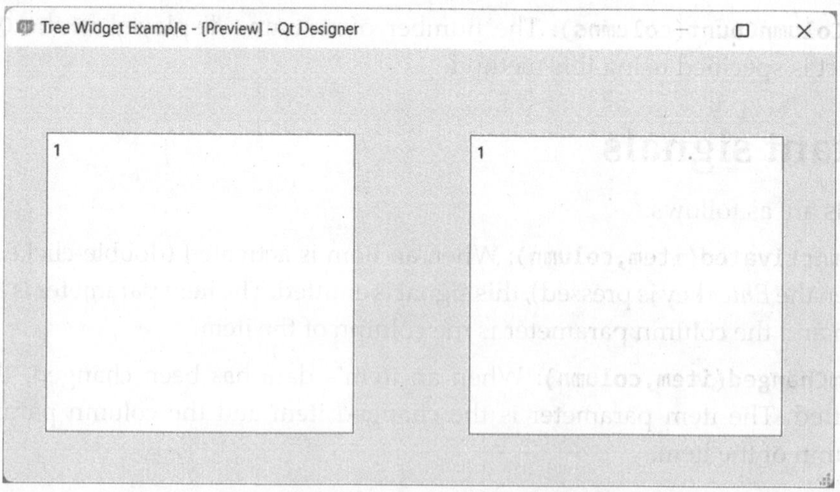

***Figure 6.15:** Qt Designer file: TreeWidget/ treeWidget_eg1.ui*

Note: The above .ui file is covered in Path: TreeWidget/run_treeWidget_eg1.ui

Consider the following code of **run_treeWidget_eg1.py**:

```
import sys
from PyQt5.QtWidgets import QMainWindow, QApplication, QTreeWidget, QTreeWidge-
tItem
from PyQt5.QtGui import QPalette, QColor
from treeWidget_eg1 import *


class MyTreeWidget(QMainWindow):
    def __init__(self):
        super().__init__()
        self.myui = Ui_MainWindow()
        self.myui.setupUi(self)

        # Initially setting the column count of the treeWidget object to 2
        self.myui.treeWidget.setColumnCount(2)

        # Set the header labels for 2 columns
        self.myui.treeWidget.setHeaderLabels(["Name", "Age"])

        # Adding items to the treeWidget object
        myitem1 = QTreeWidgetItem(["Saurabh", "34"])
        myitem2 = QTreeWidgetItem(["Nilesh", "42"])
        myitem3 = QTreeWidgetItem(["Priyanka", "30"])
        myitem4 = QTreeWidgetItem(["Pranav", "31"])
        myitem5 = QTreeWidgetItem(["Papa", "61"])
        myitem6 = QTreeWidgetItem(["Mummy", "60"])

        # For TreeWidget1
        self.myui.treeWidget.addTopLevelItem(myitem1)
        self.myui.treeWidget.addTopLevelItem(myitem2)
        self.myui.treeWidget.addTopLevelItem(myitem3)
```

```
self.myui.treeWidget.addTopLevelItem(myitem4)
self.myui.treeWidget.addTopLevelItem(myitem5)
self.myui.treeWidget.addTopLevelItem(myitem6)

# Connecting the itemClicked signal to the handle_item_click method
self.myui.treeWidget.itemClicked.connect(self.myhandle_item_click)

# Connecting the itemDoubleClicked signal to the handle_item_double_
click method
self.myui.treeWidget.itemDoubleClicked.connect(self.myhandle_item_
double_click)

# Connecting the itemActivated signal to the handle_item_activation
method
self.myui.treeWidget.itemActivated.connect(self.myhandle_item_
activation)

# For TreeWidget2
# Setting the column count to 1
self.myui.treeWidget_2.setColumnCount(1)

# Create the top-level items
self.myitemA = QTreeWidgetItem(self.myui.treeWidget_2, ["Item A"])
self.myitemB = QTreeWidgetItem(self.myui.treeWidget_2, ["Item B"])
self.myitemC = QTreeWidgetItem(self.myui.treeWidget_2, ["Item C"])

# Create the child items for Item A
self.myitemA1 = QTreeWidgetItem(self.myitemA, ["Item A_1"])
self.myitemA2 = QTreeWidgetItem(self.myitemA, ["Item A_2"])

# Create the child items for Item B
self.myitemB1 = QTreeWidgetItem(self.myitemB, ["Item B_1"])
```

```
        self.myitemB2 = QTreeWidgetItem(self.myitemB, ["Item B_2"])

        # Create the child items for Item C
        self.myitemC1 = QTreeWidgetItem(self.myitemC, ["Item C_1"])
        self.myitemC2 = QTreeWidgetItem(self.myitemC, ["Item C_2"])

        # Connect the itemExpanded and itemCollapsed signals to their
        respective slots
        self.myui.treeWidget_2.itemExpanded.connect(self.my_on_item_expanded)
        self.myui.treeWidget_2.itemCollapsed.connect(self.my_on_item_collapsed)

        self.show()

    # Method to handle item click event
    def myhandle_item_click(self,item, column):
        print("An Item is clicked:", item.text(column))

    # Method to handle item double click event
    def myhandle_item_double_click(self,item, column):
        print("An Item is double clicked:", item.text(column))

    # Method to handle item activation event
    def myhandle_item_activation(self,item, column):
        print("An Item is activated:", item.text(column))

    def my_on_item_expanded(self, item):
        # Performing some action when an item is expanded
        print(f"{item.text(0)} was expanded")

    def my_on_item_collapsed(self, item):
        # Performing some action when an item is collapsed
```

```
        print(f"{item.text(0)} was collapsed")


if __name__=="__main__":
    app = QApplication(sys.argv)
    w = MyTreeWidget()
    w.show()
    sys.exit(app.exec_())
```

Output:

Note: Each time code is run again for Case-1 to Case-4.

Default case on running initially

Refer to the following figure:

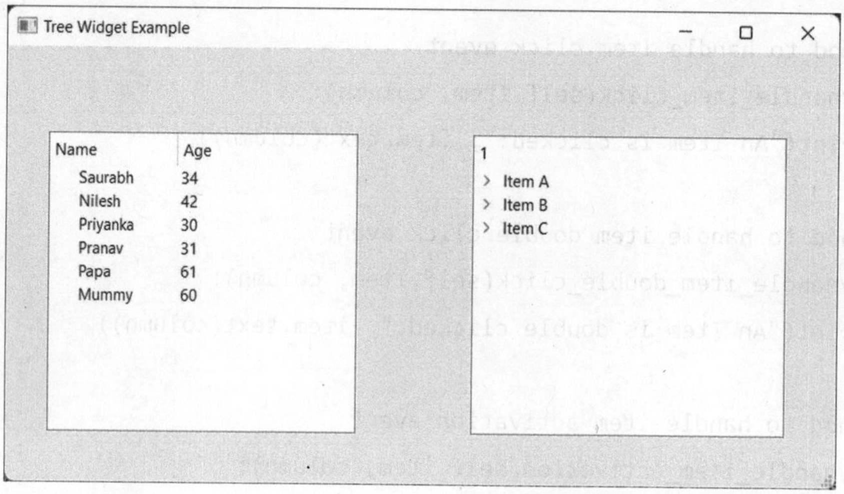

***Figure 6.16**: Default Case output of TreeWidget/ run_treeWidget_eg1.py*

Case 1: Output display when performing Item clicked event on Name = Saurabh

Refer to the following figure:

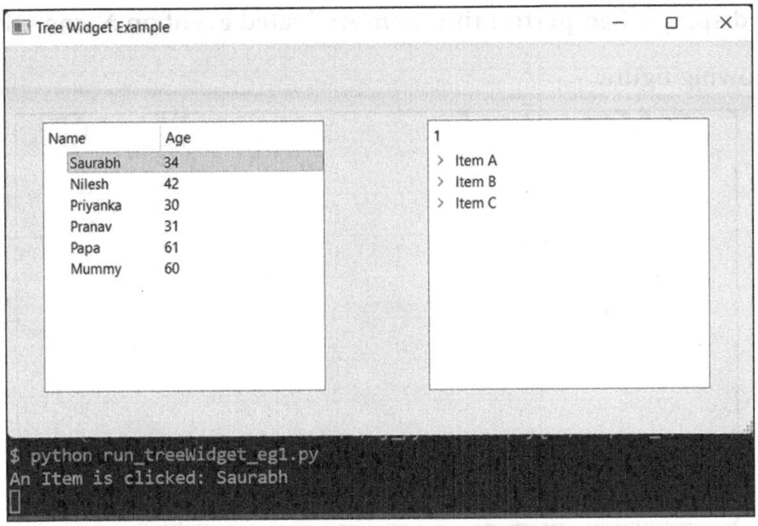

***Figure 6.17**: Case 1 output of TreeWidget/ run_treeWidget_eg1.py*

Case 2: Output display when performing Item double- clicked event on Name = Nilesh

Refer to the following figure:

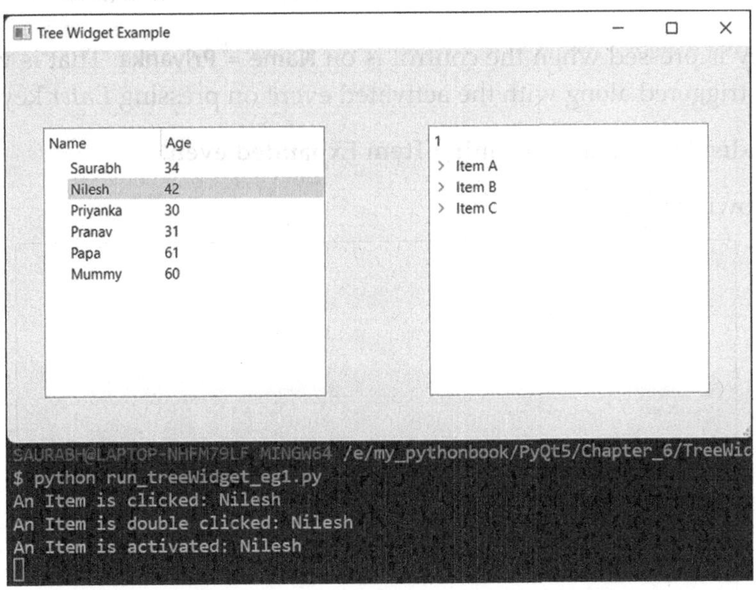

***Figure 6.18**: Case-2 output of TreeWidget/ run_treeWidget_eg1.py*

Here, on pressing double-clicked event on **Name** = **Nilesh**, the first clicked event is triggered followed by double-clicked event and then the activated event.

Case 3: Output display when performing Item Activated event on Name = Priyanka

Refer to the following figure:

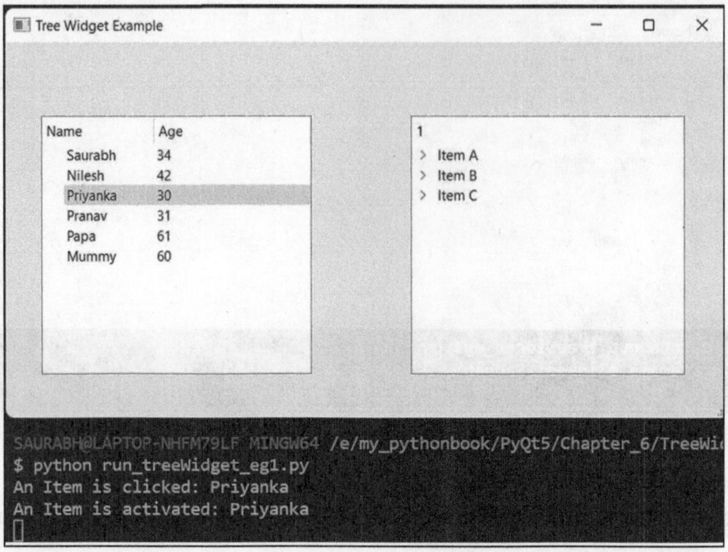

Figure 6.19: Case-3 output of TreeWidget/ run_treeWidget_eg1.py

Here , *Enter* key is pressed when the control is on **Name** = **Priyanka**. That is why the initially clicked event is triggered along with the activated event on pressing *Enter* key.

Case 4: Output display when performing Item Expanded event

Refer to the following figure:

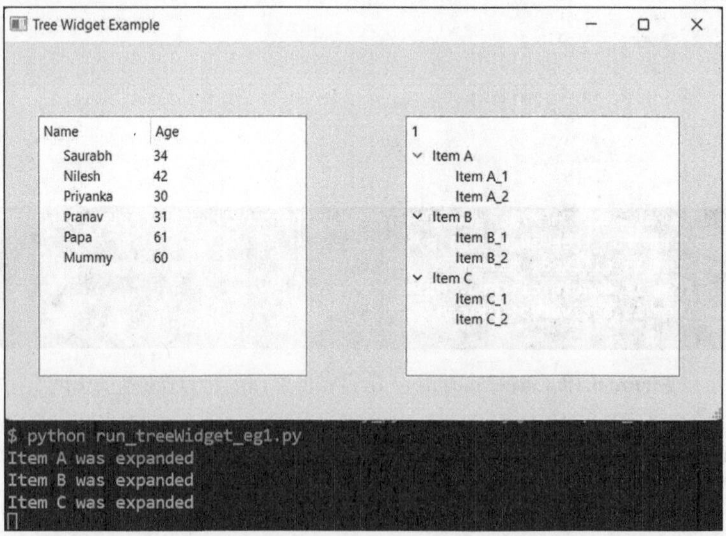

Figure 6.20: Case-4 output of TreeWidget/ run_treeWidget_eg1.py

Here, **Item A**, **Item B** and **Item C** was expanded triggering expanded event.

Case 5: Output display when performing Item Collapsed event

Refer to the following figure:

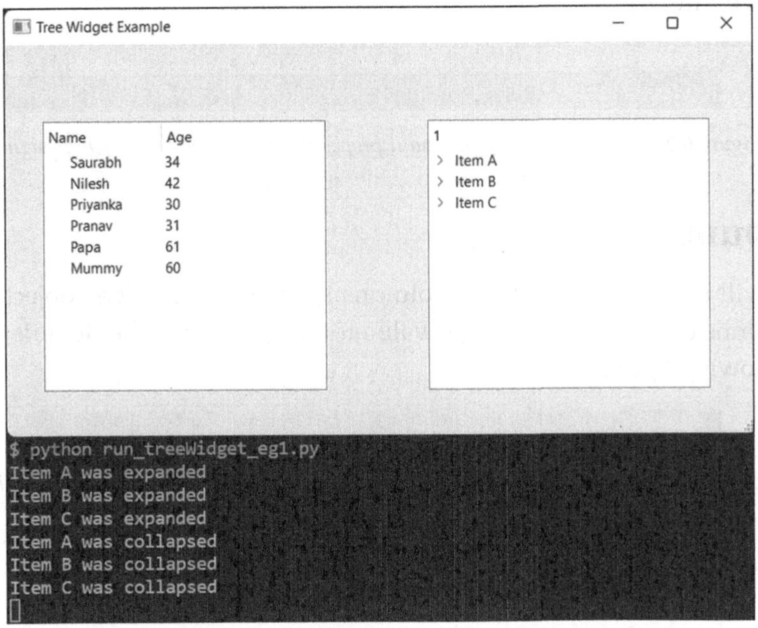

Figure 6.21: Output of TreeWidget/ run_treeWidget_eg1.py

Note: The preceding code is covered in Program Name: TreeWidget/run_treeWidget_eg1.py

Here, **Item A**, **Item B** and **Item C** was collapsed triggering collapsed event.

Table widget

A widget called **`QTableWidget`** in PyQt5 displays data in a table format with rows and columns. It supports several types of data like text, icons, and checkboxes and allows for data manipulation such as sorting and editing. Additionally, it can be used to display information from a model or database. It is comparable to **`QTableView`** but offers more efficient data-handling techniques. **`QTableWidgetItem`** provides the items for a **`QTableWidget`**.

Important properties

The properties of **`QTableWidget`** are similar to the **`QTableView`** properties seen in the previous chapter. Apart from these properties, the only other 2 properties which are added are as follows.

rowCount

This property will return the number of rows in the **QTableWidget** object. We can set the number of rows by passing an integer value to this property. The default value is set to 0. Refer to the following figure:

***Figure 6.22:** Image depicting rowCount property of QTableWidget in Qt Designer*

columnCount

This property will return the number of columns in the **QTableWidget** object. We can set the number of columns by passing an integer value to this property. The default value is set to 0. Refer to the following figure:

***Figure 6.23:** Image depicting columnCount property of QTableWidget in Qt Designer*

Important methods

Let us now go over some important methods:

- **setItem(int row, int column, QTableWidgetItem)**: This method will set the item at a specified row and column position in the **QTableWidget** object. The item may be an object of the class **QTableWidgetItem** or one of its subclasses.
- **item(int row, int column)**: The item is returned as a **QTableWidget** object at a specified row and column position if set otherwise returns **None**.
- **setCellWidget(int row, int column, QWidget)**: This method sets a widget that is to be displayed in the cell at a specified row and column position in the **QTableWidget** object. This can be useful to display data types such as a push button or a checkbox.
- **cellWidget(int row, int column)**: This method returns a widget as a **QWidget** object at a specified row and column position in the **QTableWidgetItem** object.
- **removeRow(int row)**: This method will remove a row from the **QTableWidget** object where the row number is passed as an argument.
- **removeColumn(int column)**: This method will remove a column from the **QTableWidget** object where the column number is passed as an argument.

- **`sortItems(int column[,order=Qt.AscendingOrder])`**: This method sorts the rows in the **`QTableWidget`** object based on the values in a specified column where the column number and the sort order (ascending or descending) are passed as arguments.
- **`clear()`**: Using this method, all the items and widgets are removed from the **`QTableWidget`** object.

Important signals

Some signals are as follows:

- **`itemSelectionChanged()`**: The signal is emitted when the selection in the **`QTableWidget`** object is changed.
- **`cellClicked(row,column)`**: The signal is emitted when the cell in the **`QTableWidget`** object is clicked and takes the row and column of the clicked cell as arguments.
- **`cellDoubleClicked(row,column)`**: The signal is emitted when the cell in the **`QTableWidget`** object is double-clicked and takes the row and column of the double-clicked cell as arguments.
- **`cellChanged(row,column)`**: The signal is emitted when the cell in the **`QTableWidget`** object is changed and takes the row and column of the changed cell as arguments.
- **`cellEntered(row,column)`**: The signal is emitted when the user enters a cell in the **`QTableWidget`** object and takes the row and column of the entered cell as arguments. The **`cellEntered`** signal is only triggered when the **`QTableWidget`** object has the focus, which occurs when the user clicks inside or tabs to the object.
- **`cellPressed(row,column)`**: The signal is emitted when the user presses a cell in the **`QTableWidget`** object and takes the row and column as arguments.

Now, we shall see an example of **`QTableWidget`**.

The details of the file names are as given in the following *Table 6.3*:

S No.	Qt Designer File Name (.ui)	Converting the Qt Designer file name to Python file (.py)	Creating another Python file and importing the converted Python file from Qt Designer
1	`tableWidget_eg1.ui`	`tableWidget_eg1.py`	`run_tableWidget_eg1.py`

***Table 6.3:** Details of file names*

The Qt Designer file is shown in the following figure:

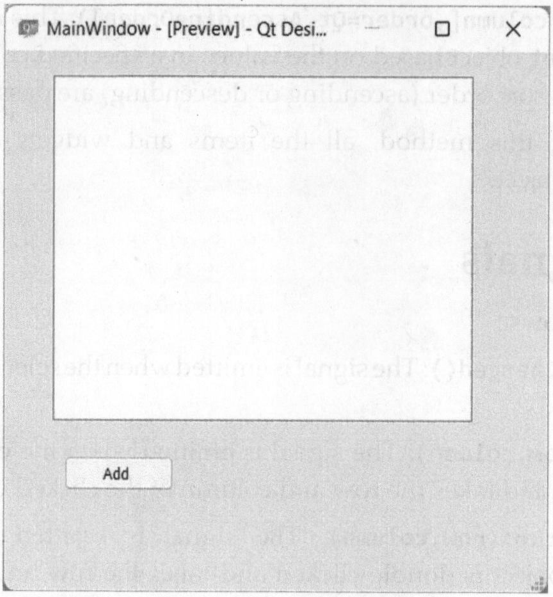

Figure 6.24: Qt Designer file: TableWidget/tableWidget_eg1..ui

Note: The above .ui file is covered in Path: TableWidget/tableWidget_eg1.ui

Consider the following code of **run_tableWidget_eg1.py**:

```
import sys
from PyQt5.QtWidgets import QMainWindow, QApplication, QTableWidgetItem, QHeaderView
from PyQt5.QtGui import QPalette, QColor
from tableWidget_eg1 import *

class MyTableWidget(QMainWindow):
    def __init__(self):
        super().__init__()
        self.myui = Ui_MainWindow()
        self.myui.setupUi(self)

        # Seting the number of rows and columns of QTableWidget object
        self.myui.tableWidget.setRowCount(2)
        self.myui.tableWidget.setColumnCount(3)
```

```
        # Set the horizontal headers for the table
        self.myui.tableWidget.setHorizontalHeaderLabels(["Name", "Age", "Sex"])

        # Adding some data to the QTableWidget object
        self.myui.tableWidget.setItem(0,0,QTableWidgetItem("Saurabh"))
        self.myui.tableWidget.setItem(0,1,QTableWidgetItem("34"))
        self.myui.tableWidget.setItem(0,2,QTableWidgetItem("Male"))
        self.myui.tableWidget.setItem(1,0,QTableWidgetItem("Aditi"))
        self.myui.tableWidget.setItem(1,1,QTableWidgetItem("30"))
        self.myui.tableWidget.setItem(1,2,QTableWidgetItem("Female"))

        #for fitting the QTableWidget object horizontally
        self.myui.tableWidget.horizontalHeader().setStretchLastSection(True)
        self.myui.tableWidget.horizontalHeader().
        setSectionResizeMode(QHeaderView.Stretch)

        # connect signals to slots
        self.myui.tableWidget.cellChanged.connect(self.mycellChanged)
        self.myui.tableWidget.cellClicked.connect(self.mycellClicked)
        self.myui.tableWidget.cellEntered.connect(self.mycellEntered)
        self.myui.tableWidget.cellPressed.connect(self.mycellPressed)

        # clicked signal of button connecting to slot btn_click
        self.myui.btn_Add.clicked.connect(self.btn_click)

        self.show()

    # defining the slots
    def mycellChanged(self, myrow, mycol):
        print("Cell is changed at row {0}, col {1}".format(myrow, mycol))

    def mycellClicked(self, myrow, mycol):
```

```
        print("Cell is clicked at row {0}, col {1}".format(myrow, mycol))

    def mycellEntered(self, myrow, mycol):
        print("Cell is entered at row {0}, col {1}".format(myrow, mycol))

    def mycellPressed(self, myrow, mycol):
        print("Cell is pressed at row {0}, col {1}".format(myrow, mycol))

    def btn_click(self):
        # inserting a new row at the end of the QTableWidget object by taking
        rowCount
        myrow = self.myui.tableWidget.rowCount()
        self.myui.tableWidget.insertRow(myrow)

        # adding fixed name, age and sex to display to the user of inserting
        new data
        self.myui.tableWidget.setItem(myrow, 0, QTableWidgetItem("Divya"))
        self.myui.tableWidget.setItem(myrow, 1, QTableWidgetItem("36"))
        self.myui.tableWidget.setItem(myrow, 2, QTableWidgetItem("Male"))

if __name__=="__main__":
    app = QApplication(sys.argv)
    w = MyTableWidget()
    w.show()
    sys.exit(app.exec_())
```

Output:

Default case on running initially

Refer to the following figure:

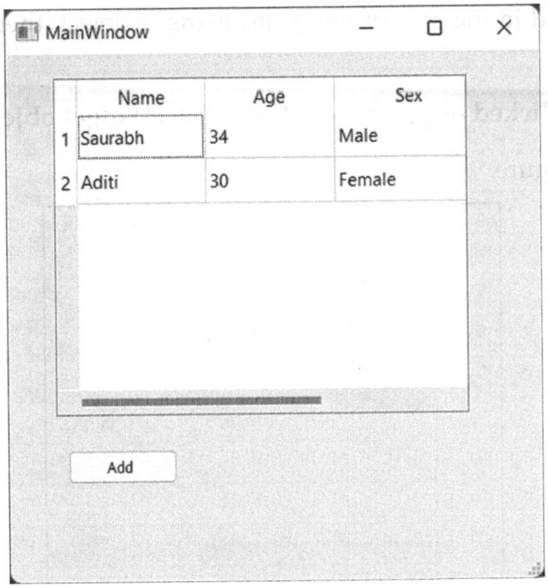

Figure 6.25: Default case output of TableWidget/ run_tableWidget_eg1.py

Case 1: When Add button is clicked on QTableWidget object

Refer to the following figure:

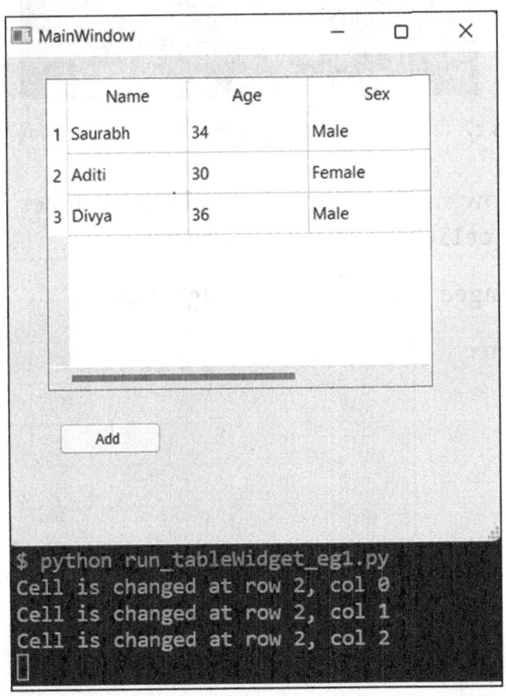

Figure 6.26: Case 1 output of TableWidget/ run_tableWidget_eg1.py

When new data is added in the row of the **QTableWidget** object, then the **cellChanged** event is triggered.

Case 2: When a cell is clicked or pressed on the QTableWidget object

Refer to the following figure:

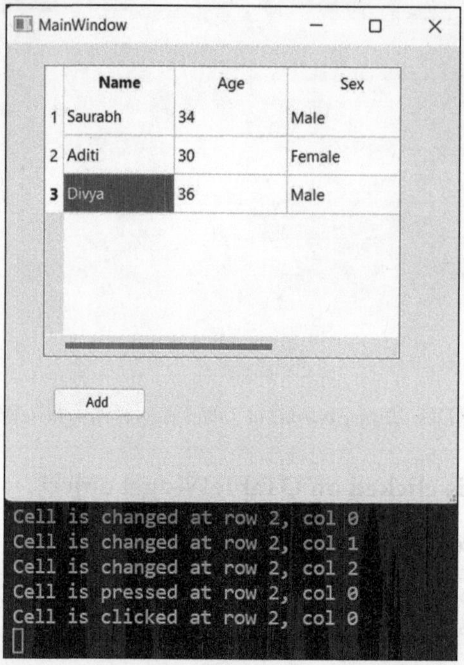

Figure 6.27*: Case-2 output of TableWidget/ run_tableWidget_eg1.py*

When a cell with data (row number as 2 and column number as 0) is clicked, then first **cellPressed** and then the **cellClicked** event is triggered.

Case 3: When a cell is changed on the QTableWidget object

Refer to the following figure:

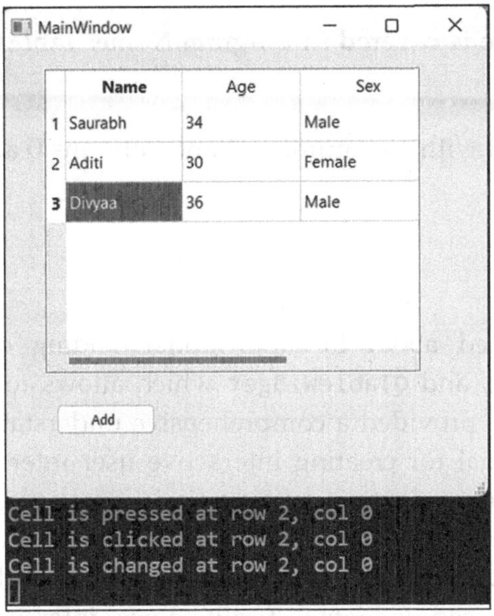

***Figure 6.28**: Case-3 output of TableWidget/ run_tableWidget_eg1.py*

When we are trying to change the data of row number 2 and column number 0, and after changing when pressing *Enter* button, the **cellChanged** event is triggered.

Case 4: When a cell is entered on the QTableWidget object

Refer to the following figure:

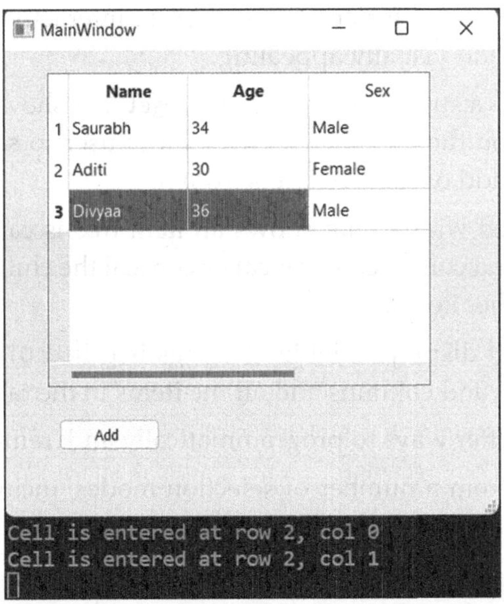

***Figure 6.29**: Output of TableWidget/ run_tableWidget_eg1.py*

Note: The preceding code is covered in Program Name: TableWidget/run_tableWidget_eg1.py

When the user enters a cell with row number 2 and columns 0 and 1, then the **cellEntered** event is triggered.

Conclusion

In this chapter, we learned about in-depth understanding of **Item Widgets**, including **QListWidget**, **QTreeWidget**, and **QTableWidget** which allows for creation of dynamic user interfaces. This chapter has provided a comprehensive understanding of **Item Widgets** in Qt Designer, which are essential for creating interactive user interfaces. By delving into their properties, functionality, customization options, and operational techniques within the Qt Designer environment, readers have gained the necessary knowledge to create and utilize item-based widgets effectively. Additionally, users have learned how to manage events and signals connected to item-based widgets to facilitate user interaction and implement desired functionality. Users will be well-prepared to develop complex yet user-friendly interfaces in Qt Designer using item-based widgets. The inclusion of solved examples with explanatory comments throughout the chapter has further enhanced the understanding and application of **Item Widgets**.

Points to remember

- **Item Widgets** will be used for creating complex, interactive user interfaces which are both user friendly and visually appealing.
- The **QListWidget** is a straightforward **List Widget** that shows a list of things in a single column. Clicking on the list's header will allow user to sort the list, add or remove items from it, and add or remove items from it.
- A more complicated widget that shows an item tree is called **QTreeWidget**. The tree can be expanded and collapsed to reveal or conceal the child objects, and things can be nested inside of other items.
- A table widget that displays a table of things is called **QTableWidget**. The table can have as many rows and columns and all the items in the table can be edited.
- All three widgets offer ways to programmatically add, remove, and modify objects.
- Users can choose from a number of selection modes, including single, multiple, and row/column selection.

Questions

1. Write short notes on Item widgets in Qt Designer.
2. Explain the List widget in Qt Designer.
3. Explain Tree widget in Qt Designer.
4. Explain the Table widget in Qt Designer.
5. Explain the important properties of the List widget in Qt Designer.
6. Explain the important properties of Tree widget in Qt Designer.
7. Explain the important properties of the Table widget in Qt Designer.

CHAPTER 7

Getting Insights of Containers in Qt Designer

Introduction

In order to organize and properly position child widgets within a parent widget, PyQt5 container widgets are used. These container widgets determine the position and size of child widgets within the parent widget and allow for the creation of a layout. If there were no container widgets, child widgets might not be properly arranged, overlap, or be hidden on the screen. Container widgets allow easy layout manipulation, such as the alignment of widgets to the left or right or the change of space between the widgets. We have already learned about layout management previously. In this chapter, we shall concentrate on different PyQt5 container widgets of Qt Designer as shown in the following *Figure 7.1:*

***Figure 7.1:** Different container widgets of Qt Designer*

The **QObject** and **QWidget** class of different container widgets are similar to that of button type class. We shall see multiple useful properties of different Qt Designer container widgets one by one.

Structure

In this chapter, we will discuss the following topics:

- Group Box
- Scroll area
- Toolbox
- Tab widget
- Stacked widget
- Frame
- Widget
- MDI Area
- Dock widget

Objectives

After reading this chapter, the reader will have a thorough knowledge of the many container widgets offered by Qt Designer, their features, and how to customize them to design aesthetically pleasing and user-friendly interfaces. The user will investigate various container widget types and will obtain knowledge of the precise features and capabilities provided by each widget and an understanding of the real-world uses for them. Users will learn what container widgets are, how they work, their different types, and their usage to create layouts. We will also explore customizing the appearance of container widgets. The idea of signal-slot connections will also be explained, and users will learn how to connect signals that widgets within container widgets send to slots in order to handle user interactions and implement desired functionality. The user will be able to use layout managers to create the layouts they want since they will have a thorough understanding of the attributes and customization options available for each container widget. To ensure that readers have a firm understanding of container widgets in Qt Designer, the chapter will also feature practical examples and exercises.

Group Box

A **QGroupBox** is a widget from the Qt GUI library that acts as a container to group other widgets together and is visually distinguished from other widgets by a title and a frame. It can be used to organize related widgets into a single unit, simplifying the interface's comprehension and navigation. The **QGroupBox** can be exclusive, which means that only one Group Box in a parent container can be checked at a time, as well as checkable, which indicates that it can be checked or unchecked by the user. Any widget from the PyQt5 can be added into the **QGroupBox** object.

Important properties

Let us go over some important properties now.

title

We can set the text that appears in the **QGroupBox** object title bar. Refer to the following figure:

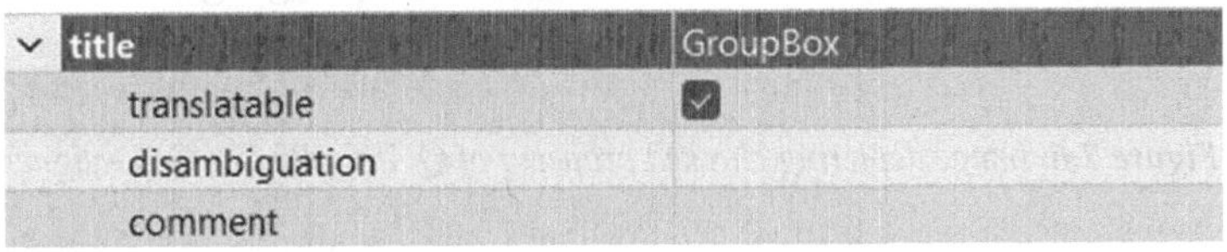

Figure 7.2: Image depicting title property of QGroupBox in Qt Designer

alignment

We can set the alignment of the title within the **QGroupBox** object's frame either vertically or horizontally. Users can choose multiple options from either of these alignments. Refer to the following figure:

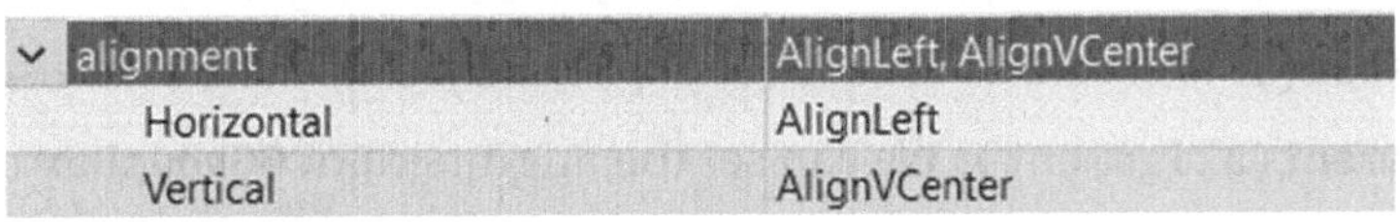

Figure 7.3: Image depicting alignment property of QGroupBox in Qt Designer

flat

We can set the appearance to be either a frame or painted flat of **QGroupBox** object. By default, it is disabled. Refer to the following figure:

Figure 7.4: Image depicting flat property of QGroupBox in Qt Designer

checkable

We can make the **QGroupBox** object title checkable with the help of this property. The title is displayed with the help of a checkbox instead of an ordinary label if set to **True**. The **QGroupBox** object's children are enabled if checked else disabled. By default, it is set to **False**. Refer to the following figure:

Figure 7.5: Image depicting checkable property of QGroupBox in Qt Designer

checked

This property will be used only if the checkable property is set to **True** for the **QGroupBox** object. By default, it is unchecked and disabled. But if the **QGroupBox** object checkable property is set to **True**, this will also be set to **True**. Refer to the following figure:

Figure 7.6: Image depicting checked property of QGroupBox in Qt Designer

Important methods

Let us now go over some important methods:

- **`setTitle(title)`**: We can set the text that appears in the **QGroupBox** object title bar with the help of this method. It will have a keyboard shortcut if the title text contains an **&** followed by a letter.
- **`setCheckable(checkable)`**: If set to **True**, **QGroupBox** object is checkable.
- **`isCheckable()`**: Will return **True** if **QGroupBox** object is checkable else **False**.
- **`setAlignment(alignment)`**: We can set the alignment of **QGroupBox** object.
- **`setFlat(flat)`**: Using this method, we can set the appearance to be either frame or painted flat of **QGroupBox** object.
- **`isChecked()`**: Will return **True** if **QGroupBox** object is checked else, **False**.

Important signals

Some important signals are as follows:

- **`clicked([checked = False])`**: Signal is emitted when the **QGroupBox** object is clicked.
- **`toggled(arg__1)`**: Signal is emitted whenever the check status of the **QGroupBox** object changes and the new state is passed as a parameter (**True** for checked, **False** for unchecked).

Now, we shall see an example of **QGroupBox** widget.

The details of the file names are given in the following *Table 7.1:*

S No.	Qt Designer file name (.ui)	Converting the QtDesigner file name to Python file (.py)	Creating another Python file and importing the converted Python file from Qt Designer
1	**groupboxWidget_eg1.ui**	**groupboxWidget_eg1.py**	**run_groupboxWidget_eg1.py**

Table 7.1: *Details of file names*

The Qt Designer file is shown in the following figure:

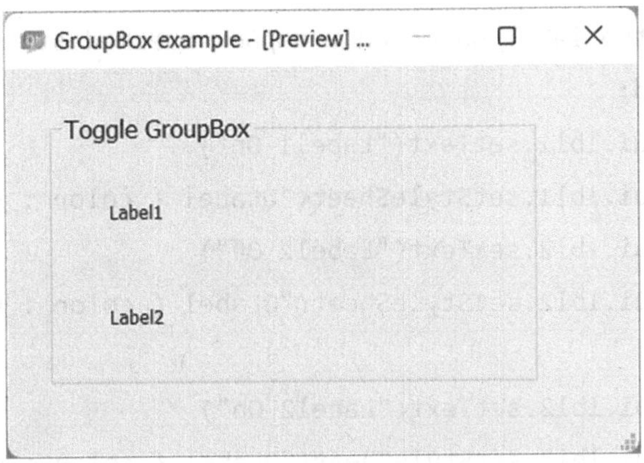

Figure 7.7: *Qt Designer file: GroupBox/groupboxWidget_eg1.ui*

Note: The above .ui file is covered in Path: GroupBox/groupboxWidget_eg1.ui

Consider the following code of **run_groupboxWidget_eg1.py**:

```
import sys
from PyQt5.QtWidgets import QMainWindow, QApplication
from groupboxWidget_eg1 import *

class MyGroupBoxWidget(QMainWindow):
    def __init__(self):
        super().__init__()
        self.myui = Ui_MainWindow()
        self.myui.setupUi(self)
        self.myui.groupBox.setCheckable(True)
        self.myui.groupBox.setChecked(False)
```

```
        # Connect the group box's toggled signal to the handle_toggled slot
        self.myui.groupBox.toggled.connect(self.mytoggle)

        self.show()

    def mytoggle(self,mychecked):
        print(mychecked)
        # Updating the label based on GroupBox checked status
        if mychecked:
            self.myui.lbl1.setText("Label1 On")
            self.myui.lbl1.setStyleSheet("QLabel { color : green; }")
            self.myui.lbl2.setText("Label2 Off")
            self.myui.lbl2.setStyleSheet("QLabel { color : red; }")
        else:
            self.myui.lbl2.setText("Label2 On")
            self.myui.lbl2.setStyleSheet("QLabel { color : green; }")
            self.myui.lbl1.setText("Label1 Off")
            self.myui.lbl1.setStyleSheet("QLabel { color : red; }")

if __name__=="__main__":
    app = QApplication(sys.argv)
    w = MyGroupBoxWidget()
    w.show()
    sys.exit(app.exec_())
```

Output:

Default Case on running initially

Refer to the following figure:

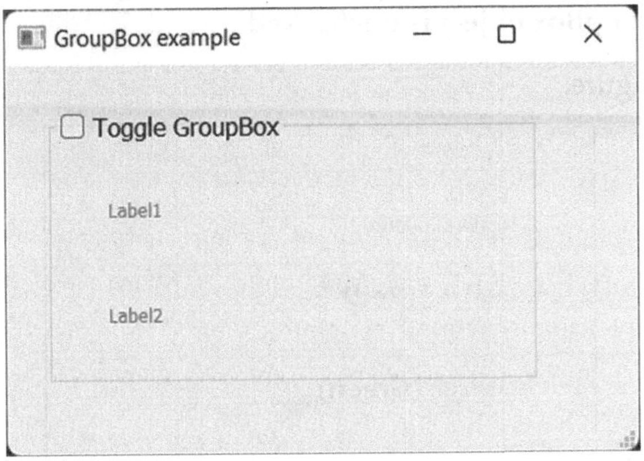

Figure 7.8: Output of GroupBox/run_groupboxWidget_eg1.py

Note: The preceding code is covered in Program Name: GroupBox/run_groupboxWidget_eg1.py

We are providing the **QGroupBox** object checkable status with initial state as unchecked.

Case-1: When the QGroupBox object is checked:

When the **QGroupBox** object is checked, then **Label1** text is set to **Label1 On,** and the color is changed to Green *(Here, legend is added as Green in bracket for better understanding of all the readers).* On the other hand, the **Label2** text is set to **Label2 Off,** and the color is set to **Red**. *(Here, legend is added as Red in bracket for better understanding of all the readers).* Refer to the following figure:

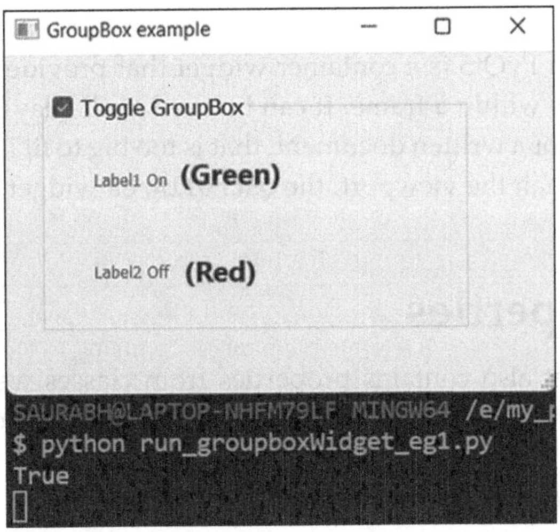

Figure 7.9: Case-1 Output of run_ groupboxWidget_eg1.py

Case-2: When the QGroupBox object is unchecked

Refer to the following figure:

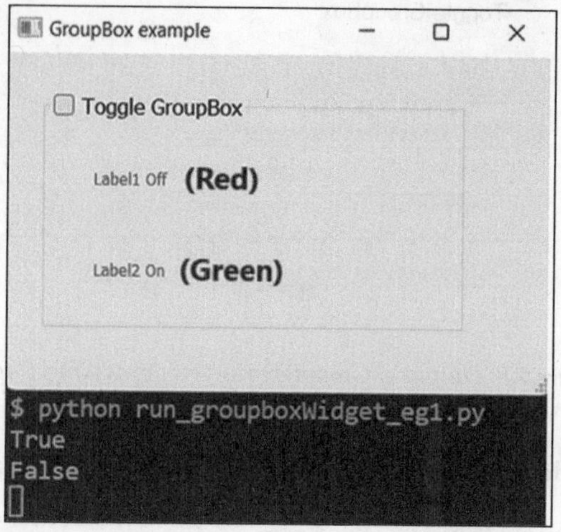

***Figure 7.10:** Case-2 Output of GroupBox/run_groupboxWidget_eg1.py*

When the **QGroupBox** object is unchecked, then the **Label2** text is set to **Label2 On,** and the color is changed to **Green** *(Here, legend is added as Green in bracket for better understanding of all the readers).* On the other hand, **Label1** text is set to **Label1 Off,** and the color is set to **Red** *(Here, legend is added as Red in bracket for better understanding of all the readers).*

Scroll area

A **QScrollArea** widget in PyQt5 is a container widget that provides scrolling capabilities for the child widget contents within a frame. It can be used to display large or complex content, such as a picture, a table, or a written document, that is too big to fit in a single viewport. When a child widget is larger than the viewport, the **QScrollArea** widget automatically adds scroll bars.

Important properties

This **QScrollArea** widget also contains properties from classes we have already discussed **QFrame** and **QAbstractScrollArea**. The extra two properties are as follows:

widgetResizable

When set to **True**, the **QScrollArea** object will automatically resize the widget to fit the viewport. The default value is set to **True**. Refer to the following figure:

Figure 7.11: Image depicting widgetResizable property of QScrollArea in Qt Designer

alignment

We can set the alignment of the title within the **QScrollArea** object's frame either vertically or horizontally. Users can choose multiple options from either of these alignments. Refer to the following figure:

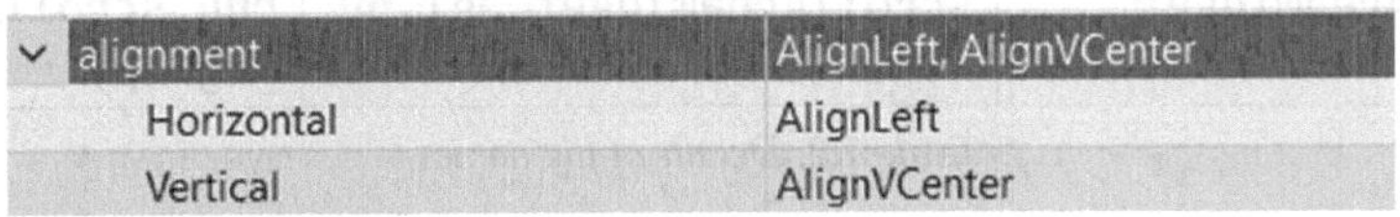

Figure 7.12: Image depicting alignment property of QScrollArea in Qt Designer

Important methods

Some important methods are as follows:

- **setWidget(widget)**: We can set the widget contained within the scroll area. The widget will be destroyed when the scroll area is deleted, as it becomes a child of the scroll area.
- **setWidgetResizable(resizable)**: Using this method, we can set the widget contained within the scroll area to be resized to fit the area.
- **ensureVisible(x,y[, xmargin=50[, ymargin=50]])**: This method ensures that the point (x, y) is visible within the scroll area, with an optional margin. The margins are specified in pixels, with the default value for both margins to be 50 pixels.
- **setAlignment(arg__1)**: We can set the alignment of the **QScrollArea** object. The default value will be aligned to the top-left of the scroll area.

Important signals

Some important signals are as follows:

scrollContentsBy(int dx, int dy)

This signal is emitted when the **QScrollArea** contents are scrolled by **dx** and **dy** pixels.

We can use the **QScrollArea** object in the following way:

1. First, create an instance of **QScrollArea** object.
2. Next, create a child widget for display within the scroll area.
3. Set the widget property of the **QScrollArea** object to the child widget.

4. Finally, add the **QScrollArea** object to the layout.

Now, we shall see an example of the **QScrollArea** widget.

The details of the file names are given in the following *Table 7.2:*

S No.	Qt Designer file name (.ui)	Converting the QtDesigner file name to Python file (.py)	Creating another Python file and importing the converted Python file from Qt Designer
1	`scrollAreaWidget_eg1.ui`	`scrollAreaWidget_eg1.py`	`run_scrollAreaWidget_eg1.py`

***Table 7.2:** Details of file names*

The Qt Designer file is shown in the following figure:

***Figure 7.13:** Qt Designer file: ScrollArea/scrollAreaWidget_eg1.ui*

Note: The above .ui file is covered in Path: ScrollArea/scrollAreaWidget_eg1.ui

Consider the following code of **`run_scrollAreaWidget_eg1.py:`**

```
import sys
from PyQt5.QtWidgets import QApplication, QMainWindow,QLabel, QPushButton,
QVBoxLayout,QHBoxLayout,QGroupBox,QWidget
from scrollAreaWidget_eg1 import *

class MyScrollAreaWidget(QMainWindow):
```

```
def __init__(self):
    super().__init__()
    self.myui = Ui_MainWindow()
    self.myui.setupUi(self)

    self.myui.top_widget = QWidget()
    self.myui.top_layout = QVBoxLayout()

    # Step-1: Already a QScrollArea object was created in Qt Designer

    # Step-2 : Creation of 8 different child widgets (groupbox having label
    and pushbutton) within the scroll area
    for loop in range(8):
        # creating groupbox widget instance
        self.myui.group_box = QGroupBox()
        # setting the groupbox title
        self.myui.group_box.setTitle('GroupBox Item No. {0}'.format(loop))
        # creating a hboxlayout instance to the groupox widget
        self.myui.layout = QHBoxLayout(self.myui.group_box)

        # creating a label object, setting the text and adding it to the
        hboxlayout instance
        self.myui.label = QLabel()
        self.myui.label.setText('Label For Item No. {0}'.format(loop))
        self.myui.layout.addWidget(self.myui.label)

        # creating a [pushbutton] object, setting the text and size and
        adding it to the hboxlayout instance
        self.myui.push_button = QPushButton()
        self.myui.push_button.setText('Display Button')
        self.myui.push_button.setFixedSize(100, 32)
        self.myui.layout.addWidget(self.myui.push_button)

        # adding the groupbox object to the vboxlayout
```

```
            self.myui.top_layout.addWidget(self.myui.group_box)

        # adding the vbox layout to the child widget
        self.myui.top_widget.setLayout(self.myui.top_layout)

        # Step-3: Setting the widget property of the QScrollArea object to the
        child widget
        self.myui.scrollArea.setWidget(self.myui.top_widget)

        # Step-4: Already the QScrollarea object is added to the vboxlayout in
        Qt Designer

        self.show()

if __name__=="__main__":
    app = QApplication(sys.argv)
    w = MyScrollAreaWidget()
    w.show()
    sys.exit(app.exec_())
```

Output:

Refer to the following figure:

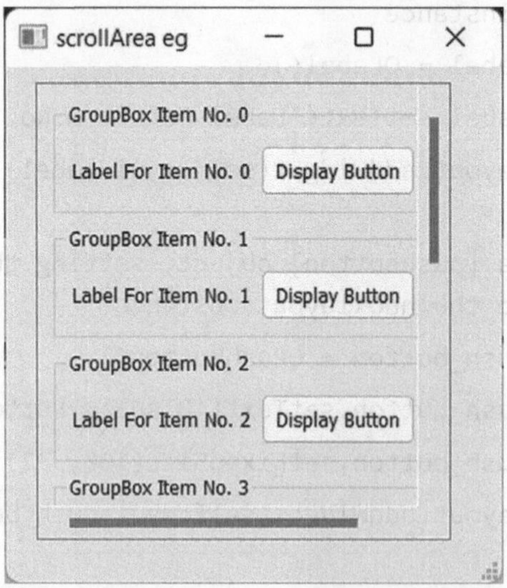

Figure 7.14: Output of ScrollArea/run_scrollAreaWidget_eg1.py

Note: The preceding code is covered in Program Name: ScrollArea/run_scrollAreaWidget_eg1.py

Toolbox

The toolbox widget is one of the widgets available in the Qt Designer to create a user interface. By dragging the toolbox item from the Containers area of the widget box onto the form in Qt Designer, the toolbox widget may be added to a form. A toolbox is a widget that shows a column of tabs stacked one on top of the other, with the current item showing up below the active tab. Each tab has a certain index location within the tab column. A **`QWidget`** is an item in a tab. The column of tabbed widget items is provided by the **`QToolBox`** class.

Important properties

Let us check some important properties.

currentIndex

This property holds the index of the **`currentItem`** of the **`QToolBox`** object. -1 value is returned for an empty **`QToolBox`** object. Refer to the following figure:

currentIndex	0

Figure 7.15: *Image depicting currentIndex property of QToolBox in Qt Designer*

currentItemText

This property holds the **`currentItemText`** of the **`QToolBox`** object. Refer to the following figure:

◢ currentItemText	Page 1
translatable	☑
disambiguation	
comment	

Figure 7.16: *Image depicting currentItemText property of QToolBox in Qt Designer*

currentItemName

This property holds the **`currentItemName`** of the **`QToolBox`** object. Refer to the following figure:

currentItemName	page

Figure 7.17: *Image depicting currentItemName property of QToolBox in Qt Designer*

currentItemIcon

This property holds the **currentItemIcon** of the **QToolBox** object. Refer to the following figure:

***Figure 7.18**: Image depicting currentItemIcon property of QToolBox in Qt Designer*

currentItemToolTip

This property holds the **currentItemToolTip** of the **QToolBox** object. Refer to the following figure:

***Figure 7.19**: Image depicting currentItemToolTip property of QToolBox in Qt Designer*

tabSpacing

This property will set the spacing between the tab bar and the pages of the **QToolBox** object. It is measured in pixels. Refer to the following figure:

***Figure 7.20**: Image depicting tabSpacing property of QToolBox in Qt Designer*

Important methods

Some important methods are as follows:

- **`addItem(widget, text)`**: This method will add a given widget in a new tab at the bottom of the **QToolBox** object where the text of the new tab is set to text.
- **`count()`**: This method will return the number of items contained in the **QToolBox** object.

- **`currentIndex()`**: This method will return the **`currentItem`** index of the **`QToolBox`** object.
- **`insertItem (index, widget, text)`**: This method will insert a widget at the index specified or the **`QToolBox`** object's bottom if the index is out of range. The text of the new item is set to text. It returns the index of the new item.
- **`itemToolTip(index)`**: This method returns the tooltip for the item at the specified index, or an empty string is returned if the index is out of range.
- **`indexOf(widget)`**: This method will return the index of the given widget, or -1 if the widget is not a child of the **`QToolBox`** object.
- **`itemText(index)`**: This method will return an empty string if the index is outside of the range or the text of the item at the position index of the **`QToolBox`** object.

Important signals

Let us check some important signals.

currentChanged(index)

This signal is emitted when the current item of the **`QToolBox`** object is changed.

Now, we shall see an example of **`QToolBoxwidget`**.

The details of the file names are given in the following *Table 7.3:*

S No.	Qt Designer file name (.ui)	Converting the QtDesigner file name to Python file (.py)	Creating another Python file and importing the converted Python file from Qt Designer
1	**`toolBoxWidget_eg1.ui`**	**`toolBoxWidget_eg1.py`**	**`run_toolBoxWidget_eg1.py`**

Table 7.3: *Details of file names*

The Qt Designer file is shown in the following figure:

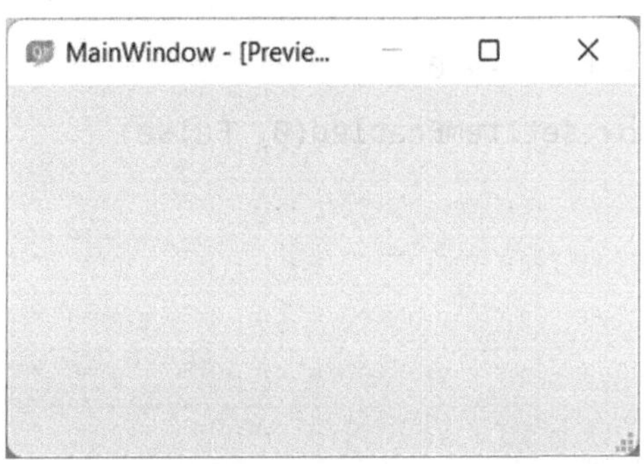

Figure 7.21: *Qt Designer file: ToolBox/toolBoxWidget_eg1.ui*

Note: The above .ui file is covered in Path: ToolBox/toolBoxWidget_eg1.ui

Consider the following code of **run_toolBoxWidget_eg1.py**:

```
import sys
from PyQt5.QtWidgets import QMainWindow,QApplication,QLabel, QToolBox
from toolBoxWidget_eg1 import *

class MyToolBox(QMainWindow):
    def __init__(self):
        super().__init__()
        self.myui = Ui_MainWindow()
        self.myui.setupUi(self)
        # creating an instance of QToolBox item
        self.myui.toolBox = QToolBox()
        # aading the widget QToolBox to the GridLayout
        self.myui.gridLayout.addWidget(self.myui.toolBox ,0,0)

        # Adding 3 Label items to the ToolBox widget
        mylbl1 = QLabel()
        self.myui.toolBox.addItem(mylbl1, "Item1")
        mylbl2 = QLabel()
        self.myui.toolBox.addItem(mylbl2, "Item3")
        mylbl3 = QLabel()
        self.myui.toolBox.addItem(mylbl3, "Item4")

        # disabling first tab --> 0
        self.myui.toolBox.setItemEnabled(0, False)
```

```
        # returns true if tems at specified positions are enabled
        print(self.myui.toolBox.isItemEnabled(0))
        print(self.myui.toolBox.isItemEnabled(1))

        # inserting Label at index specified position:1
        myitem = QLabel()
        self.myui.toolBox.insertItem(1, myitem, "Item2")

         # displaying number of items
        print(self.myui.toolBox.count())

         # mouseover tooltip at different tabs
       self.myui.toolBox.setItemToolTip(0, "This is Item1") # displaying at tab1
       self.myui.toolBox.setItemToolTip(1, "This is Item2") # displaying at tab2
       self.myui.toolBox.setItemToolTip(2, "This is Item3") # displaying at tab3
       self.myui.toolBox.setItemToolTip(3, "This is Item4") # displaying at tab4

        self.show()

if __name__ == "__main__":
    app = QApplication(sys.argv)
    screen = MyToolBox()
    screen.show()
    sys.exit(app.exec_())
```

Output:

The output can be seen in the following figure:

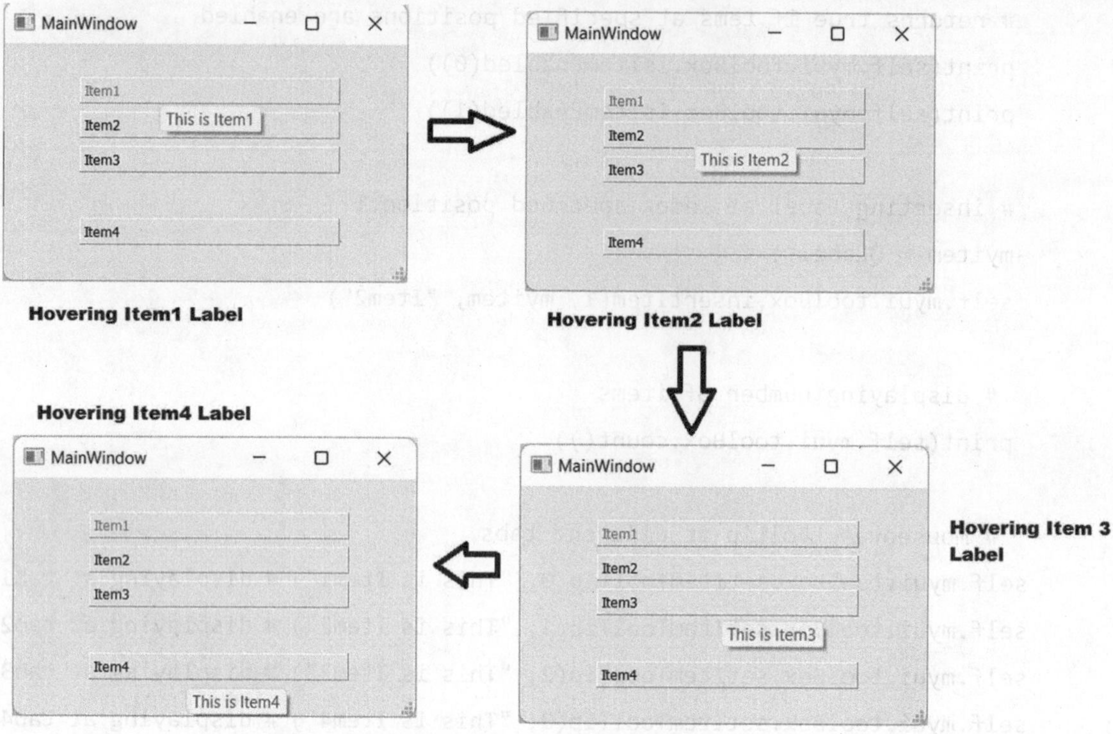

Figure 7.22: Output of ToolBox/run_toolBoxWidget_eg1.py

Note: The preceding code is covered in Program Name: ToolBox/run_toolBoxWidget_eg1.py

Tab widget

A stack of tabbed widgets is provided by the **`QTabWidget`** class. The PyQt5 library's **`QTabWidget`** class offers a tabbed widget for managing multiple widgets in a single window. A tab widget offers a tab bar and a page area where pages associated with each tab can be shown. The tab bar is displayed above the page area by default, although different configurations are available. By clicking on the tabs at the widget's top, the user can navigate between various pages of widgets. The tabs can be moved around and removed as needed, and each tab has a separate widget inside. Additionally, the **`QTabWidget`** class has signals and slots for controlling the current tab.

Important properties

Some important properties are as follows:

tabPosition

We can determine the tab's position in the **QTabWidget** object using this property. Possible values can be chosen from the drop-down menu, as the default value is **North**. Refer to the following figure:

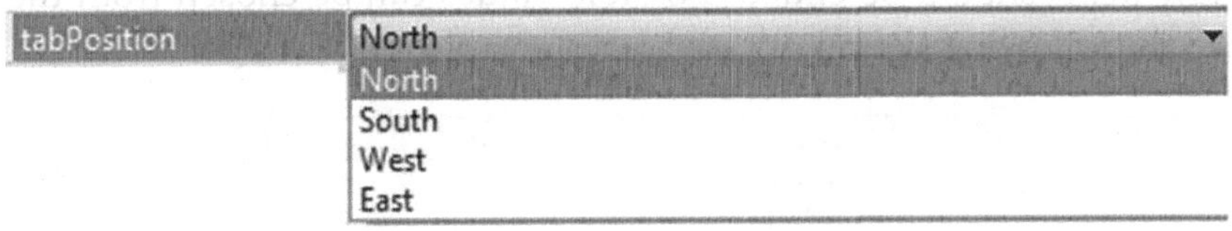

Figure 7.23: Image depicting tabPosition property of QTabWidget in Qt Designer

tabShape

We can determine the tab's shape using the above property from **QTabWidget** object. Default value is rounded as possible values can be chosen from the drop-down menu. Refer to the following figure:

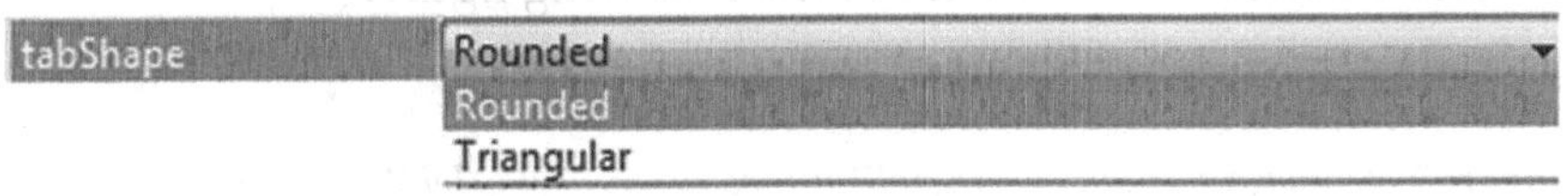

Figure 7.24: Image depicting tabShape property of QTabWidget in Qt Designer

currentIndex

We can determine the index position of the current tab page of **QTabWidget** object. Default value is -1 if there are no tabs in the **QTabWidget** object. Refer to the following figure:

Figure 7.25: Image depicting currentIndex property of QTabWidget in Qt Designer

iconSize

We can determine the icon size on the tab bar, which is a **QSize** object. Refer to the following figure:

Figure 7.26: Image depicting iconSize property of QTabWidget in Qt Designer

elideMode

When there is insufficient space to display items for a specific tab bar size, this property determines how items should be elided. Possible values can be chosen from the drop-down menu. Refer to the following figure:

Figure 7.27: Image depicting elideMode property of QTabWidget in Qt Designer

userScrollButtons

When the tab bar is too small to display all the tabs, this parameter specifies whether the tab bar should use scroll buttons or not. Refer to the following figure:

Figure 7.28: Image depicting userScrollButtons property of QTabWidget in Qt Designer

documentMode

This property, when set to **True**, that is, in document mode, tabs should be displayed as documents rather than tool buttons. Refer to the following figure:

Figure 7.29: Image depicting documentMode property of QTabWidget in Qt Designer

tabsClosable

When set to **True**, the close buttons will be automatically added to each tab of `QTabWidget` object. Refer to the following figure:

Figure 7.30: Image depicting tabsClosable property of QTabWidget in Qt Designer

movable

When set to **True**, the user can move tabs within **`QTabWidget`** object. Refer to the following figure:

Figure 7.31: Image depicting movable property of QTabWidget in Qt Designer

tabBarAutoHide

When set to **True**, the tab bar is automatically hidden when it contains less than 2 tabs. Refer to the following figure:

Figure 7.32: Image depicting tabBarAutoHide property of QTabWidget in Qt Designer

currentTabText

This property determines the text of the current tab of **`QTabWidget`** object. Refer to the following figure:

Figure 7.33: Image depicting currentTabText property of QTabWidget in Qt Designer

currentTabName

This property determines the name of the current tab of **`QTabWidget`** object. Refer to the following figure:

Figure 7.34: Image depicting currentTabName property of QTabWidget in Qt Designer

currentTabIcon

This property determines the icon of the current tab of **`QTabWidget`** object. Refer to the following figure:

Figure 7.35: *Image depicting currentTabIcon property of QTabWidget in Qt Designer*

currentTabToolTip

This property determines the tooltip of the current tab of **`QTabWidget`** object. Refer to the following figure:

Figure 7.36: *Image depicting currentTabToolTip property of QTabWidget in Qt Designer*

currentTabWhatsThis

This property determines the **What is This? Help** of the current tab of **`QTabWidget`** object. Refer to the following figure:

Figure 7.37: *Image depicting currentTabWhatsThis property of QTabWidget in Qt Designer*

Important methods

Some important methods are as follows:

- **`addTab(widget, arg__2)`**: A new tab will be added to the **`QTabWidget`** object with the given page and label as the text of the tab and the index of the tab in the **`QTabWidget`** object is returned.
- **`currentIndex()`**: The index position of the current tab page will be returned.

- `removeTab(index)`: This method will remove the tab at the specified index from the **`QTabWidget`** object.
- `count()`: This method will return the number of tabs in the **`QTabWidget`** object.
- `tabText(index)`: This method will return the tab text of the **`QTabWidget`** object at the specified index.
- `setTabText(index,text)`: This method will set the tab text by defining a new label at the specified position index's tab of the **`QTabWidget`** object.
- `insertTab(index,widget,arg__3)`: A new tab is inserted at a specified index with a given widget and a label. The new tab should be inserted at the position specified by the index parameter. A new tab is inserted at the beginning if the index is less than or equal to 0. The new tab is appended at the end if the index is more than or equal to the number of tabs that are already present.

Important signals

Some important signals are as follows.

currentChanged

When the current tab is changed, this signal is emitted. The new current tab's index is the index parameter passed to the signal handler. When the user switches between tabs, this signal can be used to update the application's state or perform other actions.

tabCloseRequested

When the user requests to close a tab, this signal is emitted. The signal handler's index parameter contains the index of the tab that the user wants to close. The user may be prompted to save any changes that have not yet been saved or to perform other actions before closing the tab using this signal.

Now, we shall see an example of **`QTabwidget`**.

The details of the file names are given in the following *Table 7.4:*

S No.	Qt Designer File name (.ui)	Converting the Qt Designer file name to Python file (.py)	Creating another Python file and importing the converted Python file from Qt Designer
1	**`tabWidget_eg1.ui`**	**`tabWidget_eg1.py`**	**`run_tabWidget_eg1.py`**

***Table 7.4:** Details of file names*

The Qt Designer file is shown in the following figure:

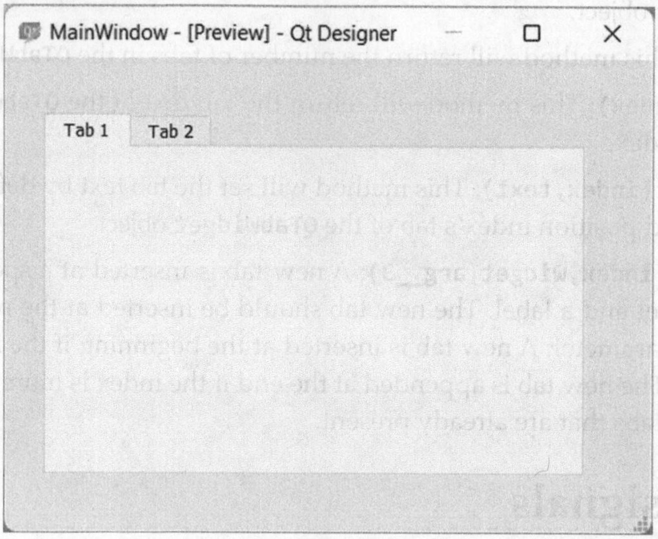

Figure 7.38: Qt Designer file: TabWidge/tabWidget_eg1.ui

Note: The above .ui file is covered in Path: TabWidget/tabWidget_eg1.ui

Consider the following code of **`run_tabWidget_eg1.py`**:

```
import sys
from PyQt5.QtCore import Qt
from PyQt5.QtWidgets import QApplication, QMainWindow, QPushButton,QFormLayout,
QLineEdit,QHBoxLayout,QRadioButton,QMessageBox, QTabWidget, QWidget
from tabWidget_eg1 import *

class MyTabWidget(QMainWindow):
    def __init__(self):
        super().__init__()
        self.myui = Ui_MainWindow()
        self.myui.setupUi(self)
        self.myui.tabWidget.clear()
        self.myui.tabWidget.setTabsClosable(True) # Allow tabs to be closed by
        the user
        self.myui.tabWidget.tabCloseRequested.connect(self.handleCloseTab) #
        Connect the tabCloseRequested signal to the handleCloseTab slot
```

```
# adding 3 LineEdit widget to tab1 and adding it to tabwidget
mylayout = QFormLayout()
mylayout.addRow("Name: ",QLineEdit())
mylayout.addRow("PhoneNo: ",QLineEdit())
mylayout.addRow("Age: ",QLineEdit())
self.tab1 = QWidget()
self.tab1.setLayout(mylayout)

# Creating Tab1 and adding widgets
self.myui.tabWidget.addTab(self.tab1, "Tab 1")

# Adding only 1 QLineEdit to tab2 of tabwidget
self.myui.tabWidget.addTab(QLineEdit(), "Tab 2")

# Adding 2 Radio Buttons to tab3 of tabwidget
mylayout2 = QFormLayout()
mysex = QHBoxLayout()
mysex.addWidget(QRadioButton("Male"))
mysex.addWidget(QRadioButton("Female"))
mylayout2.addRow("Sex",mysex)
self.tab3 = QWidget()
self.tab3.setLayout(mylayout2)
# Creating Tab3 and adding widgets
self.myui.tabWidget.addTab(self.tab3, "Tab 3")

# Change the tab position to the bottom
self.myui.tabWidget.setTabPosition(QTabWidget.South)

# Disabling the second tab
self.myui.tabWidget.setTabEnabled(1, False)
```

```
        # Setting the current tab as Tab 3
        self.myui.tabWidget.setCurrentIndex(2)
        self.show()
    def handleCloseTab(self, index):
        """
        Handling the tabCloseRequested signal by prompting the user to save
        any unsaved changes
        """
        mytab_widget = self.myui.tabWidget.widget(index)
        if isinstance(mytab_widget, QLineEdit): # if closing QLineEdit tab
            myresult = QMessageBox.question(self, "Unsaved Changes", "Do
            you want to save your changes and remove?", QMessageBox.Save |
            QMessageBox.Cancel)
            if myresult == QMessageBox.Save:
                # Save the changes
                print("Save")
                self.myui.tabWidget.removeTab(index)
                pass
            else:
                # Cancel the tab close request
                print("Cancelled")
                return
        else:
            # No unsaved changes, just remove the tab
            self.myui.tabWidget.removeTab(index)

if __name__ == '__main__':
    app = QApplication(sys.argv)
    w = MyTabWidget()
    w.show()
    sys.exit(app.exec_())
```

Output:

Refer to the following figure:

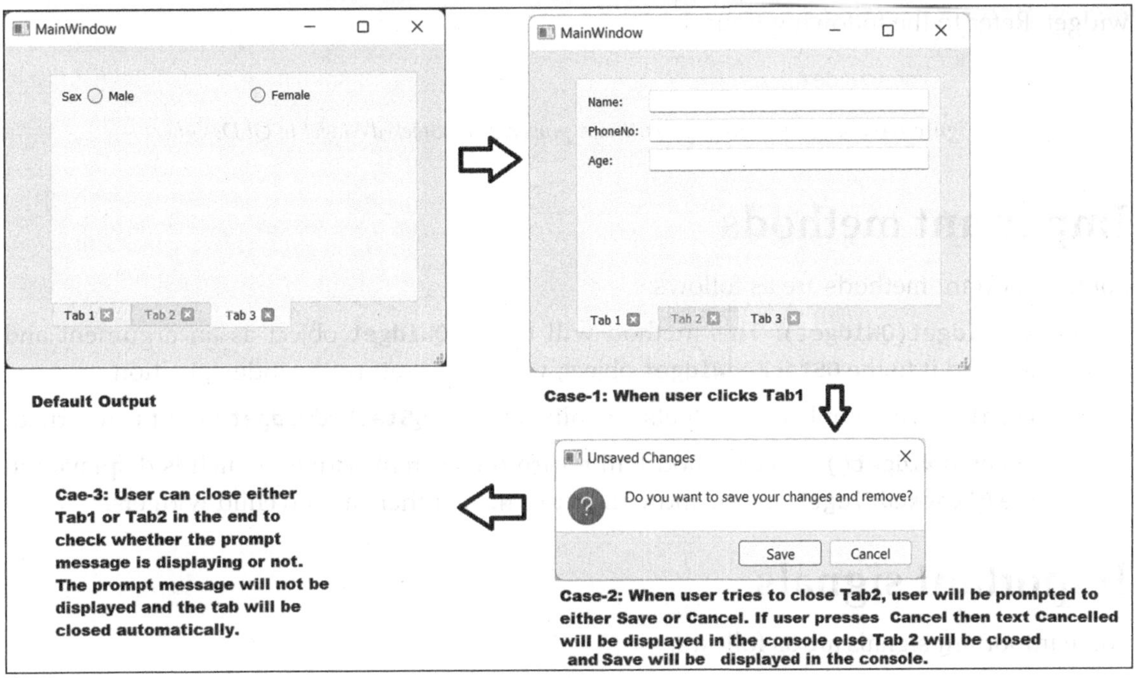

Figure 7.39: Output of TabWidget/run_tabWidget_eg1.py

Note: The preceding code is covered in Program Name: TabWidget/run_tabWidget_eg1.py

Stacked widget

In PyQt5, a stacked widget is a means to organize several widgets into a single container, each only displays one widget at a time. It is comparable to a **`QTabWidget`** but offers more layout and appearance flexibility. The **`QtWidgets`** module's stacked widget can be used to arrange multiple widgets in a stacked layout. **`QStackedWidget`** can be constructed and populated with various child widgets (pages).

Important properties

`QStackedWidget` contains **`QFrame`** class properties which we have already discussed on Item Views (*Chapter 5, Getting Insights of Item Views in Qt Designer*). Apart from that, it has **`currentIndex`** property.

currentIndex

We can determine the widget's index position which is visible. Value is -1 if there is no current widget. Refer to the following figure:

Figure 7.40: Image depicting currentIndex property of QStackedWidget in Qt Designer

Important methods

Some important methods are as follows:

- **`addWidget(QWidget)`**: This method will take a **`QWidget`** object as an argument and append it to the **`QStackedWidget`** object, which will return the index position.
- **`count()`**: The number of widgets contained by the **`QStackedWidget`** object is returned.
- **`currentWidget()`**: This method will return the current widget, which is displayed in the **`QStackedWidget`** object, and will return **`None`** if there are no child widgets.

Important signals

Some important signals are as follows.

currentChanged(arg_ _1)

This signal is emitted when the current widget in the stack changes of **`QStackedWidget`** object.

widgetRemoved

This signal is emitted when the widget is removed from the stack of **`QStackedWidget`** object.

Now, we shall see an example of **`QStackedWidget`**. Here, we are directly writing Python code and importing **`QWidget`** class.

The details of the file names are given in the following *Table 7.5:*

S No.	Creating a Python file
1	**`run_StackedWidget_eg1.py`**

Table 7.5: Details of file names

Consider the following code of **`run_StackedWidget_eg1.py`**:

```
import sys

from PyQt5.QtWidgets import *
```

```
class MyStackedWidget(QWidget):
    def __init__(self):
        super().__init__()

        self.listWidget = QListWidget()

        self.listWidget.insertItem(0,"Details")
        self.listWidget.insertItem(1,"Hobby")
        self.listWidget.insertItem(2,"Sex")

        # creating an instance of QWidget
        self.mystack1 = QWidget()
        self.mystack2 = QWidget()
        self.mystack3 = QWidget()

        self.mystack1UI()
        self.mystack2UI()
        self.mystack3UI()

        self.listWidget.currentRowChanged.connect(self.my_on_current_changed)

        self.mystackwidget = QStackedWidget(self)
        # Setting the current widget to the first one in the stack
        self.mystackwidget.setCurrentIndex(0)

        # adding the widgets to the QStackedWidget object
        self.mystackwidget.addWidget(self.mystack1)
        self.mystackwidget.addWidget(self.mystack2)
        self.mystackwidget.addWidget(self.mystack3)

        hbox = QHBoxLayout(self)
        hbox.addWidget(self.listWidget)
        hbox.addWidget(self.mystackwidget)
```

```
        self.setLayout(hbox)
        self.show()

    # Connect the currentChanged signal to a slot
    def my_on_current_changed(self,index):
        print("The current widget is changed to index no:", index)
        self.mystackwidget.setCurrentIndex(index)

    def mystack1UI(self):
        #adding the widgets to the first stack
        mylayout1 = QFormLayout()
        mylayout1.addRow("Name",QLineEdit())
        mylayout1.addRow("Age",QLineEdit())
        mylayout1.addRow("City",QLineEdit())
        self.mystack1.setLayout(mylayout1)

    def mystack2UI(self):
        #adding the widgets to the second stack
        mylayout2 = QFormLayout()
        mylayout2.addRow(QCheckBox("Playing Chess"))
        mylayout2.addRow(QCheckBox("Cooking"))
        mylayout2.addRow(QCheckBox("Reading Books"))
        self.mystack2.setLayout(mylayout2)

    def mystack3UI(self):
        #adding the widgets to the third stack
        mylayout3 = QHBoxLayout()
        mylayout3.addWidget(QLabel("Sex: "))
        mylayout3.addWidget(QRadioButton("Male"))
        mylayout3.addWidget(QRadioButton("Female"))
        self.mystack3.setLayout(mylayout3)

if __name__ == '__main__':
```

```
app = QApplication(sys.argv)
w = MyStackedWidget()
w.show()
sys.exit(app.exec_())
```

Output:

Refer to the following figure:

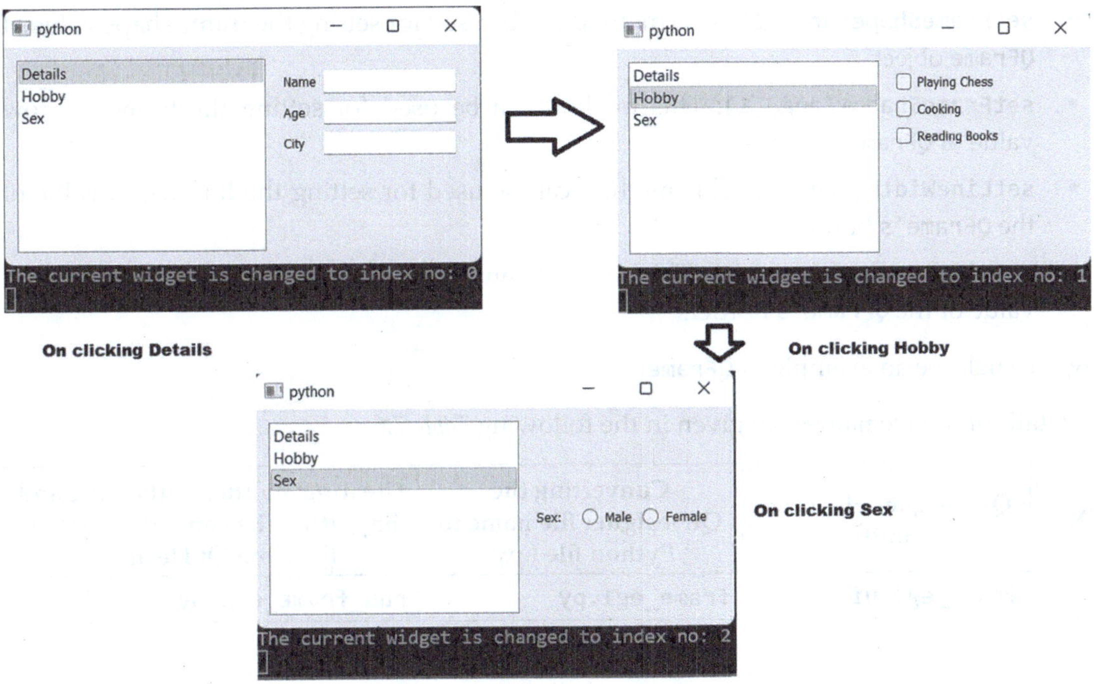

***Figure 7.41**: Output of StackedWidget/run_StackedWidget_eg1.py*

Note: The preceding code is covered in Program Name: StackedWidget/run_StackedWidget_eg1.py

Frame

The PyQt5 widget **`QFrame`** acts as a simple container for other widgets. It has characteristics like the frame form, shadow, and line width that can be used to make simple shapes or borders as well as to group other widgets together. A wide range of custom user interface components, including dialogs, Group Boxes, and custom forms, can be made with it. We can create simple placeholder frames with no contents using the **`QFrame`** class.

Important properties

We have already discussed about properties of **QFrame** when we were dealing with Item View widgets (*Chapter 5, Getting Insights of Item Views in Qt Designer*).

Important methods

Let us go over some important methods.

- **setFrameShape(arg__1)**: This method can be used for setting the frame shape value of **QFrame** object.
- **setFrameShadow(arg__1)**: This method can be used for setting the frame shadow value of **QFrame** object.
- **setLineWidth(arg__1)**: This method can be used for setting the line width value of the **QFrame's** border.
- **setMidLineWidth(arg__1)**: This method can be used for setting the mid-line width value of the **QFrame's** border.

Now, we shall see an example of **QFrame**.

The details of the file names are given in the following *Table 7.6:*

S No.	Qt designer file name (.ui)	Converting the QtDesigner file name to Python file (.py)	Creating another Python file and importing the converted Python file from Qt Designer
1	**frame_eg1.ui**	**frame_eg1.py**	**run_frame_eg1.py**

Table 7.6: *Details of file names*

The Qt Designer file is shown in the following figure:

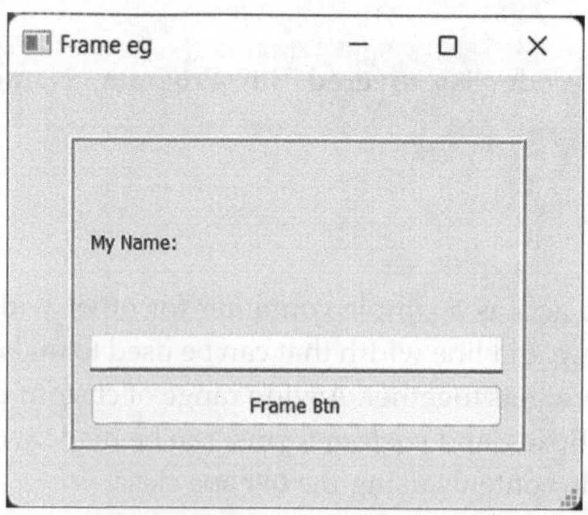

Figure 7.42: *Qt Designer file: Frame/frame_eg1.ui*

Note: The above .ui file is covered in Path: Frame/frame_eg1.ui

Consider the following code of **run_frame_eg1.py**:

```
import sys
from PyQt5.QtWidgets import QApplication, QMainWindow, QFrame, QLabel, QLineEdit,
QPushButton,QVBoxLayout
from frame_eg1 import *


class MyFrame(QMainWindow):
    def __init__(self):
        super().__init__()
        self.myui = Ui_MainWindow()
        self.myui.setupUi(self)

        # Setting the frame shape to a box
        self.myui.frame.setFrameShape(QFrame.Box)

        # Setting the frame shadow to raised
        self.myui.frame.setFrameShadow(QFrame.Raised)

        # Setting the line width of the border to 2
        self.myui.frame.setLineWidth(2)

        # Creating a QVBoxLayout to hold our widgets
        layout = QVBoxLayout()

        # Adding a label and a line edit to the layout
        layout.addWidget(QLabel("My Name:"))
        layout.addWidget(QLineEdit())
        layout.addWidget(QPushButton("Frame Btn"))

        # Adding the layout to the frame
        self.myui.frame.setLayout(layout)
```

```
        self.show()

if __name__=="__main__":
    app = QApplication(sys.argv)
    w = MyFrame()
    w.show()
    sys.exit(app.exec_())
```

Output:

Refer to the following figure:

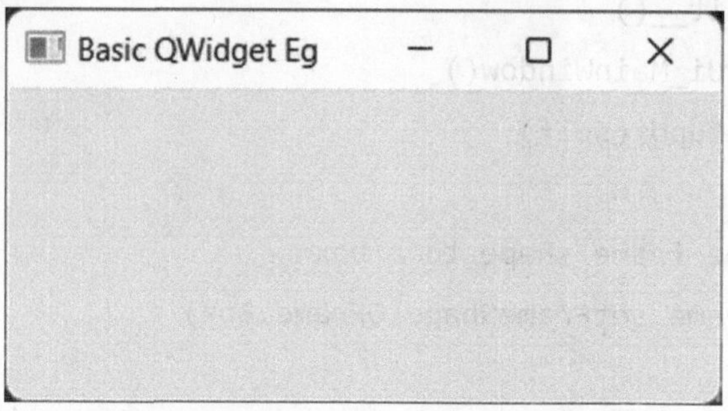

Figure 7.43: Output of Frame/ frame_eg1.py

Note: The preceding code is covered in Program Name: Frame/frame_eg1.py

Widget

The Python bindings for the Qt libraries include the class **QWidget** in PyQt5 library. In the PyQt5 library, it serves as the base class for all user interface objects. **QWidgets** can be used as containers for other widgets as well as to generate user interface components like buttons, labels, and text fields. A widget is clipped by the widgets in front of it as well as by its parent widget. A window is a widget that is not contained within a parent widget. Although it is also possible to create windows without decoration by using the appropriate window flags, windows typically feature a frame and a title bar.

Important properties

We have already seen the properties of **QWidget** in *Chapter 4, Getting Insights of Button Widgets in Qt Designer*). . The default values may be changed, but the number of properties remains the same.

Important methods

Let us go over some important methods now:

- **`setGeometry(x,y,width,height)`**: This method will set the widget geometry, including its size and position.
- **`setWindowTitle(arg__1)`**: We can set the window title containing the widget with this method.
- **`show()`**: This method will display the widget and its child widgets.
- **`resize(width,height)`**: The widget will be resized to the specified width and height using this method.
- **`move(x,y)`**: This method will help the widget to move to the specified x and y coordinates.
- **`setLayout(arg__1)`**: This method will set the layout of a widget where the first argument is the first argument is layout object which we want to set, and the second argument is the widget on which we want to set the layout on.
- **`setStyleSheet(stylesheet)`**: We can set the widget's stylesheet to the stylesheet (The Qt Style Sheets document's textual description of the widget's style modifications customizations is contained in the style sheet).

Important signals

Let us go over some important signals now:

- **`customContextMenuRequested(pos)`**: When the widget's context menu is requested, this signal is emitted. The mouse pointer's global position is supplied to it as a **`QPoint`**. When the context menu is requested, it can be connected to a slot function to carry out a specific action.
- **`windowIconChanged(icon)`**: When the window icon is changed, this signal is emitted, which passes the new icon.
- **`windowIconTextChanged(iconText)`**: When the window icon text is changed, this signal is emitted, which passes the new icon text.
- **`windowTitleChanged(title)`**: When the window title is changed, this signal is emitted, which passes the new window title.

Now, we shall see an example of **`QWidget`**.

The details of the file names are given in the following *Table 7.7:*

S No.	Creating a Python file
1	run_widget_eg1.py

***Table 7.7:** Details of file names*

Consider the following code of **run_widget_eg1.py:**

```
import sys
from PyQt5.QtWidgets import QApplication, QMainWindow, QWidget

app = QApplication(sys.argv)

# Creating an instance of QWidget and will be the main window of the application
mywidget = QWidget()

# Setting the size and position of the screen widget
mywidget.resize(350, 150)
mywidget.move(250, 250)

# Setting the widget title
mywidget.setWindowTitle("Basic QWidget Eg")

# Display the widget on the screen
mywidget.show()

sys.exit(app.exec_())
```

Output:

Refer to the following figure:

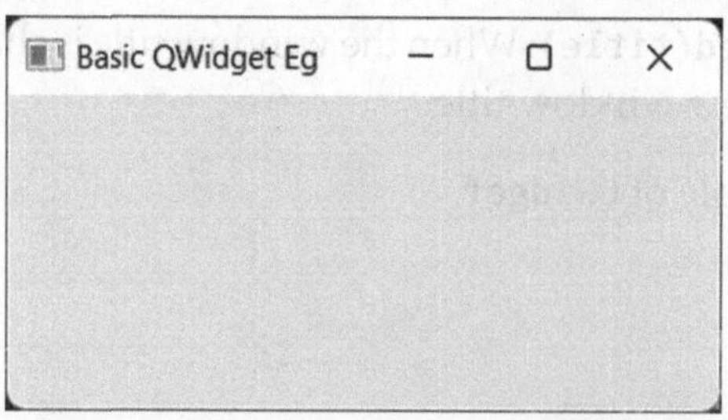

***Figure 7.44:** Output of Widget/run_widget_eg1.py*

Note: The preceding code is covered in Program Name: Widget/run_widget_eg1.py

MDI Area

The **QMdiArea** widget provides an area where **Multiple Document Interface** (**MDI**) windows can be displayed. In order to build each window separately for displaying many windows at once, **Single Document Interface** (**SDI**) can be used. Since each window may have its own menu system, toolbar, and so on, this requires extra memory resources. Applications that use the MDI interface use less memory. The sub-windows are arranged in relation to one another inside the main container, naming the container widget as **QMdiArea**. Typically, the **QMainWindow** object's center widget is the **QMdiArea** widget. The **QMdiSubWindow** class is represented by the child windows in this section. Any **QWidget** may be chosen to serve as the internal widget for the **subWindow** object. In the MDI area, sub-windows may be set up in a tiled or cascading pattern.

Important properties

Let us now go over some important properties as follows:

background

The background brush for the workspace area can be set by using this property. By default, it is a grey color. Refer to the following figure:

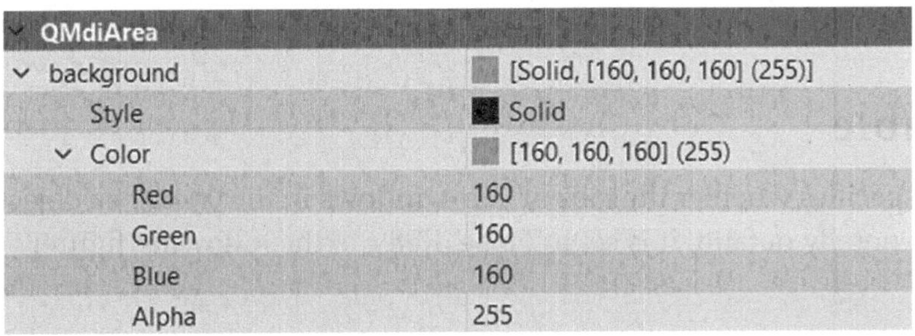

***Figure 7.45**: Image depicting background property of QMdiArea widget in Qt Designer*

activationOrder

The ordering criteria in which the sub-windows are activated are specified using this property. Refer to the following figure:

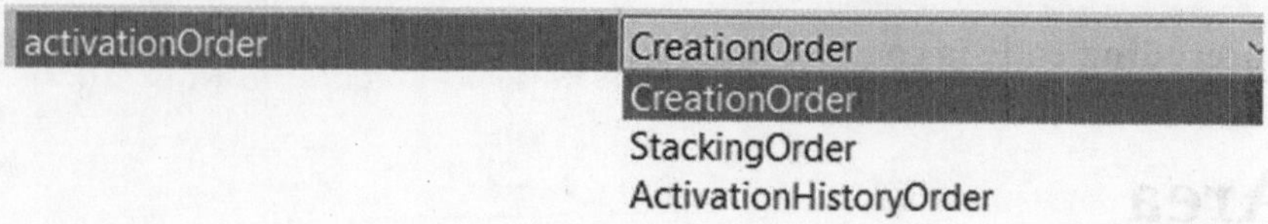

***Figure 7.46**: Image depicting activationOrder property of QMdiArea widget in Qt Designer*

viewMode

This property specifies the mode in which the sub-windows are displayed within the **`QMdiArea`** object. Refer to the following figure:

***Figure 7.47**: Image depicting viewMode property of QMdiArea widget in Qt Designer*

documentMode

This property specifies whether the Document/View architecture should be used by the **`QMdiArea`** object or not. The **`QMdiArea`** object will manage its sub-windows using this architecture if it is enabled. By default, it is **unchecked**. Refer to the following figure:

***Figure 7.48**: Image depicting documentMode property of QMdiArea widget in Qt Designer*

tabsClosable

This property specifies whether the tabs of sub-windows in the **`QMdiArea`** object should have a close button or not. By default, it is set to **False**. Refer to the following figure:

***Figure 7.49**: Image depicting tabsClosable property of QMdiArea widget in Qt Designer*

tabsMovable

This property specifies whether the tabs of sub-windows in the **`QMdiArea`** object should be movable or not. By default, it is set to **False**. Refer to the following figure:

***Figure 7.50**: Image depicting tabsMovable property of QMdiArea widget in Qt Designer*

tabShape

This property specifies the tab shape in the **QMdiArea** object. Refer to the following figure:

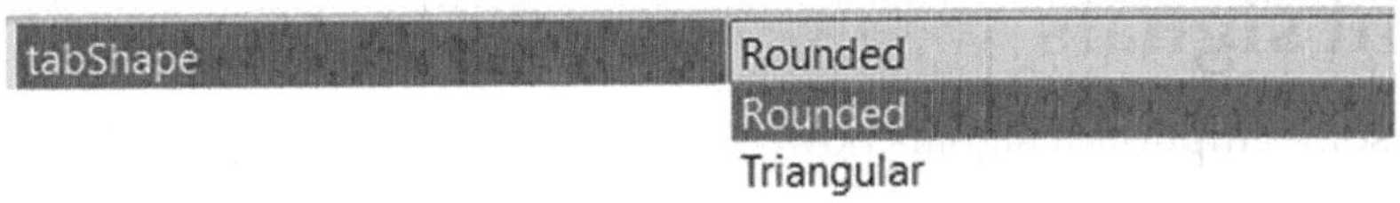

Figure 7.51: *Image depicting tabShape property of QMdiArea widget in Qt Designer*

tabPosition

This property specifies the tab position in the **QMdiArea** object. Refer to the following figure:

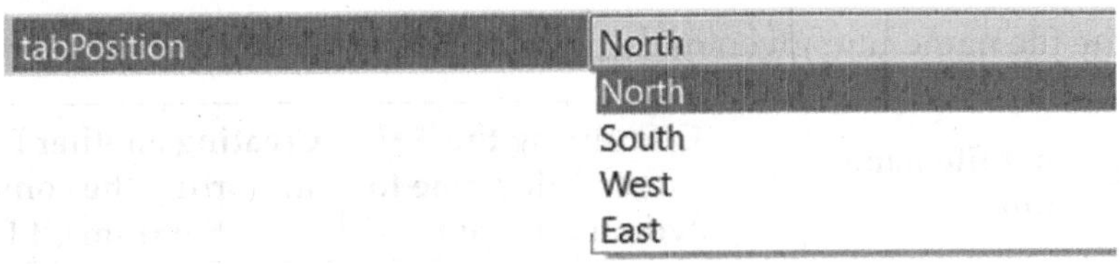

Figure 7.52: *Image depicting tabPosition property of QMdiArea widget in Qt Designer*

Important methods

Some important methods are as follows:

- **addSubWindow(widget[, flags=Qt.WindowFlags()])**: This method will add the widget as a new sub-window to the **MdiArea** which will override the flags set on the widget when **WindowFlags** are non-zero.
- **removeSubWindow(widget)**: This method will reduce the widget (which can be either an internal widget of a sub-window or a **QMdiSubWindow**) from the **MdiArea**.
- **activeSubWindow()**: A pointer is returned to the current active sub-window else, **None** is returned if no window is currently active.
- **cascadeSubWindows()**: This method will arrange all sub-windows in a cascading pattern.
- **tileSubWindows()**: This method will arrange all sub-windows in a tiled pattern.
- **closeActiveSubWindow()**: The currently active sub-window is closed using this method.
- **SubWindowList([order = CreationOrder])**: A list of sub-windows is returned in the **QMdiArea** object. The default order is the **CreationOrder,** which means sorting will be done in the order in which they were inserted into the workspace.

- **`setWidget()`**: Using this method, a **`QWidget`** is set as an internal widget of a **`QMdiSubWindow`** instance.

Important signals

Let us go over some important signals now:

subWindowActivated(arg__1)

When a sub-window within the MDI area becomes the active window, the **`subWindowActivated`** signal in **`QMdiArea`** object is emitted. **`arg__1`** refers to the newly active sub-window.

Now, we shall see an example of **`QMdiArea`**.

The details of the file names are given in the following *Table 7.8:*

S No.	Qt Designer file name (.ui)	Converting the QtDesigner file name to Python file (.py)	Creating another Python file and importing the converted Python file from Qt Designer
1	`mdiarea_eg1.ui`	`mdiarea _eg1.py`	`run_mdiarea_eg1.py`

Table 7.8: Details of file names

The Qt Designer file is shown in the following figure:

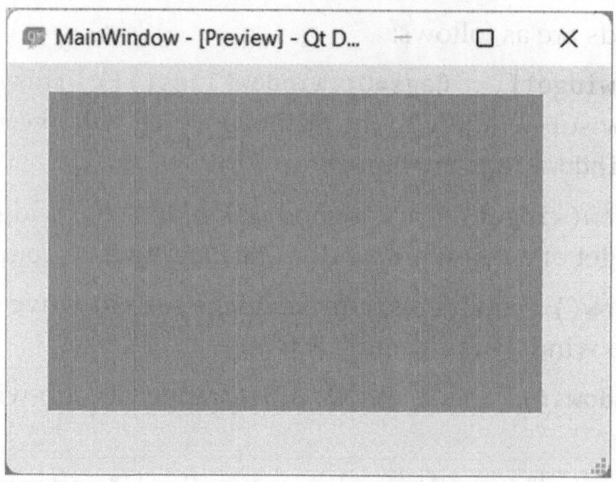

Figure 7.53: Qt Designer file: MDIArea/mdiarea_eg1.ui

Note: The above .ui file is covered in Path: MDIArea/mdiarea_eg1.ui

Consider the following code of **`run_mdiarea_eg1.py`**:

```
import sys
```

```
from PyQt5.QtWidgets import QApplication, QMainWindow, QMdiArea, QMdiSubWindow,
QTextEdit, QMenu, QMenuBar, QAction
from mdiarea_eg1 import *

class MyMdiArea(QMainWindow):
    def __init__(self):
        super().__init__()
        self.myui = Ui_MainWindow()
        self.myui.setupUi(self)

        # Setting QMdiArea object as the central widget
        self.setCentralWidget(self.myui.mdiArea)

        # Adding three QTextEdit sub-windows to the QMdiArea object
        mysub1 = QMdiSubWindow()
        mysub1.setWidget(QTextEdit())
        mysub1.setWindowTitle("Window 1")
        self.myui.mdiArea.addSubWindow(mysub1)

        mysub2 = QMdiSubWindow()
        mysub2.setWidget(QTextEdit())
        mysub2.setWindowTitle("Window 2")
        self.myui.mdiArea.addSubWindow(mysub2)

        mysub3 = QMdiSubWindow()
        mysub3.setWidget(QTextEdit())
        mysub3.setWindowTitle("Window 3")
        self.myui.mdiArea.addSubWindow(mysub3)

        # Creating a menu bar and adding two actions to it
        mymenubar = self.menuBar()
        mywindowMenu = mymenubar.addMenu("Display As")
        mycascadeAction = QAction("Cascade", self)
        mycascadeAction.triggered.connect(self.myui.mdiArea.cascadeSubWindows)
```

```
        mywindowMenu.addAction(mycascadeAction)
        mytileAction = QAction("Tile", self)
        mytileAction.triggered.connect(self.myui.mdiArea.tileSubWindows)
        mywindowMenu.addAction(mytileAction)

        self.show()

if __name__ == "__main__":
    app = QApplication(sys.argv)
    screen = MyMdiArea()
    screen.show()
    sys.exit(app.exec_())
```

Output:

Refer to the following figure:

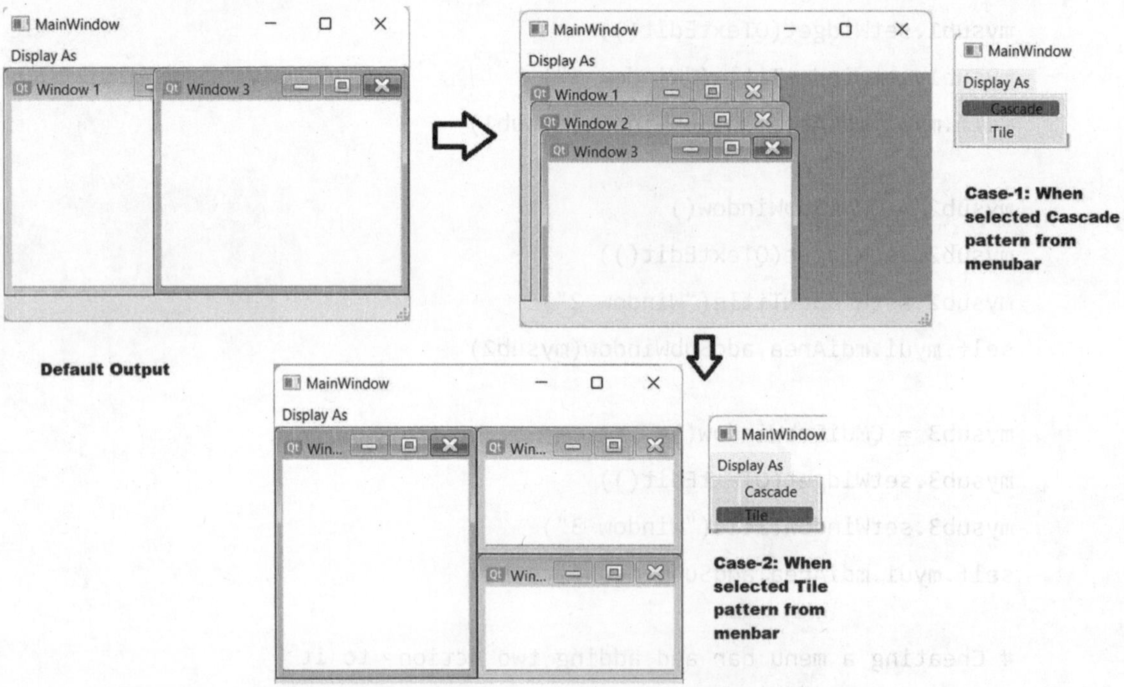

Figure 7.54: Output of MDIArea/run_mdiarea_eg1.py

Note: The preceding code is covered in Program Name: MDIArea/run_mdiarea_eg1.py

Dock widget

`QDockWidget` class allows users to add dockable windows to a main window. It offers a container widget that may be floated as a separate window or docked to the sides of a main window. The **`QDockWidget`** is capable of supporting features, including floating windows, movable and closable tabs. It is frequently used to provide users the ability to arrange the application's interface layout to meet their demands.

The idea of dock widgets, commonly referred to as tool palettes or utility windows, is presented by **`QDockWidget`**. Dock windows are secondary windows that are placed in a **`QMainWindow's`** dock widget area around the central widget. A title bar and content area make up a **`QDockWidget`**. The window title, a float button, and a close button are all displayed in the title bar of the dock widgets. The float and close buttons may be either hidden or not displayed at all depending on the state of the **`QDockWidget`**.

Important properties

Let us check some important properties now:

floating

If this Boolean property is set as **True**, then the dock widget is set as **floating**. Refer to the following figure:

***Figure 7.55**: Image depicting floating property of QDockWidget in Qt Designer*

features

This property will determine the features enabled for the dock widget, that is, can be set as movable, closable, or floatable. Refer to the following figure:

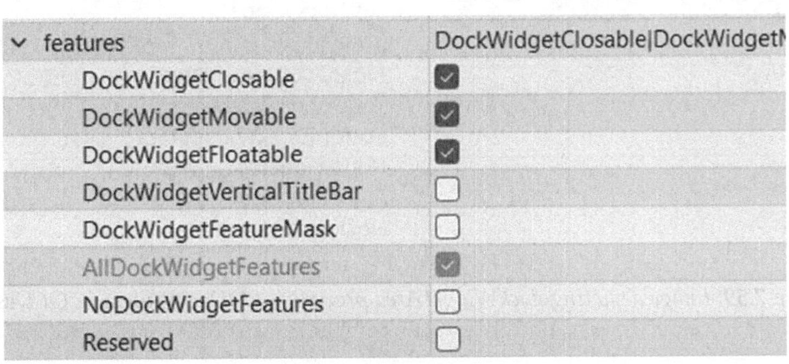

***Figure 7.56**: Image depicting features property of QDockWidget in Qt Designer*

allowedAreas

This property will determine the **`dockwidget`** areas in which the dock widget can be placed. Refer to the following figure:

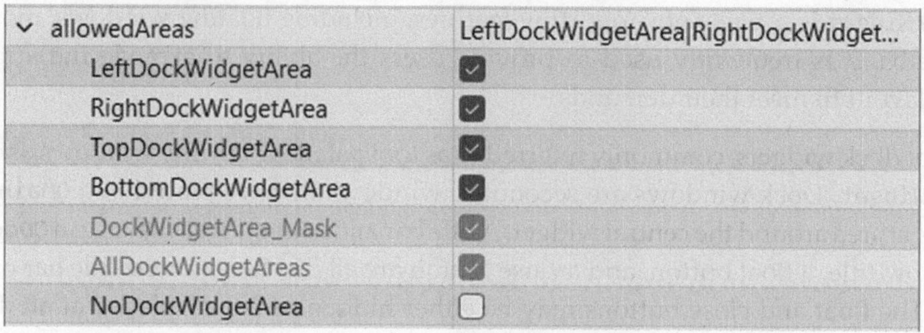

***Figure 7.57:** Image depicting allowedAreas property of QDockWidget in Qt Designer*

windowTitle

The dock widget title is set using this property. Refer to the following figure:

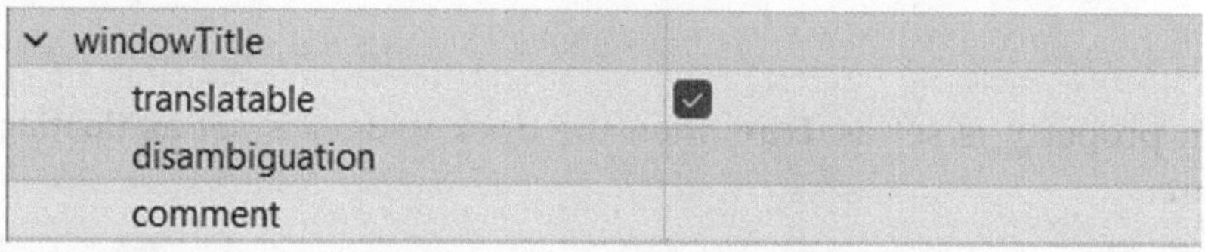

***Figure 7.58:** Image depicting windowTitle property of QDockWidget in Qt Designer*

dockWidgetArea

The current dock widget area of the dock widget is returned by using this property. Refer to the following figure:

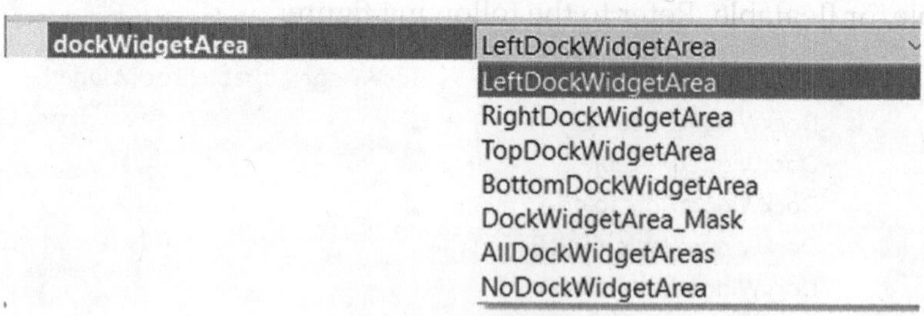

***Figure 7.59:** Image depicting dockWidgetArea property of QDockWidget in Qt Designer*

docked

By using this property, we can determine whether the dock widget is docked or floating. Refer to the following figure:

***Figure 7.60**: Image depicting docked property of QDockWidget in Qt Designer*

Important methods

Some important methods are as follows:

- **`isAreaAllowed(area)`**: A boolean value **True** is returned if the dock widget can be placed in the specified dock widget area else, **False** is returned.
- **`widget()`**: A widget is returned contained in the dock widget. If the widget has not been set, **zero** will be returned.
- **`toggleViewAction()`**: This method will return a checkable action that can be added to toolbars and menus so that the user can toggle the visibility of the dock widget.

Important signals

Some important signals are as follows:

- **`allowedAreasChanged(allowedAreas):`** The **`allowedAreasChanged`** signal is emitted when the allowed areas for a dock widget change. The argument **`allowedAreas`** specifies the new allowed areas.
- **`dockLocationChanged(area)`**: Signal is emitted when **`QDockWidget`** object is moved to a new location specified by the **area** argument.
- **`featuresChanged(features)`**: Signal is emitted when there is change in the **`QDockWidget`** object features.
- **`topLevelChanged(topLevel)`**: Signal is emitted when the dock widget changes its top-level state, that is, whether it is floated as a top-level window or docked inside a main window where the **`topLevel`** argument specifies the new state.
- **`visibilityChanged(visible)`**: Signal is emitted when **`QDockWidget`** object visibility changes.

Now, we shall see an example of **`QDockWidget`**.

The details of the file names are given in the following *Table 7.9:*

S No.	Creating a Python file
1	run_dockWidget_eg1.py

Table 7.9: Details of file names

Consider the following code of **run_dockWidget_eg1.py**:

```
import sys
from PyQt5 import QtWidgets, QtCore

myapp = QtWidgets.QApplication(sys.argv)

# Creating a main window object
mymainWindow = QtWidgets.QMainWindow()

# Creating a dock widget object
dockWidget = QtWidgets.QDockWidget("Dock Widget", mymainWindow)

# Setting the allowed dock widget areas
dockWidget.setAllowedAreas(QtCore.Qt.LeftDockWidgetArea | QtCore.
Qt.RightDockWidgetArea)

# Adding a pushbutton to the dock widget
mybtn = QtWidgets.QPushButton("This is a dock widget")
dockWidget.setWidget(mybtn)

# Adding the dock widget to the main window
mymainWindow.addDockWidget(QtCore.Qt.LeftDockWidgetArea, dockWidget)

# Checking if the dock widget is floating
if dockWidget.isFloating():
    print("Dock widget is floating")
    print('-'*50)
```

```
else:
    print("Dock widget is docked")
    print('-'*50)

# Connecting to the allowedAreasChanged signal
dockWidget.allowedAreasChanged.connect(lambda myallowedAreas: print("Allowed areas changed to", myallowedAreas))

# Connecting to the dockLocationChanged signal
dockWidget.dockLocationChanged.connect(lambda myarea: print("Dock location changed to", myarea))

# Connecting to the featuresChanged signal
dockWidget.featuresChanged.connect(lambda myfeatures: print("Features changed to", myfeatures))

# Connecting to the topLevelChanged signal
dockWidget.topLevelChanged.connect(lambda mytopLevel: print("Top level changed to", mytopLevel))

# Connecting to the visibilityChanged signal
dockWidget.visibilityChanged.connect(lambda myvisible: print("Visibility changed to", myvisible))

# Setting the dock widget floating
dockWidget.setFloating(True)

mymainWindow.show()

sys.exit(myapp.exec_())
```

Output:

Refer to the following figure:

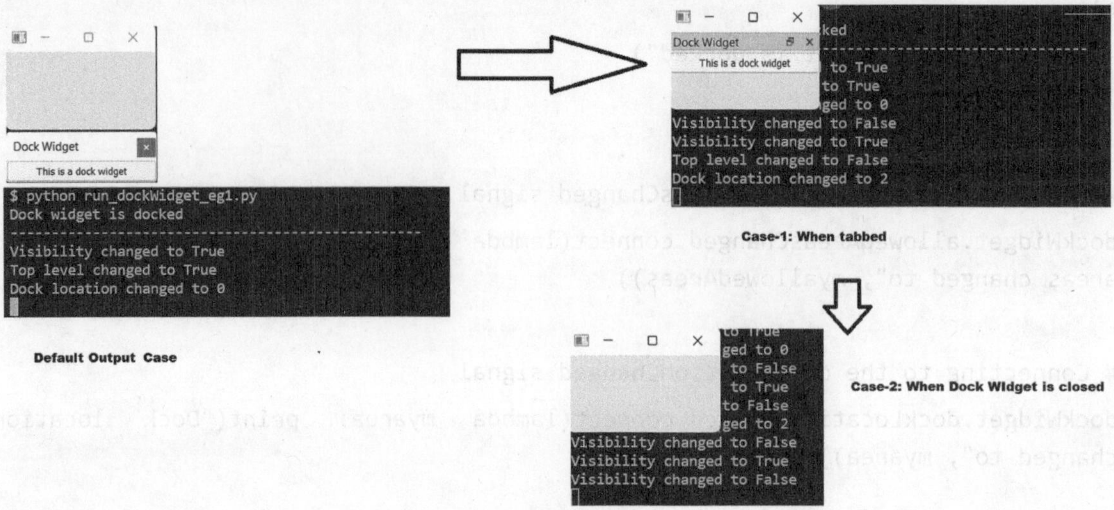

Figure 7.61: Output of run_dockWidget_eg1.py

Note: The preceding code is covered in Program Name: run_dockWidget_eg1.py

Conclusion

In this chapter, we got an in-depth understanding of many container widgets offered by Qt Designer. Readers now have a good understanding of the features and capabilities of each widget, as well as how to customize them to design aesthetically pleasing and user-friendly interfaces.

Readers specifically learned about what container widgets are and how they work, the different types of container widgets, how to use container widgets to create layouts, and how to customize the appearance of container widgets. Moreover, the readers also learned about signal-slot connections, how to connect signals that widgets within container widgets send to slots, and how to use layout managers to create the layouts we want.

To ensure that readers have a firm understanding of container widgets in Qt Designer, this chapter also featured practical examples and exercises.

Points to remember

- A **QGroupBox** is a widget from the Qt GUI library that acts as a container to group other widgets together and is visually distinguished from other widgets by a title and a frame.

- A `QScrollArea` widget in PyQt5 is a container widget that provides scrolling capabilities for the child widget contents within a frame.
- A toolbox is a widget that shows a column of tabs stacked one on top of the other, with the current item showing up below the active tab.
- A tab widget offers a tab bar and a **page area** where pages associated with each tab can be shown.
- A `QFrame` widget is used to group widgets together and provide a visual separation between them.
- The fundamental building blocks for creating **Graphical User Interfaces** (**GUI**) in PyQt5 is `QWidgets` which are visual components that can be displayed on the screen and can be interacted by the user.
- For the purpose of displaying **Numerous Document Windows** (**MDI**) in a single window, PyQt5's `QMdiArea` widget acts as a container widget. Each MDI window can be moved, resized, and closed on its own without affecting any other windows.
- The dockable windows can be added to a main window using `QDockWidget` class.

Questions

1. For what purpose, are PyQt5 container widgets used? Explain in detail.
2. Explain different container widgets of Qt designer.
3. Explain `QObject` and `QWidget` class of Qt designer.
4. Write short note on Containers in PyQt5.
5. Explain the significance and use of Group Box in Qt designer.
6. Explain the important properties of Group Box in Qt designer.
7. Explain the important signals available in Group Box in Qt designer.
8. Explain the use of Scroll Area in Qt designer.
9. Explain the important properties of Scroll Area in Qt Designer.
10. Explain the use of stacked widget in Qt Designer.
11. Explain the important properties of stacked widgets in Qt designer.
12. Explain the use of `FrameWidget` in Qt Designer.
13. Explain the important properties of `FrameWidget` in Qt designer.
14. Explain **Multiple Document Interface** (**MDI**) and its significance in Qt designer.
15. Which widget is used to add dockable windows to a main window? Explain in detail.
16. Explain the important properties of Dock Widget in Qt designer.
17. Explain the important methods of Dock Widget in Qt designer.
18. Explain the important signals of Dock Widget in Qt designer.

CHAPTER 8

Getting Insights of Input Widgets in Qt Designer

Introduction

Input widgets for PyQt5 are necessary because they provide users with an approach to input data into PyQt5 applications. As they allow user interaction and data input, these widgets are an essential component of creating a **Graphical User Interface** (**GUI**) for an application.

There are different ways to input data into the input widgets provided by PyQt5, including text input, number input, date/time input, and drop-down list selection. The developer may easily create a user-friendly interface and collect data from the user thanks to these widgets. Additionally, input widgets are a crucial component of modern applications since they let users enter and manipulate data in various ways. Different input widgets present in Qt Designer are shown in the following figure:

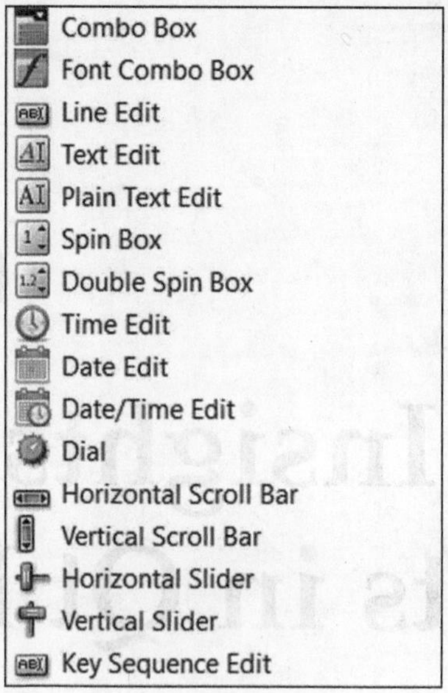

***Figure 8.1:** Different input widgets of Qt Designer*

We shall discuss the importance of each input widget one by one.

Structure

In this chapter, we will discuss the following topics:

- Combo Box
- Font Combo Box
- Line Edit
- Text Edit
- Plain Text Edit
- Spin Box
- Double Spin Box
- Date Time Edit
- Dial
- QScrollBar
- QSlider
- Key Sequence Edit

Objectives

After reading this chapter, the reader will have a thorough understanding of many input widgets that are available and how to utilize them effectively to create interactive user interfaces. By the end of this chapter, readers will have a solid understanding of input widgets, including **QLineEdit**, **QSpinBox**, **QComboBox**, **QTextEdit**, and so on, as well as their corresponding characteristics, functionality, and customization choices.

The main objective of this chapter is to give readers the knowledge needed to incorporate these input widgets into their designs so that users may enter data, select options, and interact with the program. The use of input validation methods, processing user input events, and linking signals and slots to accomplish the required functionality are also covered for the benefit of the readers. The readers will be able to develop simple and user-friendly interfaces that effectively collect user input and deliver a smooth user experience by mastering input widgets in Qt Designer. Moreover, we shall explore practical examples with useful comments at the required locations for all the input widgets in Qt Designer.

Combo Box

The combination of button and popup list is **QComboBox** widget. Users can choose an option from a drop-down list of options using the **QComboBox** widget in PyQt5. It is a frequently used widget for choosing items from a list. We can manually enter items or use a model to fill out the **QComboBox** widget. Along with text items, icons may also be displayed. Drop-down lists with different properties and options can be created using PyQt5's **QComboBox** which is a component of the **PyQt5.QtWidgets** package. The ability to make the widget editable, set the current item, set the maximum number of visible items, and the option to control the insertion policy are some noteworthy properties and options.

Important properties

Let us go over some important properties:

editable

This property will determine whether the **QComboBox** object can be edited by the user or not. The default value is **False**. Refer to the following figure:

Figure 8.2: *Image depicting editable property of QComboBox in Qt Designer*

currentText

The current text displayed in the **QComboBox** object is returned using this property. Refer to the following figure:

Figure 8.3: Image depicting currentText property of QComboBox in Qt Designer

currentIndex

The default value is **-1**, and this property will return the index of the current item selected in the **QComboBox** object. Refer to the following figure:

Figure 8.4: Image depicting currentIndex property of QComboBox in Qt Designer

maxVisibleItems

The maximum number of items to be displayed in the drop-down lists of the **QComboBox** object can be set with the help of the above property. The default value is **10**. Refer to the following figure:

Figure 8.5: Image depicting maxVisibleItems property of QComboBox in Qt Designer

maxCount

Using this property, the maximum number of items to be added to the **QComboBox** object can be set. The default value is **2147483647**. Refer to the following figure:

Figure 8.6: Image depicting maxCount property of QComboBox in Qt Designer

insertPolicy

User can set the policy where items are to appear in the **QComboBox** object. The default value is **InsertAtBottom**. Refer to the following figure:

Figure 8.7: Image depicting insertPoilcy property of QComboBox in Qt Designer

sizeAdjustPolicy

The rules policy can be set using this property for the **QComboBox** object to adjust its size when the list items change. Refer to the following figure:

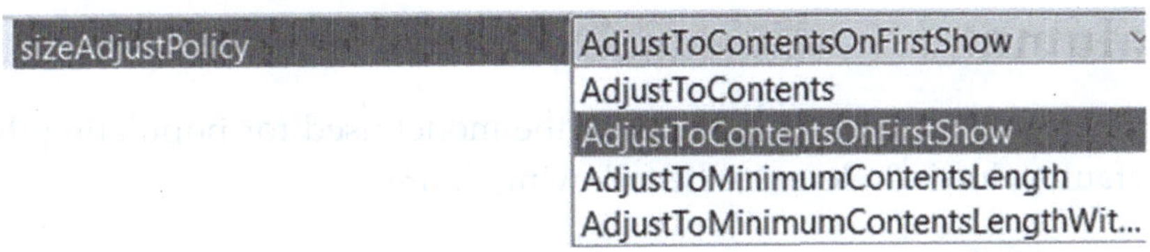

Figure 8.8: Image depicting sizeAdjustPolicy property of QComboBox in Qt Designer

minimumContentsLength

We can determine the fitting of the minimum number of characters into the **QComboBox** object. The default value is **0**. Refer to the following figure:

Figure 8.9: Image depicting minimumContentsLength property of QComboBox in Qt Designer

iconSize

The icon size to be displayed in the **QComboBox** object can be set using this property. Refer to the following figure:

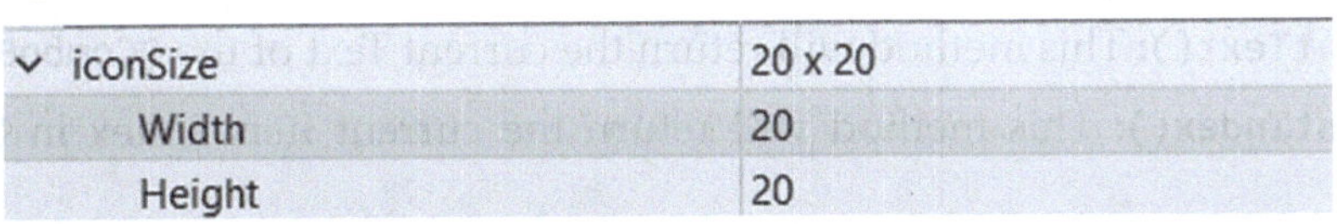

Figure 8.10: Image depicting iconSize property of QComboBox in Qt Designer

duplicatesEnabled

This Boolean property will determine whether duplicates are enabled in the **QComboBox** object. The default value is set to **False**. Refer to the following figure:

Figure 8.11: Image depicting duplicatesEnabled property of QComboBox in Qt Designer

Frame

When set to True, the **QComboBox** object draws itself inside a frame, else draws itself without any frame. Refer to the following figure:

Figure 8.12: Image depicting frame property of QComboBox in Qt Designer

modelColumn

Using this property, we can set the column of the model used for populating the **QComboBox** object. The default value is 0. Refer to the following figure:

Figure 8.13: Image depicting modelColumn property of QComboBox in Qt Designer

Important methods

Some important methods are as follows:

- **`addItem(text[,userData = None])`:** Using this method, the items will be added to the list of existing items in the **QComboBox** object with the given text and optional **userData** argument.
- **`addItems(texts)`:** This method will add a list of strings in the given texts to the **QComboBox** object.
- **`clear()`:** This method will remove all items from the **QComboBox** object.
- **`count()`:** This method will return the number of items in the **QComboBox** object.
- **`currentText()`:** This method will return the current Text of the **QComboBox** object.
- **`currentIndex()`:** This method will return the current Item index in the **QComboBox** object.
- **`setItemText(index,Text)`:** Using this method, the text of an item is changed at a specified index in the **QComboBox** object.

Important signals

Some important signals are as follows:

- **`activated(index)`:** This signal is emitted when an item in the **QComboBox** object is activated, either by using the keyboard to select or by clicking on it. The signal carries an argument index as a parameter, which is the index of the activated item.

- **`currentIndexChanged(index)`:** This signal is emitted whenever the **`QComboBox`**'s object current index changes. The new index is carried by the signal as an argument index.
- **`highlighted(index)`:** This signal is emitted when a **`QComboBox`**'s object item is highlighted, either by hovering the mouse over it or by using the keyboard to navigate to it. The index of the highlighted item is the argument index that is carried by the signal.

Now, we shall see an example of the **`QComboBox`** widget.

The details of file names are given in the following *Table 8.1*:

S No.	Qt Designer File Name (.ui)	Converting the Qt Designer file name to Python file (.py)	Creating another Python file and importing the converted Python file from Qt Designer
1	`combobox_eg1.ui`	`combobox_eg1.py`	`run_combobox_eg1.py`

Table 8.1: *Details of file names*

The Qt Designer file is shown in the following figure:

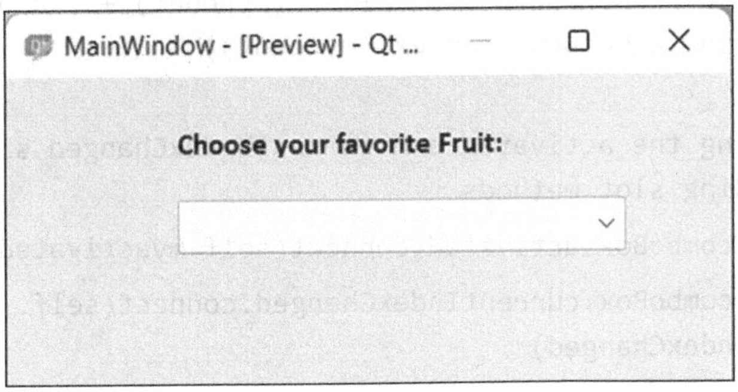

Figure 8.14: *Qt Designer file: ComboBox/combobox_eg1.ui*

Note: The above .ui file is covered in Path: ComboBox/combobox_eg1.ui

Consider the following code of **`run_combobox_eg1.py`**:

```
import sys
from PyQt5.QtWidgets import QMainWindow, QApplication
from combobox_eg1 import *

class MyComboBox(QMainWindow):
    def __init__(self):
        super().__init__()
```

```
        self.myui = Ui_MainWindow()
        self.myui.setupUi(self)

        # adding items to the QComboBox object
        self.myui.comboBox.addItems(["Orange", "Papaya", "Banana"])

        # setting the current index to 1
        self.myui.comboBox.setCurrentIndex(1)

        # inserting the item at index position 0 of QComboBox widget
        self.myui.comboBox.insertItem(0, "Mango")

        # display of all the items of QComboBox widget
        for mycount in range(self.myui.comboBox.count()):
            print("Current Index is: " + str(mycount) + " and the text is: " +
            self.myui.comboBox.itemText(mycount))

        # connecting the activated and currentIndexChanged signals to the
        corresponding slot methods
        self.myui.comboBox.activated.connect(self.myactivated)
        self.myui.comboBox.currentIndexChanged.connect(self.
        mycurrentIndexChanged)

        self.show()

    def myactivated(self, myindex):
        self.myui.mylbl2.setText("Item Activated is: " + self.myui.comboBox.
        currentText())

    def mycurrentIndexChanged(self, myindex):
        self.myui.mylbl3.setText("Index is: " + str(myindex) + " & Text is: "
        + self.myui.comboBox.currentText())

if __name__=="__main__":
    app = QApplication(sys.argv)
```

```
w = MyComboBox()
w.show()
sys.exit(app.exec_())
```

Output:

Refer to the following figure:

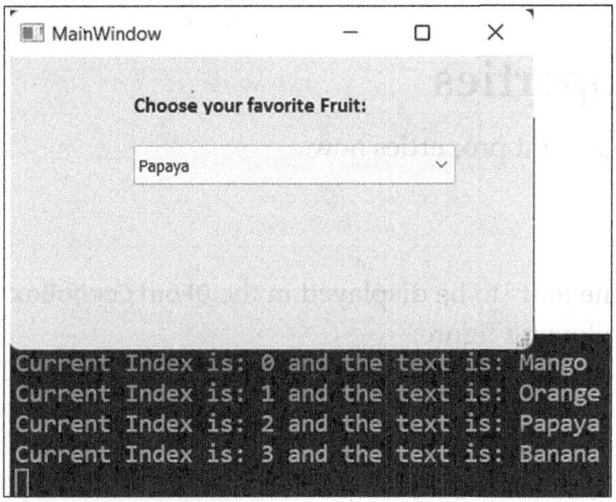

***Figure 8.15**: Output of ComboBox/run_combobox_eg1.py*

Note: The preceding code is covered in Program Name: ComboBox/run_combobox_eg1.py

From *Figure 8.15*, since the **Current Index** was set to **1** before inserting the item **Mango**, that is why it displayed **Papaya** in the **QComboBox** widget to the user.

From *Figure 8.16*, we can view the output when the item **Orange** is selected. Refer the following figure:

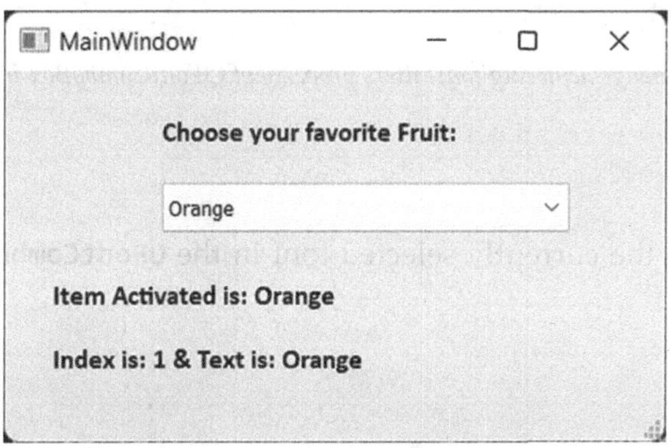

***Figure 8.16**: Output When Orange text is selected in ComboBox/run_combobox_eg1.py*

Font Combo Box

In PyQt5, a **QFontComboBox** widget is a combobox that enables users to select a font family from a list of system fonts. The **currentFontChanged()** signal is sent when a font is selected from a drop-down list of font family names displayed by the widget. Along with two **QToolButtons** for bold and italic formatting and a **QComboBox** for adjusting font size, **QFontComboBox** is frequently used in toolbars.

Important properties

Let us go over some important properties now.

writingSystem

The writing system of the fonts to be displayed in the **QFontComboBox** object is held using this property. Refer to the following figure:

***Figure 8.17**: Image depicting writingSystem property of QFontComboBox in Qt Designer*

fontFilters

This property will hold the font filters that limit the available font families in the **QFontComboBox** object. Refer to the following figure:

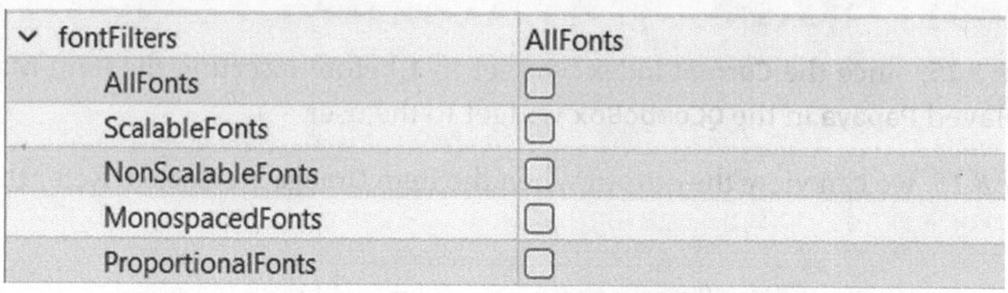

***Figure 8.18**: Image depicting fontFilters property of QFontComboBox in Qt Designer*

currentFont

This property will hold the currently selected font in the **QFontComboBox** object. Refer to the following figure:

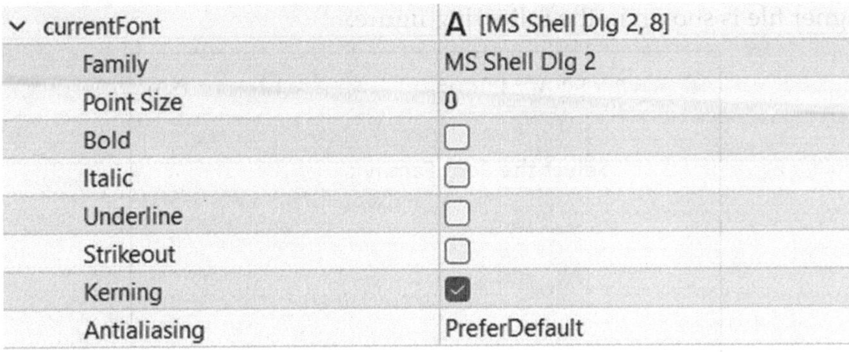

Figure 8.19: *Image depicting currentFont property of QFontComboBox in Qt Designer*

Important methods

Some important methods are as follows:

- **`setCurrentFont(QFont):`** This method will set the currently selected font in the **`QFontComboBox`** object.
- **`setFontFilters(FontFilters):`** This method will set the font filters used to limit the available font families in the **`QFontComboBox`** object.
- **`setWritingSystem(WritingSystem):`** This method will set the writing system of the fonts to be displayed in the **`QFontComboBox`** object.

Important signals

Let us now check an important signal.

currentFontChanged(QFont)

This signal is emitted when the currently selected font in the **`QFontComboBox`** object changes. A **`QFont`** object is taken as a parameter representing the newly selected font.

Now, we shall see an example of the **`QFontComboBox`** widget.

The details of file names are given in the following *Table 8.2*:

S No.	Qt Designer File Name (.ui)	Converting the Qt Designer file name to Python file (.py)	Creating another Python file and importing the converted Python file from Qt Designer
1	**`fontcombobox_eg1.ui`**	**`fontcombobox_eg1.py`**	**`run_fontcombobox_eg1.py`**

Table 8.2: *Details of file names*

The Qt Designer file is shown in the following figure:

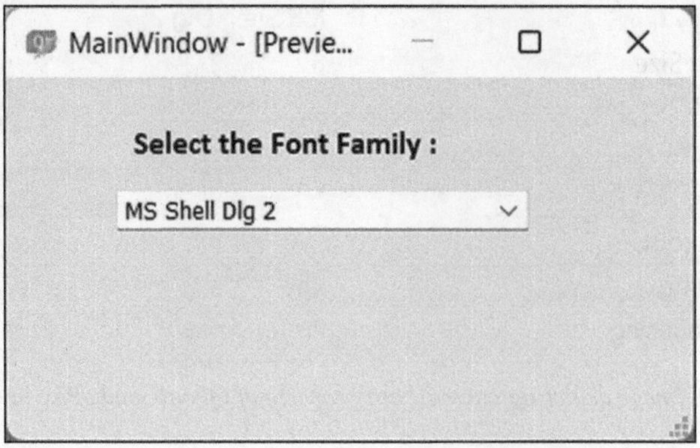

Figure 8.20: Qt Designer file: FontComboBox/fontcombobox_eg1.ui

Note: The above .ui file is covered in Path: FontComboBox/fontcombobox_eg1.ui

Consider the following code of **run_fontcombobox_eg1.py**:

```
import sys
from PyQt5.QtWidgets import QMainWindow, QApplication, QFontComboBox
from fontcombobox_eg1 import *


class MyFontComboBox(QMainWindow):
    def __init__(self):
        super().__init__()
        self.myui = Ui_MainWindow()
        self.myui.setupUi(self)

        # setting the font filters which are used to limit the available font
        families of QFOntComboBox object
        self.myui.fontComboBox.setFontFilters(QFontComboBox.NonScalableFonts)

        # Connecting the currentFontChanged signal of QFOntComboBox object to
        the myfontchanged slot
        self.myui.fontComboBox.currentFontChanged.connect(self.myfontchanged)

        self.show()
```

```
    def myfontchanged(self, myfont):
        self.myui.mylb2.setText("Current font changed to:" + myfont.family())


if __name__=="__main__":
    app = QApplication(sys.argv)
    w = MyFontComboBox()
    w.show()
    sys.exit(app.exec_())
```

Output:

Refer to the following figure:

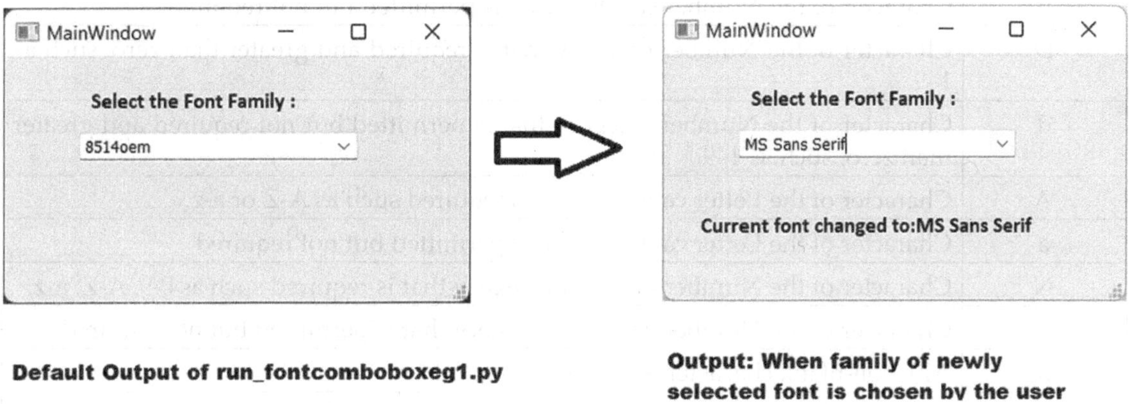

***Figure 8.21:** Output of FontComboBox/run_fontcombobox_eg1.py*

> **Note: The preceding code is covered in Program Name: FontComboBox/run_fontcombobox_eg1.py**

Line Edit

One of the most commonly used single-line text editors of Qt Designer is **`QLineEdit`** widget. It is frequently used to display text or to accept text input from users. Various properties, including font, input mask, placeholder text, and so on, can be changed. Additionally, it offers signals like **`editingFinished`** and **`textChanged`** that are emitted when a user interacts with the widget.

Important properties

Let us go over some important properties now.

inputMask

This property defines a string that specifies a validation input mask. A valid input format is defined by the mask, such as any phone number, IP Address, date, and so on. An empty string is returned if no mask is set. Some of the different mask characters and meanings can be found in the following *Table 8.3:*

Mask Characters	Meaning
9	Character of the Number category that is required such as 0–9.
0	Character of the Number category that is permitted but not required
D	Character of the Number category that is required and greater than zero, such as 1–9.
d	Character of the Number category that is permitted but not required and greater than zero, such as 1–9.
A	Character of the Letter category that is required such as A-Z or a-z.
a	Character of the Letter category that is permitted but not required
N	Character of the Number or Letter category that is required such as 0-9, A-Z, a-z.
n	Character of the Number or Letter category that is permitted but not required
X	Any non-blank character is required.
x	Any non-blank character is permitted but not required.
#	+/- sign or character of the number category is permitted but not required.
H	Requirement of the hexadecimal character A-F, a-f , 0-9.
h	Hexadecimal character is permitted but not required.
B	Requirement of the binary character 0-1.
b	Binary character is permitted but not required.
<	Makes all the alphabetic characters to lowercase.
>	Makes all the alphabetic characters to uppercase.
!	Case conversion is switched off.
\	Special character escapes for using them as separators.
{}	A user-defined character is represented to define a custom character set.

***Table 8.3:** Masked characters and their meanings*

Refer to the following figure:

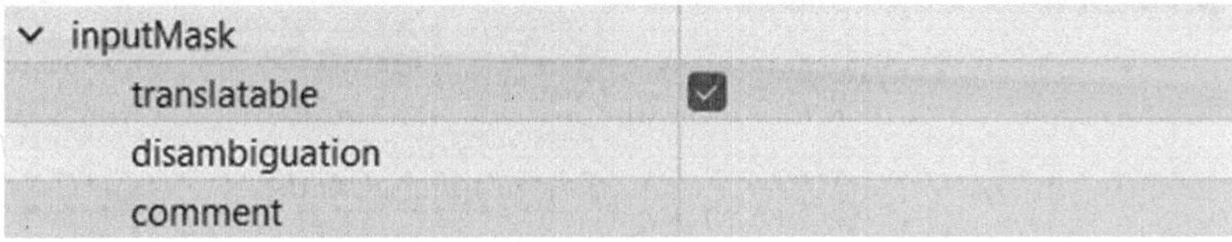

***Figure 8.22:** Image depicting inputMask property of QLineEdit in Qt Designer*

text

QLineEdit's object is held using this property. The default value is an empty string. Refer to the following figure:

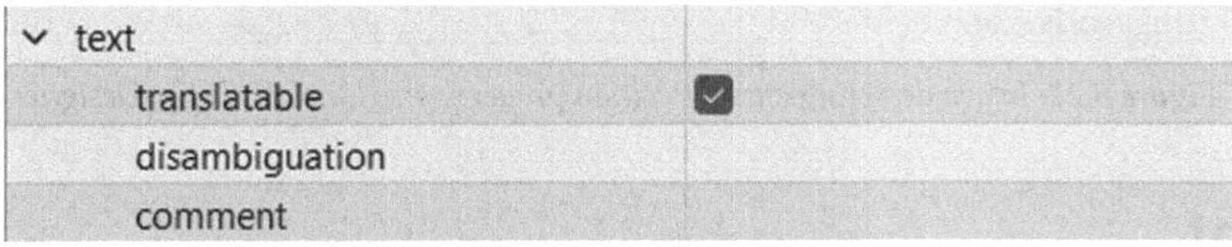

***Figure 8.23:** Image depicting text property of QLineEdit in Qt Designer*

maxLength

The maximum allowed length of the text in the **QLineEdit** object is set using this property. Refer to the following figure:

***Figure 8.24:** Image depicting maxLength property of QLineEdit in Qt Designer*

frame

If checked, the **QLineEdit** object will be drawn itself inside a frame. Refer to the following figure:

***Figure 8.25:** Image depicting frame property of QLineEdit in Qt Designer*

echoMode

This property will decide how the text entered in the **QLineEdit** object will be displayed to the user. Refer to the following figure:

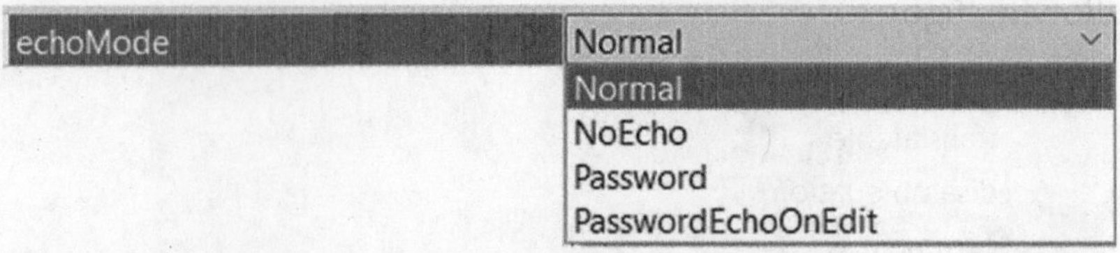

***Figure 8.26:** Image depicting echoMode property of QLineEdit in Qt Designer*

cursorPosition

The current cursor position will be held for the **`QLineEdit`** object. The default value is **`0`**. Refer to the following figure:

***Figure 8.27:** Image depicting cursorPosition property of QLineEdit in Qt Designer*

alignment

Using this property, the alignment of **`QLineEdit`** object is held where we can align both horizontal and vertical alignment. Refer to the following figure:

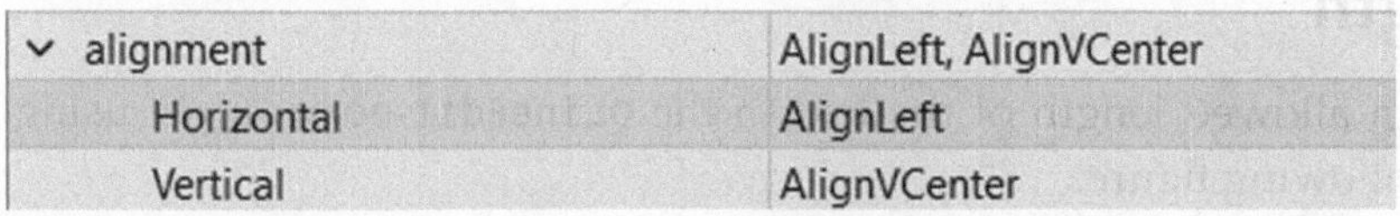

***Figure 8.28:** Image depicting alignment property of QLineEdit in Qt Designer*

dragEnabled

This property allows the user to press and move the mouse inside the **`QLineEdit`** object. When enabled, it allows the dragging of its contents. Refer to the following figure:

***Figure 8.29:** Image depicting deagEnabled property of QLineEdit in Qt Designer*

readOnly

This property is disabled by default and indicates that text inside the **`QLineEdit`** object is **readOnly**. The user cannot edit the text but can copy or drag and drop the text. Refer to the following figure:

***Figure 8.30:** Image depicting readOnly property of QLineEdit in Qt Designer*

placeholderText

We can set and display the placeholder text in the **QLineEdit** object when it is empty and not focused. Refer to the following figure:

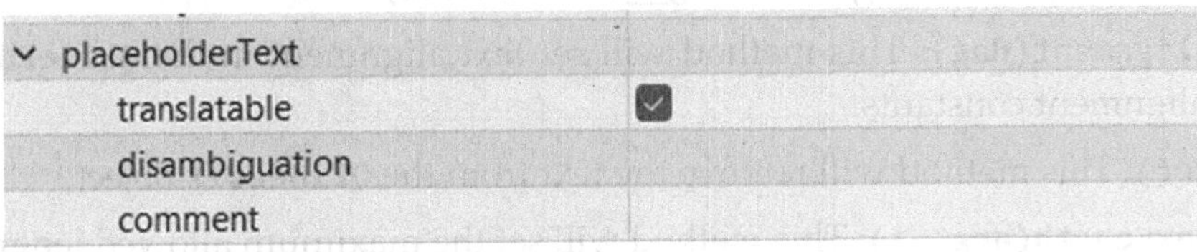

Figure 8.31: *Image depicting placeholderText property of QLineEdit in Qt Designer*

cursorMoveStyle

We can set the way or movement style of the cursor in the **QLineEdit** object. Refer to the following figure:

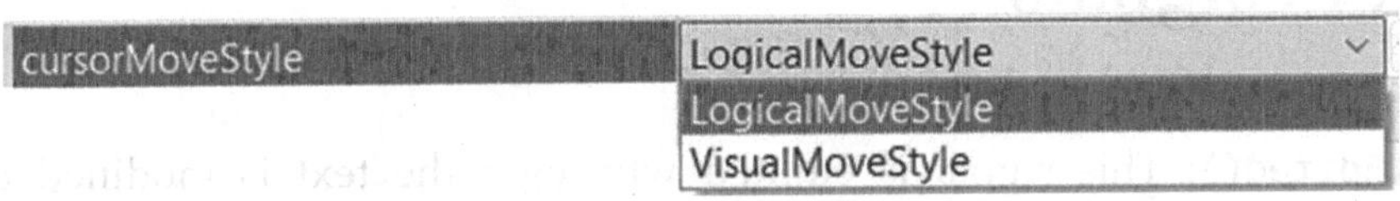

Figure 8.32: *Image depicting cursorMoveStyle property of QLineEdit in Qt Designer*

clearButtonEnabled

This property will indicate whether the **QLineEdit** object will have a clear button when it is not empty. It is disabled by default. Refer to the following figure:

Figure 8.33: *Image depicting clearButtonEnabled property of QLineEdit in Qt Designer*

Important methods

Let us go over some important methods:

- **`setText(arg__1)`:** Using this method, the text is set in the **`QLineEdit`** object to the specified argument string.
- **`setValidator(arg__1)`:** The input validator for the **`QLineEdit`** object is set using this method. The validator parameter **`arg__1`** is a **`QValidator`** instance or one of its subclasses. The input conforms to a specified format ensured by the validator.
- **`setInputMask(inputMask)`:** An input mask is set for the **`QLineEdit`** object using this method. The input format is specified by the **`inputMask`** argument, which is a string.

- **`setFont(arg__1)`:** The font is set using this method to display the text in the **`QLineEdit`** object to the specified argument **`arg__1`**. This is an instance of the **`QFont`** object.
- **`setEchoMode(arg__1)`:** The display mode of the text entered into the **`QLineEdit`** object is set to the specified argument **`arg__1 (EchoMode)`**.
- **`setAlignment(flag)`:** This method will set text alignment in the **`QLineEdit`** object as per alignment constants.
- **`clear()`:** This method will remove the text from the **`QLineEdit`** object.
- **`setMaxLength(arg__1)`:** This method will set the maximum allowed length of the text in the **`QLineEdit`** object to the specified argument **`arg__1`** of type **`int`**.
- **`setReadOnly(arg__1)`:** The read-only status of the **`QLineEdit`** object is set to the specified Read Only Boolean value **`arg__1`**. If Read Only is set as True, the user cannot modify the text in the **`QLineEdit`** object.

Important signals

Some important signals are as follows:

- **`textEdited()`:** This signal is emitted whenever the text is modified by the user, including additions or deletions in the **`QLineEdit`** object.
- **`textChanged()`:** This signal is emitted whenever any **`QLineEdit`** object text is changed, including changes made programmatically.
- **`editingFinished()`:** This signal is emitted when the user completes editing the text in the **`QLineEdit`** object by pressing the *Enter* key or leaving the widget.
- **`returnPressed()`:** This signal is emitted by pressing the *Enter* key while editing the text in the **`QLineEdit`** object.
- **`selectionChanged()`:** This signal is emitted when the selected text in the **`QLineEdit`** object is changed.
- **`cursorPositionChanged()`:** This signal is emitted when the cursor is moved and its position is changed in the **`QLineEdit`** object.

Now, we shall see an example of the **`QLineEdit`** widget.

The details of file names are given in the following *Table 8.4*:

S No.	Qt Designer File Name (.ui)	Converting the Qt Designer file name to Python file (.py)	Creating another Python file and importing the converted Python file from Qt Designer
1	**`lineedit_eg1.ui`**	**`lineedit_eg1.py`**	**`run_lineedit_eg1.py`**

***Table 8.4:** Details of file names*

The Qt Designer file is shown in the following figure:

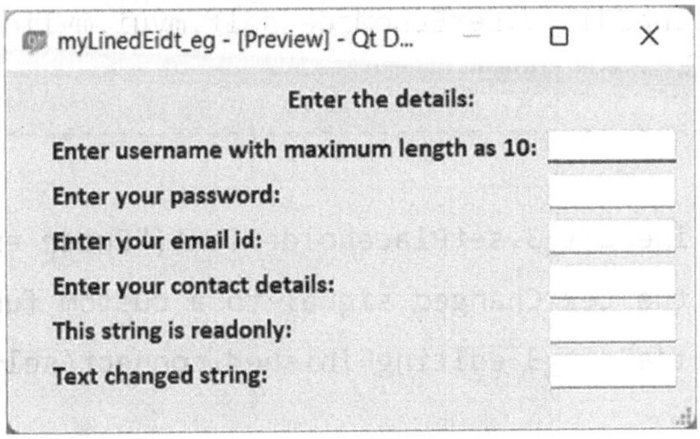

Figure 8.34: Qt Designer file: LineEdit/lineedit_eg1.ui

Note: The above .ui file is covered in Path: LineEdit/lineedit_eg1.ui

Consider the following code of **run_lineedit_eg1.py**:

```
import sys
import re
from PyQt5.QtWidgets import QMainWindow, QApplication, QMessageBox
from PyQt5.QtGui import QFont
from lineedit_eg1 import *

class MyLineEdit(QMainWindow):
    def __init__(self):
        super().__init__()
        self.myui = Ui_MainWindow()
        self.myui.setupUi(self)

        # LineEdit1 ---------------------------------------------------------
        ------------

        # Set the maximum number of characters that can be entered
        self.myui.mylineEdit_1.setMaxLength(10)
        self.myui.mylineEdit_1.setFont(QFont("Calibri",16))
        self.myui.mylineEdit_1.setPlaceholderText("Enter username")

        # LineEdit2 ---------------------------------------------------------
        ------------
```

```
        self.myui.mylineEdit_2.setPlaceholderText("Enter password")
        self.myui.mylineEdit_2.setEchoMode(self.myui.mylineEdit_2.Password)

        # LineEdit3 ------------------------------------------------------------
------------
        self.myui.mylineEdit_3.setPlaceholderText("Enter email @ is must")
        # Connecting the textChanged signal to a custom function
        self.myui.mylineEdit_3.editingFinished.connect(self.myvalidate_email)

        # LineEdit4 ------------------------------------------------------------
------------
        self.myui.mylineEdit_4.setInputMask("+99_99999_99999")

        # LineEdit5 ------------------------------------------------------------
------------
        self.myui.mylineEdit_5.setText("Only Read Only Text")
        self.myui.mylineEdit_5.setReadOnly(True)

        # LineEdit6 ------------------------------------------------------------
------------
        self.myui.mylineEdit_6.textChanged.connect(self.mytextchanged)

        self.show()

    def myvalidate_email(self):
        # Regex for valid email addresses
        myemail_regex = re.compile(r"[^@]+@[^@]+\.[^@]+")

        # Getting the text from the QLineEdit widget
        myemail = self.myui.mylineEdit_3.text()

        # Checking if the email address is valid
        if not myemail_regex.match(myemail):
            # Set the input method to invalid if the email address is not valid
```

```
                self.myui.mylineEdit_3.setStyleSheet("border: 1px solid red")

                # Displaying an error message
                QMessageBox.warning(self, "Error!", "Email address is invalid")

                # focusing on the LineEdit if wrong email id is entered
                self.myui.mylineEdit_3.setFocus()
            else:
                # Set the input method to valid if the email address is valid
                self.myui.mylineEdit_3.setStyleSheet("border: 1px solid green")

    def mytextchanged(self, mytext):
        print("Changed contents: "+ mytext)


if __name__ == "__main__":
    app = QApplication(sys.argv)
    screen = MyLineEdit()
    screen.show()
    sys.exit(app.exec_())
```

Output:

Refer to the following figure:

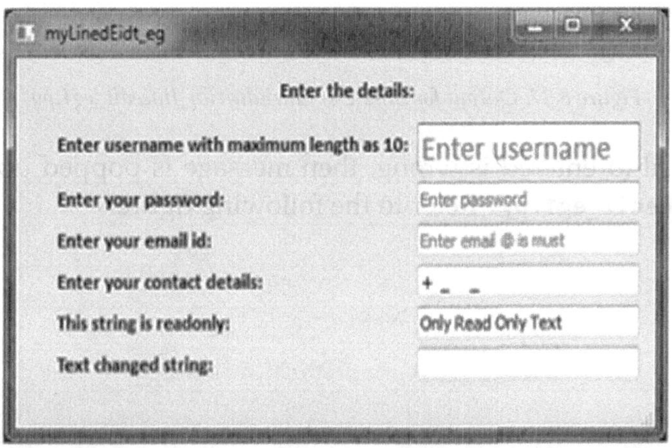

***Figure 8.35**: Default output for LineEdit/run_lineedit_eg1.py*

Case 1: When **`LineEdit1`** is focused on entering the username with max length as 10 for **`LineEdit/run_lineedit_eg1.py`**. Refer to the following figure:

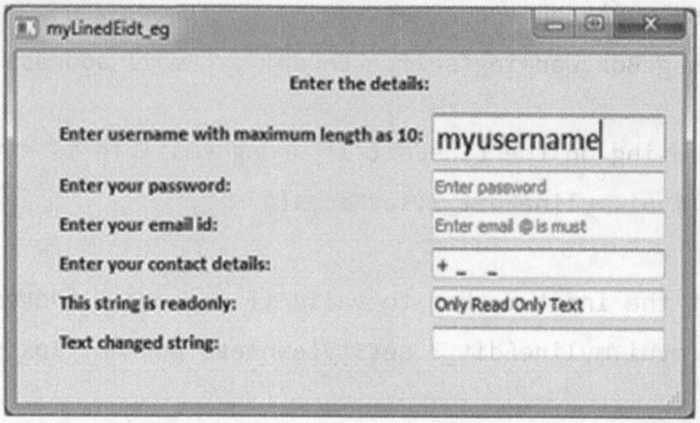

Figure 8.36: Output for Case-1 of LineEdit/run_lineedit_eg1.py.

Case 2: When **`LineEdit2`** is focused and user is required to enter the password for **`LineEdit/run_lineedit_eg1.py.`** Refer to the following figure:

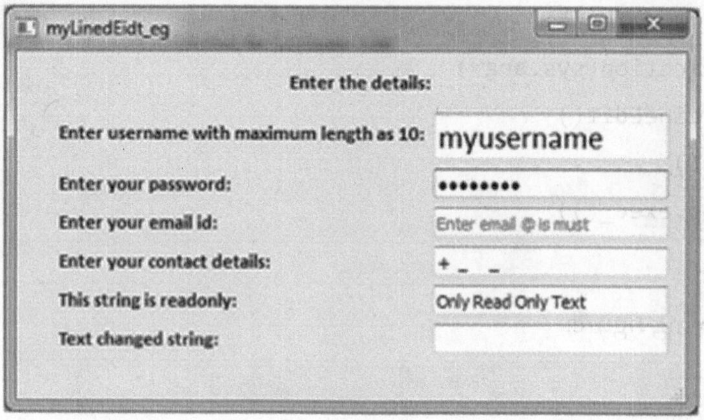

Figure 8.37: Output for Case-2 of LineEdit/run_lineedit_eg1.py.

Case 3: When email id entered is wrong, then message is popped up in **`LineEdit3`** for **`LineEdit/run_lineedit_eg1.py.`** Refer to the following figure:

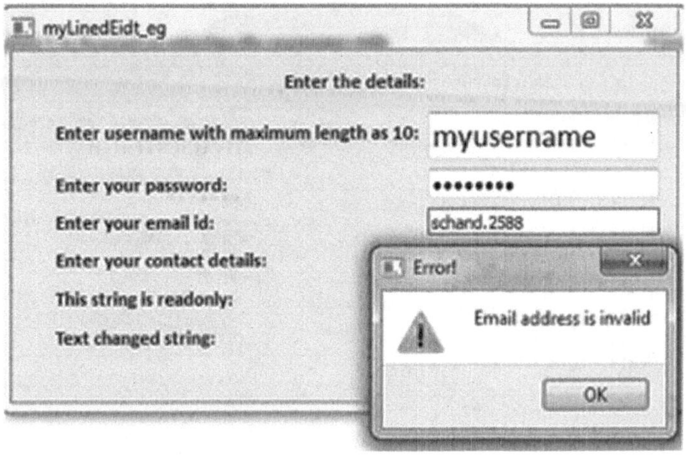

Figure 8.38: Output for Case-3 of LineEdit/run_lineedit_eg1.py.

Case 4: When email id entered is correct in **`LineEdit3`** for **`LineEdit/run_lineedit_eg1.py.`** Refer to the following figure:

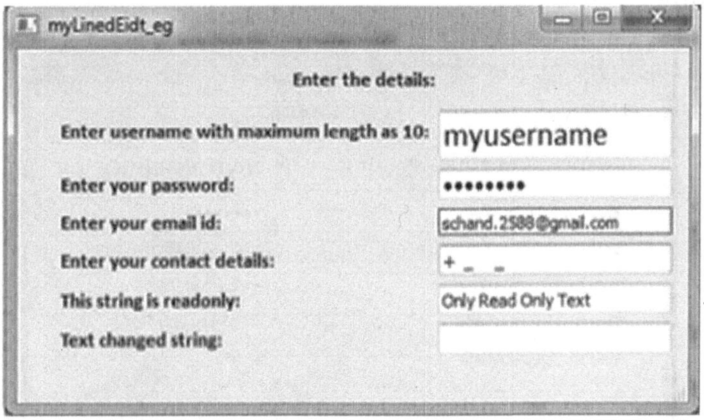

Figure 8.39: Output for Case-4 of LineEdit/run_lineedit_eg1.py.

Case 5: When contact details are entered correctly in **`LineEdit4`**. Also, in **`LineEdit5`** read only text is displayed. User cannot edit anything in the above **`LineEdit`** widget for **`LineEdit/run_lineedit_eg1.py.`** Refer to the following figure.

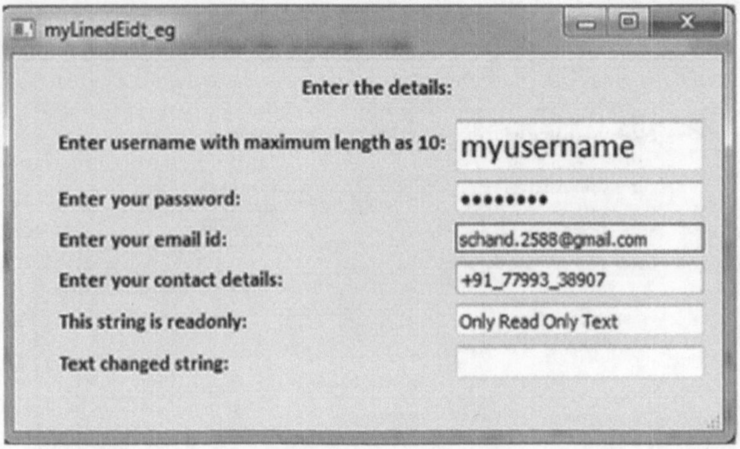

Figure 8.40: Output for Case-5 of LineEdit/run_lineedit_eg1.py.

Case 6: When user enters **`hithere`** text, textchanged event of **`LineEdit6`** is triggered to a method for the display of text to the console for **`LineEdit/run_lineedit_eg1.py.`** Refer to the following figure:

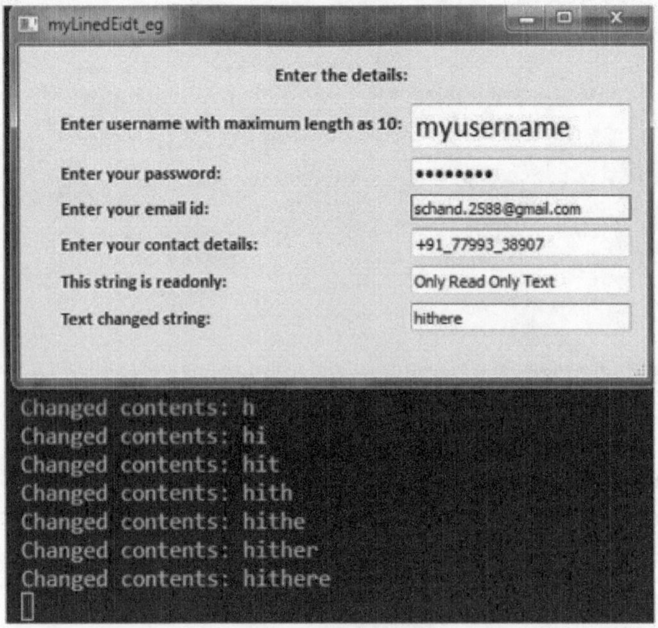

Figure 8.41: Output for Case-6 of LineEdit/run_lineedit_eg1.py.

Note: The preceding code is covered in Program Name: LineEdit/run_lineedit_eg1.py

TextEdit

The PyQt5 widget **`QTextEdit`** offers a multi-line text area for editing and displaying documents in plain text or HTML. It includes undo and redo capability and extensive text formatting options like bold, italic, and underlining. It can be utilized to develop simple text editors, email clients, and other programs that require the ability to edit and display text.

Important properties

Let us check some important properties now.

autoFormatting

This property will determine enabling of automatic formatting features like text completion, spelling correction, and so on, of the **`QTextEdit`** object. The default value is **AutoNone**. For enabling all automatic formatting, the user may select **AutoAll**. Refer to the following figure:

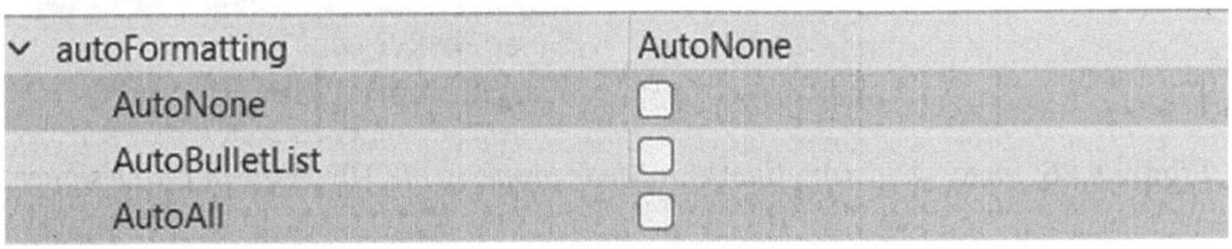

Figure 8.42: *Image depicting autoFormatting property of QTextEdit in Qt Designer*

tabChangeFocus

On pressing the *Tab* key, this property determines whether the focus will be changed to the next widget or a tab character is inserted into the **`QTextEdit`** object. The default value is **False**. Refer to the following figure:

Figure 8.43: *Image depicting tabChangeFocus property of QTextEdit in Qt Designer*

documentTitle

This property will hold the document title parsed from the text. For a newly created empty document, this property contains an empty string by default. Refer to the following figure:

Figure 8.44: *Image depicting documentTitle property of QTextEdit in Qt Designer*

undoRedoEnabled

This property will determine whether functionality, like undo and redo, is enabled. The default value is **True**. Refer to the following figure:

***Figure 8.45**: Image depicting undoRedoEnabled property of QTextEdit in Qt Designer*

lineWrapMode

This property will hold the mode of line wrap and determine the way the text will be wrapped when it reaches the end of the line. The default mode is **`WidgetWidth`**, and the words will be wrapped at the right edge of the **`QTextEdit`** object. Refer to the following figure:

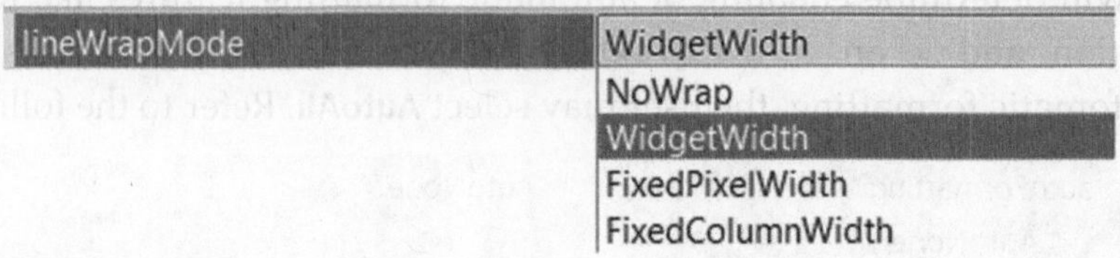

***Figure 8.46**: Image depicting lineWrapMode property of QTextEdit in Qt Designer*

lineWrapColumnOrWidth

This property will determine the position (width in pixels or columns) depending on the selection of warp mode in which text will be wrapped in the **`QTextEdit`** object. Refer to the following figure:

***Figure 8.47**: Image depicting lineWrapColumnOrWidth property of QTextEdit in Qt Designer*

readOnly

This property, when set to **True**, will make the text in the **`QTextEdit`** object read-only, that is, it cannot be edited. The default value is **False**. Refer to the following figure:

***Figure 8.48**: Image depicting readOnly property of QTextEdit in Qt Designer*

html

An HTML interface is provided for the text of the **`QTextEdit`** object. Refer to the following figure:

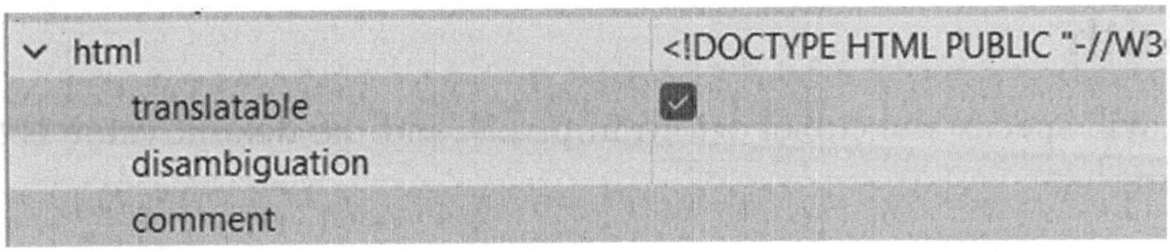

***Figure 8.49**: Image depicting html property of QTextEdit in Qt Designer*

overwriteMode

This property will overwrite the existing text with a text entered by the user when set. The default value is **False**, indicating that the new text will not overwrite the existing text. Refer to the following figure:

***Figure 8.50**: Image depicting overwriteMode property of QTextEdit in Qt Designer*

tabStopWidth

This property will hold the width of **`tabStop`** in pixels where the default value is **`80`** pixels. Refer to the following figure:

***Figure 8.51**: Image depicting tabStopWidth property of QTextEdit in Qt Designer*

tabStopDistance

This property will hold the distance of **`tabStop`** in pixels. Refer to the following figure:

***Figure 8.52**: Image depicting tabStopDistance property of QTextEdit in Qt Designer*

acceptRichText

This property will determine whether richtext, such as HTML, is accepted in the **`QTextEdit`** object. The default value is **True**. Refer to the following figure:

***Figure 8.53**: Image depicting acceptRichText property of QTextEdit in Qt Designer*

cursorWidth

This property will specify the cursor width in pixels, and the default value is **1**. Refer to the following figure:

Figure 8.54: *Image depicting cursorWidth property of QTextEdit in Qt Designer*

textInteractionFlags

This property will determine how the **QTextEdit** object will interact with mouse and keyboard events. Refer to the following figure:

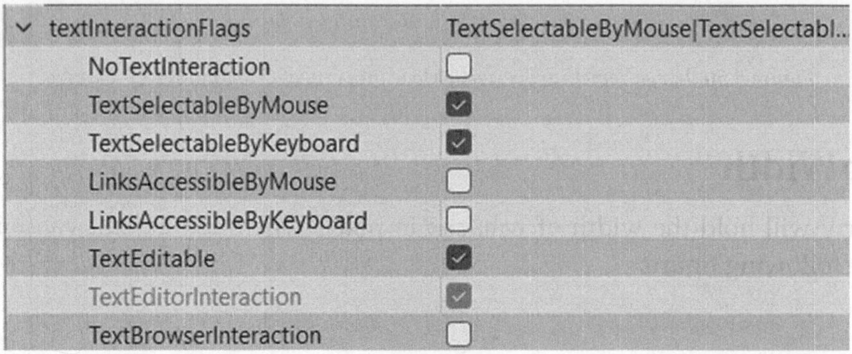

Figure 8.55: *Image depicting textInteractionFlags property of QTextEdit in Qt Designer*

placeholderText

This property will hold the placeholder text displayed in the **QTextEdit** object when it is not focused and empty. Refer to the following figure:

Figure 8.56: *Image depicting placeholderText property of QTextEdit in Qt Designer*

Important methods

Let us go over some important methods:

- **append(text):** The specified argument **text** of type string is added to the end of the current document in the **QTextEdit** object.

- **`insertHtml(text)`:** The specified argument **`text`** of type string is inserted and formatted as HTML into the **`QTextEdit`** object at the current cursor position.
- **`insertPlainText(text)`:** The specified argument **`text`** of type string is inserted as plain text into the **`QTextEdit`** object at the current cursor position.
- **`setCurrentFont(f)`:** The selected text font or text at the cursor position is changed to argument **`f`**, a **`QFont`** object.
- **`clear()`:** This method will delete all the text in the **`QTextEdit`** object.
- **`setPlainText(text)`:** This method will replace the current text in the **`QTextEdit`** object with the specified **`text`** formatted as plain text.
- **`setHtml(text)`:** This method will replace the current text in the **`QTextEdit`** object with the specified **`text`** formatted by providing an HTML interface. The interpretation of input text will be as rich text in HTML format.

Just prepend **`set`** to all the properties discussed, followed by the parameters. This will add to the list of methods. We have discussed only a few methods.

Important signals

Some important signals are as follows:

- **`textChanged()`:** This signal is emitted when the text in the **`QTextEdit`** object is changed.
- **`undoAvailable(b)`:** This signal is emitted when the availability of an undo operation changes. Parameter **`b`** is a Boolean value indicating whether an undo operation is available.
- **`redoAvailable(b)`:** This signal is emitted when the availability of a redo operation changes. Parameter **`b`** is a Boolean value indicating whether a redo operation is available.
- **`copyAvailable(b)`:** This signal is emitted when the availability of a copy operation changes. Parameter **`b`** is a Boolean value indicating whether a copy operation is available.

Now, we shall see an example of the **`QTextEdit`** widget.

The details of file names are given in the following *Table 8.5:*

S No.	Qt Designer File Name (.ui)	Converting the Qt Designer file name to Python file (.py)	Creating another Python file and importing the converted Python file from Qt Designer
1	`textedit_eg1.ui`	`textedit_eg1.py`	`run_textedit_eg1.py`

***Table 8.5:** Details of file names*

The Qt Designer file is shown in the following figure:

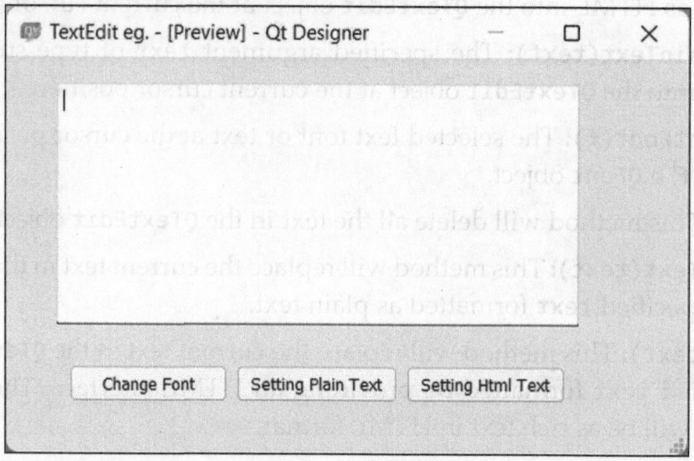

Figure 8.57: Qt Designer file: TextEdit/textedit_eg1.ui

Note: The above .ui file is covered in Path: TextEdit/textedit_eg1.ui

Consider the following code of **run_textedit_eg1.py**:

```
import sys
import re
from PyQt5.QtWidgets import QMainWindow,QApplication, QFontDialog
from textedit_eg1 import *

class MyTextEdit(QMainWindow):
    def __init__(self):
        super().__init__()
        self.myui = Ui_MainWindow()
        self.myui.setupUi(self)
        self.myui.mybtn1.clicked.connect(self.my_btn1)
        self.myui.mybtn2.clicked.connect(self.my_btn2)
        self.myui.mybtn3.clicked.connect(self.my_btn3)

        # replacing the text of TextEdit object with 'Hello'
        self.myui.textEdit.setText("Hello")
```

```
        self.show()

    def my_btn1(self):
        # prompting the user to select the font family, font style, size
        myfont, imok = QFontDialog.getFont()
        # on pressing Ok replacing the text in the TextEdit object with the
        selected font
        if imok:
            self.myui.textEdit.setCurrentFont(myfont)

    def my_btn2(self):
        # replacing the text of TextEdit object with plain text on button click
        self.myui.textEdit.setPlainText("Hi Friends!\nWelcome to study PyQt5
        textEdit widget")

    def my_btn3(self):
        # replacing the text of TextEdit object with text formatted by
        providing an html interface on button click
        self.myui.textEdit.setHtml("<font color='green' size='7'>Hi Friends!\
        nHello</font>")

if __name__ == "__main__":
    app = QApplication(sys.argv)
    screen = MyTextEdit()
    screen.show()
    sys.exit(app.exec_())
```

Output:

Refer to the following figure:

Default output:

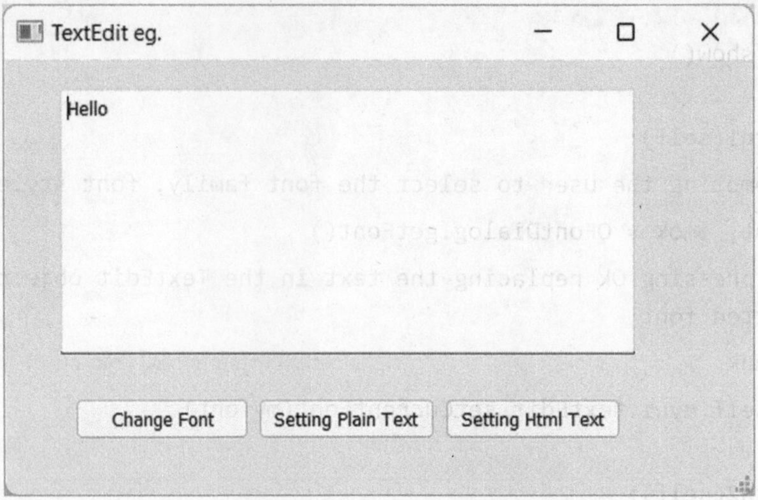

Figure 8.58: Default output of TextEdit/run_textedit_eg1.py

Case 1: First text inside the **`QTextEdit`** is selected and then selecting the font, font style and Size from **`QFontDialog`**.

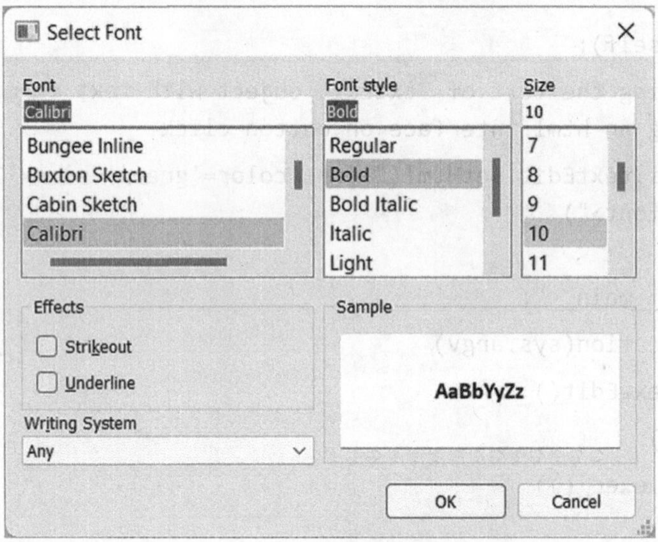

Figure 8.59: Case1 output of TextEdit/run_textedit_eg1.py

Case 2: The text inside the **`QTextEdit`** is changed as per choice selected from QFontDialog Box.

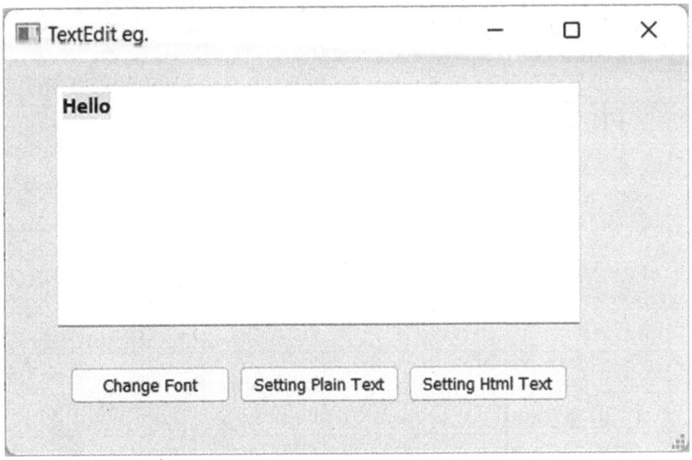

***Figure 8.60**: Case2 output of TextEdit/run_textedit_eg1.py*

Case 3: On clicking **Setting Plain Text** button.

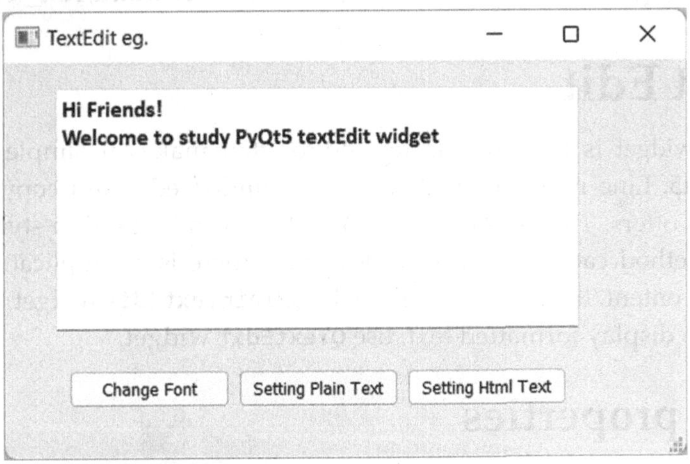

***Figure 8.61**: Case3 output of TextEdit/run_textedit_eg1.py*

Case 4: On clicking **Setting Html Text** button.

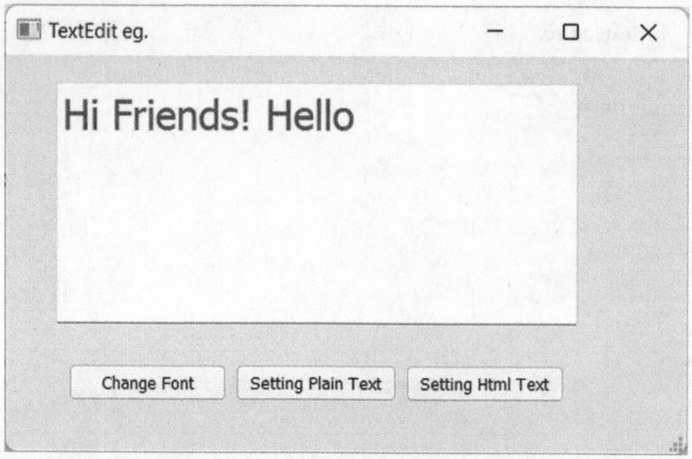

Figure 8.62: *Case4 output of TextEdit/run_textedit_eg1.py*

Note: The preceding code is covered in Program Name: TextEdit/run_textedit_eg1.py

Plain Text Edit

`QPlainTextEdit` widget is a multi-line text editor that makes it simple to view and edit plain text in PyQt5. Line numbers, text wrapping, undo/redo, and copy/paste are among the few features it offers. The **`setPlainText()`** method can be used to style the text, and the **`toPlainText()`** method can be used to retrieve it. If there is an application requirement to display plain text content, then we need to use the **`QPlainTextEdit`** widget. Otherwise, if there is a requirement to display formatted text, use **`QTextEdit`** widget.

Important properties

Maximum properties are similar to that of the Text Edit widget. The other extra properties are explained in the following section.

plainText

This property will hold the plain text displayed in the **`QPlainTextEdit`** object. The text displayed in the **`QPlainTextEdit`** can be either get or set using this property. By default, this object contains an empty string. Refer to the following figure:

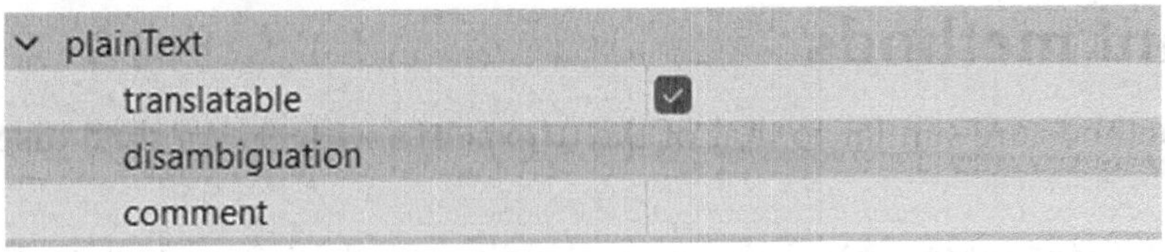

Figure 8.63: Image depicting plainText property of QPlainTextEdit in Qt Designer

maximumBlockCount

This property will determine the maximum number of blocks visible in the `QPlainTextEdit` object. An unlimited number of blocks can be contained by the `QPlainTextEdit` object if the value is set as **0** or **-1**. Refer to the following figure:

Figure 8.64: Image depicting maximumBlockCount property of QPlainTextEdit in Qt Designer

backgroundVisible

This property determines whether the palette background is visible outside of the document area. The default value is **False**. Refer to the following figure:

Figure 8.65: Image depicting backgroundVisible property of QPlainTextEdit in Qt Designer

centerOnScroll

This property will determine whether the cursor will be centered on the screen when `QPlainTextEdit` object is scrolled. The default value is **False**. The text will always be seen in the middle of the widget if the value is **True**, which centers the view. When the value is set to **False**, the view scrolls normally and the text moves up or down as the widget is scrolled. Refer to the following figure:

Figure 8.66: Image depicting centerOnScroll property of QPlainTextEdit in Qt Designer

Important methods

Most of the methods are similar to that of the **QTextEdit** widget. We shall discuss the useful ones:

- **appendPlainText(text):** This method will add the given text to the end of the **QPlainTextEdit** object.
- **insertPlainText(text):** This method will insert the given text at the current cursor position of the **QPlainTextEdit** object.
- **setPlainText(text):** This method will set the **QPlainTextEdit** object content with the given text.
- **clear():** This method will delete all the **QPlainTextEdit** object content.
- **toPlainText(text):** This method will return **QPlainTextEdit** object content.

Important signals

Some important signals are as follows:

- **textChanged():** This signal is emitted when the text in the **QPlainTextEdit** object is changed.
- **cursorPositionChanged():** This signal is emitted whenever the cursor position in the **QPlainTextEdit** object changes.
- **blockCountChanged(newBlockCount):** This signal is emitted when the number of blocks, that is, lines in the **QPlainTextEdit** object changes.
- **selectionChanged():** This signal is emitted by a **QPlainTextEdit** object when its selection changes.

Now, we shall see an example of the **QPlainTextEdit** widget.

The details of file names are given in the following *Table 8.6:*

S No.	Qt Designer File Name (.ui)	Converting the Qt Designer file name to Python file (.py)	Creating another Python file and importing the converted Python file from Qt Designer
1	plaintextedit_eg1.ui	plaintextedit_eg1.py	run_plaintextedit_eg1.py

Table 8.6: Details of file names

The Qt Designer file is shown in the following figure:

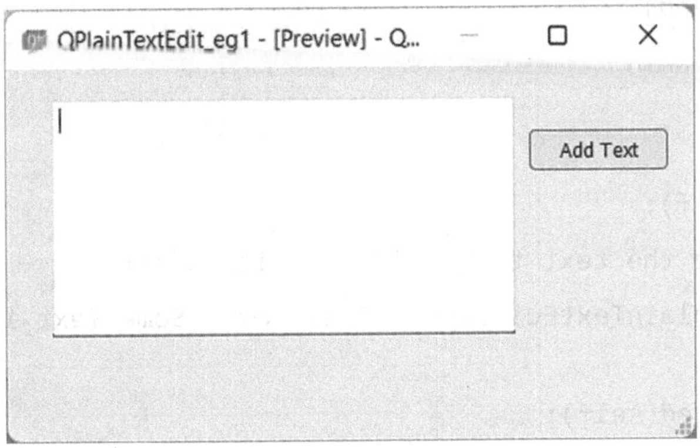

Figure 8.67: Qt Designer file: PlainTextEdit/plaintextedit_eg1.ui

Note: The above .ui file is covered in Path: PlainTextEdit/plaintextedit_eg1.ui

Consider the following code of **run_plaintextedit_eg1.py**:

```
import sys
import re
from PyQt5.QtWidgets import QMainWindow,QApplication, QFontDialog
from plaintextedit_eg1 import *

class MyPlainTextEdit(QMainWindow):
    def __init__(self):
        super().__init__()
        self.myui = Ui_MainWindow()
        self.myui.setupUi(self)
        # setting the placeholder text in the QPlainTexEdit object
       self.myui.plainTextEdit.setPlaceholderText("Kindly enter any plain text")
        self.myui.plainTextEdit.textChanged.connect(self.mytextchanged)
        self.myui.plainTextEdit.cursorPositionChanged.connect(self.my_on_
        cursor_position_changed)
        self.myui.mybtn.clicked.connect(self.my_btn1)
        # Connecting the blockCountChanged signal to the my_on_block_count_
        changed slot
```

```
        self.myui.plainTextEdit.blockCountChanged.connect(self.my_on_block_
        count_changed)

        self.show()

    def my_btn1(self):
        # appending the text to QPlainTextEdit object
        self.myui.plainTextEdit.appendPlainText("Some Text is Added")

    def mytextchanged(self):
        self.myui.mylbl.setText("QPlainTextEdit signal is emitted")

    # Method for the cursorPositionChanged signal
    def my_on_cursor_position_changed(self):
        mycursor = self.myui.plainTextEdit.textCursor()
        print("Cursor position is changed to column no.:", mycursor.position())

    # Method for the blockCountChanged signal
    def my_on_block_count_changed(self, my_new_block_count):
        print("Block count changed to:", my_new_block_count)


if __name__ == "__main__":
    app = QApplication(sys.argv)
    screen = MyPlainTextEdit()
    screen.show()
    sys.exit(app.exec_())
```

Output:

Refer to the following figure:

Default output:

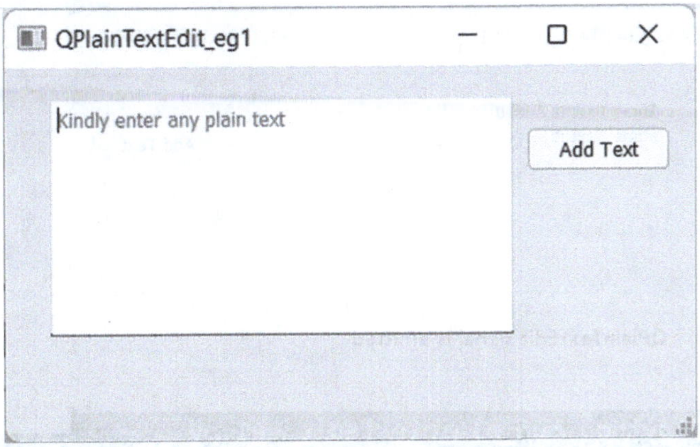

Figure 8.68: Default output of PlainTextEdit/run_plaintextedit_eg1.py

Case 1: On clicking **Add Text** button, **`textChanged`** and **`cursorPositionChanged`** signal is being emitted.

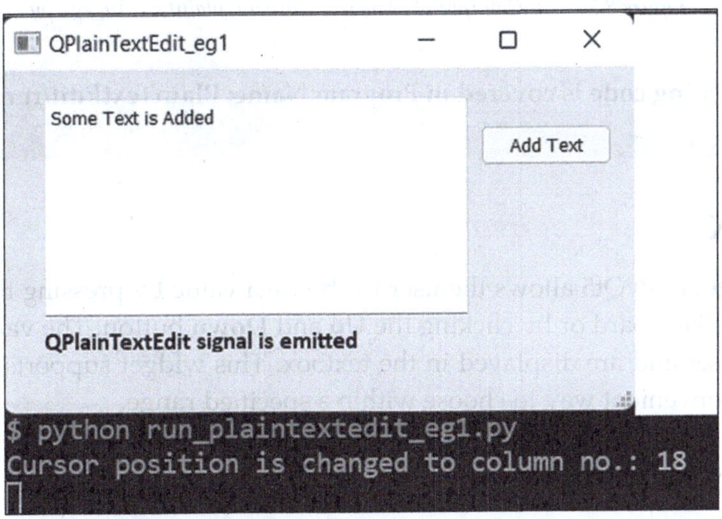

Figure 8.69: Case1 output of PlainTextEdit/run_plaintextedit_eg1.py

Case 2: On again clicking **Add Text** button, all the three signals **`textChanged`**, **`cursorPositionChanged`** and **`blockCountChanged`** signal are emitted.

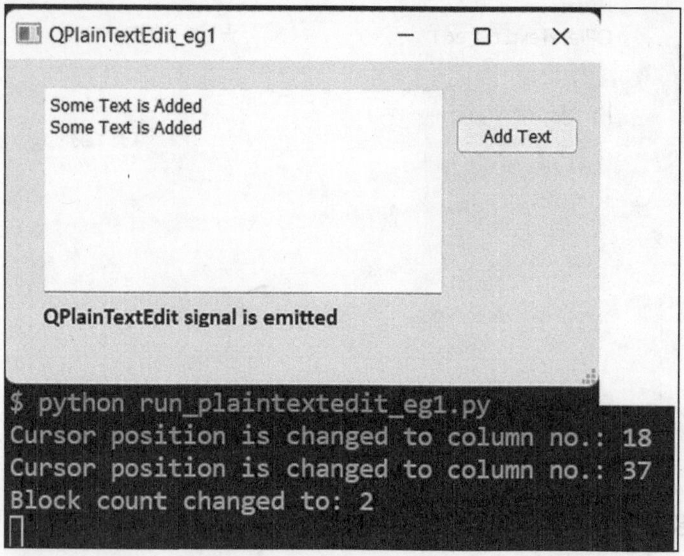

Figure 8.70: *Case2 output of PlainTextEdit/run_plaintextedit_eg1.py*

Note: The preceding code is covered in Program Name: PlainTextEdit/run_plaintextedit_eg1.py

Spin Box

A Spin Box widget in PyQt5 allows the user to choose a value by pressing the Up and Down arrow keys of the keyboard or by clicking the **Up** and **Down** button. The values can be typed directly by the user and are displayed in the textbox. This widget supports integer numbers and may find a convenient way to choose within a specified range.

Important properties

Some important properties are discussed in the next section.

wrapping

When the **`QSpinBox`** object hits or reaches its minimum or maximum value, this property determines whether or not it should wrap around. To enable wrapping, set it to **True**; to disable it, set it to **False** (default value). Refer to the following figure:

Figure 8.71: *Image depicting wrapping property of QSpinBox in Qt Designer*

frame

This property will determine whether **QSpinBox** object should have a frame or not. The default value is set as **checked**. Refer to the following figure:

Figure 8.72: *Image depicting frame property of QSpinBox in Qt Designer*

alignment

This property will set the content alignment within the **QSpinBox** object. Refer to the following figure:

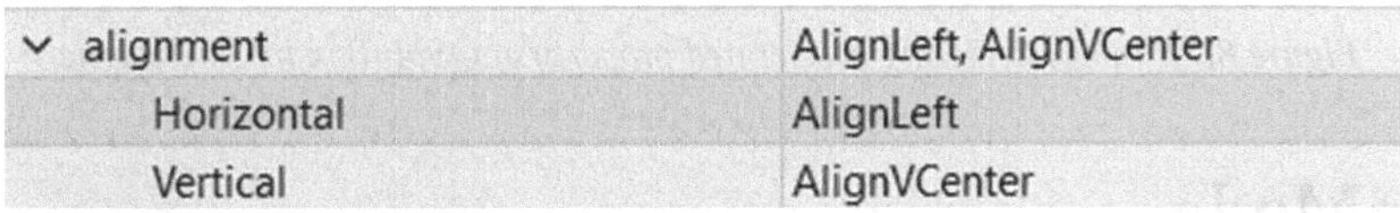

Figure 8.73: *Image depicting alignment property of QSpinBox in Qt Designer*

readOnly

This property will allow **QSpinBox** object to **readOnly** when set to **True**. Refer to the following figure:

Figure 8.74: *Image depicting readOnly property of QSpinBox in Qt Designer*

buttonSymbols

This property will set the symbol in the up and down button of **QSpinBox** object. Refer to the following figure:

Figure 8.75: *Image depicting buttonSymbols property of QSpinBox in Qt Designer*

specialValueText

This property will set and display the special value text in the **QSpinBox** object when the value is set to minimum or maximum of the range and the object is in special value mode. Refer to the following figure:

***Figure 8.76:** Image depicting specialValueText property of QSpinBox in Qt Designer*

accelerated

This property will decide whether the **`QSpinBox`** object value changes should be accelerated. Refer to the following figure:

***Figure 8.77:** Image depicting accelerated property of QSpinBox in Qt Designer*

correctionMode

This property will determine the behavior of the **`QSpinBox`** object if the user enters an invalid value. Refer to the following figure:

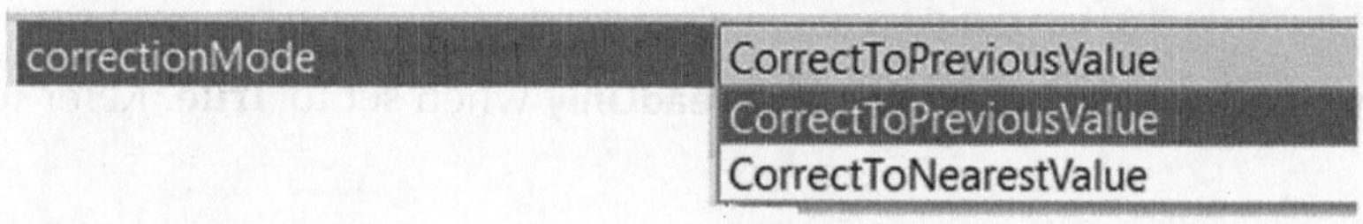

***Figure 8.78:** Image depicting correctionMode property of QSpinBox in Qt Designer*

keyboardTracking

This property will determine the tracking of keyboard inputs in the **`QSpinBox`** object. Refer to the following figure:

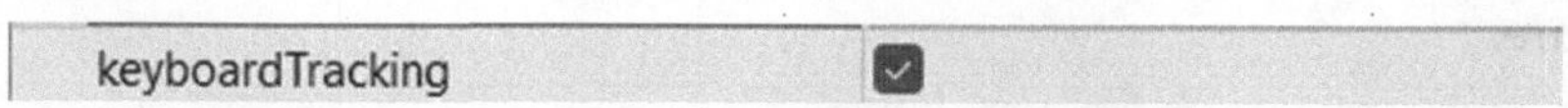

***Figure 8.79:** Image depicting keyboardTracking property of QSpinBox in Qt Designer*

showGroupSeparator

This property will determine whether the **`QSpinBox`** object should display a group separator. Refer to the following figure:

***Figure 8.80:** Image depicting showGroupSeparator property of QSpinBox in Qt Designer*

suffix

This property will set a string that will be appended to the current value of the **QSpinBox** object. Refer to the following figure:

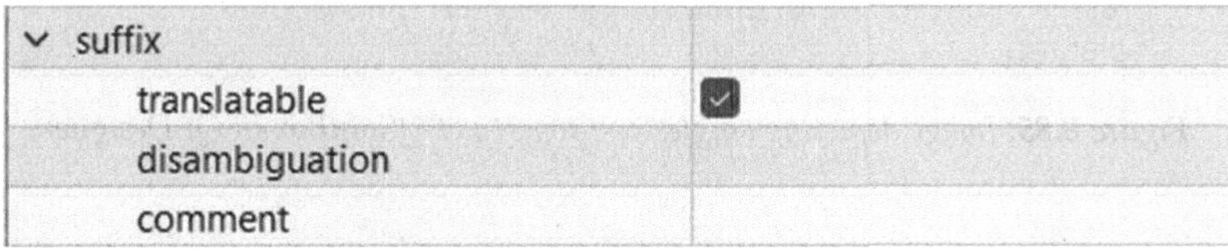

Figure 8.81: *Image depicting suffix property of QSpinBox in Qt Designer*

prefix

This property will set a string that will be prepended to the current value of the **QSpinBox** object. Refer to the following figure:

Figure 8.82: *Image depicting prefix property of QSpinBox in Qt Designer*

minimum

This property will set the minimum value that can be entered in the **QSpinBox** object. Refer to the following figure:

Figure 8.83: *Image depicting minimum property of QSpinBox in Qt Designer*

maximum

This property will set the maximum value that can be entered in the **QSpinBox** object. Refer to the following figure:

Figure 8.84: *Image depicting maximum property of QSpinBox in Qt Designer*

singlestep

This property will set the step size for incrementing or decrementing the value in the **QSpinBox** object. Refer to the following figure:

Figure 8.85: Image depicting singlestep property of QSpinBox in Qt Designer

value

This property will set or return the current value of the **QSpinBox** object. Refer to the following figure:

Figure 8.86: Image depicting value property of QSpinBox in Qt Designer

displayIntegerBase

This property will set the base for displaying the value in the **QSpinBox** object. Refer to the following figure:

Figure 8.87: Image depicting displayIntegerBase property of QSpinBox in Qt Designer

Important methods

Some important methods are as follows:

- **setMinimum(min):** This method will set the minimum value that can be entered in the **QSpinBox** object where the **min** parameter is the minimum value. The default value is 0.
- **setMaximum(max):** This method will set the maximum value that can be entered in the **QSpinBox** object where the **max** parameter is the maximum value. The default value is 99.
- **setRange(min,max):** This method will set the minimum and maximum values for the **QSpinBox** object in one call. Here, the **min** parameter is the minimum value, and the **max** parameter is the maximum value.
- **setValue(val):** This method will set the current value of the **QSpinBox** object where the **val** parameter is the value to be set.
- **value():** This method will return the current value of the **QSpinBox** object.

- `cleanText()`: This method will return the text of the **QSpinBox** object, excluding prefix/suffix or trailing/leading whitespace.
- `setDisplayIntegerBase(base)`: The base for displaying the value of the **QSpinBox** object is set by this method.

Important signals

Let us discuss an important signal.

valueChanged(arg__1)

This signal is emitted when the value of the **QSpinBox** object changes either by entering a new value or spinning the wheel. The **arg__1** parameter is an integer type representing the new value of the **QSpinBox** object.

Now, we shall see an example of the **QSpinBox** widget.

The details of file names are given in the following *Table 8.7:*

S No.	Qt Designer File Name (.ui)	Converting the Qt Designer file name to Python file (.py)	Creating another Python file and importing the converted Python file from Qt Designer
1	spinbox_eg1.ui	spinbox_eg1.py	run_spinbox_eg1.py

Table 8.7: *Details of file names*

The Qt Designer file is shown in the following figure:

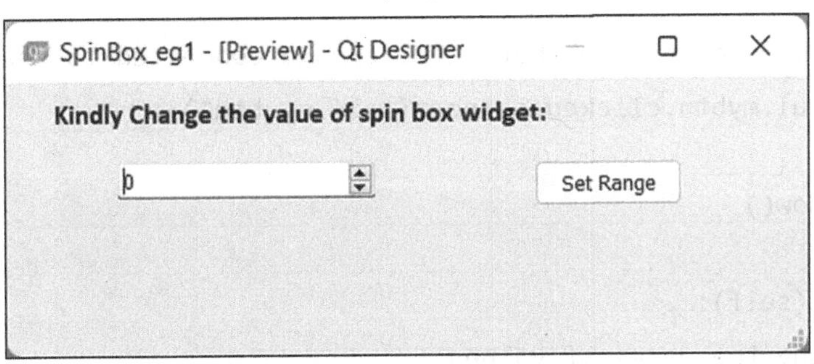

Figure 8.88: *Qt Designer file: SpinBox/spinbox_eg1.ui*

Note: The above .ui file is covered in Path: SpinBox/spinbox_eg1.ui

Consider the following code of **run_spinbox_eg1.py**:

```
import sys
import re
```

```
from PyQt5.QtWidgets import QMainWindow,QApplication
from spinbox_eg1 import *

class MySpinBoxEdit(QMainWindow):
    def __init__(self):
        super().__init__()
        self.myui = Ui_MainWindow()
        self.myui.setupUi(self)

        # Setting the initial value
        self.myui.spinBox.setValue(0)

        # Setting the minimum value
        self.myui.spinBox.setMinimum(-2)

        # Setting the maximum value
        self.myui.spinBox.setMaximum(2)

        # signal is emitted when the QSpinBox object value changes
        self.myui.spinBox.valueChanged.connect(self.my_valuechange)

        # signal is emitted on button click and connected to the method my_btn1
        self.myui.mybtn.clicked.connect(self.my_btn1)

        self.show()

    def my_btn1(self):
        # Setting the range of values
        self.myui.spinBox.setRange(-3, 3)

    def my_valuechange(self,myval):
        self.myui.mylbl2.setText("My current value is:"+str(myval))
```

```
if __name__ == "__main__":
    app = QApplication(sys.argv)
    screen = MySpinBoxEdit()
    screen.show()
    sys.exit(app.exec_())
```

Output:

Refer to the following figure:

Default output:

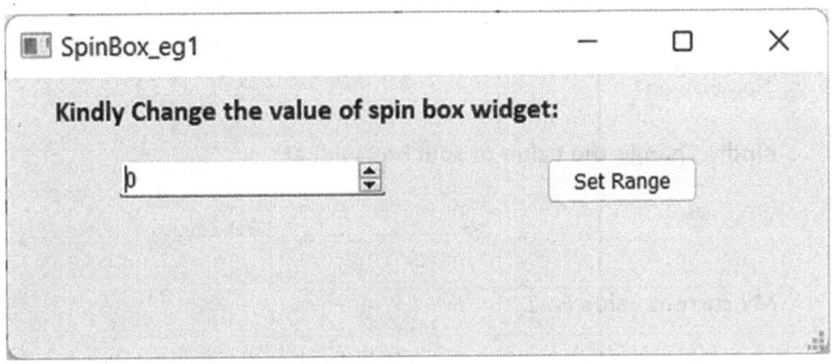

Figure 8.89: Default output of SpinBox/run_spinbox_eg1.py

Case 1: When Up button of spin box widget is clicked once, then its **valueChanged** signal is triggered.

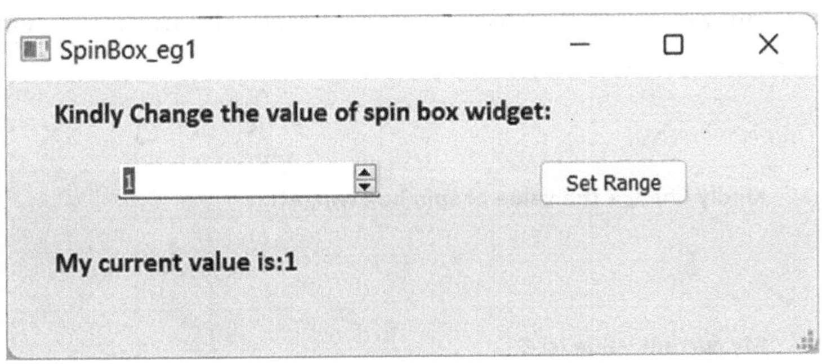

Figure 8.90: Case1 output of SpinBox/run_spinbox_eg1.py

Case 2: Here, Up button of spin box widget is clicked many times. The maximum value of the widget is **2**.

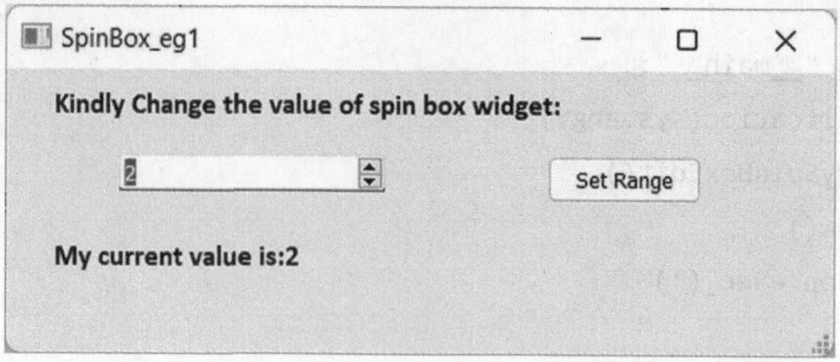

Figure 8.91: Case2 output of SpinBox/run_spinbox_eg1.py

Case 3: Here, Down button of spin box widget is clicked many times. The minimum value of the widget is **-2**.

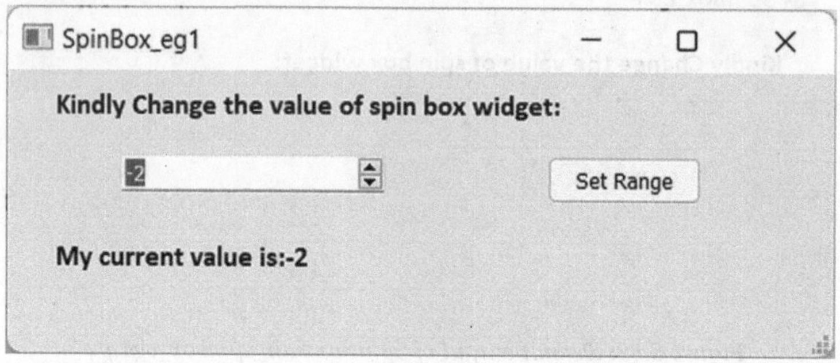

Figure 8.92: Case3 output of SpinBox/run_spinbox_eg1.py

Case 4: Here, Set Range button is clicked and the maximum and minimum value is set as **3** and **-3**. Down button of spin box widget is clicked many times. The minimum value of the widget is **-3**.

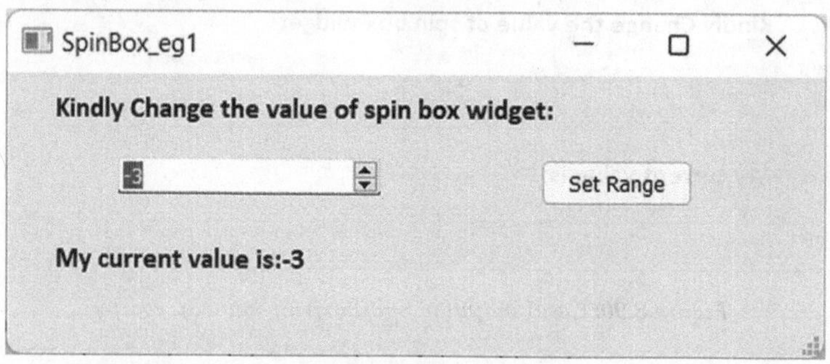

Figure 8.93: Case4 output of SpinBox/run_spinbox_eg1.py

Case 5: Now, Up button of spin box widget is clicked many times. The maximum value of the widget is **3**.

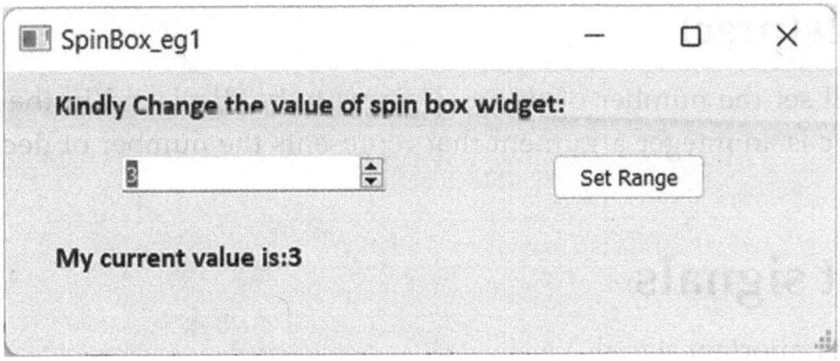

Figure 8.94: Case5 output of SpinBox/run_spinbox_eg1.py

Note: The preceding code is covered in Program Name: SpinBox/run_spinbox_eg1.py

Double Spin Box

This **`QDoubleSpinBox`** class in PyQt5 allows the user to choose a value by either using the up or down arrow keys from the keyboard or directly entering the text field. It is a spinbox widget for supporting double-type values.

Important properties

The properties of the Double Spin Box widget are similar to that of the Spin Box Widget. It has a decimals property instead of **`displayIntegerBase`** and properties of minimum, maximum, value, and **`singleStep`** is of type double.

decimals

This property will specify the number of decimal places to be displayed in the **`QDoubleSpinBox`** object, that is, precision. Refer to the following figure:

Figure 8.95: Image depicting decimals property of QDoubleSpinBox in Qt Designer

Important methods

All the methods of the **`QSpinBox`** widget discussed are almost similar to that of the **`QDoubleSpinBox`** widget, except for one method. Instead of the **`setDisplayIntegerBase()`** method, this widget has the **`setDecimals()`** method.

setDecimals(prec)

This method will set the number of decimal places to be displayed in the **QDoubleSpinBox** object. Here, **prec** is an integer argument that represents the number of decimal places to be displayed.

Important signals

Let us discuss an important signal.

valueChanged(arg__1)

This signal is emitted when the value of the **QDoubleSpinBox** object changes either by entering a new value or spinning the wheel. The **arg__1** parameter is of double type, representing the new value of the **QDoubleSpinBox** object.

Now, we shall see an example of the **QDoubleSpinBox** widget.

The details of file names are given in the following *Table 8.8:*

S No.	Qt Designer File Name (.ui)	Converting the Qt Designer file name to Python file (.py)	Creating another Python file and importing the converted Python file from Qt Designer
1	`doublespinbox_eg1.ui`	`doublespinbox_eg1.py`	`run_doublespinbox_eg1.py`

Table 8.8: Details of file names

The Qt Designer file is shown in the following figure:

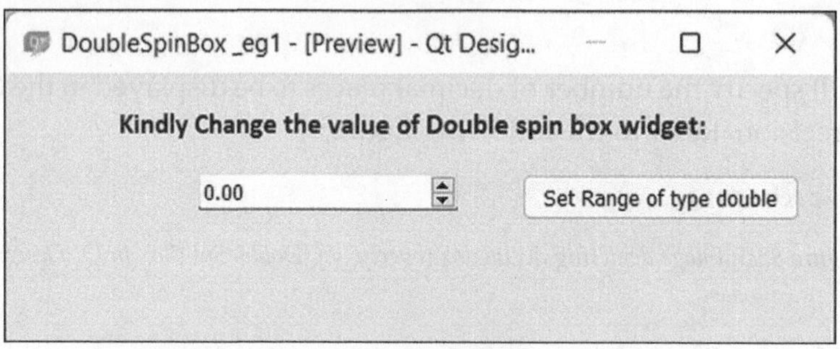

***Figure 8.96:** Qt Designer file: DoubleSpinBox/doublespinbox_eg1.ui*

Note: The above .ui file is covered in Path: DoubleSpinBox/doublespinbox_eg1.ui

Consider the following code of **run_doublespinbox_eg1.py**:

```
import sys
```

```
import re
from PyQt5.QtWidgets import QMainWindow,QApplication
from doublespinbox_eg1 import *

class MyDoubleSpinBoxEdit(QMainWindow):
    def __init__(self):
        super().__init__()
        self.myui = Ui_MainWindow()
        self.myui.setupUi(self)

        # Setting the initial value of QDoubleSpinBox object
        self.myui.doubleSpinBox.setValue(0.10)

        # Setting the minimum value of QDoubleSpinBox object
        self.myui.doubleSpinBox.setMinimum(-1.10)

        # Setting the maximum value of QDoubleSpinBox object
        self.myui.doubleSpinBox.setMaximum(1.10)

        # Setting the step value to 0.2 of QDoubleSpinBox object
        self.myui.doubleSpinBox.setSingleStep(0.2)

        # signal is emitted when the QDoubleSpinBox object value changes
        self.myui.doubleSpinBox.valueChanged.connect(self.my_valuechange)

        # signal is emitted on button click and connected to the method my_btn1
        self.myui.my_btn.clicked.connect(self.my_btn1)

        self.show()

    def my_btn1(self):
        # Setting the range of values of QDoubleSpinBox object
        self.myui.doubleSpinBox.setRange(-2.10, 2.10)
```

```
    def my_valuechange(self,myval):
        # setting the label text when valueChanged signal is emitted
        self.myui.mylbl2.setText("My current value is:"+str(myval))

if __name__ == "__main__":
    app = QApplication(sys.argv)
    screen = MyDoubleSpinBoxEdit()
    screen.show()
    sys.exit(app.exec_())
```

Output:

Refer to the following figure:

Default output:

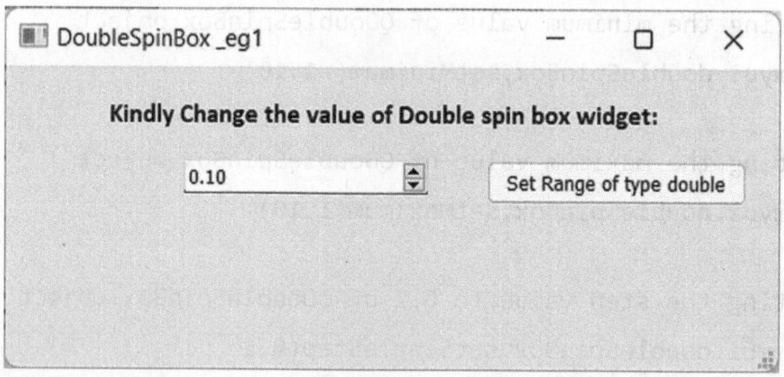

Figure 8.97: Default output of DoubleSpinBox/run_doublespinbox_eg1.py

Case 1: When Up Button of double spin box widget is clicked once, then **valueChanged** signal is emitted.

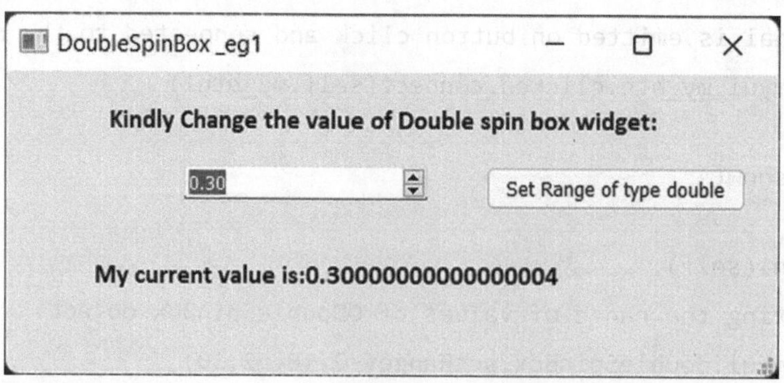

Figure 8.98: Case1 output of DoubleSpinBox/run_doublespinbox_eg1.py

Case 2: Up Button of double spin box widget is clicked many times and it reached its maximum value. The maximum value of the widget is set as **1.10**.

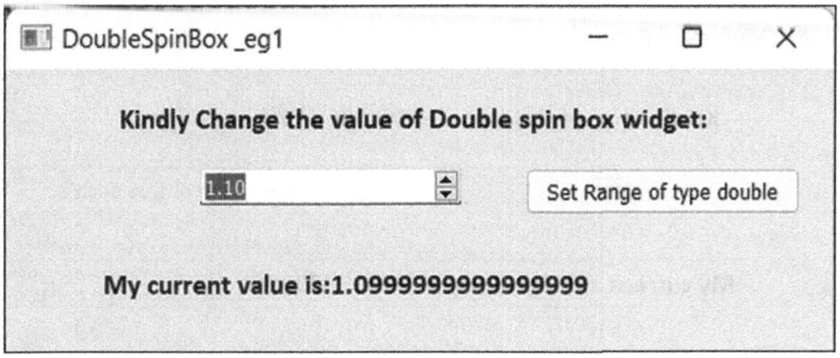

Figure 8.99: *Case2 output of DoubleSpinBox/run_doublespinbox_eg1.py*

Case 3: Down Button of double spin box widget is clicked many times and it reached its maximum value. The minimum value of the widget is set as **-1.10**:

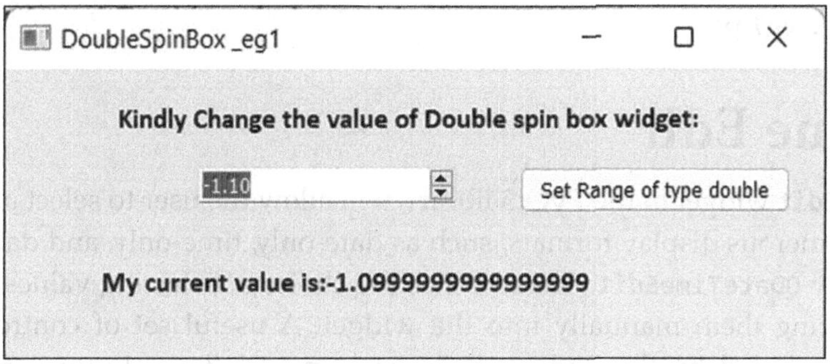

Figure 8.100: *Case3 output of DoubleSpinBox/run_doublespinbox_eg1.py*

Case 4: "**Set Range of type double button**" is clicked and the maximum and minimum range is set as **2.10** and **-2.10**. Down button of double spin box widget is clicked many times till it reached the minimum value. The minimum value of the widget is set as **-2.10**.

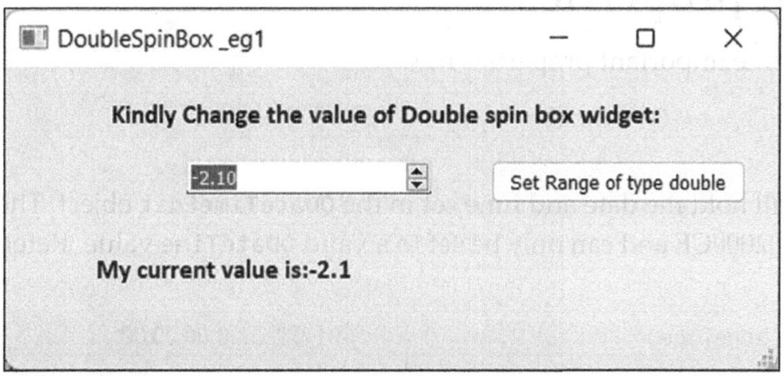

Figure 8.101: *Case4 output of DoubleSpinBox/run_doublespinbox_eg1.py*

Case 5: Up button of double spin box widget is clicked many times till it reached the maximum value. The maximum value of the widget is set as **2.10**:

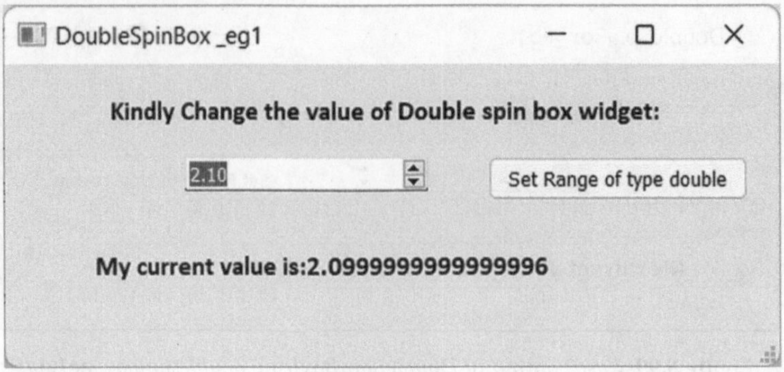

Figure 8.102: Case5 output of DoubleSpinBox/run_doublespinbox_eg1.py

Note: The preceding code is covered in Program Name: DoubleSpinBox/run_doublespinbox_eg1.py

Date/Time Edit

The **QDateTimeEdit** widget in the PyQt5 library will allow the user to select and edit date and time values. Numerous display formats, such as date-only, time-only, and date-time displays, are supported by **QDateTimeEdit**. The user has the choice of selecting values from a calendar pop-up or entering them manually into the widget. A useful set of controls for adjusting values is also included by the widget, including up and down buttons for incrementing and decrementing the date and time. Additionally, **QDateTimeEdit** provides various input validation and user interaction features, including read-only displays, the ability to step through values incrementally, minimum and maximum dates and times, and so on.

Important properties

Let us discuss some important properties now.

dateTime

This property will hold the date and time set in the **QDateTimeEdit** object. The default value is set to the start of 2000CE and can only be set to a valid **QDateTime** value. Refer to the following figure:

Figure 8.103: Image depicting dateTime property of QDateTimeEdit in Qt Designer

date

This property will hold the date that is currently set in the widget. The default value is set to the date of **1st Jan 2000**. The object is **QDate**. Refer to the following figure:

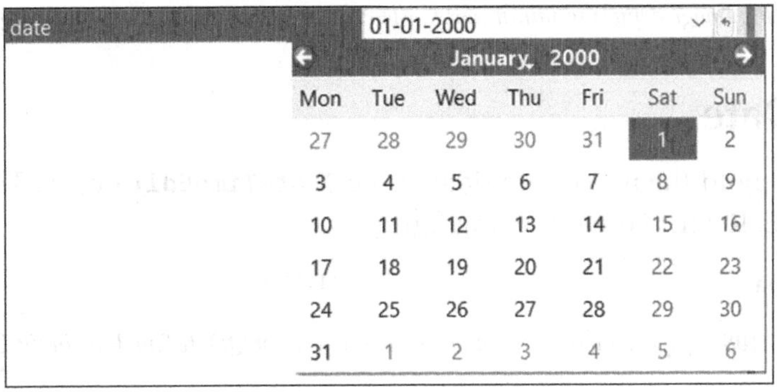

***Figure 8.104:** Image depicting date property of QDateTimeEdit in Qt Designer*

time

This property will hold the time that is currently set in the widget. The default value contains the time of **00:00:00** and 0 milliseconds. The object is **QTime**. Refer to the following figure:

***Figure 8.105:** Image depicting time property of QDateTimeEdit in Qt Designer*

maximumDateTime

This property will hold the maximum date and time values that are allowed to be set for the **QDateTimeEdit** object. The **minimumDateTime** is adjusted on setting this property. Only this property can be set to a valid **QDateTime** value. The end of **9999** CE is the latest date that is accepted. The default value is **23:59:59** and 999 milliseconds for the time. Refer to the following figure:

***Figure 8.106:** Image depicting maximumDateTime property of QDateTimeEdit in Qt Designer*

minimumDateTime

This property will hold the minimum date and time values that are allowed to be set for the **QDateTimeEdit** object. The **maximumDateTime** is adjusted on setting this property. Only this property can be set to a valid **QDateTime** value. The start of 100CE is the earliest date and time that is accepted. The default value is **14th Sep 1752** for the date and **00:00:00** and 0 milliseconds for the time. Refer to the following figure:

***Figure 8.107:** Image depicting minimumDateTime property of QDateTimeEdit in Qt Designer*

maximumDate

This property will hold the maximum date of the **`QDateTimeEdit`** object. The default value is the end of **9999** CE. Refer to the following figure:

***Figure 8.108:** Image depicting maximumDate property of QDateTimeEdit in Qt Designer*

minimumDate

This property will hold the minimum date of the **`QDateTimeEdit`** object. The default value is **14th Sep, 1752**. Refer to the following figure:

***Figure 8.109:** Image depicting minimumDate property of QDateTimeEdit in Qt Designer*

maximumTime

This property will hold the maximum time of the **`QDateTimeEdit`** object. The default value is **23:59:59** and 999 milliseconds. Refer to the following figure:

***Figure 8.110:** Image depicting maximumTime property of QDateTimeEdit in Qt Designer*

minimumTime

This property will hold the minimum time of the **`QDateTimeEdit`** object. The default value is **00:00:00** and 0 milliseconds. Refer to the following figure:

***Figure 8.111:** Image depicting minimumTime property of QDateTimeEdit in Qt Designer*

currentSection

This property will hold the section of date/time of the **QDateTimeEdit** object, which has a focus such as year, month, day, hour, minute, or second. Refer to the following figure:

currentSection	DaySection

Figure 8.112: *Image depicting currentSection property of QDateTimeEdit in Qt Designer*

displayFormat

This property will set the date and time format in the **QDateTimeEdit** object. The default format is **dd-MM-yyyy HH:mm**. Refer to the following figure:

⌄ displayFormat	dd-MM-yyyy HH:mm
translatable	☑
disambiguation	
comment	

Figure 8.113: *Image depicting displayFormat property of QDateTimeEdit in Qt Designer*

calendarPopup

When a user clicks on the **QDateTimeEdit** widget, this property determines whether or not a calendar pop-up is shown. When the pop-up is enabled, the user can choose a date from the calendar, and the **QDateTimeEdit** widget will update accordingly. Refer to the following figure:

calendarPopup	☐

Figure 8.114: *Image depicting calendarPopup property of QDateTimeEdit in Qt Designer*

currentSectionIndex

The **QDateTimeEdit** widget's currently active section index is returned by this property. Refer to the following figure:

currentSectionIndex	0

Figure 8.115: *Image depicting currentSectionIndex property of QDateTimeEdit in Qt Designer*

timeSpec

The **QDateTimeEdit** widget's time specification, which establishes the time zone and whether daylight saving time is used, is set by this property. Local time, **Coordinated Universal Time (UTC)**, or a particular time zone can all be specified as the time specification. Refer to the following figure:

Figure 8.116: *Image depicting timeSpec property of QDateTimeEdit in Qt Designer*

Important methods/signals

All the properties of the above widget if prepended with the word **set** can be used as methods. We shall discuss the important ones:

- **dateTime():** This method will return the currently selected date and time as a **QDateTime** object.
- **setMaximumDateTime(dt):** This method will set the maximum date and time which can be set in the **QDateTimeEdit** object by taking the **QDateTime** object as a parameter.
- **dateChanged(date):** This signal is emitted when the date in the **QDateTimeEdit** object changes. Here, the **date** argument is a **QDate** object representing the new date.
- **dateTimeChanged(dateTime):** This signal is emitted when the date and time in the **QDateTimeEdit** object is changed. Here, the **dateTime** argument is a **QDateTime** object representing the new date and time.
- **timeChanged(time):** This signal is emitted when time in the **QDateTimeEdit** object is changed. Here, the **time** argument is a **QTime** object representing the new time.

Now, we shall see an example of the **QDateTimeEdit** widget.

The details of file names are given in the following *Table 8.9:*

S No.	Qt Designer File Name (.ui)	Converting the Qt Designer file name to Python file (.py)	Creating another Python file and importing the converted Python file from Qt Designer
1	**datetimeedit_eg1.ui**	**datetimeedit_eg1.py**	**run_datetimeedit_eg1.py**

Table 8.9: *Details of file names*

The Qt Designer file is shown in the following figure:

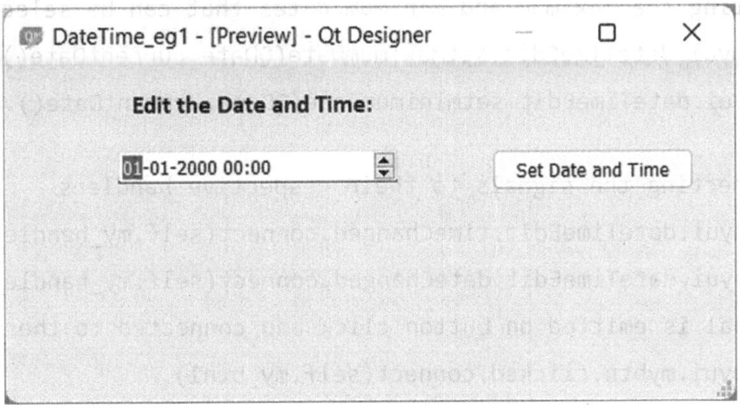

Figure 8.117: *Qt Designer file: DateorTimeEdit/datetimeedit_eg1.ui*

Note: The above .ui file is covered in Path: DateorTimeEdit/ datetimeedit_eg1.ui

Consider the following code of **run_datetimeedit_eg1.py**:

```
import sys
from PyQt5.QtWidgets import QMainWindow,QApplication
from PyQt5.QtCore import *
from datetimeedit_eg1 import *

class MyDateTimeEdit(QMainWindow):
    def __init__(self):
        super().__init__()
        self.myui = Ui_MainWindow()
        self.myui.setupUi(self)

        # setting the date and time for the widget
        self.myui.dateTimeEdit.setDateTime(QDateTime.currentDateTime())

        # Setting the display format for the QDateTimeEdit widget
        self.myui.dateTimeEdit.setDisplayFormat("yyyy-MM-dd hh:mm:ss")

        # Setting the calendar popup to be enabled
        self.myui.dateTimeEdit.setCalendarPopup(True)
```

```
        # Setting the maximum and minimum dates that can be selected
        self.myui.dateTimeEdit.setMaximumDate(QDate.currentDate().addYears(1))
        self.myui.dateTimeEdit.setMinimumDate(QDate.currentDate().addDays(-365))

        # Connecting the signals to their respective handlers
        self.myui.dateTimeEdit.timeChanged.connect(self.my_handle_time_changed)
        self.myui.dateTimeEdit.dateChanged.connect(self.my_handle_date_changed)
        # signal is emitted on button click and connected to the method my_btn1
        self.myui.mybtn.clicked.connect(self.my_btn1)

        self.show()

    def my_btn1(self):
        self.myui.mylbl2.setText("Displaying Date and Time to: " + str(self.
        myui.dateTimeEdit.dateTime()))

    def my_handle_time_changed(self, time):
        self.myui.mylbl2.setText("Time changed to: " + time.toString())

    def my_handle_date_changed(self, date):
        self.myui.mylbl2.setText("Date changed to: " + date.toString())

if __name__ == "__main__":
    app = QApplication(sys.argv)
    screen = MyDateTimeEdit()
    screen.show()
    sys.exit(app.exec_())
```

Output:

Refer to the following figure:

Default output:

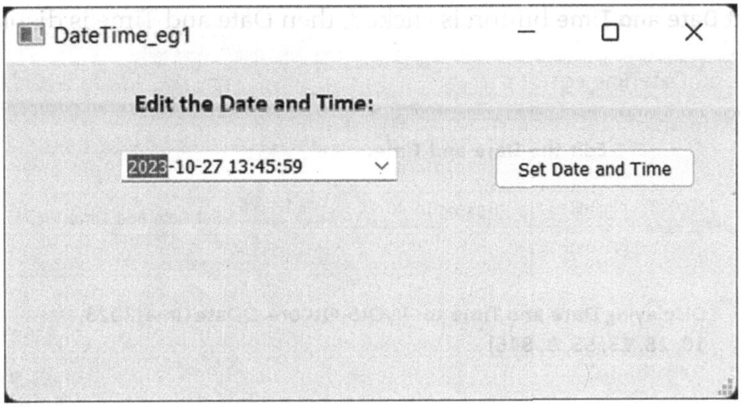

***Figure 8.118:** Default output of DateorTimeEdit/run_datetimeedit_eg1.py*

Case 1: When date is changed, **`dateChanged`** signal is emitted.

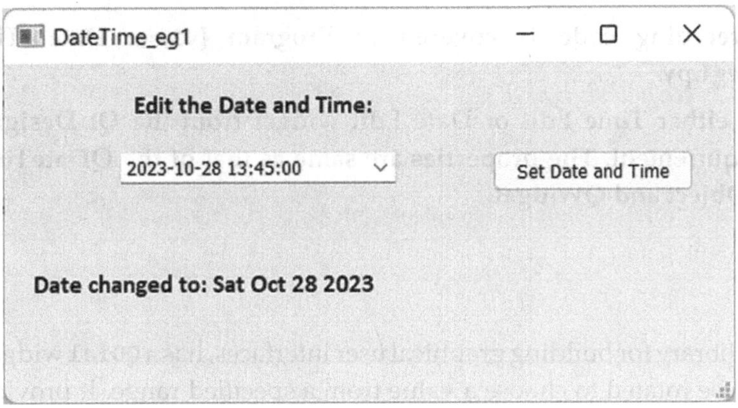

***Figure 8.119:** Case1 output of DateorTimeEdit/run_datetimeedit_eg1.py*

Case 2: When time is changed, **`timeChanged`** signal is emitted.

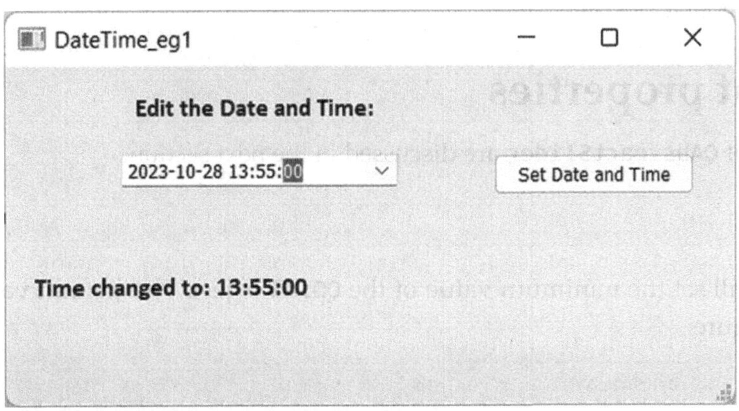

***Figure 8.120:** Case2 output of DateorTimeEdit/run_datetimeedit_eg1.py*

Case 3: When **Set Date and Time** button is clicked, then Date and Time is displayed.

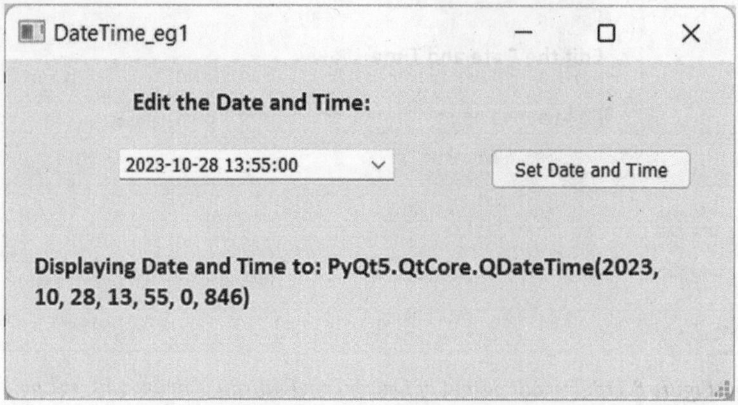

***Figure 8.121:** Case3 output of DateorTimeEdit/run_datetimeedit_eg1.py*

> **Note: The preceding code is covered in Program Name: DateorTimeEdit/ run_datetimeedit_eg1.py.**
>
> **We can select either Time Edit or Date Edit widget from the Qt Designer as per our application requirement. The properties are same as that of the QDateTimeEdit widget along with QObject and QWidget.**

Dial

PyQt5, a Python library for building graphical user interfaces, has a **`QDial`** widget. A circular dial called **`QDial`** can be rotated to choose a value from a specified range. It provides a convenient method for the user to change a numerical value, like a brightness or volume setting. **`QDial`**'s features, including the value range, the number of notches, the dial's appearance, and how it behaves to drags and clicks, can all be changed. **`QDial`** behaves similarly to a slider because it derives from **`QAbstractSlider`**.

Important properties

The properties of **`QAbstractSlider`** are discussed in the next section.

minimum

This property will set the minimum value of the **`QDial`** object. The default value is **`0`**. Refer to the following figure:

***Figure 8.122:** Image depicting minimum property of QDial in Qt Designer*

maximum

This property will set the maximum value of the **QDial** object. The default value is **99**. Refer to the following figure:

Figure 8.123: *Image depicting maximum property of QDial in Qt Designer*

singleStep

This property will hold the step size for single steps of the **QDial** object. The default value is **1**. If this property is set as 5, then on rotating the **QDial** object, the 'value' property will be changed by 5. Refer to the following figure:

Figure 8.124: *Image depicting singleStep property of QDial in Qt Designer*

pageStep

This property will hold the step size for page steps of the **QDial** object. The default value is **10**. If this property is set as **10**, then on clicking the background of the **QDial** object, the 'value' property will be changed by 10. Refer to the following figure:

Figure 8.125: *Image depicting pageStep property of QDial in Qt Designer*

value

This property will hold the current value of the **QDial** object and is always between the minimum and maximum values. It will be updated when the **QDial** object is clicked or rotated. The default value is **0**. Refer to the following figure:

Figure 8.126: *Image depicting value property of QDial in Qt Designer*

sliderPosition

This property will hold the current value of the **QDial** object. Refer to the following figure:

Figure 8.127: *Image depicting sliderPosition property of QDial in Qt Designer*

tracking

This property will determine whether the dial's value is updated continuously while it is moved or only when the mouse button is released. When tracking is enabled, the **`valueChanged`** signal is continuously emitted, and the value of the dial is updated as it is dragged. Refer to the following figure:

***Figure 8.128:** Image depicting tracking property of QDial in Qt Designer*

orientation

This property will specify the orientation of the **`QDial`** object either vertically or horizontally. Refer to the following figure:

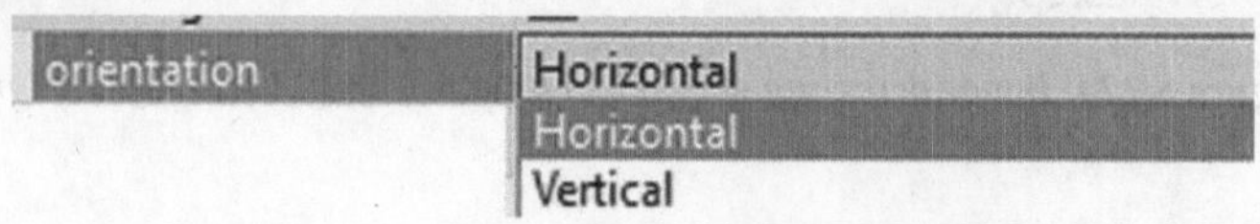

***Figure 8.129:** Image depicting orientation property of QDial in Qt Designer*

invertedAppearance

This property will specify whether the **`QDial`** object appearance is inverted. The default value is **False**. Refer to the following figure:

***Figure 8.130:** Image depicting invertedAppearance property of QDial in Qt Designer*

invertedControls

This property will specify whether the **`QDial`** object controls are inverted. The default value is **False**. Refer to the following figure:

***Figure 8.131:** Image depicting invertedControls property of QDial in Qt Designer*

Properties of QDial

The properties of **QDial** are discussed in the next section.

wrapping

This property will determine whether wrapping is enabled or not. When enabled, the arrow on the **QDial** object can be pointed in any direction. If the arrow is disabled, it can only go to the top of the **QDial** object; if it moves to the bottom of the **QDial** object, it is clamped to the end of the valid range of values closest to it. Refer to the following figure:

Figure 8.132: *Image depicting wrapping property of QDial in Qt Designer*

notchTarget

The target number of pixels between notches is held by this property. The number of pixels **QDial** tries to place in between the notch is known as the **notchTarget**. The default value is 3.7 pixels. Refer to the following figure:

Figure 8.133: *Image depicting notchTarget property of QDial in Qt Designer*

notchesVisible

This property will determine whether the **QDial** object should display notches or not. Refer to the following figure:

Figure 8.134: *Image depicting notchesVisible property of QDial in Qt Designer*

Important methods/signals

If we prepend the **set** word with all **QDial** properties, that is, wrapping, **notchTarget**, and **notchesVisible**, then we will get methods (**setwrapping(on)**, **setnotchTarget(target)**, **setNotchesVisible(visible)**). The **QDial** object will constantly emit a **valueChanged()** signal as the slider is being moved.

Now, we shall see an example of a **QDial** widget.

The details of file names are given in the following *Table 8.10:*

S No.	Qt Designer File Name (.ui)	Converting the Qt Designer file name to Python file (.py)	Creating another Python file and importing the converted Python file from Qt Designer
1	`dial_eg1.ui`	`dial_eg1.py`	`run_dial_eg1.py`

***Table 8.10:** Details of file names*

The Qt Designer file is shown in the following figure:

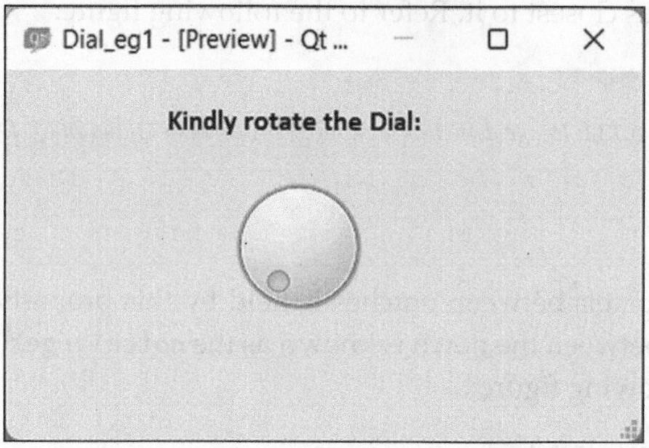

***Figure 8.135:** Qt Designer file: Dial/dial_eg1.ui*

Note: The above .ui file is covered in Path: Dial/dial_eg1.ui

Consider the following code of **`run_dial_eg1.py`**:

```
import sys

from PyQt5.QtWidgets import QMainWindow,QApplication

from dial_eg1 import *


class MyDateTimeEdit(QMainWindow):

    def __init__(self):

        super().__init__()

        self.myui = Ui_MainWindow()

        self.myui.setupUi(self)

        # set the min and max values of the dial
```

```
        self.myui.dial.setRange(0, 100)
        # default value is set to 30
        self.myui.dial.setValue(30)

        # the dial will move by increment of 1
        self.myui.dial.setNotchTarget(1.0)

        # valueChanged signal will be emitted continuously as the dial is rotated
        self.myui.dial.setTracking(True)

        # the dial value will wrap around from the max value to the min value
        and vice versa
        self.myui.dial.setWrapping(True)

        # connecting the valueChanged signal of the dial to my_labelupdate method
        self.myui.dial.valueChanged.connect(self.my_labelupdate)

        self.show()

    def my_labelupdate(self, myval):
        self.myui.mylbl1.setText("Value is: " + str(myval))

if __name__ == "__main__":
    app = QApplication(sys.argv)
    screen = MyDateTimeEdit()
    screen.show()
    sys.exit(app.exec_())
```

Output:

Refer to the following figure:

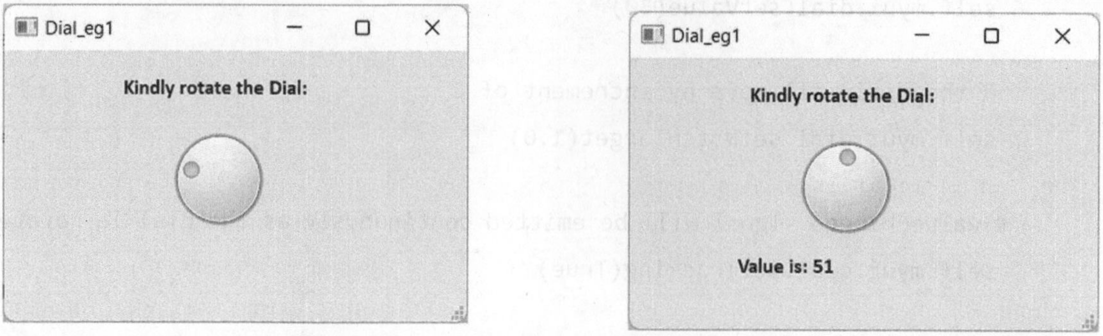

Default Output

When the slider is moved, valueChanged signal is emitted and the value is displayed in the QLabel object

Figure 8.136: *Output of Dial/run_dial_eg1.py*

Note: The preceding code is covered in Program Name: Dial/run_dial_eg1.py

QScrollBar

Let us go through the **`QScrollBar`** now:

- For horizontal scrollbar, class is **`QScrollBar`**
  - Contains properties of **`QAbstractSlider`**. Here, the default value of orientation is Horizontal, and the **`invertedControls`** property is checked.
- For vertical scrollbar, class is **`QScrollBar`**
  - Contains properties of **`QAbstractSlider`**. Here, the default value of orientation is Vertical, and the **`invertedControls`** property is checked.

Now, we shall see an example of the **`QScrollBar`** widget.

The details of file names are given in the following *Table 8.11:*

S No.	Qt Designer File Name (.ui)	Converting the Qt Designer file name to Python file (.py)	Creating another Python file and importing the converted Python file from Qt Designer
1	`scrollbar_eg1.ui`	`scrollbar_eg1.py`	`run_scrollbar_eg1.py`

Table 8.11: *Details of file names*

The Qt Designer file is shown in the following figure:

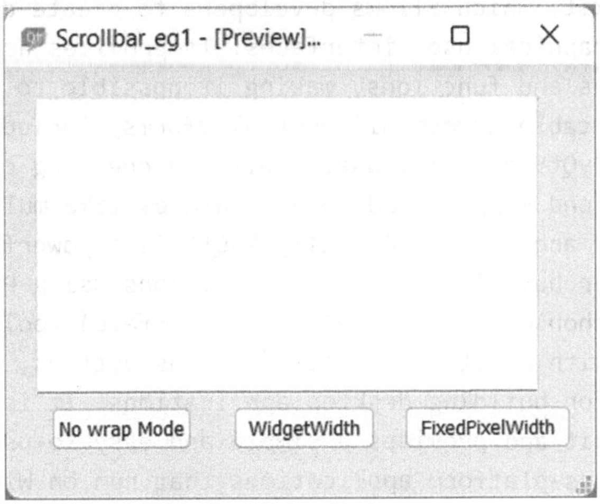

Figure 8.137: Qt Designer file : Scrollbar/scrollbar_eg1.ui

Note: The above .ui file is covered in Path: Scrollbar/scrollbar_eg1.ui

Consider the following code of **run_scrollbar_eg1.py**:

```
import sys
from PyQt5.QtWidgets import QApplication, QMainWindow, QTextEdit
from PyQt5.QtCore import Qt
from scrollbar_eg1 import *

class MyScrollbar(QMainWindow):
    def __init__(self):
        super().__init__()
        self.myui = Ui_MainWindow()
        self.myui.setupUi(self)

        # signal is emitted on button click and connected to the method my_btn1
        self.myui.btn1.clicked.connect(self.my_btn1)
        self.myui.btn2.clicked.connect(self.my_btn2)
        self.myui.btn3.clicked.connect(self.my_btn3)

        # Set some initial text to show in the text edit
```

```
        self.myui.mytextEdit.setPlainText("PyQt5 is a Python binding for the
        Qt GUI toolkit, which allows developers to create desktop applications
        with rich graphical user interfaces. It provides access to a wide range
        of Qt classes and functions, making it possible to create applications
        that are portable across different platforms, including Windows, Linux,
        and macOS. PyQt5 also includes tools for creating custom widgets and
        interfaces, and supports advanced features like multithreading, network
        programming, and OpenGL. Overall, PyQt5 is a powerful and flexible
        framework for building desktop applications using Python. Tkinter is a
        built-in Python GUI (Graphical User Interface) toolkit that provides
        developers with a set of widgets, such as buttons, labels, text boxes,
        and menus, for building desktop applications. It is based on the Tcl/
        Tk GUI toolkit and provides a simple and easy-to-use interface for
        creating cross-platform applications that run on Windows, Linux, and
        macOS. With Tkinter, developers can create event-driven applications
        that respond to user input, such as mouse clicks and keyboard events.
        It also provides tools for creating custom dialogs, message boxes,
        and other types of pop-up windows.Tkinter supports a wide range of
        features, such as internationalization, drag-and-drop support, and
        support for various font types and colors. It also provides tools for
        creating animated graphics, simple games, and multimedia applications.
        Overall, Tkinter is a powerful and flexible toolkit for creating desktop
        applications using Python. Its simplicity and cross-platform support
        make it a popular choice for developers who want to create simple GUI
        applications without the overhead of more complex frameworks.")

    def my_btn1(self):
        # set the text wrap mode to NoWrap
        self.myui.mytextEdit.setLineWrapMode(QTextEdit.NoWrap)
    def my_btn2(self):
        # set the text wrap mode to WidgetWidth
        self.myui.mytextEdit.setLineWrapMode(QTextEdit.WidgetWidth)
    def my_btn3(self):
        # set the text wrap mode to FixedPixelWidth
        self.myui.mytextEdit.setLineWrapMode(QTextEdit.FixedPixelWidth)

if __name__ == '__main__':
    myapp = QApplication(sys.argv)
```

```
    mywidget = MyScrollbar()
    mywidget.show()
    sys.exit(myapp.exec_())
```

Output:

Refer to the following figure:

Default output:

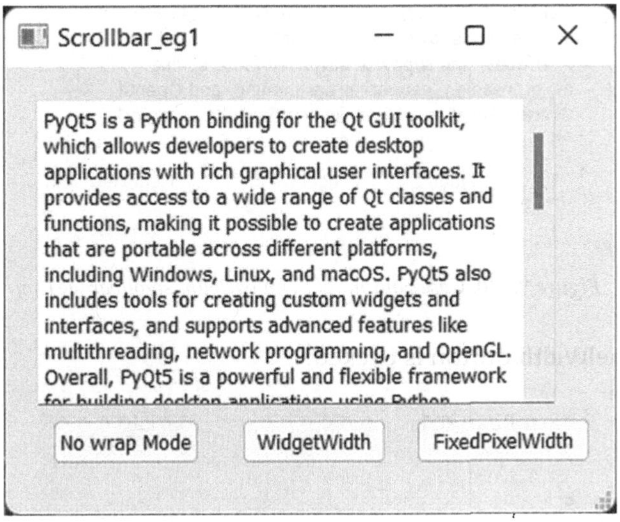

***Figure 8.138**: Default output of Scrollbar/run_scrollbar_eg1.py*

Case 1: When **No wrap Mode** button is clicked

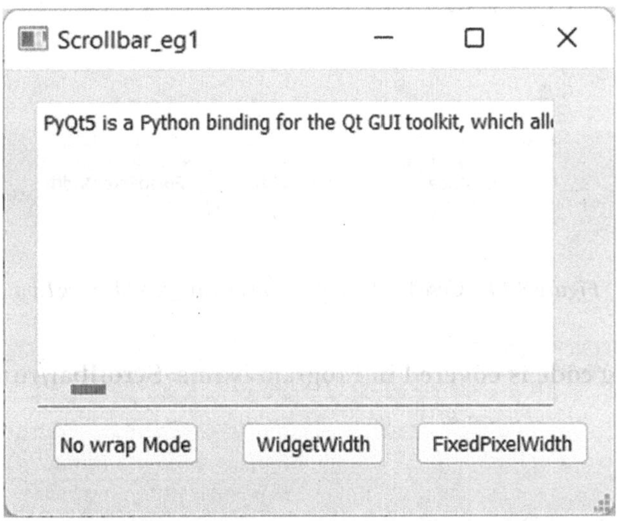

***Figure 8.139**: Case1 output of Scrollbar/run_scrollbar_eg1.py*

Case 2: When **WidgetWidth** button is clicked:

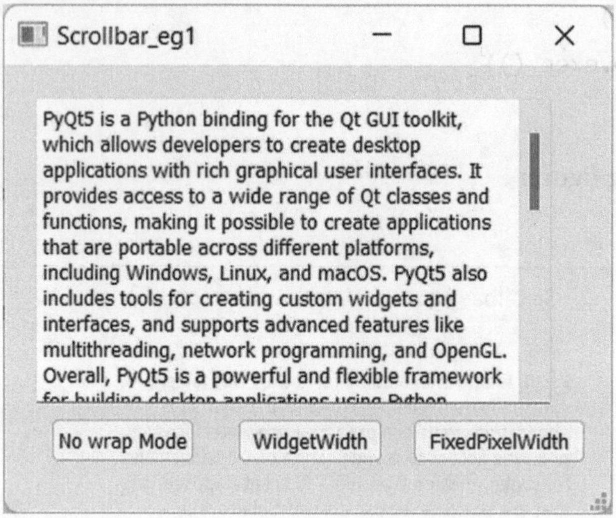

Figure 8.140: Case2 output of Scrollbar/run_scrollbar_eg1.py

Case 3: When **FixedPixelWidth** button is clicked:

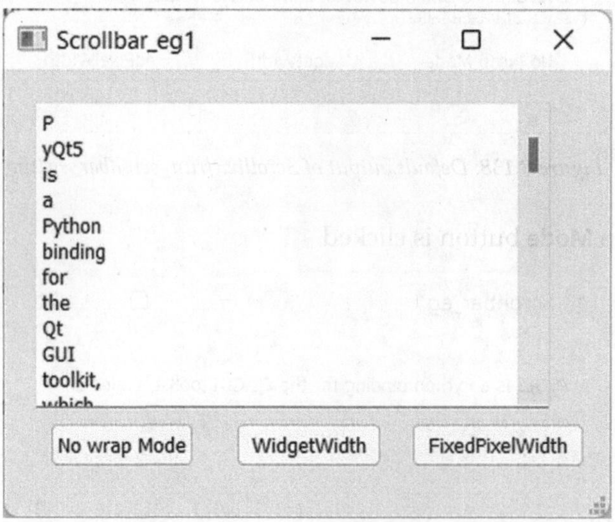

Figure 8.141: Case3 output of Scrollbar/run_scrollbar_eg1.py

Note: The preceding code is covered in Program Name: Scrollbar/run_scrollbar_eg1.py

QSlider

Let us now learn about **`QSlider`**:

- For both Vertical and Horizontal slider, the class is **`QSlider`**.

Important properties

It comprises the properties of **`QAbstractSlider`**. The other properties are as follows.

tickPosition

This property will control the tick position (small marks placed across the slider for indicating specific values) in the **`QSlider`** object. The default value is **NoTicks**. Refer to the following figure:

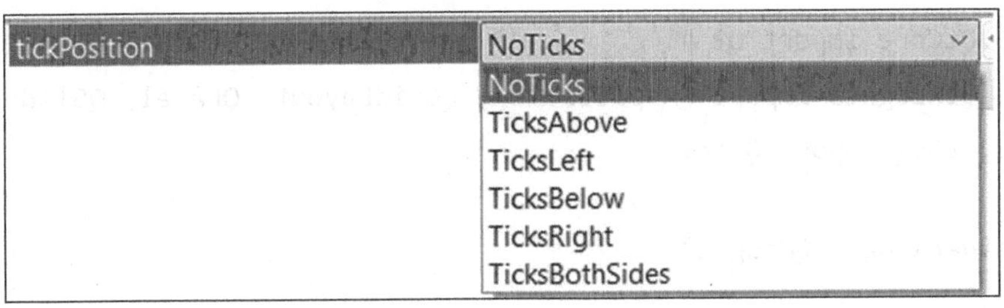

Figure 8.142: *Image depicting tickPosition property of QSlider in Qt Designer*

tickInterval

This property will hold the value interval and not the pixel interval between tickmarks, that is, spacing between the ticks in the **`QSlider`** object. The default value is **`0`**. Refer to the following figure:

Figure 8.143: *Image depicting tickInterval property of QSlider in Qt Designer*

Important methods/signals

Some important methods / signals are as follows:

- **`valueChanged()`:** This signal is emitted when the value of the **`QSlider`** object is changed.
- **`sliderPressed()`:** This signal is emitted when the user will start to drag the **`QSlider`** object.
- **`sliderMoved()`:** This signal is emitted when the user drags the **`QSlider`** object.
- **`sliderReleased()`:** This signal is emitted when the user releases the **`QSlider`** object.

Important properties

The properties and methods/signals are similar to the ones discussed in Horizontal slider.

Now, we shall see an example of **QScrollBar** widget.

The details of file names are given in the following *Table 8.12:*

S No.	Creating a Python file
1	run_slider_eg1.py

Table 8.12: Details of file names

Consider the following code of **run_slider_eg1.py**:

```
import sys
from PyQt5.QtCore import Qt
from PyQt5.QtWidgets import QApplication, QGridLayout, QLabel, QSlider, QWidget
from PyQt5.QtGui import QFont

class MySliderWidget(QWidget):

    def __init__(self):
        super().__init__()

        # Creating a label object for the horizontal slider
        myhlabel = QLabel('Horizontal')
        myhlabel.setAlignment(Qt.AlignCenter)

        # Creating a horizontal slider object
        myhslider = QSlider(Qt.Horizontal)
        myhslider.setFocusPolicy(Qt.NoFocus)
        myhslider.setRange(0, 100)
        myhslider.setValue(30)
        myhslider.setTickInterval(10)
        myhslider.setTickPosition(QSlider.TicksBelow)

        # Create a label object for the vertical slider
```

```
myvlabel = QLabel('Vertical')
myvlabel.setAlignment(Qt.AlignCenter)

# Creating a vertical slider
myvslider = QSlider(Qt.Vertical)
myvslider.setFocusPolicy(Qt.NoFocus)
myvslider.setRange(0, 100)
myvslider.setValue(40)
myvslider.setTickInterval(10)
myvslider.setTickPosition(QSlider.TicksLeft)

# Creating a label object to show the value of the horizontal slider
myhvalue = QLabel(str(myhslider.value()))
myhvalue.setAlignment(Qt.AlignCenter)

# creating a font object for myhvalue and myvvalue
myfont = QFont()
myfont.setPointSize(12)
myfont.setBold(True)
myhvalue.setFont(myfont)

# Creating a label object to show the value of the vertical slider
myvvalue = QLabel(str(myvslider.value()))
myvvalue.setAlignment(Qt.AlignCenter)
myvvalue.setFont(myfont)

# Creating a grid object layout to organize the widgets
mygrid = QGridLayout()
mygrid.setSpacing(10)

# Adding the horizontal slider and label object to the grid
mygrid.addWidget(myhlabel, 0, 0)
mygrid.addWidget(myhslider, 1, 0)
```

```
        mygrid.addWidget(myhvalue, 2, 0)

        # Adding the vertical slider and label object to the grid
        mygrid.addWidget(myvlabel, 0, 1)
        mygrid.addWidget(myvslider, 1, 1)
        mygrid.addWidget(myvvalue, 2, 1)

        # Connecting the valueChanged signal of myhslider object to its label
        obj myhvalue
        myhslider.valueChanged.connect(lambda value: myhvalue.
        setText(str(value)))

        # Connecting the valueChanged signal of myvslider object  to its label
        obj myvvalue
        myvslider.valueChanged.connect(lambda value: myvvalue.
        setText(str(value)))

        self.setLayout(mygrid)

        self.setGeometry(400, 400, 400, 400)
        self.setWindowTitle('My Sliders and Labels eg')
        self.show()

if __name__ == '__main__':
    myapp = QApplication(sys.argv)
    myslider_widget = MySliderWidget()
    sys.exit(myapp.exec_())
```

Output:

Refer to the following figure:

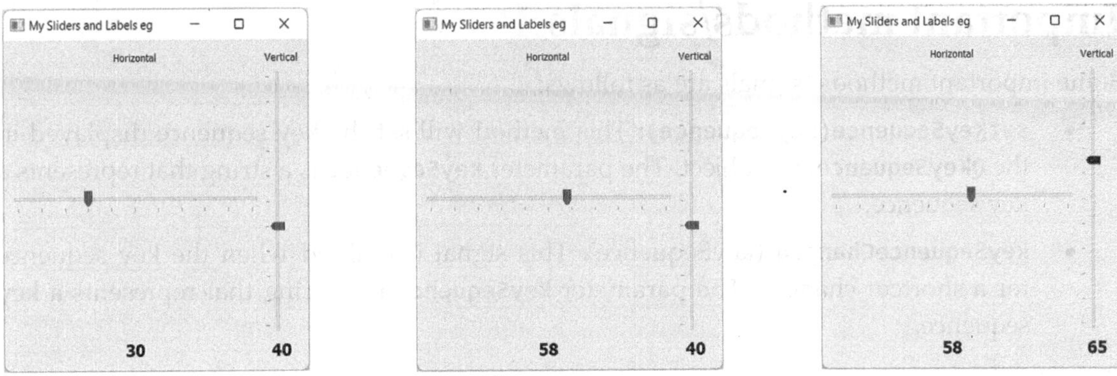

Default Output

When horizontal slider is dragged, the label value is set to 58.

When vertical slider is dragged, the label value is set to 65.

Figure 8.144: Output of Slider/run_slider_eg1.py

Note: The preceding code is covered in Program Name: Slider/run_slider_eg1.py

Key Sequence Edit

This widget in PyQt5 will allow the user to select a keyboard shortcut, that is, to input a `QKeySequence`. The recording starts when the widget gets the user's attention and concludes one second after the last key is released.

Important properties

Let us discuss an important property now.

keySequence

This property is used to set the key sequence that `QKeySequenceEdit` object represents. Refer to the following figure:

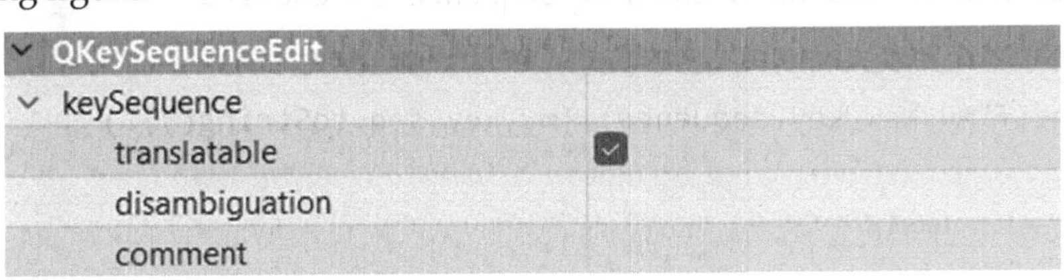

Figure 8.145: Image depicting keySequence property of QKeySequenceEdit in Qt Designer

Important methods/signals

Some important methods/signals are as follows:

- **setKeySequence(keySequence):** This method will set the key sequence displayed in the **QKeySequenceEdit** object. The parameter **keySequence** is a string that represents a key sequence.
- **keySequenceChanged** (keySequence): This signal is emitted when the key sequence for a shortcut changes. The parameter **keySequence** is a string that represents a key sequence.

Consider the following code of **run_keysequenceedit_eg1.py**:

```
import sys
from PyQt5.QtWidgets import QApplication, QMainWindow, QKeySequenceEdit
from PyQt5.QtGui import QKeySequence
from PyQt5.QtCore import Qt

class MyKeySequence(QMainWindow):
    def __init__(self):
        super().__init__()

        # Create a QKeySequenceEdit widget
        self.my_key_edit = QKeySequenceEdit(self)
        self.my_key_edit.setKeySequence(QKeySequence(Qt.CTRL + Qt.Key_H))
        self.my_key_edit.keySequenceChanged.connect(self.my_handle_key_
        sequence_changed)
        self.setCentralWidget(self.my_key_edit)

    # Slot method called when the key sequence is changed
    def my_handle_key_sequence_changed(self, my_key_seq):
        print(f"My New key sequence: {my_key_seq.toString()}")

if __name__ == '__main__':
    myapp = QApplication(sys.argv)
    mywidget = MyKeySequence()
    mywidget.show()
```

```
myapp.exec_()
```

Output:

Refer to the following figure:

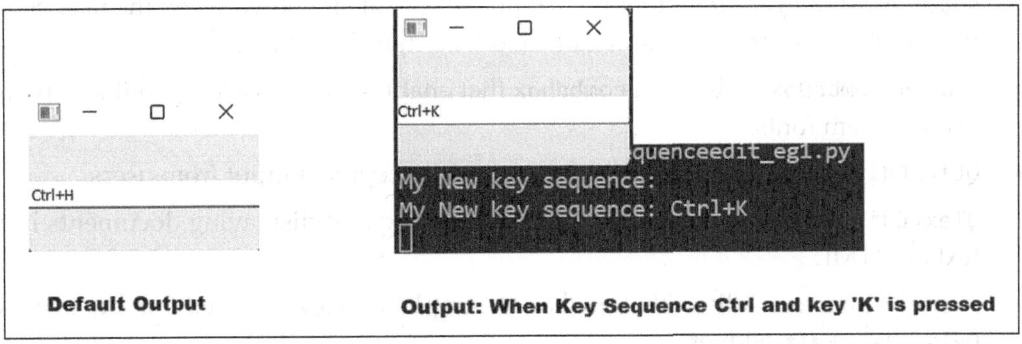

Figure 8.146: Output of KeySequenceEdit/run_keysequenceedit_eg1.py

Note: The preceding code is covered in Program Name: KeySequenceEdit/run_keysequenceedit_eg1.py

Conclusion

In this chapter, we learned about the concepts of various input widgets available in Qt and how to effectively utilize them to create interactive user interfaces. After completing this chapter, readers gained a solid understanding of input widgets such as **`QLineEdit`**, **`QSpinBox`**, **`QComboBox`**, **`QTextEdit`**, and others, including their characteristics, functionality, and customization options. We explored the knowledge required to incorporate these input widgets into their designs, enabling users to enter data, select options, and interact with the program seamlessly. Moreover, this chapter covers essential topics such as input validation methods, processing user input events, and linking signals and slots to achieve the desired functionality. By mastering these concepts, users can now develop simple and user-friendly interfaces that effectively collect user input and deliver a smooth user experience using input widgets in Qt Designer.

Furthermore, practical examples with helpful comments are provided throughout the chapter, showcasing the implementation of input widgets in Qt Designer. These examples serve as valuable resources, aiding readers in understanding the usage and application of each input widget effectively. Finally, users have gained the necessary skills and knowledge to confidently utilize input widgets in Qt Designer, empowering them to create interactive and user-friendly interfaces that meet the requirements of their projects.

Points to remember

- Users can choose from a drop-down list of options in the **QComboBox** widget in PyQt5. Since it displays the item that is now selected, it occupies the least amount of screen space. A list of every item that is currently accessible is shown when the user clicks on the widget. After then, the user can choose an item from the list.
- A **QFontComboBox** widget is a **combobox** that enables users to select a font family from a list of system fonts.
- **QLineEditWidget** is used to display text or to accept text input from users.
- **QTextEdit** offers a multi-line text area for editing and displaying documents in plain text or HTML.
- A multi-line text editor that makes it simple to view and edit plain text is the **QPlainTextEdit** widget.
- A Spin Box widget in PyQt5 allows the user to choose a value by pressing the Up and Down arrow keys of the keyboard or by clicking the Up and Down button.
- The **QDoubleSpinBox** widget is a **spinbox** widget supporting double-type values.
- The **QDateTimeEdit** widget will allow the user to select and edit date and time values supporting display formats, such as date-only, time-only, and date-time displays.
- A circular dial called **QDial** can be rotated to choose a value from a specified range which provides a convenient method for the user to change a numerical value, like brightness or volume setting.
- **QKeySequence** will allow the user to select a keyboard shortcut.

Questions

1. Explain any five input widgets in the Qt designer system.
2. Explain the method for input of date and time in the Qt designer system.
3. Explain the use of the Combo Box widget in detail.
4. Explain the important properties of the Combo Box widget in the Qt designer system.
5. Explain the important methods of the Combo Box widget in the Qt designer system.
6. Explain the important signals of the Combo Box widget in the Qt designer system.
7. Give a comparison of Combo Box and Font Combo Box.
8. Explain important properties of the Font Combo Box widget.
9. Explain important signals of the Font Combo Box widget.
10. Which widget is used for single-line text editing? Explain in detail.
11. Explain important properties of the Line Edit widget.

12. Explain important signals of the Line Edit widget.
13. Which widget is used for multi-line text editing? Explain in detail.
14. Explain important properties of the Text Edit widget.
15. Explain important signals of the Text Edit widget.
16. Explain the significance of the Spin Box widget in GUI designing in Qt Designer.
17. Explain the use of the Double Spin Box widget in GUI designing in Qt Designer.
18. How to select and edit date and time values? Explain the widget used for this purpose.
19. Explain the Key Sequence Edit widget in Qt Designer.

CHAPTER 9
Getting Insights of Display Widgets in Qt Designer

Introduction

Till now, we have seen how to create GUI forms using different widgets in the Qt Designer. In this chapter, we will deal with some display widgets that are used for enhancing the graphical representation of the GUI and its experience.

Structure

In this chapter, we will discuss the following topics:

- Introduction to the display widgets in Qt Designer
- Label
- Text browser
- Calendar widget
- LCD number
- Progress bar

Objectives

After reading this chapter, the reader will have a thorough understanding of display widgets in Qt Designer. We will learn how to display static text or images using labels and change their font, color, alignment, and size. Moreover, we will discuss how labels can improve the GUI's visual presentation of information. We will examine the text browser widget's features and learn how to display and control rich text content. The chapter also discusses adding hyperlinks, graphics, and formatting choices to text displays to make them dynamic and interactive. Next, we will explore how to add a calendar widget to our GUI application. We shall discover how to customize the calendar widget's look, structure, and behavior to meet specific application requirements. We will learn how to display numerical values, such as counters using the LCD Number widget, and how to modify the LCD number widget's digit count, decimal accuracy, look, and style. Finally, we explore the progress bar widget to show how a task or operation is progressing. We will learn how to dynamically update the progress bar based on our application.

Introduction to the display widgets in Qt Designer

This is the final chapter on Qt Designer. In this chapter, we will deal with some display widgets of Qt Designer. Refer to *Figure 9.1:*

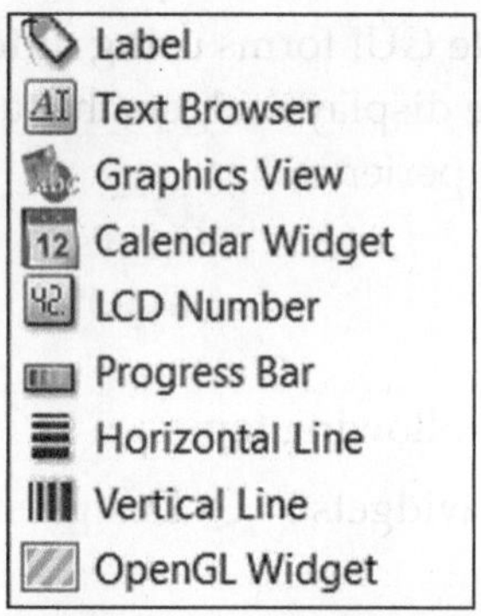

Figure 9.1: *Different input widgets of Qt Designer*

We shall discuss the importance of each input widget one by one.

Label

A **`QLabel`** widget in PyQt5 is a display widget used to display text, an image, or any animated GIF on a GUI form page. It can be used to inform the user, by displaying **PlainText**, **RichText**, or an image.

Important properties

Let us check some important properties now.

text

This property will hold the **`QLabel`** object text. Refer to *Figure 9.2:*

Figure 9.2: *Image depicting text property of QLabel in Qt Designer*

textFormat

This property will hold the **`QLabel`** object text format. Default format selected is **AutoText**. Refer to *Figure 9.3:*

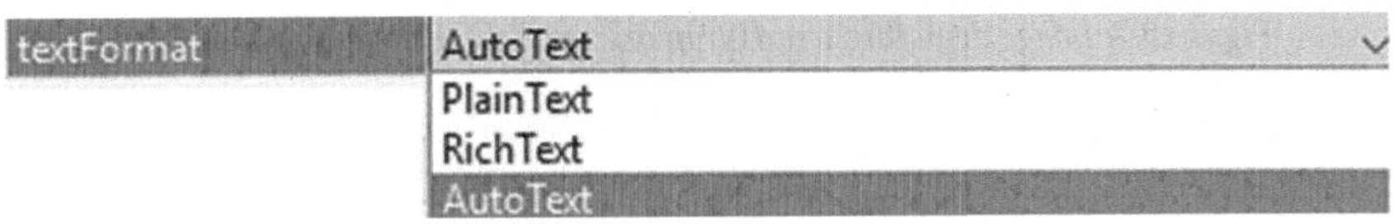

Figure 9.3: *Image depicting textFormat property of QLabel in Qt Designer*

pixmap

This property will hold the **`QLabel`** object **pixmap**. Refer to *Figure 9.4:*

Figure 9.4: *Image depicting pixmap property of QLabel in Qt Designer*

scaledContents

This property will hold whether **`QLabel`** object will scale its contents to fill all the available space. Refer to *Figure 9.5:*

Figure 9.5: *Image depicting scaledContents property of QLabel in Qt Designer*

alignment

This property will hold **QLabel** object content alignment. Refer to *Figure 9.6:*

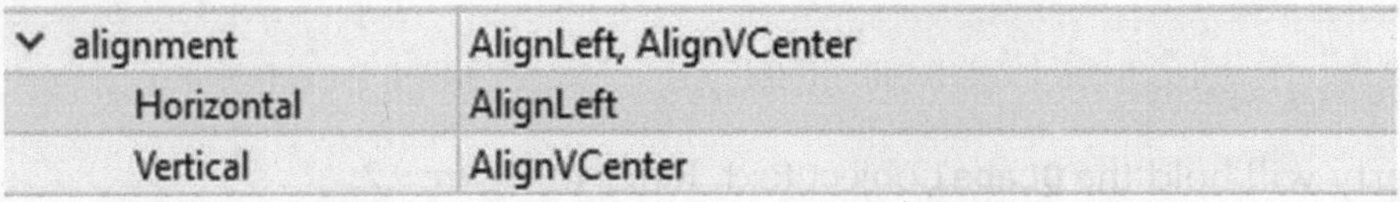

***Figure 9.6:** Image depicting alignment property of QLabel in Qt Designer*

wordWrap

This property will determine whether **QLabel** object will wrap the text at necessary word breaks. The default value is **False**. Refer to the following *Figure 9.7:*

***Figure 9.7:** Image depicting wordWrap property of QLabel in Qt Designer*

margin

This property will hold the width of the margin (separation between the innermost pixel of frame and outermost pixel of content) surrounding the **QLabel** object content. Refer to the following *Figure 9.8:*

***Figure 9.8:** Image depicting margin property of QLabel in Qt Designer*

indent

This property will hold the **QLabel** object text indent in pixels. Refer to *Figure 9.9:*

***Figure 9.9:** Image depicting indent property of QLabel in Qt Designer*

openExternalLinks

This property will specify whether the **QLabel** object should automatically open external links using **openUrl()** instead of **linkActivated()** signal emitting. The default value is **False**. Refer to *Figure 9.10:*

***Figure 9.10:** Image depicting openExternalLinks property of QLabel in Qt Designer*

textInteractionFlags

This property will describe how the **QLabel** object should respond to user interaction if it displays text. Refer to the following *Figure 9.11:*

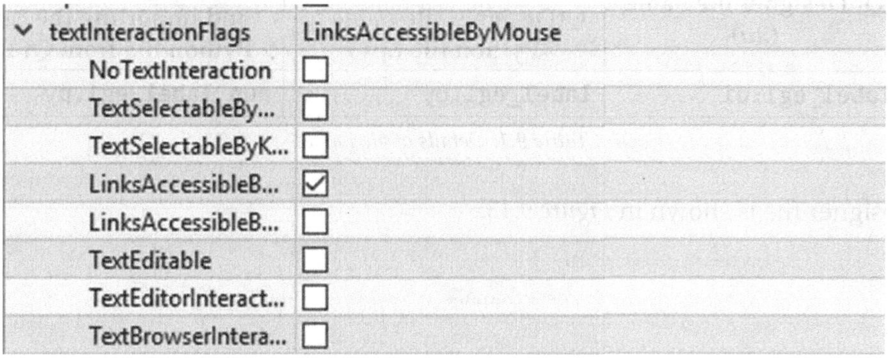

***Figure 9.11:** Image depicting textInteractionFlags property of QLabel in Qt Designer*

buddy

This property will hold the **QLabel** object buddy widget. A widget is connected to another widget using the buddy mechanism so that they can be used in combination. Refer to the following *Figure 9.12:*

***Figure 9.12:** Image depicting buddy property of QLabel in Qt Designer*

Important methods/signals

Let us check some important methods and signals:

- **setText(arg__1):** This method will set the text of the **QLabel** object to the specified **argument arg__1,** which is of type string.
- **setPixmap(arg__1):** This method will set the image or **pixmap** to the **QLabel** object to the specified **argument arg__1,** which is of **QPixmap** object.
- **setTextInteractionFlags(flags):** This method will set the text interaction flags of **QLabel** object, and the flags will determine how the user will interact with the text in the **QLabel** object.
- **linkActivated(link):** This signal is emitted when the link (URL of the activated link) in **QLabel** object is activated.
- **linkHovered(link):** This signal is emitted when the mouse hovers over a link in **QLabel** object.

Now, we shall see an example of **QLabel** widget.

The details of file names are given in *Table 9.1*:

S No.	Qt Designer file name (.ui)	Converting the QtDesigner file name to Python file (.py)	Creating another Python file and importing the converted Python file from Qt Designer
1.	**label_eg1.ui**	**label_eg1.py**	**run_label_eg1.py**

***Table 9.1:** Details of file names*

The Qt Designer file is shown in *Figure 9.13:*

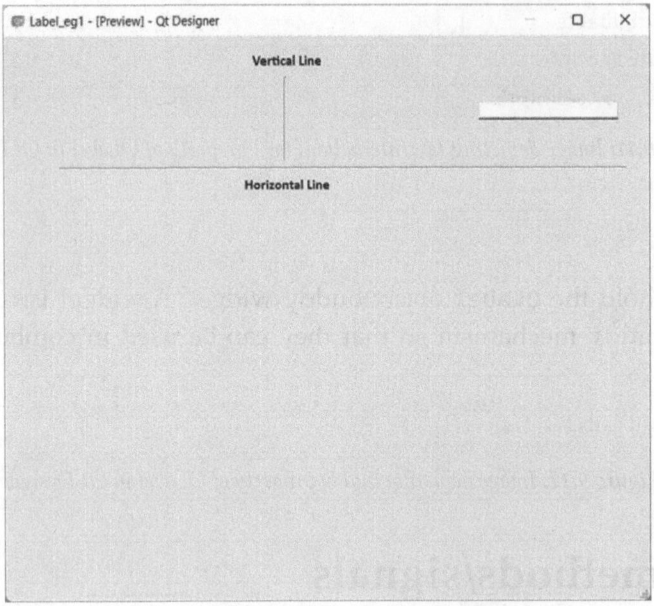

***Figure 9.13:** Qt Designer file: Label/label_eg1.ui*

Note: The above .ui file is covered in Path: Label/label_eg1.ui

Consider the following code of **run_label_eg1.py**:

```
import sys
from PyQt5.QtWidgets import QMainWindow, QApplication
from PyQt5.QtGui import QPixmap
from label_eg1 import *

class MyLabel(QMainWindow):
```

```
    def __init__(self):
        super().__init__()
        self.myui = Ui_MainWindow()
        self.myui.setupUi(self)

        # displaying rich text
        self.myui.mylbl1.setText("Displaying plain text.")

        # displaying rich text
        self.myui.mylbl2.setText("<font color='green'>Displaying rich text.</
        font>")

        self.myui.lineEdit.setText("Buddy with Label")
        # setting the buddy property of the label to the LineEdit object
        self.myui.mylbl2.setBuddy(self.myui.lineEdit)

        # displaying image
        self.myui.mylbl3.setPixmap(QPixmap("myimage.jpg"))

        self.show()

if __name__ == "__main__":
    app = QApplication(sys.argv)
    screen = MyLabel()
    screen.show()
    sys.exit(app.exec_())
```

Output:

Refer to *Figure 9.14:*

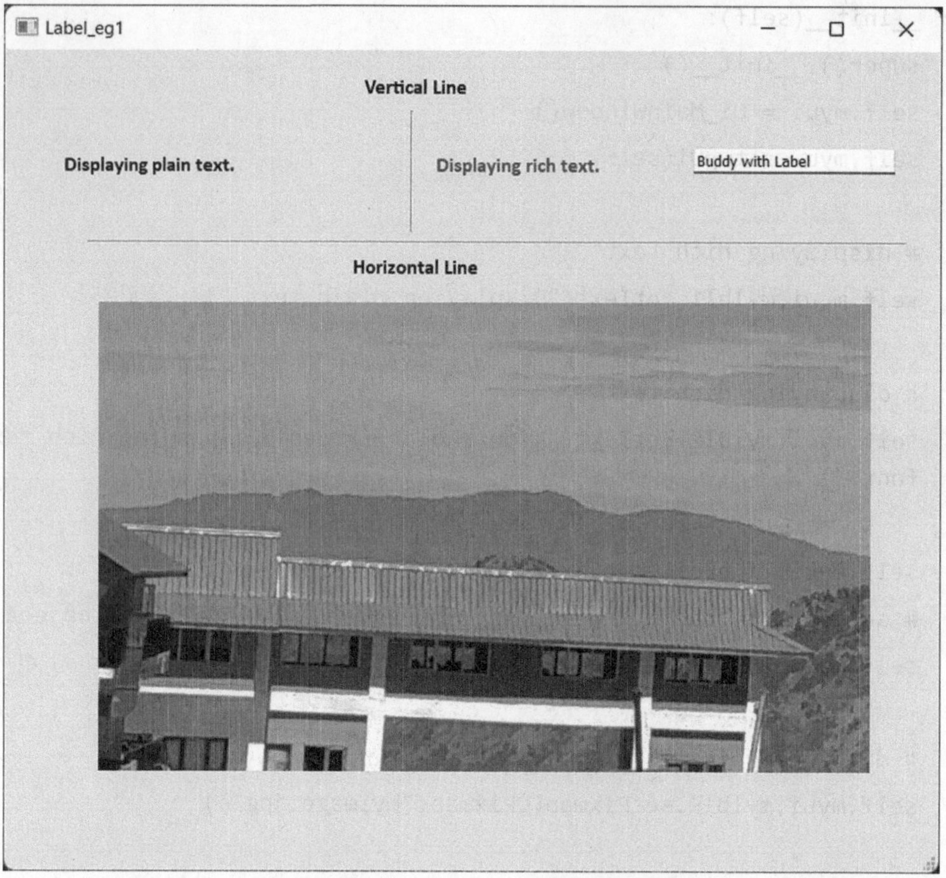

Figure 9.14: Output of Label/run_label_eg1.py

Note: The preceding code is covered in program name: Label/run_label_eg1.py

In this example, we have used *horizontal* and *vertical* lines, which are class lines. These lines are typically used as separators to visually divide sections of the GUI page. They can be used to group related widgets together, making the form more organized and easier to navigate.

Text browser

A rich text browser with hypertext navigation capabilities is offered by PyQt5's **`QtextBrowser`** class. The user can interact with the text by clicking on links and selecting the text, and it is used to display formatted text, including images and links. The read-only **`QtextBrowser`** class extends the **`QtextEdit`** class and offers more functionality for displaying and navigating hypertext. It supports a number of text types, including plain text, HTML, and Markdown. **Cascading Style Sheets** (**CSS**) and inline HTML tags can be used to style the text.

Important properties

It contains properties of **QtextEdit**. The other properties are discussed in the following sections.

Source

The URL of the current document displayed in the **QtextBrowser** object can be set or obtained using this property. Both the **source()** method and **setSource()** method can be used to get and set it. Refer to the following *Figure 9.15:*

***Figure 9.15**: Image depicting source property of QTextBrowser in Qt Designer*

searchPaths

This property will hold the search paths used by the **QtextBrowser** object to search for resources such as images and documents. Refer to the following *Figure 9.16:*

***Figure 9.16**: Image depicting source searchPaths of QTextBrowser in Qt Designer*

openExternalLinks

This property determines whether links that lead to external URLs should be opened within **QTextBrowser** object or as a separate application. The default value is **False**. Refer to the following *Figure 9.17:*

***Figure 9.17**: Image depicting openExternalLinks property of QTextBrowser in Qt Designer*

openLinks

If the user attempts to activate links using the mouse or keyboard, **QTextBrowser** should automatically open those links, according to this property. The default value is **True**. Refer to the following *Figure 9.18:*

***Figure 9.18**: Image depicting openLinks property of QTextBrowser in Qt Designer*

Important methods/signals

Let us go over some important methods and signals:

- `isBackwardAvailable()`: If the backward history is available to navigate in the `QTextBrowser` object, then this method will return **True**; else will return **False**.
- `isForwardAvailable()`: If the forward history is available to navigate in the `QTextBrowser` object, then this method will return **True**; else will return **False**.
- `anchorClicked(arg_ _1)`: This signal is emitted when a hyperlink is clicked in the `QTextBrowser` object.
- `sourceChanged(arg_ _1)`: This signal is emitted when the source of the **`QTextBrowser`** object changes.

Now, we shall see an example of **`QTextBrowser`** widget.

The details of file names are given in *Table 9.2*:

S No.	Qt Designer file name (.ui)	Converting the QtDesigner file name to Python file (.py)	Creating another python file and importing the converted Python file from Qt Designer
1.	`textbrowser_eg1.ui`	`textbrowser_eg1.py`	`run_textbrowser_eg1.py`

Table 9.2: *Details of file names*

The Qt Designer file is shown in *Figure 9.19:*

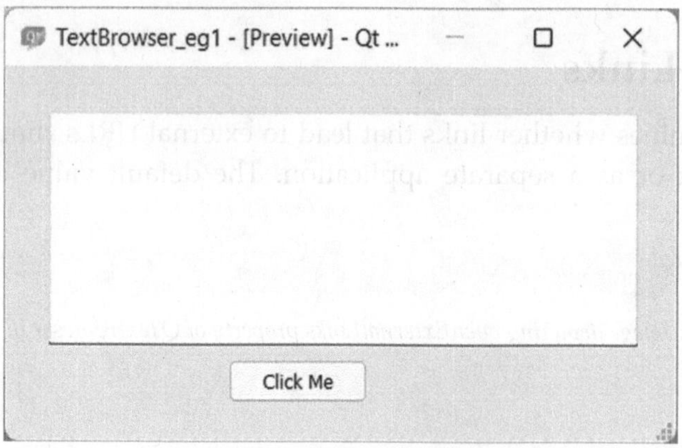

Figure 9.19: *Qt Designer file : TextBrowser/textbrowser_eg1.ui*

Note: The above .ui file is covered in Path: TextBrowser/textbrowser_eg1.ui

Consider the following code of **run_textbrowser_eg1.py:**

```
import sys
from PyQt5.QtWidgets import QMainWindow,QApplication
from PyQt5.QtGui import QTextCursor
from textbrowser_eg1 import *


class MyTextBrowser(QMainWindow):
    def __init__(self):
        super().__init__()
        self.myui = Ui_MainWindow()
        self.myui.setupUi(self)

        self.myui.textBrowser.setOpenExternalLinks(True)
        self.myui.textBrowser.setStyleSheet('font-size: 24px;')

        self.myui.btn.clicked.connect(self.my_btn_clickme)

        self.show()

    def my_btn_clickme(self):
        self.myui.textBrowser.moveCursor(QTextCursor.Start)
        self.myui.textBrowser.append('Displaying Bolloywood movies list')
        self.myui.textBrowser.append('<a href=https://en.wikipedia.org/wiki/
        List_of_Hindi_films_of_2023>Bollywood Movies 2023</a>')


if __name__ == "__main__":
    app = QApplication(sys.argv)
    screen = MyTextBrowser()
    screen.show()
    sys.exit(app.exec_())
```

Output:

Refer to the following *Figure 9.20:*

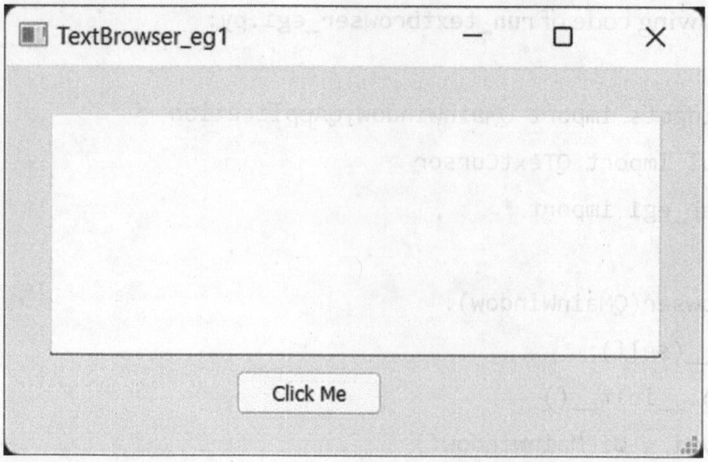

Figure 9.20: Default output of TextBrowser/run_textbrowser_eg1.py

Case: When **Click Me** button is clicked, then the text will be appended in the **text browser** widget. User may click the hyperlink text **Bollywood Movies 2023** and if connected to internet, then it will navigate to that web page.

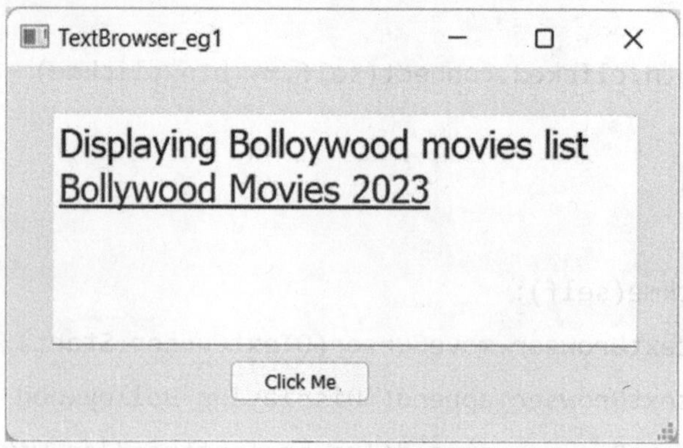

Figure 9.21: Output of TextBrowser/run_textbrowser_eg1.py when Click Me button is clicked

Note: The preceding code is covered in Program Name: TextBrowser/run_textbrowser_eg1.py

Calendar widget

The PyQt5 widget **QCalendarWidget** offers a monthly calendar view and allows users to select a date. Events, appointments, and other time-based information can be displayed using the above widget. Numerous customization options are available for the widget, including choosing the first day of the week, specifying a minimum and maximum date range, and enabling or disabling certain dates. Programmatic retrieval of the selected date or range is also possible or through signals emitted by the widget.

Important properties

Let us explore some important properties now.

selectedDate

This property view will hold the currently selected date, which must be within the **dateRange** specified by the **minimumDate** and **maximumDate** property of **QCalendarWidget** object. Refer to the following *Figure 9.22:*

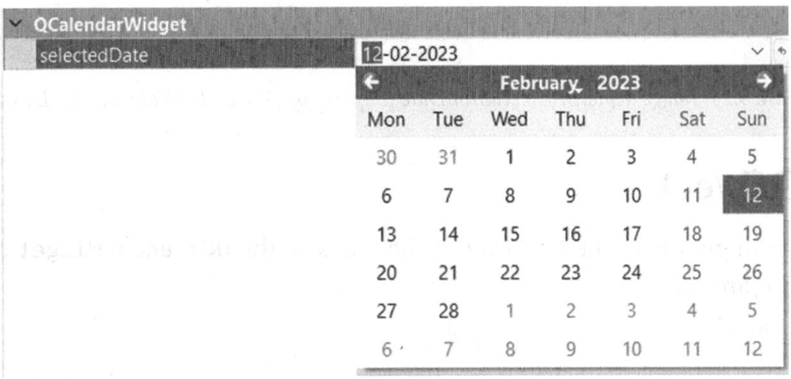

***Figure 9.22**: Image depicting selectedDate property of QCalendarWidget in Qt Designer*

minimumDate

The minimum date of the currently specified date range of **QCalendarWidget** object is held by this property. Refer to the following *Figure 9.23:*

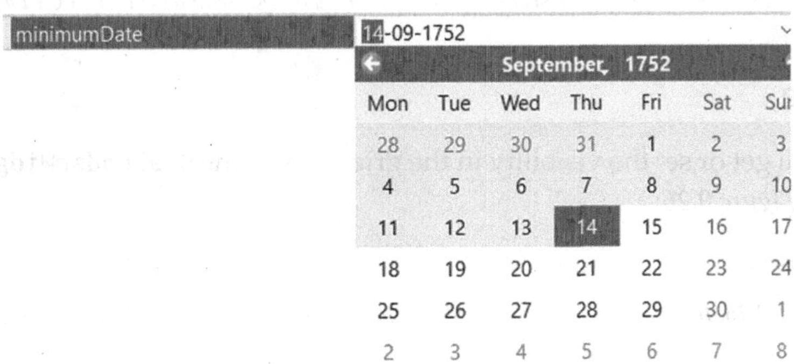

***Figure 9.23**: Image depicting minimumDate property of QCalendarWidget in Qt Designer*

maximumDate

The maximum date of the currently specified date range of **`QCalendarWidget`** object is held by this property. Refer to the following *Figure 9.24:*

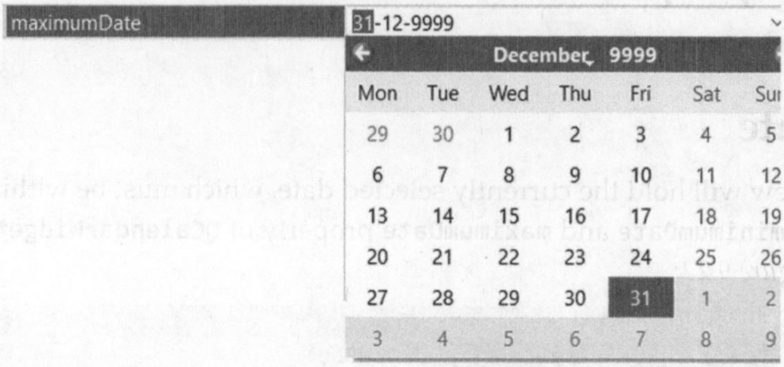

Figure 9.24: *Image depicting maximumDate property of QCalendarWidget in Qt Designer*

firstDayOfWeek

This property will get or set the first day of the week in the **`QCalendarWidget`** object. Refer to the following *Figure 9.25:*

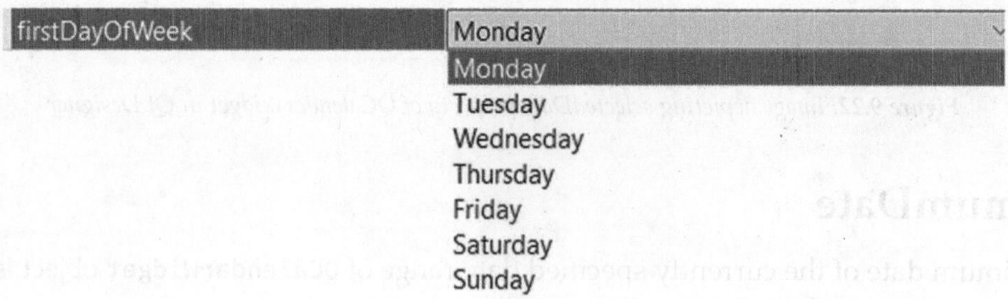

Figure 9.25: *Image depicting firstDayOfWeek property of QCalendarWidget in Qt Designer*

gridVisible

This property will get or set the visibility in the grid lines in the **`QCalendarWidget`** object. Refer to the following *Figure 9.26:*

Figure 9.26: *Image depicting gridVisible property of QCalendarWidget in Qt Designer*

selectionMode

This property will hold the selection type the user can make in the **QCalendarWidget** object. The user will be unable to select the dates on **NoSelection** or can select a date within the minimum and maximum allowed dates on **SingleSelection**. Refer to the following *Figure 9.27:*

***Figure 9.27**: Image depicting selectionMode property of QCalendarWidget in Qt Designer*

horizontalHeaderFormat

This property will get or set the format of the horizontal header. Refer to the following *Figure 9.28:*

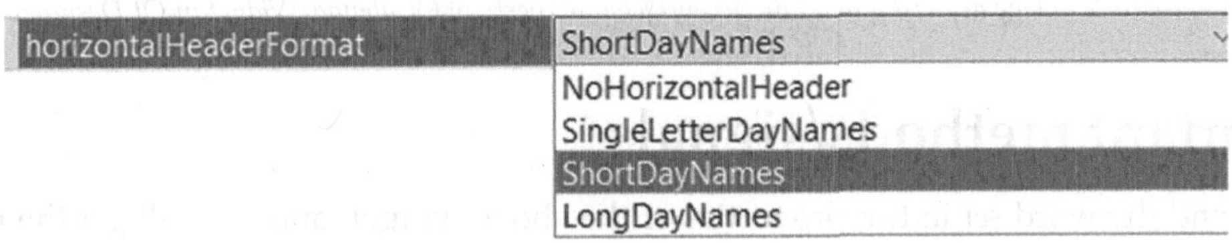

***Figure 9.28**: Image depicting horizontalHeaderFormat property of QCalendarWidget in Qt Designer*

verticalHeaderFormat

This property will get or set the format of the vertical header. Refer to the following *Figure 9.29:*

***Figure 9.29**: Image depicting verticalHeaderFormat property of QCalendarWidget in Qt Designer*

navigationBarVisible

This property will determine whether the navigation bar is to be displayed or not in the **QCalendarWidget** object. Refer to the following *Figure 9.30:*

***Figure 9.30**: Image depicting navigationBarVisible property of QCalendarWidget in Qt Designer*

dateEditEnabled

This property determines whether the date edit popup is enabled or not. Refer to the following *Figure 9.31:*

Figure 9.31: *Image depicting dateEditEnabled property of QCalendarWidget in Qt Designer*

dateEditAcceptDelay

This property specifies the time delay (default value is **1500** in milliseconds) the date edit will remain active following the most recent user input. The popup is closed once the time has elapsed, thus accepting the date specified in the date edit. Refer to the following *Figure 9.31:*

Figure 9.32: *Image depicting dateEditAcceptDelay property of QCalendarWidget in Qt Designer*

Important methods/signals

Just prepend the word *set* in the properties of the above widget, and we will get the required methods. We will discuss an important signal in this section.

selectionChanged()

This signal is emitted when the user changes the currently selected date in the **`QCalendarWidget`** object.

Now, we shall see an example of **`QCalendarWidget`**.

The details of file names are given in the following *Table 9.3*:

S No.	Qt Designer file name (.ui)	Converting the QtDesigner file name to Python file (.py)	Creating another Python file and importing the converted Python file from Qt Designer
1.	**`calendarwidget_eg1.ui`**	**`calendarwidget_eg1.py`**	**`run_calendarwidget_eg1.py`**

Table 9.3: *Details of file names*

The Qt Designer file is shown in *Figure 9.33:*

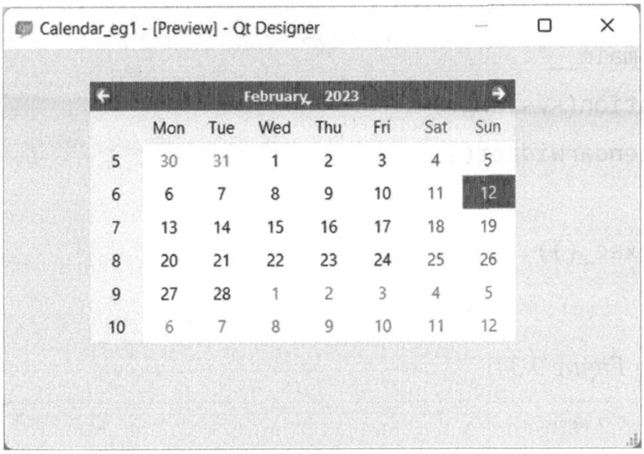

***Figure 9.33**: Qt Designer file : CalendarWidget/calendarwidget_eg1.ui*

Note: The above .ui file is covered in Path: CalendarWidget/calendarwidget_eg1.ui

Consider the following code of **run_calendarwidget_eg1.py**:

```
import sys
from PyQt5.QtWidgets import QMainWindow,QApplication
from calendarwidget_eg1 import *

class MyCalendarWidget(QMainWindow):
    def __init__(self):
        super().__init__()
        self.myui = Ui_MainWindow()
        self.myui.setupUi(self)

        # Connect the calendar's selectionChanged signal to the update_label
        method
        self.myui.calendarWidget.selectionChanged.connect(self.my_display_date)

        self.show()

    # Define a method to set the label object text with the selected date
    def my_display_date(self):
        self.myui.mylbl.setText('Selected date is: {}'.format(self.myui.
        calendarWidget.selectedDate().toString()))
```

```
if __name__ == "__main__":
    app = QApplication(sys.argv)
    screen = MyCalendarWidget()
    screen.show()
    sys.exit(app.exec_())
```

Output:

Refer to the following *Figure 9.34:*

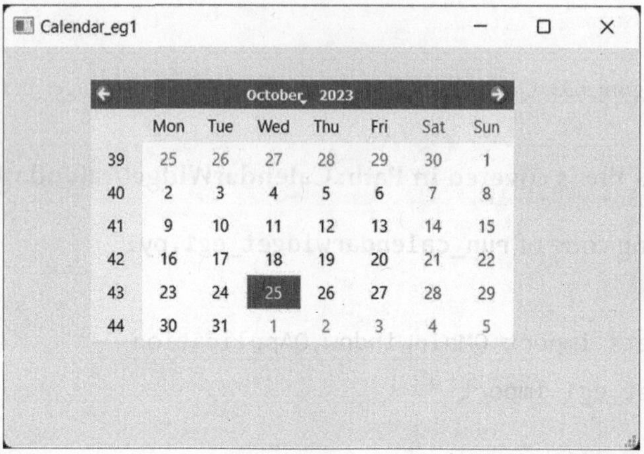

***Figure 9.34**: Default output of CalendarWidget/run_calendarwidget_eg1.py*

Case: When any date is selected from the **QCalendarWidget** object, the selected date will be displayed in the label widget.

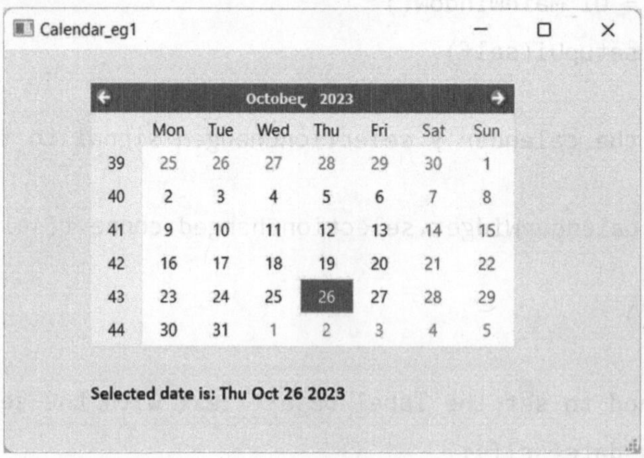

***Figure 9.35**: Output of CalendarWidget/run_calendarwidget_eg1.py when any date is selected from the QCalendar widget object*

Note: The preceding code is covered in program name: CalendarWidget/run_calendarwidget_eg1.py

LCD number

The PyQt5 widget **`QLCDNumber`** shows a numerical value in a seven-segment LCD display. In GUI forms, it is commonly used to display numerical data, such as sensor, timer, and other measurements. As a **`QFrame`** subclass, **`QLCDNumber`** offers a number of methods and properties to control the LCD display's appearance and behavior.

Important properties

Let us check some important properties now.

smallDecimalPoint

This property will hold the decimal point style of **`QLCDNumber`** object. The default value is **False**, indicating that the decimal point is displayed as a large dot. When set to **True**, the decimal point is displayed as a small dot. Refer to the following *Figure 9.36:*

***Figure 9.36**: Image depicting smallDecimalPoint property of QLCDNumber in Qt Designer*

digitCount

This property will set the current number of digits displayed in the **`QLCDNumber`** object. The default value is **5**. Refer to the following *Figure 9.37:*

***Figure 9.37**: Image depicting digitCount property of QLCDNumber in Qt Designer*

mode

This property will set the current display mode of the **`QLCDNumber`** object which can be hexadecimal, decimal, octal or binary. The default value is **Dec**. Refer to the following *Figure 9.38:*

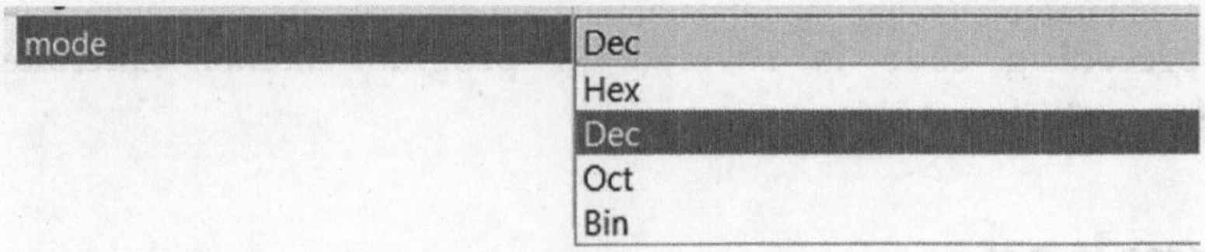

Figure 9.38: Image depicting mode property of QLCDNumber in Qt Designer

segmentStyle

This property will set the style of the **QLCDNumber** object. Raised segments filled with background color are produced when style is **Outline** filled. Raised segments filled with foreground color are produced when style is **Filled** (default value). Flat segments filled with foreground color are produced when style is **Flat**. Refer to the following *Figure 9.39:*

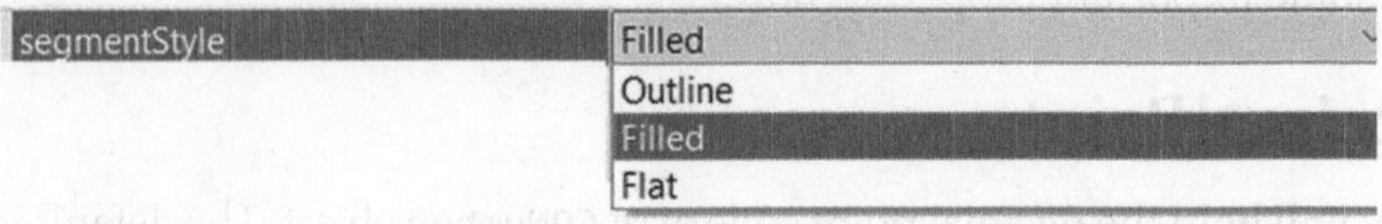

Figure 9.39: Image depicting segmentStyle property of QLCDNumber in Qt Designer

value

This property will set the numeric value displayed in the **QLCDNumber** object. Value can be integer or float value. Refer to the following *Figure 9.40:*

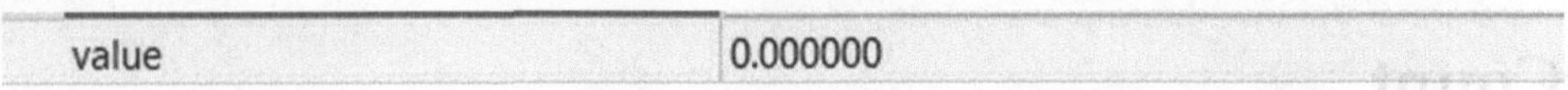

Figure 9.40: Image depicting value property of QLCDNumber in Qt Designer

intValue

This property will be truncated to the nearest integer to the current value displayed by the **QLCDNumber** object. Refer to the following *Figure 9.41:*

Figure 9.41: Image depicting intValue property of QLCDNumber in Qt Designer

Important methods/signals

An important method/signal is the following:

display(num)

This method will set the numeric value displayed in the **QLCDNumber** object. The parameter **num** can be of integer or double type.

Now, we shall see an example of **QLCDNumber** widget.

The details of file names are given in *Table 9.4*:

S No.	Qt Designer file name (.ui)	Converting the Qt Designer file name to Python file (.py)	Creating another Python file and importing the converted Python file from Qt Designer
1	lcdnumber_eg1.ui	lcdnumber_eg1.py	run_lcdnumber_eg1.py

Table 9.4: *Details of file names*

The Qt Designer file is shown in *Figure 9.42:*

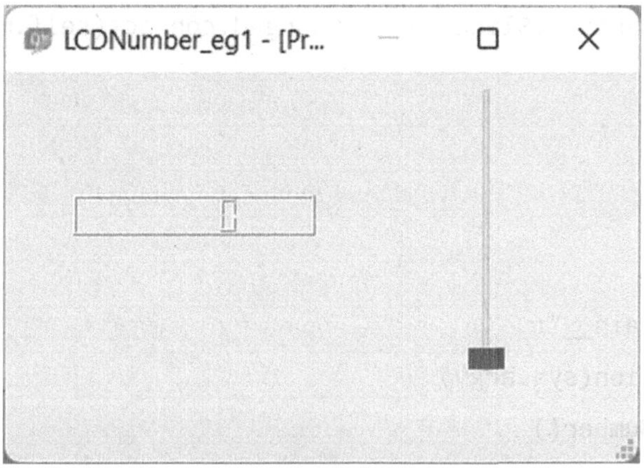

Figure 9.42: *Qt Designer file: LCDNumber/lcdnumber_eg1.ui*

Note: The above .ui file is covered in Path: LCDNumber/lcdnumber_eg1.ui

Consider the following code of **run_lcdnumber_eg1.py:**

```
import sys
from PyQt5.QtWidgets import QMainWindow,QApplication, QLCDNumber
from lcdnumber_eg1 import *
```

```
class MyLCDNumber(QMainWindow):
    def __init__(self):
        super().__init__()
        self.myui = Ui_MainWindow()
        self.myui.setupUi(self)

        # Set the minimum and maximum values for the vertical slider
        self.myui.verticalSlider.setMinimum(0)
        self.myui.verticalSlider.setMaximum(100)
        self.myui.verticalSlider.setValue(0)

        # change the segment style to flat
        self.myui.lcdNumber.setSegmentStyle(QLCDNumber.Flat)


        # Connect the slider's valueChanged signal to the lcd's display slot
        self.myui.verticalSlider.valueChanged.connect(self.myui.lcdNumber.
        display)

        self.show()



if __name__ == "__main__":
    app = QApplication(sys.argv)
    screen = MyLCDNumber()
    screen.show()
    sys.exit(app.exec_())
```

Output:

Refer to *Figure 9.43:*

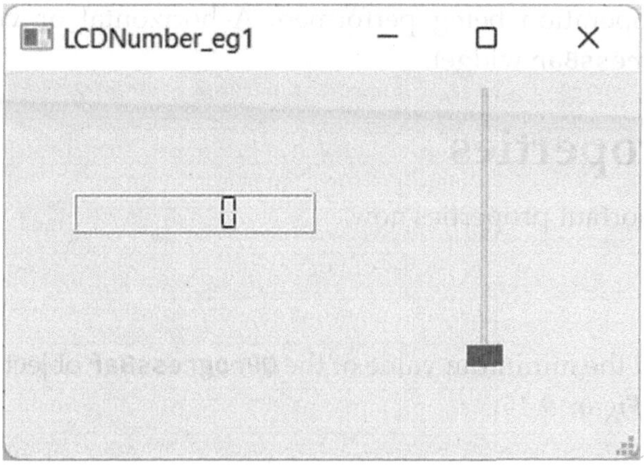

Figure 9.43: *Default output of LCDNumber/run_lcdnumber_eg1.py*

Case: The numeric value in the **LCDNumber** widget is displayed when the vertical slider is moved.

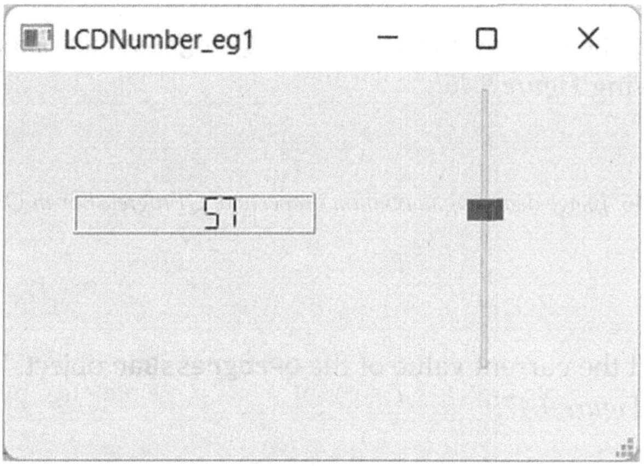

Figure 9.44: *Output of LCDNumber/run_lcdnumber_eg1.py when the vertical slider is moved.*

Note: The preceding code is covered in program name: LCDNumber/run_lcdnumber_eg1.py

Progress bar

In PyQt5, the **`QProgressBar`** widget is used to display an operation's progress. It is often used to display the status of a task when the user must wait for the operation to finish, such as a file download or data transfer. The **`QProgressBar`** widget provides a visual indication that displays the operation's progress. The progress bar grows in length as long as the operation progresses. Additionally, the widget provides a label that may be used to display a message which describes the operation being performed. A horizontal or vertical progress bar is provided by the **QProgressBar** widget.

Important properties

Let us check some important properties now.

minimum

This property will hold the minimum value of the **QProgressBar** object. The default value is **0**. Refer to the following *Figure 9.45:*

minimum	0

***Figure 9.45:** Image depicting minimum property of QProgressBar in Qt Designer*

maximum

This property will hold the maximum value of the **QProgressBar** object. The default value is **100**. Refer to the following *Figure 9.46:*

maximum	100

***Figure 9.46:** Image depicting maximum property of QProgressBar in Qt Designer*

value

This property will hold the current value of the **QProgressBar** object. The default value is **24**. Refer to the following *Figure 9.47:*

value	24

***Figure 9.47:** Image depicting value property of QProgressBar in Qt Designer*

alignment

This property will represent the alignment of the **QProgressBar** object. User may choose the options for both horizontal and vertical alignment. Refer to the following *Figure 9.48:*

˅ alignment	AlignLeft, AlignVCenter
Horizontal	AlignLeft
Vertical	AlignVCenter

***Figure 9.48:** Image depicting alignment property of QProgressBar in Qt Designer*

textVisible

This property will determine whether **QProgressBar** object's value should be displayed as text or not. The default value is **True**. Refer to the following *Figure 9.49:*

Figure 9.49: *Image depicting textVisible property of QProgressBar in Qt Designer*

orientation

This property will represent the orientation of the **QProgressBar** object, which can be set to either horizontal or vertical. The default value is **Horizontal**. Refer to the following *Figure 9.50:*

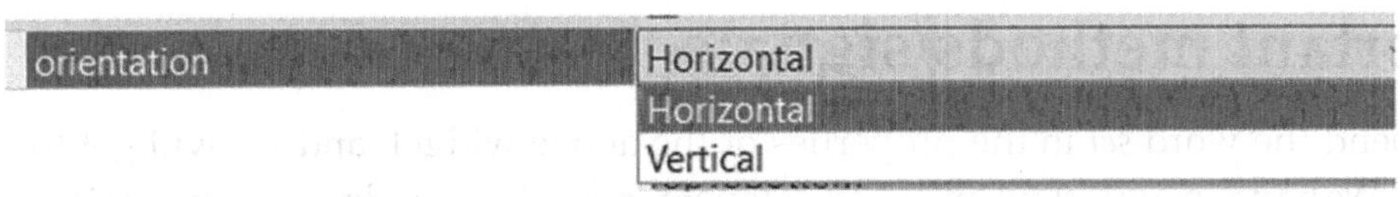

Figure 9.50: *Image depicting orientation property of QProgressBar in Qt Designer*

invertedAppearance

This property will determine whether the appearance of **QProgressBar** object should be inverted or not. The default value is **False**. Refer to the following *Figure 9.51:*

Figure 9.51: *Image depicting invertedAppearance property of QProgressBar in Qt Designer*

textDirection

This property will have no impact on the horizontal **QProgressBar** object and will hold the text reading direction on vertical **QProgressBar** object. The default value is **TopToBottom**. Refer to the following *Figure 9.52:*

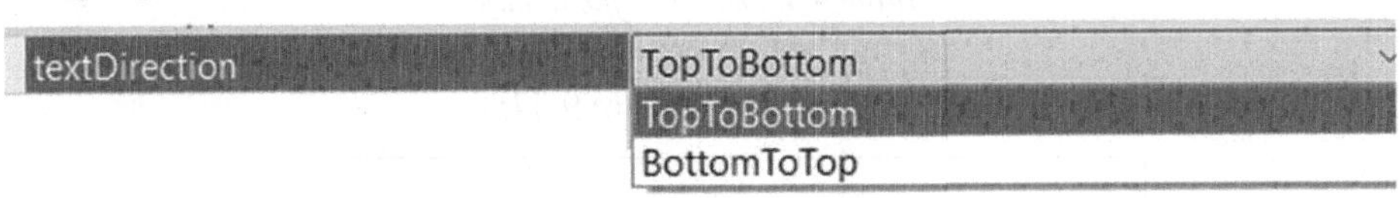

Figure 9.52: *Image depicting textDirection property of QProgressBar in Qt Designer*

format

This property will represent the **QProgressBar** object's text format where **%p** is replaced by percentage completed, **%m** for the total number of steps, and **%v** for the current value. The default value is **%p%**. Refer to the following *Figure 9.53:*

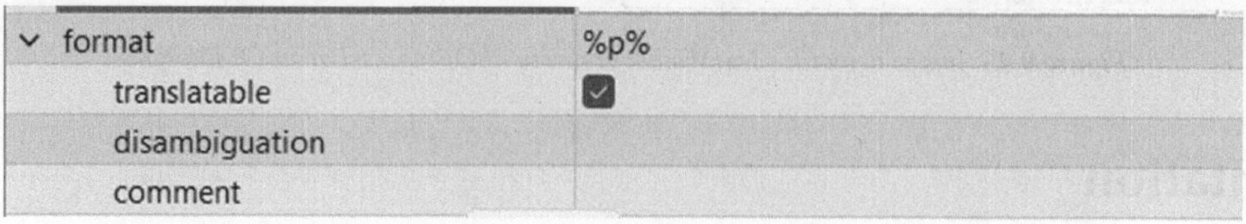

Figure 9.53*: Image depicting format property of QProgressBar in Qt Designer*

Important methods/signals

Just prepend the word *set* in the properties of the above widget, and we will get the required methods. We have an important and useful signal for the above widget which is **valueChanged()** signal.

valueChanged(value)

This signal is emitted whenever the value in the **QProgressBar** object changes programmatically or due to user interaction. The *value* argument is of type int, which is the new value of **QProgressBar** object after the change.

Now, we shall see an example of **QProgressBar**.

The details of file names are given in the following *Table 9.5*:

S No.	Qt Designer file name (.ui)	Converting the Qt Designer file name to Python file (.py)	Creating another Python file and importing the converted Python file from Qt Designer
1	**progressbar_eg1.ui**	**progressbar_eg1.py**	**run_progressbar_eg1.py**

Table 9.5: *Details of file names*

The Qt Designer file is shown in the following *Figure 9.54:*

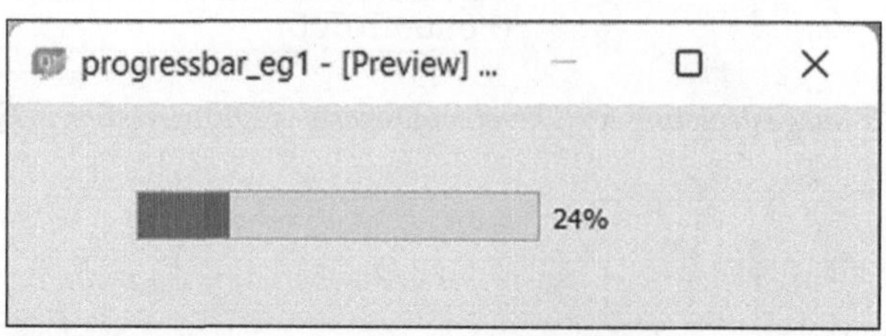

Figure 9.54*: Qt Designer file: ProgressBar/progressbar_eg1.ui*

Consider the following code of **run_progressbar_eg1.py**:

```
import sys
from PyQt5.QtWidgets import QMainWindow,QApplication
from progressbar_eg1 import *

class MyProgressBar(QMainWindow):
    def __init__(self):
        super().__init__()
        self.myui = Ui_MainWindow()
        self.myui.setupUi(self)

    def my_start_counting(self):
        self.myui.progressBar.setRange(0, 1000)
        self.myui.progressBar.setValue(0)
        for i in range(1, 1001):
            self.myui.progressBar.setValue(i)
            self.myui.mylbl.setText(f"Count No is: {i}")
                QApplication.processEvents() # processing any pending events for
updating the UI

if __name__ == "__main__":
    app = QApplication(sys.argv)
    myprogress_bar_widget = MyProgressBar()
    myprogress_bar_widget.show()
    myprogress_bar_widget.my_start_counting()
    sys.exit(app.exec_())
```

Output:

Refer to the following *Figure 9.55:*

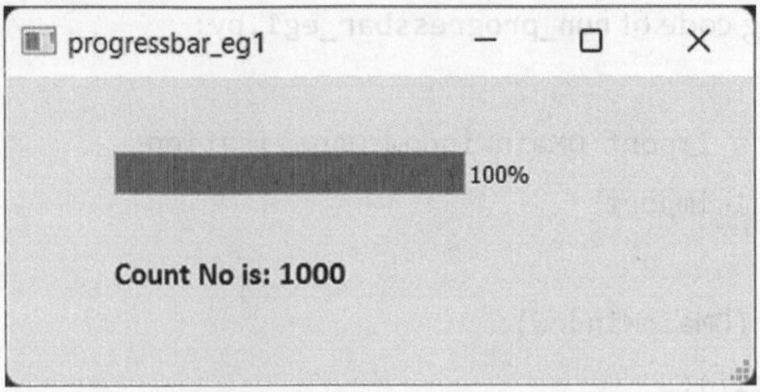

Figure 9.55: Output of ProgressBar/run_progressbar_eg1.py

Note: The preceding code is covered in program name: ProgressBar/run_progressbar_eg1.py

There are other widgets which are **`Graphics View`** and **`OpenGL`** widget which the reader can explore on their own.

Conclusion

In this chapter, we have learned about concepts of various display widgets available in Qt and how to effectively utilize them to create interactive user interfaces. Through the exploration of various widgets, we have gained knowledge on how to effectively display static text or images using labels, along with the ability to customize their font, colour, alignment, and size. Furthermore, we have recognized the significance of labels in enhancing the visual presentation of information in a graphical user interface. The **`TextBrowser`** widget has been thoroughly examined, enabling us to grasp its features for displaying and controlling rich text content. We have learned how to incorporate hyperlinks, graphics, and formatting choices to create dynamic and interactive text displays. This knowledge opens up opportunities for creating engaging and versatile user interfaces. Moreover, the chapter delved into adding a calendar widget to our GUI application. By understanding how to customize its appearance, structure, and behavior, we are equipped to tailor the calendar widget to meet the specific requirements of our application. The **`LCDNumber`** widget has been introduced as a means to display numerical values, such as counters, with the added capability of modifying its digit count, decimal accuracy, look, and style. This widget provides a visually appealing and customizable way to present numeric data to users. Finally, we explored the **`ProgressBar`** widget, which enables us to visualize the progress of a task or operation. Understanding how to dynamically update the progress bar based on our application's needs allows for effective feedback and user engagement. Armed with this knowledge, the user is now equipped to create visually appealing, interactive, and functional graphical user interfaces.

Points to remember

- A **QLabel** widget in PyQt5 is a display widget used to display text, an image, or any animated GIF on a GUI form page.
- A rich text browser with hypertext navigation capabilities is offered by PyQt5's **QTextBrowser** class.
- The PyQt5 widget **QCalendarWidget** offers a monthly calendar view and allows users to select a date which allows display of events, appointments, and other time-based information.
- The PyQt5 widget **QLCDNumber** shows a numerical value in a seven-segment LCD display.
- In PyQt5, the **QProgressBar** widget is used to display an operation's progress and is also used for displaying the status of a task when the user must wait for the operation to finish, such as a file download or data transfer.

Questions

1. State the importance of display widgets in Qt Designer for GUI applications.
2. List the different input widgets of Qt Designer and explain any one in detail.
3. Which widget is used to display text, an image, or any animated GIF on a GUI form page? Explain in detail.
4. Explain **text** and **textFormat** properties of the **Label** widget in Qt Designer.
5. Explain the following properties of the **Label** widget in Qt Designer:
   a. **pixmap**
   b. **scaledContents**
   c. **alignment**
   d. **wordWrap**
   e. **margin**
   f. **indent**
   g. **openExternalLinks**
   h. **textInteractionFlags**
   i. **buddy**
6. What is the purpose of the methods **setText(arg__1)** and **setPixmap(arg__1)** in **Label** in Qt Designer?
7. Explain the widget used for rich text browser with hypertext navigation capabilities access in Qt Designer.

8. State the utilization of the following properties in the text browser widget in Qt Designer:
   a. **searchPaths**
   b. **source**
   c. **openExternalLinks**
   d. **openLinks**
9. Explain the importance of the following methods in context to the Text Browser widget in Qt designer:
   a. **isBackwardAvailable()**
   b. **isForwardAvailable()**
   c. **anchorClicked(arg_ _1)**
   d. **sourceChanged(arg_ _1)**
10. What is the purpose of the **Calendar** widget in Qt Designer for GUI applications? Explain in detail any two essential properties.
11. Explain how to set minimum and maximum dates in Qt Designer.
12. Explain the following properties of the **Calendar** widget in Qt Designer:
    a. **firstDayOfWeek**
    b. **gridVisible**
    c. **selectionMode**
    d. **horizontalHeaderFormat**
    e. **verticalHeaderFormat**
    f. **navigationBarVisible**
13. Explain the widget used to display numerical data, such as sensor, timer, and other measurements in Qt Designer.
14. State the use of **smallDecimalPoint** and **digitCount** properties of **QLCDNumber** widget in Qt Designer.
15. Explain the widget used to provide a visual indication that displays the operation's progress in Qt Designer.
16. Explain the **QProgressBar** widget in Qt Designer.
17. State the importance of the following properties of **QProgressBar** widget in Qt Designer:
    a. **textDirection**
    b. **format**
    c. **invertedAppearance**
    d. **orientation**

Index

A

B

C

D

E

F

M

P

Q

T

U

W